THE ILLUSTRATED HISTORY OF
THE 20th CENTURY

ISBN 1-85613-083-5

Manufactured in Spain

Produced by Ted Smart
Author Rupert Matthews
Designed by Sara Cooper
Picture Research by Seni Glaister

All the photographs in this book
are the copyright of
Popperfoto

The publishers would like to thank Popperfoto and in
particular Ian Blackwell for his help and co-operation
in making this book possible.

This edition produced by Ted Smart for
The Book People Ltd,
Guardian House,
Borough Road,
Godalming,
Surrey GU7 2AE

THE ILLUSTRATED HISTORY OF
THE 20th CENTURY

TED SMART

CONTENTS

INTRODUCTION

More than any other this has been a century of change. Empires which took generations to build have been swept away, monolithic superstates founded on ideology have been created and destroyed, technology we now take for granted was not even dreamed of at the beginning of the century.

In the year 1900 Europe dominated the world, with the USA starting to become an international power. The British Empire ruled over a quarter of the people on Earth, knitting them together in a web of trade, commerce and power which set the agenda for diplomacy and wars. Asia was divided between the three empires of British India, enjoying prosperity as never before, China, on its last legs as an empire, and the Tsar's Russia which appeared stronger than any other. Europe was ruled by the autocratic emperors of Russia, Austria and Germany while Italy, France and Britain had democratic governments.

The everyday life of the average person was little changed from that of their fathers. The bulk of the population lived by farming, using techniques and tools which would have been familiar a century earlier. Even in the most industrialised nations the dominance of steam and vast factories had increased little since the latter half of the century before.

It was this world order which was swept away in the maelstrom of the Great War. The Austrian Empire was fragmented into numerous small states, the German Empire was broken and the Russian Empire collapsed from within as the age-old certainties of Tsarist rule were replaced by Socialist ideology run riot. Even among the winners the seeds of destruction were sown. The world trade pattern on which the British Empire was founded was smashed after generations of careful nurturing. Those who had built the colonies were replaced by new men with new ideas. Collapse was only a matter of time. The Great Depression which impoverished the world in the later 1920s and early 1930s hurried the ending of the old orders, finally crushed by the Second World War and its aftermath.

Standards of living have risen with the technology on which it feeds. In 1900 no person had ever flown in an aircraft, now transoceanic flights in jetliners are taken as a matter of course. The automobile, in 1900 a plaything of the wealthy, is now owned by the masses in industrialised nations. Everywhere the exclusive privilege has become a common occurrence and the futuristic dream is reality. Who could have imagined the computers, space craft and microtechnology which we now take for granted.

Since the 1950s the world has been searching for a new order and a fresh start. The collapse of the Soviet Union leaves only China as the final state built on an ideology. Everywhere new nations are emerging from suppression and the peoples of the world are striving to construct fresh webs of friendship. A new trade pattern to replace that lost in 1914 may be at hand. As the 20th Century draws to a close the world finds itself on the edge of a great future, with the bloodshed and tribulations of the century of change left behind.

1900-1909

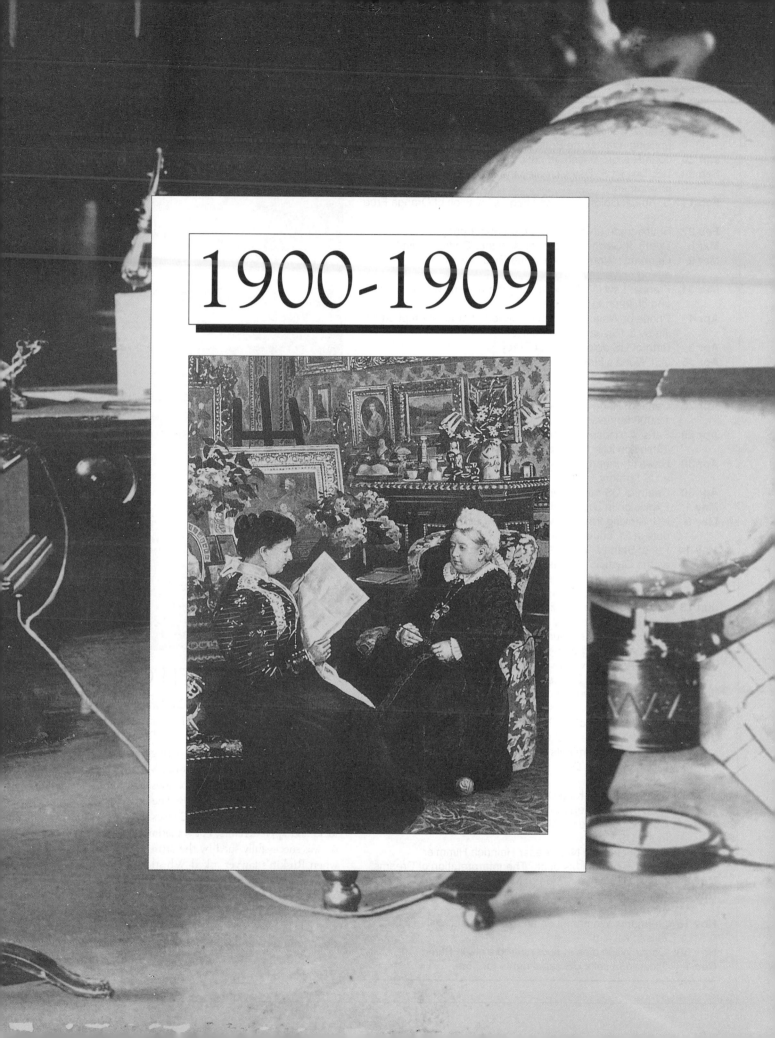

Jan 2	First electric omnibus installed in New York City
Jan 5	Ireland: Nationalist leader John Redmond calls for uprising against the British
Jan 20	John Ruskin, British art critic and social theorist, dies
Feb 9	US: Dwight F. Davis creates the Davis Cup tennis tournament
Feb 11	S. Africa: Colonel Hannay begins invasion of Orange Free State
Feb 27	British trade unions create the Labour party
Mar 6	Death of German motor car designer Gottleib Daimler
Mar 9	Germany: Women petition the Reichstag for the right to attend university
Mar 31	France: Law is passed limiting the working day for women and children to 11 hours
Apr 4	Prince of Wales escapes uninjured after an attempt on his life by a 16 year old anarchist
Apr 5	Birth of US actor Spencer Tracy
Apr 16	US: World's first book of stamps is issued
Apr 24	Johannesburg: Explosion at engineering works kills 10 people
Apr 26	Canada: Huge fire destroys Ottawa and Hull leaving 12,000 homeless
Apr 29	Paris: Collapse of a footbridge at the Great World Exhibition kills 10 people
Apr 30	Hawaii (formerly the British Sandwich Islands) becomes a US territory
Apr 30	Death of US railway engineer Casey Jones
May 1	Explosion in Utah coal mine kills 200
May 9	US: Striking tramway workers blow up tramcar during riots in St. Louis
May 14	Paris: Start of "World Amateur Championships" known as the Olympic Games
May 27	Belgium: World's first experiment in proportional representation is made in the general election
Jun 13	Boxer Rebellion in China
Jun 25	Birth of British military commander and last Viceroy of India, Lord Louis Mountbatten
Jul 4	Louis Armstrong born
Jul 9	Royal Assent given to the Act creating Federal Commonwealth of Australia
Jul 13	Earl of Hopetown appointed first Governor General of Australia
Jul 19	Paris: Opening of the Metro underground system
Jul 23	Canada: The Federal Government forbids immigration of paupers and criminals
Jul 30	Death of Alfred, Duke of Edinburgh, Queen Victoria's second son
Jul 30	Death of Italian King Umberto, shot dead by an anarchist
Aug 4	Birth of the Queen Mother
Aug 31	Coca Cola arrives in Britain 14 years after it went on sale in the US
Oct 7	Birth of German Nazi leader Heinrich Himmler
Oct 14	Freud publishes his book "The Interpretation of Dreams"
Nov 8	Birth of US writer Margaret Mitchell
Nov 15	France: Madrid to Paris express train derails, killing 17 including the Peruvian ambassador
Nov 16	Germany: Woman hurls an axe at Kaiser Wilhelm but fails to kill him
Nov 30	Oscar Wilde dies in poverty and exile in Paris
Dec 1	Nicaragua sells US canal rights for $5m

THE DEATH OF RUSKIN

When John Ruskin died on 20th January, Britain lost a man who[ ]been called the archetypal Victorian. Born in 1819 to a prospe[ ]London wine merchant, the young Ruskin was allowed to indulge[ ]tastes for architecture and art during extensive tours through Eur[ ]In 1843 Ruskin published his work *Modern Painters*, which establis[ ]his reputation as an art critic of unusual insight and clarity. Nume[ ]works on art followed and in 1869 he became Slade Professor of Ar[ ]Oxford, holding the post for 12 years. His commentary on the arts[ ]lucid and approachable, but sometimes got him into trouble. In 1[ ]he was successfully sued by the artist J.M. Whistler. The case tur[ ]when Ruskin's lawyer asked Whistler how he could possibly ch[ ]200 guineas for a painting which took only two days to prod[ ]Whistler glared "I do not ask it for two days work, I ask it for[ ]knowledge of a lifetime". When not engaging in art criticism, Ru[ ]worked hard for social reform, never missing an opportunity to crit[ ]the crushing conditions of the poor in industrial towns. His devo[ ]to both fine art and conditions for the poor mark a high poin[ ]Victorian philosophy.

Clark Gable was born on 1st February in Cadiz , Ohio. After a short stage career he took to the movies and became a major star. He is seen here in **Gone with the Wind**, *made in 1939. Below left: The German engineer Gottlieb Daimler, the man who is widely credited with inventing the automobile. After working for many years for an English engineering company, Daimler returned home and spent the 1870s and 1880s working on a variety of gas, oil and petrol engines. Eventually he perfected the internal combustion engine and by 1891 the Daimler Company was producing motorised carriages capable of 12 miles per hour. Below: The great jazz trumpet player Louis Armstrong was born on 4th July. Brought up in a New Orleans bordello he quickly gained a reputation as the finest jazz man in the city. In 1922 he moved to Chicago and so on to international fame.*

Oscar Wilde Dies in Disgrace

On 30th November a poverty-struck and obscure Irishman died in Paris. His name had once been the talk of London and the toast of Society. His name was Oscar Wilde. Born in Dublin in 1856, Wilde blazed a dazzling academic career at Trinity College, Dublin, and at Oxford before embarking on a high-profile career as poet, writer and bon-viveur. The 1880s and early 1890s were marked by brilliant plays and novels of great technical skill and wit. His conversation was widely acclaimed to be even more amusing and witty than his works, Wilde being the master of the throwaway comment. In 1895 his reign as Society idol ended in dramatic fashion. The Marquis of Queensbury, angered by Wilde's friendship with his son, made an accusation of sodomy. Wilde sued for libel, but lost the case and was at once prosecuted for homosexuality, then a criminal offence. He served two years in gaol before fleeing to Paris and poverty.

Left: Princess Mary of Teck, wife of the Duke of York w[ho] later came to the British throne as George V. Princess M[ary] became especially popular in 1900 and 1901 when she und[er]took an arduous series of tours throughout the Empire. Be[low] left: An early photo of Lady Elizabeth Bowes-Lyon, born [on] 4th August, who later married Princess Mary's second s[on] George VI. Below: The Prince of Wales, later Edward VII [in] flamboyant dress. Facing page top: The Upper Pool [of] London in 1900 when the docks handled the trade of [the] Empire. Facing page bottom: St. Pancras Station showing [the] tram rails and cobbles which were soon to vanish.

Birth of Australia

A new nation came into being on 9th July when Queen Victoria gav[e] the Royal Assent to an Act of Parliament which created the Feder[al] Commonwealth of Australia. Until that time Australia had been a num[-]ber of colonies ruled by Britain, though with varying degrees of sel[f-]government. The establishment of the new nation recognised tha[t] Australia enjoyed a common culture and outlook, although inter-col[o-]nial rivalries were keenly felt. Only Western Australia, separated fro[m] other centres of population by vast expanses of desert, felt slight[ly] estranged and the feeling has persisted. At the time of the Act th[e] Australian colonies had a higher per capita income than did Britai[n] and a rapidly developing economy. Ties with Britain remained clos[e] with Australia joining the war against Germany in 1914 without ques[-]tion.

The Boxer Rebellion

The Society of the Harmonious Fists, known as Boxers, spread a wave of fear, panic and violence across the ailing Chinese Empire, culminating in open warfare in the long summer of 1900. For many years the spread of missionaries, salesmen and technology throughout the countryside led to intense resentment and anger among traditionalists. Prince Tuan's anti-Western faction at court orchestrated the anger at a national level and supplied the Society with arms. In May the southern provinces exploded in violence with many Western missionaries being killed and their heads spiked on poles as triumphal symbols. On 20th June riots in Peking led to the killing of the German ambassador and 300,000 Boxers from the rural regions poured into the city. Within days the foreign legations were under siege. Only a co-ordinated army with troops from many nations saved the trapped westerners, the siege being raised on 14th August. The Imperial Court, backed by Western pressure, put down the Boxers with great ferocity and loss of life.

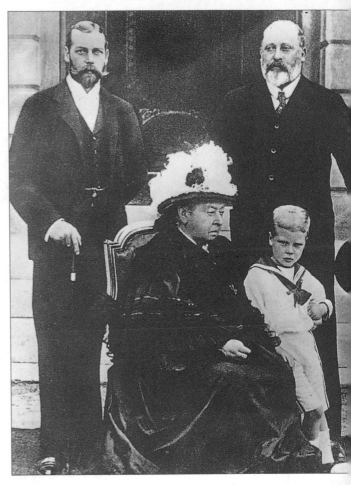

Above: The Duke and Duchess of York, later King George V and Queen Mary, in India. This was the high-point of the British Raj in India. The Duke and Duchess are surrounded by army officers, civil administrators, a highly decorated Gurkha and two Indian cavalrymen. At this time India was a patchwork of states, ruled by native princes, others by British residents and still others by the army. The area was enjoying economic growth and social improvements. Widespread discontent with British rule came later. Above right: Queen Victoria, in her last year of life, is flanked on her left by her son, later Edward VII, and on her right by her grandson, later George V. Her grandson, later the controversial Edward VIII who occupied the throne for less than a year, stands by her knee.

On 22nd November the po[pu]lar composer Sir Arthur Seymour Sullivan died. H[is] massive output was receiv[ed] with enthusiasm by his Victorian audience, but on[ly] a few of his works remain [well] known today. The most of[ten] performed works are the li[ght] operettas he produced with W.S. Gilbert between 1871 and 1896. **The Mikado,** **Pirates of Penzance** *and* **[HMS]** **Pinafore** *are three of these works. The partnership w[ith] Gilbert, a well known com[ic] writer, was highly product[ive] but rarely amicable. The [pair] parted in 1896 after an a[rgu]ment about the position o[f a] rug on stage. However, Sullivan always considere[d] himself to be a serious mu[si]cian. He produced a num[ber] of operas, a symphony, ch[urch] music and songs. Few of t[he] more serious works are remembered today.*

HEINRICH HIMMLER

On 7th October Heinrich Himmler, later to earn infamy as the leader of the Nazi SS, was born. Himmler first gained infamy in June 1934 when he masterminded the liquidation of several senior Nazis whose loyalty to Hitler was not absolute. His SS quickly rose from being an unofficial militia to take on the role of state police and elite military unit. His total ruthlessness combined with the exact niceties of a brain schooled in bureaucratic procedure to create a formidable talent. Responsible from an early date for political prisons, Himmler acquired control of the extermination camps in which millions of Jews and others, including communists and trade unionists, were tortured and murdered during the second world war.

A Boer Commando poses outside Mafeking. The failure of the Boers to capture this rail junction, defended by Baden-Powell, was an early sign of weakness in their war against British control in South Africa. The Boers went to war in October 1899 and for several months won a string of victories against the British. The arrival of Kitchener with massive reinforcements in November threw the Boers on to the defensive. The war dragged on with great loss of life on both sides until May 1902.

Jan 1	Commonwealth of Australia is formed.
Jan 10	World's largest oil strike in Texas
Jan 14	Explosion in hat factory in Manchester kills 12
Jan 22	Death of Queen Victoria
Jan 27	Death of Giuseppe Verdi
Feb 1	Birth of US film actor Clark Gable
Feb 2	Funeral of Queen Victoria
Feb 5	First Billion Dollar business deal: J. Pierpont Morgan buys up a billion dollars worth of mines and steel mills
Feb 6	Paris : First public telephones at railway stations
Feb 14	King Edward VII opens his first parliament
Feb 22	Mail steamer sinks in San Francisco Harbour, killing 128
Mar 4	Inauguration of President McKinley
Mar 6	Germany : Anarchist attempts to assassinate Kaiser Wilhelm, who escapes with face wounds
Mar 13	Death of 23rd US President, Benjamin Harrison
Mar 18	Birth of Russo German dancer Tatiana Gsovsky
Mar 19	Boer leader Botha rejects Kitchener's terms
Mar 25	UK: The first diesel motor goes on show
Apr 14	US actors are arrested in NY at the Academy of Music for wearing costumes on Sunday
Apr 24	200 are killed in chemical explosion at Griesheim, Germany
Apr 29	Birth of Crown Prince Hirohito
May 7	Birth of US actor Gary Cooper
May 24	78 miners die in Caerphilly, South Wales
Jun 24	First Picasso exhibition in Paris
Jun 26	France : Professional chauffeurs in Paris protest at a move to prevent them from wearing moustaches
Jul 2	400 die in New York heatwave
Jul 13	France : Brazilian aviator Santos-Dumont crashes his drigible at Boulogne after circling the Eiffel Tower
Aug 4	Gold strike in South African Rand
Aug 9	Colombian troops invade Venezuela
Aug 21	Cadillac Car Company is formed in Detroit
Sep 6	President McKinley shot at a public reception
Sep 9	Death of French painter Toulouse-Lautrec
Sep 10	US : Anarchist Emma Goldman arrested for her part in the plot to kill President McKinley
Sep 14	Theodore Roosevelt is elected as President of US - youngest at 42
Sep 30	France : Registration becomes compulsory for cars doing more than 20 mph
Oct 2	Vickers launches Britain's first submarine Holland 1
Oct 23	General Buller is sacked in South Africa for indiscretion
Oct 24	Incorporation of the Eastman Kodak company
Oct 28	34 die in race riots sparked by a dinner at the White House
Nov 1	Chicago : Dr J. E. Gillman announces an X-Ray treatment for breast cancer
Nov 10	North West Frontier province is incorporated into India
Nov 18	Birth of US journalist and statistician George Gallup
Dec 2	The US Supreme Court decides that Puerto Ricans do not qualify for US citizenship
Dec 5	Walt Disney born
Dec 12	Italian physicist Marconi receives the first trans-atlantic wireless signals at St. Johns, Newfoundland
Dec 21	Norway : Women vote for the first time
Dec 27	Marlene Dietrich born

THE END OF AN ERA

On 22nd January an era ended with the death of Queen Victoria. The majestic monarch had reigned for nearly 64 years and had presided over an era of British power and might unsurpassed in history. During her reign the industrial revolution changed the face of Britain forever. Yet when she ascended the throne in 1837 it was as a slight 18 year old who had grown up in a tight and closed family estranged from the Court. The young queen learnt quickly, benefiting from the experience of her husband, Prince Albert, who she married in 1840. They enjoyed a good marriage and his death in 1861 threw her into deep mourning, but though she abandoned public appearances she continued to play an active part in Court, Church and political life. It has been said that her careful nurturing of the role of the constitutional monarchy laid the foundations for today's style of government in Britain. Her numerous children married into royal families across Europe, providing a close network of relationships which eased diplomacy, but ultimately failed in 1914 with the start of World War 1. Victoria is shown (opposite) with Princess Beatrice in 1880. Her death propelled Edward VII to the throne. He is shown (above) with his wife Queen Alexandra and her sister.

MCKINLEY SHOOTING

The United States was stunned on 6th September when President William McKinley was shot by an anarchist in Buffalo, New York. A native of Ohio, McKinley served in the Civil War rising from the rank of private to Major before becoming a lawyer in civilian life. After serving as both a Congressman and as Governor of Ohio for two terms, McKinley was elected President in 1896. He pursued a vigorous economic policy based on the gold standard and trade tariffs. He also went to war with Spain over Cuba and annexed Hawaii. Re-elected in 1900 with a larger majority than before, McKinley looked set to continue his prudent policies. His frail wife, however, was uneasy and suffered repeated bouts of illness. McKinley was attending a music reception at the Pan American Exposition when Leon Czolgosz shot him twice at point blank range. McKinley seemed well on the way to recovery when he suffered a sudden relapse, muttered "Goodbye. It is God's way." and died on 14th September.

Top right: Walt Disney, the cartoon genius who was born in Chicago on 5th December. He first entered animated films in 1923, but did not become famous until the creation of his famous Mickey Mouse in 1928.

Thereafter Disney built up a vast business built on his unique artistic talents and business skills.
Right: Marlene Dietrich who was born in Berlin on 27th December hit the movie headlines for her role in **The Blue Angel** *in 1930.*

The Submarine

On 2nd October a new era in sea warfare opened as Britain's Royal Navy, the largest and most powerful in the world, launched its first submarine. HMS *Holland 1,* displaced 105 tons and was designed for coastal duties. The hazardous petrol engine which powered the craft was a drawback which later diesel models avoided. The Royal Navy was soon left behind in the submarine area for it concentrated on small coastal patrol craft while other navies, Germany's in particular, developed larger long distance craft. During the First World War this disparity would almost prove fatal to Britain. German U-boats hunted British ships on the high seas and only the development of sophisticated counter measures saved Britain from starvation.

Top left: An Italian officer prepares to lead his men towards Peking to relieve the foreign legations under siege from the Chinese Boxer rebels. Above left: Marchers in an anti-foreigner demonstration pause to read a poster in Peking as Boxer unrest grew to violent proportions. Above: Toulouse-Lautrec admires one of his famous posters. The artist died on 9th September, aged 36, after a decade of illness, heavy drinking and mental problems. Left: Gugliemo Marconi beside the experimental radio receiver which picked up a Morse code signal sent from Canada to Cornwall, thus proving long distance radio communication to be practical.

1902

Jan 9	US: New York State introduces a bill to stop public flirting	**Jun 18**	Death of British writer and satarist, Samuel Butler
Jan 17	Earthquake in Mexico City kills 300	**Jun 23**	Germany, Austria-Hungary and Italy renew Triple Allianc
Jan 18	US Commission chooses Panama as site of canal	**Jul 6**	King Edward treats 456,000 poor people of London to dinner
Feb 1	Women's foot binding is abolished in China	**Jul 15**	The 1,000 year old bell tower of St Mark's Square collapses
Feb 4	Birth of US aviator Charles Lindbergh		
Feb 15	Berlin's first underground railway opens	**Aug 1**	100 miners die in pit explosion in Wollongang, Australia
Feb 19	France: Vaccination against smallpox becomes obligatory	**Aug 8**	Coronation of Edward VII
Feb 20	Spain: 500 are reported dead in Barcelona strike clashes	**Aug 25**	New York: The intrepid Harry de Windt successfully completes his 248 day trek from Paris to New York
Feb 25	US: Hubert Cecil Booth founds Vacuum Cleaner Company Ltd	**Sep 13**	First conviction in Britain on fingerprint evidence
Feb 27	Birth of US author John Steinbeck	**Sep 14**	20,000 in Dublin demonstate against the British government
Mar 4	US: Creation of AAA (American Automobile Association)		
Mar 10	Turkey: Earthquake wipes out entire town of Tochangri	**Sep 28**	15,000 requests in a week are received for gold mining permits in South Africa
Mar 26	Death of statesman Cecil John Rhodes	**Sep 29**	Emile Zola, French novelist, dies
Mar 29	Sir William Walton born	**Oct 16**	First borstal institution opens
Apr 5	Glasgow: 20 people die when a stand collapses at the Ibrox Park Stadium during an England-Scotland match	**Oct 17**	US: The first Cadillac motor car is produced
		Nov 9	Birth of British film director Anthony Asquith
Apr 7	Texaco Oil Co., formed in the US	**Nov 8**	Death of German steel magnate, Friedrich Krupp
Apr 8	Russia agrees to withdraw troops from Manchuria	**Nov 22**	Williamsburg bridge across the East River is destroyed b fire
Apr 13	New car speed record of 74 mph set in France		
May 1	Tornado kills 416 in Dacca, India	**Nov 26**	New Zealand: Fifth consecutive general election victory for the Progressive Party
May 8	Volcano Mount Pelee on Martinique erupts, 30,000 die		
May 12	France: Aviator Auguste Seveno dies when his airship explodes over Paris	**Dec 10**	Aswan Dam opens
		Dec 19	Sir Ralph Richardson born
May 31	Peace of Vereeniging is signed, ending the Boer War		

THE END OF RHODES

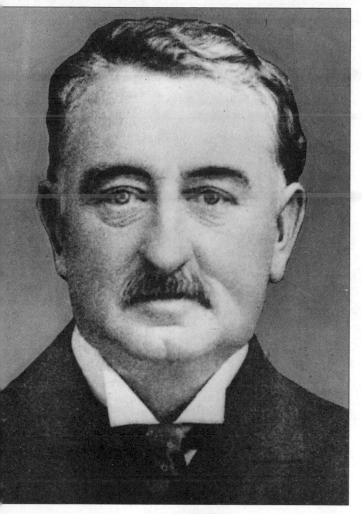

On 26th March Cecil Rhodes, the only man to have a nation named after him, died at his home in South Africa. Rhodes was sent to southern Africa in 1870 for his health. In 1889, at the age of 36, he succeeded in amalgamating the various private claims in the diamond fields and so established his massive fortune. In the years which followed Rhodes combined his own business ventures with Imperial policy. He managed to add thousands of square miles to British control after his commercial interests infiltrated the area. Rhodes resigned from politics in 1896 after he conspired to form an uprising in Boer territory. He later travelled alone to negotiate peace with the warlike Matabele. Matabeleland and adjacent territories became independent in 1965 as Rhodesia, now Zimbabwe. Left: Cecil Rhodes. Below: Rhodes and Kimberley notables in 1894.

*ight: Henry Ford with
*rney Oldsfield and his 999
*cing chassis of 1902. Ford
*recognised as the founder of
*e US automobile industry
*d an engineer of genius.
*rn in 1863, Ford helped on
*s father's farm but later
*oved to Detroit to work as
*engineer. In 1892 he built
*s first car and in 1902 pro-
*ced a pair of racing cars.
*e following year he founded
*Ford Motor Company. He
*n his great success in 1909
*th the Model T. This car
*s mass produced on simple
*es to enable the cars to be
*d at a price which ordinary
*rkers could afford. Facing
*ge: A tram runs through
*e prosperous town of Hull in
*rthern England, then the
artland of British industry.

When Edward VII ascended to the throne of Britain in 1901 he showed he would be very different from his mother Victoria. He refused to give up his sporting interests, or the fun-loving crowd which had surrounded him in his years as Prince of Wales. Nevertheless, Edward proved to be a popular king. The coronation was set for June 1902, but was cancelled when the king fell ill. The ceremony finally went ahead on 9th August. Below: Edward VII recovers from illness. Remaining pictures: The Coronation. Overleaf: In 1902 Britain recognised the efforts of General Kitchener in the Boer War by creating him a Viscount and awarding him the Order of Merit. Almost at once he was appointed Commander in Chief in India, a post he held until 1909.

an 1	King Edward VII proclaimed Emperor of India.
an 2	US: President Roosevelt closes post office in Missouri for refusing to employ a black postmistress.
an 10	Birth of British sculptress Barbara Hepworth
an 19	Paris: A new bicycle race is announced called the "Tour de France"
eb 3	British capture Kano from Nigerian rebels
eb 26	Death of US inventor of the rapid-fire gun, Richard Gatling
Mar 3	Scott in Antarctic reaches furthest point South
Mar 3	Bill passed by Congress to ban undesirables from entering the US
Mar 3	Man arrested in St. Louis for spitting
Mar 10	Paris: The Academy of Medicine issues a report denouncing alcohol as detrimental to health
Mar 10	Birth of US jazz musician Bix Beiderbecke
Mar 14	Birth of US painter, Adolph Gottlieb
Mar 22	New York: The US side of the Niagra Falls runs dry
Apr 2	Bloody clashes between students and police in Spain
Apr 6	Dreyfus documents are proved army forgeries in France
Apr 29	Turkey : Earthquake in Van kills 860
May 2	Dr Benjamin Spock, American pediatrician, born
May 8	Death of French painter Paul Gauguin
May 26	Paris to Madrid motor race is banned after 6 deaths
May 28	Constantinople : Earthquake kills 2,000 people
May 29	Bob Hope born
un 10	Army officers kill King and Queen of Serbia
un 16	Ford Motor Company is formed

Jun 26	Birth of British writer Eric Blair, alias George Orwell
Jul 11	Ireland: World's first power boat race takes place, organised by the Royal Cork Yacht Club
Aug 9	Pope Plus X is crowned in Rome
Aug 15	New York: Joseph Pulitzer gives $2 million to Columbia University to start a school of jounalism
Sep 1	Helen Keller graduates with honours from Radcliffe College in the US
Sep 3	New York: US yacht Reliance beats British Shamrock to win America's Cup
Sep 21	First "Wild West" film, called "Kit Carson"
Sep 26	US: Connecticut gives women the vote in State elections
Oct 5	Berlin: Siemens electric train reaches 125 mph.
Oct 7	US: Professor Samuel Langley fails in his attempt to fly a heavier-than-air machine
Oct 10	UK: The Women's Socal and Political Union formed with Emmeline Pankhurst as leader
Oct 13	First baseball World Series, won by Boston Red Sox
Oct 28	British novelist Evelyn Waugh born
Nov 1	Death of German historian Theodor Mommsen
Nov 2	President Roosevelt sends 3 gunships to Panama
Nov 6	US Government recognises Panama's independence
Nov 18	US and Panama sign canal treaty
Dec 10	Marie Curie becomes first woman to win a Nobel Prize
Dec 17	Wright brothers make first heavier-than-air flight at Kittyhawk, North Carolina
Dec 31	578 die in a theatre fire in Chicago

Above: Mrs Emmeline Pankhurst speaking at a public meeting. In 1903 she formed the Women's Social and Political Union which led the campaign for women's suffrage in Britain. Mrs Pankhurst worked tirelessly for reform. She took part in numerous events including window-smashing, assault and even planting small bombs to draw attention to her cause. Votes were eventually won by women in 1918. Left: Marie Curie won the Nobel Prize for Physics jointly with her husband in 1903 for their studies on radioactivity and the discovery of radium. Her husband died in 1906, and Marie continued his work. In 1911 she won the Nobel Prize for Chemistry on her own.

Murder of a King

On 11th June a group of army officers rushed the private rooms of King Alexander of Serbia. They hacked the king to death before turning on the terror-struck Queen Draga and killing her. The murder plot had been hatched in March when King Alexander overthrew the constitution in favour of totalitarian rule by himself. He turned his back on Serbia's traditional friendship with Russia and alienated many vested interests. With Alexander's death, the Royal line was extinct. The throne passed to Peter Karageorge, a popular nobleman and grandson of the national hero who led the Serbian revolt against the Turks in 1804. King Peter returned to the Russian camp, encouraged Slav nationalism and reorganised the army. In 1914 it was a Serbian Slav nationalist who shot Archduke Ferdinand and so brought about the First World War.

Below: Robert Scott who returned from a skiing expedition in the Antarctic to announce he had reached 82 degrees south, further than any other human. Right: Alfred Dreyfus, French army officer who was pardoned for crimes he had not committed. Convicted of spying in 1894, Dreyfus later showed that evidence against him had been forged and that the army had refused to accept his innocence to protect the reputation of senior officers.

THE FIRST FLIGHT

On 17th December the era of manned flight began when the Wright Brothers first aircraft made a powered flight of 852 feet. The brothers, Wilbur and Orville, ran a bicycle repair shop in Dayton, Ohio, but devoted all their spare time and energies to flight. In 1900 they began building gliders. Over the next three years they gradually solved various practical aeronautical problems. In December 1903 they bolted a petrol engine to their best glider and so made their first flight. The problem of tail spin quickly emerged as a problem with powered aircraft. Orville solved this by adding forward winglets and, in 1905, covered 24 miles in 38 minutes. For a while the brothers ran a successful aircraft manufacturing company, but they failed to keep up with more inventive competitors. Their first aircraft is preserved in a Washington museum. Facing page, top: The first flight of a heavier than air machine. Orville Wright was the pilot on this historic flight with Wilbur running alongside the aircraft in case of mishap. Facing page, bottom left: Wilbur Wright about the time of the flight. Facing page, bottom right: Orville Wright photographed in old age.

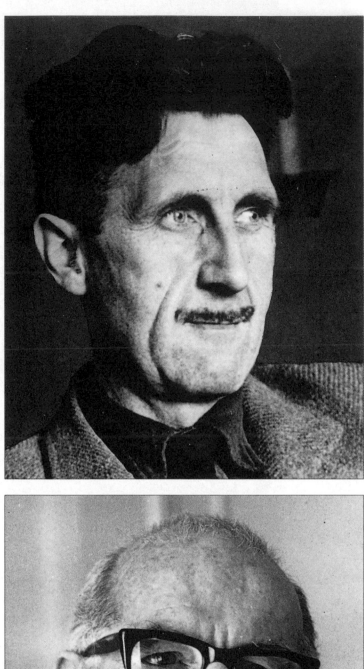

Top left: George Orwell, who was born as Eric Blair on 25th June. Educated at Eton, Orwell fought for the Socialists in the Spanish Civil War but is most famous as a writer. His novels **1984** and **Animal Farm** are particularly popular. Top right: The abstract sculptress Barbara Hepworth was born on 10th January. She is seen here with her work Meridian, which stands on London's High Holborn. Left: Benjamin Spock, born in 1903, went on to cause outrage and continuing controversy with his book **Baby and Childcare.** Published in 1946 the book advocated freedom of expression and lack of discipline for children. Above: Thomas Edison and his famous protege Henry Ford. Ford founded his motor company in 1903 with just $28,000.

Jan 4	US: Supreme Court says Puerto Ricans can enter US freely, but stops short of granting citizenship
Jan 8	Pope Pius X hits out against low cut evening gowns
Jan 10	British troops massacre 1,000 Dervishes in Somaliland.
Jan 12	US: Henry Ford sets new land speed record of 91.37 mph in his motor car "999" on frozen Lake St. Clair.
Jan 14	Birth of British photographer Cecil Beaton
Jan 18	Birth of British-born US film actor Cary Grant
Jan 22	Norway: Fire destroys the city of Alesund leaving 10,000 people destitute.
Feb 1	London: UK agrees with France that it will remain neutral if Japan and Russia go to war
Feb 5	America ends its occupation of Cuba
Feb 6	Maryland disenfranchises black voters
Feb 10	Japanese night attack cripples Russian fleet at Port Arthur
Mar 1	Birth of US band leader Glenn Miller
Mar 22	US: The "Daily Illustrated Mirror" carries the first colour photographs in a newspaper
Apr 13	Russian loses battleship Petropavlovsk and 600 men in an ill-fated sortie from Port Arthur
Apr 14	London: First attempt at "talking pictures" at Fulham Theatre, using cinematography and phonograph
Apr 14	Birth of British actor John Gielgud
Apr 24	Birth of US painter Willem de Kooning
Apr 24	Death of German industrialist Friedrich Siemens
May 1	Death of Bohemian composer Antonin Dvorak
May 2	Birth of US singer and actor Bing Crosby
May 4	Charles Rolls and Henry Royce agree to make cars
May 11	Birth of Spanish painter Salvador Dali
May 21	Birth of US jazz musician Fats Waller
May 25	Far East: 4,500 Japanese and 3,000 Russians die at Nanshan; Oku seals off Port Arthur by land and sea
May 30	London: Strike begins of 3,000 cabbies
Jun 2	US swimmer and actor Johnny Weissmuller born
Jun 15	A church outing turns to disaster when fire breaks out aboard the steamer General Slocum - 1000 die
Jun 23	President Roosevelt nominated for another term
Jun 25	Birth of German actor Peter Lorre
Jun 28	UK : Over 700 Scandinavian immigrants are killed when the steamer Norge is wrecked off Ireland
Jul 1	Third summer Olympic Games of modern times open at St. Louis
Jul 14	Death of S. African Boer leader Paul Kruger
Jul 15	Death of Russian writer Anton Chekhov
Jul 21	Trans-Siberian railway is completed
Aug 4	First Atlantic weather forecast is received by wireless telegraph
Sep 7	US: Alabama mob of 2,000 burns black man accused of murder
Sep 20	US Army rejects heavier-than-air flying machines
Oct 2	British novelist Graham Greene born
Oct 31	John Fleming invents radio valve
Nov 8	Theodore Roosevelt wins US election
Nov 17	Southampton: The first underwater journey of a submarine, across the Solent to the Isle of Wight
Nov 18	Gold discovered in Rhodesia
Dec 13	London's first 'tube' train goes electric
Dec 27	First showing of Peter Pan

...ove: Salvador Dali was ...rn on 11th May. As a surre-...ist painter, Dali exhibited ...uch talent but his true ...nius lay in self-publicity, self-...agery and a capacity for ...hibitionism which amounted ...near genius. His first exhibi-tion was mounted in Paris in 1929 and in 1934 his New York show left sceptical critics speechless. Never one to avoid controversy, Dali angered the art world by establishing close links with the regime of Franco in Spain.

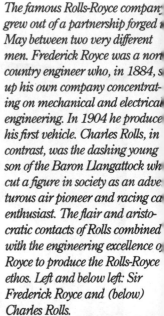

The famous Rolls-Royce company grew out of a partnership forged in May between two very different men. Frederick Royce was a north country engineer who, in 1884, set up his own company concentrating on mechanical and electrical engineering. In 1904 he produced his first vehicle. Charles Rolls, in contrast, was the dashing young son of the Baron Llangattock who cut a figure in society as an adventurous air pioneer and racing car enthusiast. The flair and aristocratic contacts of Rolls combined with the engineering excellence of Royce to produce the Rolls-Royce ethos. Left and below left: Sir Frederick Royce and (below) Charles Rolls.

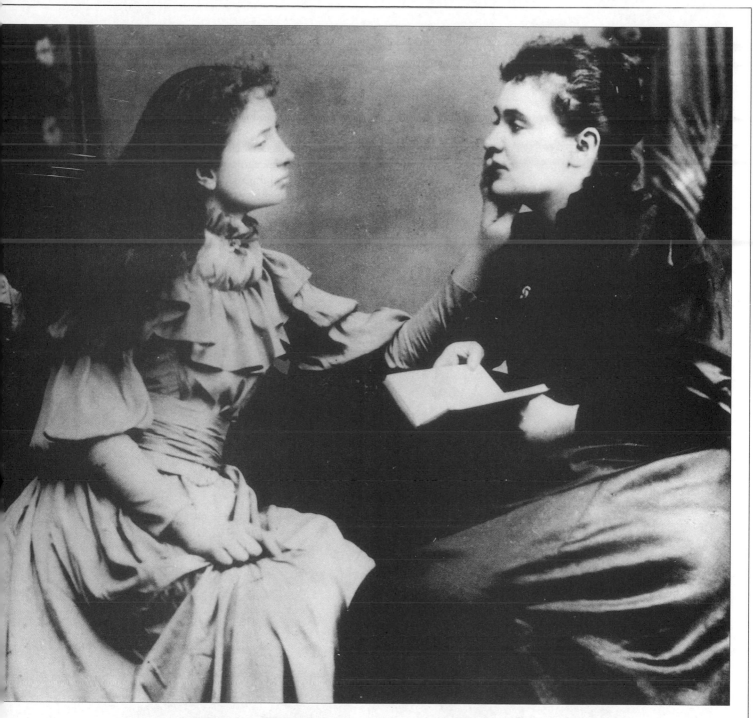

HELEN KELLER'S ACHIEVEMENT

n 1st September a special student graduated with honours from
adcliffe College in Boston, Massachusetts. Helen Keller's
hievement made the world headlines because she had been a
af and blind mute from the age of 2. The disability resulted
om a severe bout of scarlet fever, then a real hazard in child-
od. Helen Keller was born at Tuscumbia, Alabama, on 27th
ne 1880. Despite her disability the young girl showed clear
ns of being a lively and intelligent child. At the age of seven,
elen was enrolled at the Perkin Institute of the Blind, Boston,
ere she was placed in the care of Miss Anna Sullivan. With
finite patience and total dedication, Miss Sullivan taught
elen to read braille, to type and to 'hear' by placing her fingers
the lips of a person talking to her. At the age of 20 Helen

finally mastered the art of speaking. Two years later Helen
enrolled at the Cambridge School for Young Ladies in Boston
and, accompanied by Miss Sullivan, attended lectures at
Radcliffe College. Progress was slow for all lecture notes and
course work had to be converted to braille for Helen to understand it and her writings needed to be reproduced in normal type
for the staff to read and mark. Helen took time out from her
studies to write her autobiography, entitled *The Story of my Life*,
which was published in 1902. After graduating, Helen went on
to produce a number of other books detailing the problems and
opportunities of those suffering from sense deprivation. As her
skills at lip-reading and speaking improved she led and increasingly full social life.

Left: Sir John Gielgud as Julius Caesar in the 1969 film of that name. Gielgud was born on 14th April, the same day as the first attempts to produce a talking movie were made in Fulham, London. Bottom left: Cary Grant, born on 18th January. He left his native Britain at an early age and forged a successful career in the American film industry. His screen persona as a suave and sophisticated man about town provided endless light entertainment to millions of moviegoers. Below: The athletic Johnny Weissmuller who was born in Chicago on 2nd June. In 1927 he took the world title in freestyle swimming for the 100, 220, 300 and 200 yards. In 1932 he entered the movies as the muscular ape man Tarzan, going on to successfully repeat the role a number of times. Facing page: Explorer Sir Henry Stanley who died on 10th May. Stanley opened up vast regions of Africa, making a number of excellent maps. He is best known for his words "Dr Livingstone, I presume", uttered on meeting Livingstone in the depth of the African jungle.

1905

Jan 1	Italy: Belgian Henri Oedenkoven founds world's first vegetarian organisation
Jan 1	Trans-Siberian Railway officially opens
Jan 1	Russians surrender Port Arthur to the Japanese
Jan 21	Birth of French fashion designer Christian Dior
Jan 22	March of Russian strikers fired on, 500 die
Feb 2	Russia: Maxim Gorky is released from prison
Feb 5	Chicago: Polar bear freezes to death in the zoo after three nights of -15 degrees F.
Feb 8	Paris: Court declares all gramophone recordings of published music to be in breach of copyright
Feb 10	US: Wisconsin passes a tax on bachelors over 30
Feb 17	The Grand Duke Sergei is assassinated when a bomb, filled with nails, is thrown into his lap
Feb 23	The Rotary Club founded in Chicago
Mar 4	US : President Roosevelt declares "No weak nation should have cause to fear us... no strong power can attack us"
Apr 2	Birth of French dancer Serge Lifar
Apr 2	Simplon tunnel through Alps officially opens
Apr 4	Indian earthquake kills 10,000
Apr 4	Death of Belgian artist and sculptor Constantin Meunier
Apr 11	St. Petersburg: Government lifts censorship on private telegrams
Apr 19	UK: Judge decides the public have no right of way to Stonehenge.
Apr 30	Tsar Nicholas II guarantees freedom of conscience
May 1	Poland: 100 people die when troops fire into the May Day demonstrators in Warsaw
May 13	London: A bill to give women the vote fails
May 16	Birth of US actor Henry Fonda
May 25	France: The first flight of a motorised aeroplane in Europe
May 27	Russian fleet annihilated by Japanese
May 29	Birth in UK of US comedian Bob Hope
Jun 7	Norway gains independence from Sweden
Jun 21	Birth of French writer and philosopher Jean-Paul Sartre
Jun 29	UK: Automobile Association is founded
Jul 1	Australia: Salvation Army General Booth buys 20,000 acres of land on which to settle poor immigrants
Jul 1	Albert Einstein proposes his "Theory of Relativity"
Jul 3	Separation of Church and State in France
Jul 10	UK: Parliamentary reshuffle means 22 fewer Irish MPs
Jul 11	UK: 124 die in Glamorgan pit disaster
Aug 11	Leicester: Australian swimmer B. B. Kieran swims half-mile in record 11 mins 28 seconds
Sep 5	Russians and Japanese sign peace treaty
Sep 9	Thousands die in earthquake in Calabria, Italy
Sep 12	Japanese Navy's flagship 'Mikasa' sinks, 544 die
Sep 18	Birth of Swedish actress Greta Garbo
Sep 19	Death of Irish-born doctor, Thomas John Barnardo
Oct 5	US : Wright brothers make longest flight yet of 38 minutes three seconds.
Oct 13	Death of English actor Sir Henry Irving
Nov 1	A performance of Shaw's play "Mrs Warren's Profession" was closed by police and the actors were arrested for offences against public decency.
Nov 28	Sinn Fein founded in Dublin by Arthur Griffith
Dec 19	London: First-ever motorised ambulance service for traffic accident victims
Dec 24	Birth of US industrialist Howard Hughes

Russia Humbled

In May the military might of Russia was battered in a battle which marked the first defeat of a Western power by an Eastern nation. Hoping to turn the tide of the war against Japan, Tsar Nicholas II sent a powerful fleet from the Baltic to the Far East. The fleet of 45 warships, including 7 battleships and 6 cruisers, was met in the Tsushima Straits by the Japanese Admiral Togo who commanded a fleet of similar size. Battle raged all through the afternoon of the 27th May and recommenced at dawn next day. All but 12 Russian ships were sunk or captured and the Tsar had to accept a humiliating peace treaty which allowed Japan extensive gains in northern China. The Battle of Tsushima forced the rest of the world to accept Japan as a major power. It was a significant achievement for a nation which until 1854 had been a feudal state closed to the outside world.

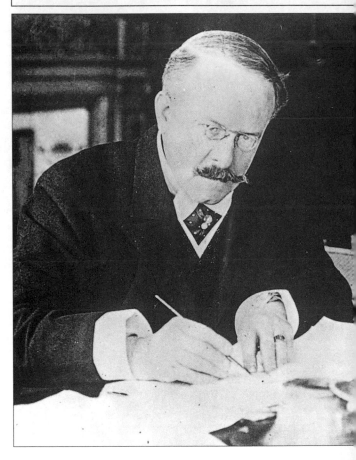

Above: Dr Thomas Barnardo who died on 19th September the age of 60. Intending to be a medical missionary, Barnar trained at the London Hospital but decided that work need to be done in the London slums. He soon concentrated helping destitute children and in 1866 founded his first hor His policy of never closing the door to a destitute child ma the home famous and attracted numerous bequests. Fac page, bottom left: On 1st July Albert Einstein published Special Theory of Relativity. The work touched off inter controversy, not least because so few people understood it. late as 1922 a group of scientists denounced the work as tion, but it has, however, gained universal acceptance sin Einstein went on to produce a General Theory of Relativ and work in the electro-magnetic field. His outspoken paci comments and virulent anti-Nazi statements led to his ab doning Germany for Britain.

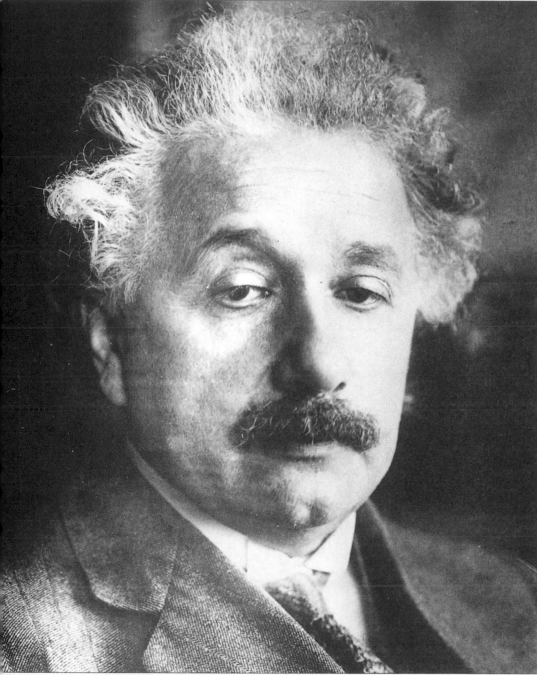

Top left: A sailing ship aground on the Grandsands. Sailing ships provided a sizeable amount of world shipping in 1905, but steam power was destined to take over within a decade. Top right: Born on 18th September in Stolkholm, Greta Gustafson changed her name to Garbo when she abandoned a job as a clerk for the movie screen in 1925. After just one film in her native Sweden, Garbo moved to Hollywood under contract to Metro-Goldwyn-Mayer where she made the silent classic **The Temptress**. The coming of sound movies revealed her soft, foreign accent to an enthralled audience and she went on to even greater success. Above: Ten year old Prince Albert, later King George VI, in highland garb during the Royal Family's summer break at Balmoral.

New Nation In Europe

In the summer of 1905 a nation was reborn in northern Europe. Since the end of the Napoleonic Wars Norway had been a self-governing subject to the Swedish king. In July the provincial Parliament voted to cut off relations with Sweden. A plebiscite backed the plan by 386,208 to 184 votes in August after the entire Norwegian government had resigned in protest at the action of the Swedish king in refusing to give his assent to a bill establishing a consular service. On 18th November the Norwegian Parliament elected Prince Carl, a younger son of the King of Denmark, to be their monarch. When the news arrived in Denmark Carl was at an official banquet. His elder brother, Crown Prince Frederick, leapt to his feet and proposed a toast to the new king. Carl took the name of Haakon VII, in deference to a line of Norwegian kings the first of which, in 961, went by the propitious name of Haakon the Good.

Above: George Bernard Shaw experienced his great success in 1905 when his plays **Major Barbara** *and* **Man and Superman** *played to packed houses in London simultaneously. Top right: Pablo Picasso's famous work* **Acrobate et jeune Arlequin** *was produced in 1905 to a somewhat indifferent art world. His great fame began with cubism in 1907 and only then was the value of his earlier work appreciated. Right: The great French philosopher and socialist writer Jean-Paul Sartre who was born on 21st June and went on to win the Nobel Prize for Literature in 1964.*

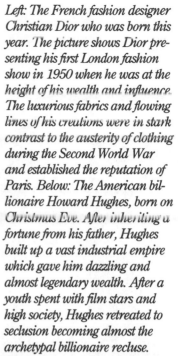

Left: The French fashion designer Christian Dior who was born this year. The picture shows Dior presenting his first London fashion show in 1950 when he was at the height of his wealth and influence. The luxurious fabrics and flowing lines of his creations were in stark contrast to the austerity of clothing during the Second World War and established the reputation of Paris. Below: The American billionaire Howard Hughes, born on Christmas Eve. After inheriting a fortune from his father, Hughes built up a vast industrial empire which gave him dazzling and almost legendary wealth. After a youth spent with film stars and high society, Hughes retreated to seclusion becoming almost the archetypal billionaire recluse.

Centre left: The fabulous Cullinan diamond which was found in the Premier Mine, Pretoria, South Africa on 25th January. Uncut it weighed 3106 carats, about 1lb 6oz. Above: The nine largest gems cut from the Cullinan, now part of the British Crown Jewels.

The First Duma

In May 1906 the Tsar of Russia set up a Du, or Parliament, elected by universal male suffrage. The move came as a conciliatory gesture to forces demanding democracy after riots, demonstrations and a naval mutiny in the previous year. The opening ceremony, on 10th May, was a grand affair accompanied by all the impressive pomp which the Tsarist regime could muster. The brilliant hopes of the early sessions of the Du were short lived. It soon became clear that Tsarist ministers were intent on stifling opposition. By judicious use of patronage, threats and ballot rigging they managed to reduce the Du to little more than a talking shop. Demands for democracy became more bitter.

n 18th April a massive earthquake struck San ancisco, tumbling the wealthy American city into ns. Fire broke out almost at once as gas mains frac- ed and some 500 people were killed and around 000 acres flattened. Facing page, top: City Hall after e earthquake. Facing page bottom: Devastation ng Sacremento Street. Top: Gutted remains of a nsion. Above: American President Theodore osevelt, left, about to be presented with the Nobel ace Prize for his work in negotiating an end to the sso-Japanese War.

Jan 4	US dancer Isadora Duncan banned by Belgian police
Jan 20	Birth of Greek shipping tycoon Aristotle Onassis
Feb 2	Paris: 530 injured in dispute over Church property
Feb 7	Liberal landslide in British General Election
Feb 8	Typhoon hits Tahiti, 10,000 feared dead
Feb 23	US: Chicago "Bluebeard" Johann Koch, said to have murdered at least one of his 50 wives, is executed
Mar 3	France: The first trials of an aeroplane with tyres take place at Montesson, Seine-et-Marne
Mar 11	1,200 miners die in explosion at pit in Northern France
Mar 14	British parliament accepts principle of old age pensions
Mar 22	Paris: England win the first rugby international against France by 35 to 8
Mar 28	New York: The State Meteororological Office says that the science of forecasting the weather is "within our grasp"
Apr 6	Sir John Betjeman born
Apr 7	Eruption of Vesuvius in Italy kills hundreds
Apr 13	Birth of Franco-Irish playwright Samuel Beckett
Apr 16	US: Supreme Court rules against inter-state divorce
Apr 18	Severe earthquake in San Francisco, more than 500 die
Apr 19	French physicist Pierre Curie killed in a road accident
May 8	Birth of Italian film director Roberto Rossellini
May 10	First Duma meets in St.Petersburg
May 22	Wilbur Wright patents his airplane
May 28	Russia: Government decides to redistribute 25 million acres of land to peasants
Jun 7	British liner Lusitania was launched
Jun 14	London: Bill banning women from dangerous sports following the death of a woman parachutist
Jun 22	Washington: Roosevelt sues John D. Rockefeller's Standard Oil Co. for operating monopoly
Jun 26	First motor racing Grand Prix is run at Le Mans
Jul 12	Alfred Dreyfus awared French Legion of Honour
Jul 12	10 Londoners on a day trip to Brighton are killed in a bus crash
Jul 15	London: House of Commons agrees to create a separate government ministry for Wales
Jul 21	Martial law declared in Russia
Aug 5	John Huston, film director, born
Aug 18	Massive earthquake in Chile kills hundreds
Sep 9	100 Jews murdered in Siedlce, Poland
Sep 20	Launch of British liners 'Mauretania' and 'Adriatic'
Sep 30	Paris: First international hot-air balloon race sets off
Oct 3	SOS established as international distress signal
Oct 9	US: Death of Joseph Glidden, inventor of barbed wire
Oct 16	British New Guinea becomes part of Australia
Oct 17	First transmission of a picture by telegraph
Oct 22	Death of Paul Cezanne
Oct 24	11 suffragettes jailed for demonstrations in London
Nov 2	Leon Trotsky exiled to Siberia for life
Nov 6	London: Sylvia Pankhurst released from prison
Nov 15	Launch of the world's biggest battleship in Japan, the 'Satsuma'
Dec 10	Roosevelt receives Nobel peace prize
Dec 14	First submarine, U1, enters German Navy
Dec 19	Birth of Soviet Leader Leonid Brezhnev

Facing page: A family of Italian immigrants arrives on Ellis Island in New York Harbour together with their meagre belongings. About 5,000 people a day were passing through Ellis Island in 1906. Many stayed in the city, or moved to equally crowded centres along the eastern seaboard. Here they tended to congregate together in areas dominated by a single nationality. Right: The Greek shipping magnate Aristotle Onassis was born on 15th January. Below: A self portrait of Paul Cezanne, who died on 22nd October. Born in Aix en Provence in 1839, Cezanne began life as a banker, but in 1863 began the study of art full time. His early success was modest but in the 1870s he turned to Impressionism and perfected the technique to produce some magnificent landscapes and portraits.

Crisis In Morocco

The ailing Sultanate of Morocco led to crisis talks between European powers in March. The nominally independent Sultan had for many years been gradually losing power as he became increasingly dependent on French, Spanish and German business and subsidies for financial security. It was concern by Germany that her financial stake in Morocco was under threat from Franco-Spanish power which led to the crisis. In March 1906 the three powers reached an agreement under which there would be a commercial open door policy, linked to a joint French-Spanish police force which reported jointly to the diplomatic corps and to the Sultan, still nominally independent. The agreement was at once thrown into turmoil when the Sultan Abd-el-Aziz was overthrown by his brother Mulai Hafid who refused to accept the deal negotiated by the Europeans.

Above: The smoking peak of Vesuvius, the Italian volcano which erupted on 10th April. The sudden blast of hot gases and ashes caught the surrounding countryside by surprise and killed hundreds. Over 105 were killed when the Church of San Giuseppe collapsed in Naples. For some weeks afterwards the mountain continued to pour forth molten rock and white hot ash, which covered large areas and forced thousands to flee from their homes. The disaster destroyed many homes and the entire village of Ottajano. It was easily the most violent of the recent eruptions of Vesuvius.

Jan 1	China: 4 million are feared to be starving owing to heavy rains and crop failure
Jan 2	France: Latest anti-clerical law comes into force, which forbids the crucifix in schools
Jan 7	England beats France 41-13 in the first Rugby meeting held in the UK between the two countries
Jan 14	Earthquake devastates Kingston, Jamaica
Jan 19	Mohammad Ali Mirza becomes new Shah of Persia
Jan 22	Strike by music hall artistes
Jan 26	Strauss's opera Salome is banned as obscene in New York
Jan 28	164 miners die in pit explosion at Saarbruchen, Germany
Feb 10	Death of British journalist Sir William Howard Russell
Feb 21	Birth of British poet Wystan Hugh Auden
Feb 27	The Central Criminal Court 'Old Bailey' opens in London
Mar 1	New York: Salvation Army sets up a suicide counselling bureau
Mar 12	French battleship 'Jena' explodes at Toulon, killing 118
Mar 14	New York: The Stock Exchange suffers the worst crash since 1901
Mar 22	Gandhi starts civil disobedience campaign in South Africa
Mar 22	75 Suffragettes are jailed in Britain for refusing to pay fines
Apr 25	Channel Tunnel Bill is killed by British Government
May 1	Canada: Death reported of Neil Brodie, the nation's dirtiest man who only bathed when ordered to do so by law
May 10	Mother's Day first held in Philadelphia
May 13	Birth of British novelist Daphne du Maurier
May 22	Birth of British actor Laurence Olivier
May 22	Birth of Belgian creator of "Tintin", Georges Remi, alias Herge

May 25	Finland: Opening of the World's first Parliament with women members
May 26	John Wayne born
Jun 1	Birth of Sir Frank Whittle, inventor of jet propulsion
Jun 6	British Government says it will never leave India
Jun 10	Northamptonshire score 12 runs in an innings against Gloucestershire
Jul 6	Brooklands motor racing track opens
Jul 6	London: Tom Reece ends billiards break of 499,135 begun on June 3rd
Jul 20	471 miners are killed in Japanese pit disaster
Jul 25	Japan makes Korea a protectorate
Jul 26	US author Mark Twain receives Honorary Doctorate
Jul 29	Boy Scout movement originated by Baden-Powell
Jul 30	British troops sent to quell unrest in Belfast
Aug 1	US Army forms first military air force
Sep 4	Death of Norwegian composer Edvard Grieg
Sep 26	New Zealand becomes a dominion
Oct 15	US: Town of Fontanet is almost entirely destroyed when a gunpowder factory explodes
Oct 26	The Territorial Army is established in Britain
Nov 16	Oklahoma is admitted as 46th US State
Dec 6	America's worst mining disaster, 361 die at Monongah, West Virginia
Dec 10	Rudyard Kipling is awarded the Nobel prize for literature
Dec 12	New York: New rules force woman to sign affidavits as to their age and good character before they marry

The year 1907 was one of optimism and confidence for many around the world. In most countries the standard of living was rising steadily as were levels of health care, food provision and overall life expectancy. The growing confidence led to demands for improved rights. The Suffragette movement, demanding voting rights for women, was a particularly widespread cause. In Finland women got the vote in March with Norway following in June. The new invention, aeroplanes, took two steps forward. An experimental helicopter flew in November while the French Voisin brothers established the first aircraft factory in March. Other inventions continued to tumble out of the laboratories and workshops, leading to a feeling that human ingenuity could, given time, achieve almost anything. In June the first colour photographs capable of easy reproduction were produced by the Lumiere brothers. The motor car was given its toughest test to date when six vehicles entered the Peking to Paris road race. The 8,000 mile course ran through rugged terrain and wilderness areas with great range of climate. However, not all was well. In Russia revolutionaries assassinated over 1,000 Tsarist officials as unrest continued. In the Balkans tensions mounted over the fate of Bosnia and war threatened.

Left: The American financial and industrial magnate John Pierpont Morgan who, in 1907, began handing his business affairs over to his son and thus retiring from public life. Born in 1837 to a wealthy Connecticut family, Morgan joined a banking company at the age of 20, founding his own bank just seven years later. J.P. Morgan & *Co of New York quickly established itself as the leading financial institution in America with a prudent policy and vast funds. Through the institution Morgan funded much of the railway building of the 1880s and 1890s and established the United States Steel Trust with the then unheard of capital of £220 million. Morgan died in 1913.*

Gandhi In South Africa

In March the world heard the first of a man who would go on to dominate world headlines during the 1930s. Mohandas Gandhi, an Indian living in South Africa, was incensed by a new law passed by the Transvaal Colony assembly which placed restrictions on Asian immigrants. Gandhi, possessed of a fine legal mind and with a flourishing attorney's practice set out to fight the measure by a process of civil disobedience and legal challenges. The campaign cost Gandhi his legal work, which he abandoned to take up political agitation full time. In 1908 he threw himself and his team into humanitarian relief work following the Natal Revolt and so gained credibility with colonial authorities. In 1914 the Indian's Relief Act was passed, thus achieving much which Gandhi had worked for in South Africa. Soon afterwards he left for India, where he became a leader of the nationalist cause.

Top left: Lord and Lady Baden-Powell who conceived his idea for the Boy Scouts movement in 1907 and founded it the following year. Baden-Powell gained fame as the hero of the siege of Mafeking during the Boer War and placed great military value on scouting. Left:

Pablo Picasso who, in 1907, produced a startling work in a style he called 'cubist'. Above: Movie star John Wayne born as Marion Morrison in Iowa in 1907. He went on to become a giant star, attracting more people to see his films than any other actor.

Birth Of New Zealand

In September New Zealand lost its colonial status to become a Dominion. The move marked the first step towards nationhood for the island peoples. Britain had claimed sovereignty in 1840 and a series of wars with the native Maoris followed until peace was achieved in the 1870s. The Maoris, due to their vigorous culture and tough attitude to Europeans have fared rather better than other peoples, such as the North American Indians and Australian Aborigines, in coming to terms with a large influx of white settlers. The move to Dominion status entailed increased powers of self-government, but the Statute of Westminster, granting full independence was not given assent until 1947.

Facing page: Laurence Olivier, born on 22nd May, starring opposite Gertrude Lawrence in Noel Coward's **Private Lives.** *Top left: The British novelist Daphne Du Maurier who wrote such classics as* **Rebecca** *and* **The Birds.** *Left: American novelist Mark Twain, real name Samuel Clemens, was awarded an honourary doctorate in July for his services to literature. Above: J.M. Barrie whose most popular work,* **Peter Pan,** *first appeared in book form in 1907, having originated as a stage play at the Duke of York in London in 1904.*

1908

Jan 1	US:State of Georgia introduces alcohol prohibition.
Jan 6	UK: 2,000 textile workers strike in Oldham,Lancashire
Jan 8	Count von Zeppelin will build airship to hold 100 people
Jan 9	Birth of French writer Simone de Beauvoir
Jan 22	British Labour Party decides to adopt socialism
Jan 30	General Smuts frees Gandhi in South Africa
Feb 1	King Carlos I and Crown Prince are murdered in Portugal
Feb 22	Birth of actor John Mills
Feb 27	Oklahoma becomes the 46th state of the US
Mar 4	New York: The whip is banned as a means of corporal punishment in schools
Mar 7	First German dreadnought battleship is launched
Mar 16	Florence Nightingale is awarded the freedom of the City of London
Mar 21	Frenchman Henri Farman pilots first passenger flight
Mar 23	Birth of Joan Crawford
Apr 5	Birth of Bette Davis
Apr 8	Herbert Asquith becomes new British Liberal PM
Apr 8	US: Injunction issued by Roosevelt allowing blacks to use the same train carriages as whites in the South
Apr 13	Floods in China kill 2,000
May 7	British OAPs to get 5 shillings a week
May 15	Monet destroys paintings worth £20,000 saying they were unsatisfactory
May 16	Britain's first diesel submarine is launched
May 20	Birth of US actor James Stewart
May 22	The Wright brothers patent their aeroplane
May 26	State of North Carolina adopts alcohol prohibition
May 28	Birth of British writer Ian Fleming
Jun 4	An attempt is made on the life of Major Alfred Dreyfus
Jun 6	France: A new law grants automatic divorce after three years separation
Jun 11	Rotherhithe Tunnel under Thames is opened
Jun 20	Russian composer Rimsky-Korsakov dies
Jun 22	Six blacks accused of murder are lynched in Texas, US
Jun 24	Former US President Grover Cleveland dies
Jun 24	Spain: Steamer Larache sinks killing 85 people
Jul 3	Death of US author Joel Chandler Harris, writer of the Brer Rabbit stories
Jul 26	Federal Bureau of Investigation is established in Washington DC
Jul 27	Fourth Olympic Games open in London
Aug 14	The first international beauty contest is held in Britain
Aug 27	Birth of US President, Lyndon Baines Johnson
Sep 12	Wedding of Winston Churchill and Clementine Hozier
Sep 16	Buick and Oldsmobile merge to form General Motors
Sept 17	A passenger of Orville Wright's becomes first man to be killed in a plane crash
Oct 1	Model T Ford goes on sale for first time in the US, at $900
Sep 5	Bulgaria proclaims independence from Ottoman Empire
Oct 14	Chicago Cubs win World Series
Oct 16	First aeroplane flight in Britain
Nov 3	William Taft elected President of the US
Nov 5	Cullinan diamond is cut for Queen Alexandra
Nov 9	Britain's first woman mayor is elected
Dec 2	Child emperor Pu Yi ascends Chinese throne at the age of 2
Dec 28	Messina, on island of Sicily, damaged by earthquake

FLORENCE NIGHTINGALE

Facing page: Florence Nightingale who, in 1908, became the first woman [to] receive the Order of Merit. It was as the Lady with the Lamp, the hero[ic] nurse of the Crimean War, that Florence Nightingale became famo[us] though she was involved in many other good works during her long and pr[o]ductive life. Born in 1820 to a Derbyshire gentleman, Florence abandon[ed] the standard upbringing for a country girl of a good family when in 1850 s[he] visited a German religious hospital which specialised in hygiene and care. [In] 1854, disturbed by reports from the Crimean War of the horrific conditio[ns] in military hospitals, Florence gathered 37 nurses and set out for the ma[in] hospital at Scutari, arriving on 4th November. At first the military did n[ot] take her seriously, and refused to accept her advice. Her determination an[d] at times, blazing anger combined with her unfailing good judgment won h[er] many concessions so that within months the death rate in hospital fell fr[om] 42% to just 2%. After the war she founded a home for training nurses [in] London and worked ceaselessly to improve the care for the sick.

Above: President William Taft with his family in a photograph taken days after the election in 1908 which gave him the White House. Taft was a large and impressive man who was able to swing crowds with his orato- *ry, but was a man whom man[y] suspected of being without mu[ch] substance or political acumen He served as both Governor o[f] the Philippines and Secretary [of] War before becoming Preside[nt] He later served as Chief Justic[e]*

46

Right: Winston Churchill and Clementine Hozier, photographed a week before their wedding. Below right: Miss Clementine arrives at the church. Below: The most famous image of the 1908 London Olympics, held in July. The Italian runner Dorando Pietri reached the stadium at the end of the Marathon well ahead of the other competitors and staggered towards the finishing line suffering from obvious exhaustion. Before he breasted the tape a well meaning steward gave him a helping hand, thus ensuring the hapless Pietri both disqualification and enormous public support. Bottom left: Britain's George Larner winning the 10 mile walk at the London Olympics. British athletes took all three medals in this event.

The Travels Of King Edward

Britain's King Edward VII undertook a series of gruelling diplomatic tours in 1908 as the cut and thrust of European international relations became increasingly complex and situations and loyalties changed rapidly. Already well known and much admired in France, King Edward travelled to Russia in June to meet Tsar Nicholas II. The visit helped ease tension in Persia and Afghanistan between the two empires. It also marked the historic first visit of a British monarch to the Russian Empire. In August the king travelled to Germany to see Kaiser Wilhelm II in an effort to reproduce his Russian success. Difficulties with Germany largely revolved around the comparative sizes of the Royal and Imperial navies. However, Edward failed to win over the Kaiser. In October the German monarch made abrasive remarks which contained many anti-British and sabre-rattling statements. The tension between Britain and Germany remained.

Left: Classic film star Bette Davis, born in Massachusetts this year. After a successful Broadway career, Davis moved to Hollywood. Fame came with **The Man who played God** *in 1932. Below: Hollywood leading man James Stewart, born in Pennsylvania in 1908. He began his film career as a sidekick of leading villains, but soon established his screen persona as a gangling idealist not always aware of the realities around him. Bottom: The great cricketer W.G. Grace who dominated English cricket as much by his personality as by his amazing ability.*

12th August a new era in transport began when the first Model T Ford ne off the assembly lines. The Model T was the first car to be produced a conveyor belt system of assembly and was deliberately kept simple and in so as to ensure a low price. It went on sale for $850, putting motor s into the reach of the middle classes for the first time. The Model T atinued to be produced, in various styles, until 1928 by which time over million had been sold. It was the innovation of simple mechanics and cost which established the Ford Company, which by the time the del T stopped production was the third largest in the USA.

1909

Jan 1	London: Astronomers report they may have sighted another planet beyond Neptune
Jan 3	Birth of Victor Borge
Jan 5	Colombian government recognises independence of Panama
Jan 5	Riots between Hindus and Muslems in Calcutta
Jan 9	Ernest Shackleton's expedition gets closest yet to South Pole
Jan 11	Four murderers are guillotined publicly in N. France
Jan 12	Turkey accepts cash for loss of Bosnia and Herzegovina
Jan 15	Italy: At least 200,000 die in Europe's worst earthquake
Jan 18	New Zealand: Brewers abolish barmaids and ban women from buying alcohol in bars
Jan 21	US: State of Tennessee adopts alcohol prohibition
Feb 3	Birth of French philosopher Simone Weil
Feb 9	London: A court rules that a wife if not entitled to a divorce, even if she has been deserted by her husband
Feb 17	Death of Apache chief Geronimo
Feb 24	Colour films are shown to the public for the first time
Mar 4	William Taft inaugurated as US President
Mar 15	Selfridges opens in Oxford Street
Mar 24	President Taft approves the Income Tax Bill
Mar 25	Madame Papova arrested for 300 murders in Russia
Apr 3	Memorial to Keats and Shelley is unveiled in Rome
Apr 6	US Commander Robert Peary reaches N. Pole
Apr 10	Death of British poet Algernon Charles Swinburne
Apr 23	Muslem fanatics massacre 80,000 Armenians in Turkey
Apr 30	Juliana, Queen of Netherlands, born
May 15	Birth of British actor James Mason
May 18	Fred Perry born
May 18	Death of British novelist George Meredith
May 26	Sir Matt Busby born
May 30	Benny Goodman, American band leader, born
Jun 1	US: Opening of Seattle World Fair
Jun 10	SOS distress signal broadcast for first time
Jun 11	Earthquake in Provence, France, kills 60
Jun 13	Shackleton arrives in Dover, England, after his Antarctic expedition
Jun 18	Joan of Arc beatified by the Pope 478 years after the English burned her at the stake in Rouen
Jun 20	Errol Flynn born
Jun 26	London: King Edward VII opens Victoria and Albert Museum
Jun 29	120 suffragettes arrested outside Houses of Parliament
Jul 1	Indian terrorist kills Anglo-Indian Sir Curzon Wylie
Jul 16	Revolution in Persia places 12 year old prince on throne
Jul 24	Aristide Briant becomes French PM
Jul 25	Louis Bleriot makes first flight across the English Channel
Aug 22	Five US workers die in steel industry riots
Aug 30	Floods in Mexico kill 1,400
Sep 4	The first Boy Scout rally takes place at Crystal Palace
Oct 2	First rugby match is played at Twickenham
Oct 13	Yerren, leader of anti-clerical party, executed in Spain
Oct 26	Prince Ito of Japan is assassinated by Korean terrorist
Nov 5	First Woolworth's store opened in Britain
Nov 9	Katharine Hepburn born
Dec 17	Albert I becomes King of the Belgians

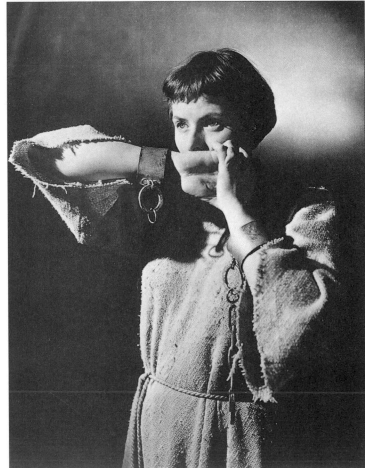

Joan of Arc was beatified on 18th June by Pope Pius X. The warrior maid who defeated English troops had long been regarded as a saint by the French people, but it took 478 years for the Church to take the claims seriously. She was canonised in 1919. Left: Ingrid Bergman in the role of Joan in Honegger's opera. Above: Apache chief Geronimo who held out against the United States army a bitter guerrilla campaign until 1886, died on 17th February.

The struggle for women's suffrage continued unabated in 1909. Above: Muriel Manners receives plenty of male assistance before taking off in a balloon to drift over the Palace of Westminster and shout suffragette slogans at MPs arriving for the official opening of Parliament. Miss Manners had earlier attracted attention by chaining herself to the public gallery in the House of Commons.

THE PEOPLE'S BUDGET

In 1909 the great Liberal politician, Lloyd George, introduced a revolutionary budget which was quickly hailed by his supporters as 'The People's Budget", but caused his opponents to brand him a demagogue. Born in 1863, the South Wales lawyer entered Parliament aged only 27. There his legendary oratory skills were honed to a fine art. He could keep an audience spellbound and convert even the bitterest critic to his views. In 1908 he made a speech warning against German aggression which was so powerful that the German ambassador persuaded the Kaiser to resolve the Agadir Crisis peacefully. He followed up his 1909 budget with the 1911 National Insurance Bill and in 1916 took over as Prime Minister and proved to be an inspired war leader. He resigned the Premiership in 1922 and sadly watched the decline of the Liberal Party as a force in national politics.

BLERIOT CROSSES THE CHANNEL

A milestone in the history of flight was reached on 25th July when Frenchman Louis Bleriot became the first human to fly across a large body of open water in an heavier than air machine by crossing the English Channel. The attempt was prompted by a £1,000 cash prize offered by a British newspaper for the first to complete the flight. Three men took up the challenge. Count de Lambert tried on 19th July, but was grounded by mechanical failure. Hubert Latham took off next and had reached halfway when, at a record height of 1,000 feet, his engine stalled and he crashed into the sea to be rescued by the French navy. Bleriot took off at 5 am on the 25th, and completed the flight in just 37 minutes. Although the flight was without incident, Bleriot suffered bruising when his landing resulted in a slight crash. Bleriot not only claimed his prize, but was awarded the Legion d'Honneur by the French government. Bleriot made some notable technical improvements to aircraft design in the years before the outbreak of war, but faded from the scene as more advanced aircraft appeared. Facing page, top: Louis Bleriot at the controls of the monoplane in which he made his historic flight. Facing page, bottom: Bleriot (centre) shows his machine, with wings folded, to neighbours and friends.

Left: Commander Robert Peary of the US Navy in his polar exploration clothing, based closely on Eskimo originals. He became the first man to reach the North Pole on 6th April. But his claim at once plunged him into international controversy. A former colleague, Frederick Cook returned from the polar regions to claim *that he reached the Pole the previous year. Scientific societies eventually decided in favour of Peary claim. However, more recent research has cast some doubt on this finding. Above: Ernest Shackleton, the British explorer who returned from an unsuccessful attempt to reach the South Pole in 1909.*

Naval Rivals Come to Grips

In March the British First Lord of Admiralty shocked the nation when he announced that the global supremacy of the Royal Navy was under threat and that, unless urgent action was taken, it would be lost within months. The naval supremacy had come to be taken for granted since 1805 when a British fleet under Admiral Nelson utterly destroyed the combined might of France and Spain at the Battle of Trafalgar. Since then none had dared to challenge the Royal Navy. But in 1909 it became clear that the German Imperial Navy was not only challenging but overtaking the Royal Navy. It was learnt that Germany had laid down thirty battle ships of the latest design, each one capable of outgunning most ships in the Royal Navy. The British government reacted swiftly. The Naval dockyards were ordered to begin a massive shipbuilding programme which was to continue unabated until the First World War.

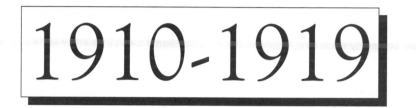

1910-1919

1910

THE KING AND A TSAR

Facing page: A picture of King Edward VII surrounded by his family at Cowes Week. Seated beside him is Tsar Nicholas II of Russia on one of several visits to England. Seated in front of the two monarchs is the sickly heir to the Russian throne, Alexis. The Tsar believed his power to rule came from divine right and consistently refused to allow the type of constitutional monarchy followed by the British. He lost his throne to a Revolution precipitated by misgovernment and defeat in the war with Germany. In 1918 Tsar Nicholas, his wife and children were shot dead by Communist revolutionaries.

New Nation In Africa

On 1st July the Union of South Africa was born out of the disparate colonies of Cape Colony, Natal, Transvaal and the Orange Free State. So different were these colonies that some predicted the Union would not last, and indeed there were early tensions. The Transvaal and Orange Free State originated as republics established by Boer farmers who trekked north from the Cape in the 1830s to escape British rule. Their subjugation in the Boer War was completed only in 1902, and their relationship with the British dominated Cape Colony and Natal was uneasy. Tensions between the provinces of the new Union reflected very different lifestyles, religions and views on morality. Though these faded with time they remained potent political factors for many years.

Above: Inspector Drew escorts a muffled Dr Crippen into custody. Crippen became the first man caught by radio when the captain of the ship on which he travelled radioed the police. Top right: Mark Twain died on 21st April. Right: Leo Tolstoy, the author of **War and Peace,** died on 21st November.

Below: Actor David Niven, born on 1st March in Kirriemuir, Scotland. He first acted in 1935 and quickly became established as a gifted player of British gentlemen. On the outbreak of the Second World War, Niven joined the Commandos and reached the rank of Colonel, returning to acting with the coming of peace.

Right: The funeral cortege of King Edward VII, who died on 6th May, arrives at Windsor Castle. Below right: Kaiser Wilhelm II, King George V, Duke of Connaught, Prince of Wales and Prince Albert at the funeral. Bottom right: Douglas Bader, born this year, gained fame as a fighter pilot during World War II.

Fall Of The House Of Braganza

When, in 1640, the Duke of Braganza was declared to be King John IV of Portugal it was a turning point in the history of the Iberian Peninsula. No longer could the rulers of Castille claim to speak on behalf of all the Christians in the Peninsula. When the last of the Braganza monarchs, Manuel II, was forced to flee his native home it was, yet again a turning point. Manuel's troubles had various causes, but essentially stemmed from inept government which many suspected of being both corrupt and incapable of dealing with Portugal's problems. Secret societies, such as the notorious Carbonari who had earlier fomented trouble in Italy, encouraged unrest. On 4th October the army stepped in by occupying the capital and establishing a ruling junta. Within hours Manuel II had fled with a fortune in jewels, leaving Portugal a republic. By August the following year a constitution was in place and elections were held.

Hope Of Misfortune

In January a new record was set for the price of a gem stone when the Hope Diamond was bought by American businessman Ned McLean for $300,000. The Hope diamond was a flawless gem, deep blue in colour which weighed some 44 carats. The diamond had originally been found in India during the Middle Ages and had passed through various hands as war booty or as a diplomatic gift before it came into the possession of French King Louis XIV. By this time, the beautiful stone had already acquired something of a reputation for bad luck. No doubt this was influenced by the sudden and violent deaths not uncommon among Indian princes during the 17th and 18th centuries. The grim name was enhanced when Louis XIV was overthrown by the French Revolution and executed. Louis XVI also owned the stone when he took the French throne, but sold the gem after he lost it temporarily to Napoleon in 1815. It then passed to a banker named Hope, after whom it took its name, and thence to America and Mr. McLean. The McLeans had it set in a tiara which was worn by the younger Mrs McLean at formal occasions.

Above: Norwegian explorer Roald Amundsen became the first man to reach the South Pole on 14th December. Amundsen's bid for the Pole began in January when his ship anchored in the Bay of Whales on the Ross Ice Shelf. After enduring the Antarctic winter, Amundsen set out in October with a small team which carried only light equipment on sleds drawn by specially trained husky dogs.

Jan 2	Nicaragua: President Taft recognises Jose Estrada's new government and orders withdrawal of troops
Jan 17	Paris: Attempt is made on the life of French premier Aristide Briand
Jan 21	Start of first Monte Carlo rally
Jan 25	US Cavalry sent to Rio Grande in Mexican Civil War
Feb 6	Ramsay MacDonald succeeds Keir Hardie as Chairman of the Labour Party
Feb 6	King George V opens his first parliament
Feb 6	Large area of Constantinople is destroyed by fire
Feb 6	Birth of actor and US President Ronald Reagan
Feb 22	Canada votes to remain in British Empire
Mar 8	Britain says it will not support France if it is attacked
Mar 17	Norway's first first woman member of parliament takes her seat
Mar 26	Birth of US playwright Tennessee Williams
Apr 4	US: Massachusetts state legislature refuses women the right to vote
Mar 31	British shopworkers win fight for 60 hour week
May 3	Lloyd George introduces National Health Insurance Bill
May 4	UK: Britain's first airship is wrecked at Aldershot
May 18	Gustav Mahler, Austrian composer, dies in Venice
May 25	Mexican dictator Porfirio Diaz ousted after 45 years
May 30	W. S. Gilbert (collaborator with Arthur Sullivan) dies
May 30	Indianapolis 500 inaugurated
May 31	White Star liner 'Titanic' is launched
Jun 7	Earthquake kills over 100 in Mexico City
Jun 13	First performance of Stravinsky's ballet 'Petrushka'
Jun 24	Birth of Argentinian racing driver Juan Fangio
Jun 20	City of Leeds begins Britain's first trolley-bus service
Jun 22	Coronation of George V
Jun 22	Liverpool's Liver Clock begins recording time
Jul 5	Birth of French President Georges Pompidou
Jul 13	Investiture of Edward, Prince of Wales
Jul 16	Ginger Rogers born
Jul 20	Nine rioters are shot by troops in Wales
Aug 3	North Africa: First military use of aeroplanes
Aug 6	Birth of US comedienne Lucille Ball
Aug 8	50,000 troops assemble to fight riots in Liverpool
Aug 14	South Wales miners lift strike after 10 months
Aug 21	The Mona Lisa was stolen from the Louvre, to be found two years later
Aug 31	The Director of the Louvre is sacked following the theft of the Mona Lisa
Sep 4	100,000 die in Yangtse River floods in China
Sep 14	Duke Ellington gets rapturous reception on Soviet tour
Sep 14	Russian Premier Peter Stolypin is shot
Sep 19	Birth of British writer William Golding
Sep 28	Italy declares war on Turkey
Sep 30	Italy mounts an assault on Turks in Tripoli harbour
Oct 2	Mexico: Francisco Madero is elected President
Oct 6	Barbara Castle born
Oct 10	Robert Borden succeeds Wilfred Laurier as PM of Canada
Oct 11	US: 700 are killed in an earthquake in California
Oct 30	Chinese Emperor Pu Yi grants a constitution
Nov 1	First ever aerial bombing by Italians in Tripolitania
Nov 15	The Chevrolet Motor Company is incorporated
Nov 29	Death of US journalist Joseph Pulitzer
Dec 14	Roald Amundsen becomes first man to reach the South Pole

The coronation of Britain's King George V took place on 22nd June, a year and a month after his accession. The delay reflected the elaborate preparations for the ceremony, arguably the grandest ever staged for a British monarch and was in stark contrast to mediaeval monarchs who took the crown as quickly as possible. Above left: The Royal Carriage arriving at Westminster. Above: The new king and queen in their elaborate coronation robes and magnificent jewels. Left: The newly crowned king returns to Buckingham Palace after the ceremony. Facing page: King George and Queen Mary on board the Medina en route to the even more lavish Delhi Durbar when they were enthroned as Emperor and Empress of India. At the Durbar Indian princes paid homage in a ceremony which owed much to mediaeval Indian practice.

Facing page: Queen Mary,
crowned Queen-Empress of
Britain on 22nd June and photographed soon after. Already popular with the British public,
Queen Mary quickly established
herself as an effective, dignified
and widely admired queen. Born
in 1867 to the family of the Duke
of Teck, Mary lived largely in
Florence and Richmond before she
was betrothed to the Duke of
Clarence, heir to the British
throne, in 1891. He died in 1892
and within five months she was
engaged to the Duke of York, later
George V. The royal pair were
married in 1893 and remained
close until his death in 1936. Top
left: Ginger Rogers, seen here with
Fred Astaire, was born in
Missouri on 16th July. Above:
Playwright Tennessee Williams,
also born in Missouri in 1911.
Left: Ramsay MacDonald who
was elected leader of Britain's
Labour Party on 6th February.

Jan 1	UK: The National Telephone Company is taken over by the Post Office
Jan 6	New Mexico becomes 47th US State
Jan 17	Scott reaches South Pole to find Amundsen has beaten him
Jan 28	Birth of US artist Jackson Pollock
Feb 10	Death of Lord Lister, founder of antiseptic surgery
Feb 14	Arizona becomes 48th US State
Feb 27	Birth of British poet and writer Lawrence Durrell
Mar 1	Albert Berry (US) makes 1st successful parachute jump
Mar 3	Martial Law is declared in Peking
Mar 7	Frenchman Henri Seimet becomes the first man to fly non-stop from Paris to London
Mar 17	Lawrence Oates, Captain Scotts companion, dies on the way back from the South Pole on his 32nd birthday, his last words: "I am just going outside, and may be some time"
Mar 27	Birth of British Prime Minister James Callaghan
Mar 28	London: Both boats sink in the University boat race
Mar 29	Captain Scott dies in Antarctica
Apr 4	Chinese Republic is proclaimed in Tibet
Apr 15	The Titanic sinks with the loss of over 1,500 passengers on her maiden voyage
Apr 16	American pilot Harriet Quimby became first woman to fly the English Channel
May 5	First issue of revolutionary Russian paper Pravda
May 11	Phil Silvers born
May 24	Joan Hammond, New Zealand soprano, born
May 26	UK: Transport strikes paralyse the country
May 28	US: Titanic enquiry gives verdict of negligence
May 31	US Marines land in Cuba to quell slave revolt
Jun 16	Enoch Powell born
Jun 22	William Taft is nominated for 2nd term as US President
Jun 23	Bridge over Niagara Falls collapses, killing 47
Jul 1	Morocco is declared a French protectorate
Jul 1	London: First Royal Command Performance at Palace Theatre
Jul 15	National Insurance begins in Britain
Jul 23	Modesty League protests against tight dresses
Jul 30	Japanese Emporer Meiji Tenno dies - Yoshihito succeeds
Aug 23	Gene Kelly born
Sep 1	Uprising in Morocco quelled by French troops
Oct 8	Montenegro declares war on Turkey
Oct 14	Turkey invades Serbia
Oct 18	Italy and Turkey sign peace treaty at Lausanne
Oct 19	Bulgarian and allied armies invade Turkey
Nov 5	Woodrow Wilson elected US President
Nov 5	Roy Rogers born
Nov 27	Spain and France sign treaty over Morocco
Nov 28	Albania declares independence
Nov 30	Bulgaria and Turkey sign armistice
Dec 18	The Piltdown Skull discovered, later to be proved a hoax
Dec 25	Italy sends troops to Albania to deal with uprising

SCOTT OF THE ANTARCTIC

Captain Robert Scott's expedition to Antarctica of 1910-1912 was a triumph of scientific research, but ended in tragedy and death. The all male team included geologists, biologists and physicists along with technical crew and, for the first time on such an expedition, a movie cameraman. The photographer, Herbert Ponting, produced a remarkable record of the expedition. After carrying out their scientific tasks, Scott and four companions - Bowers, Oates, Evans and Wilson - set out for the South Pole in November 1911. They reached the Pole on 16th January only to find that the Norwegian Roald Amundsen had got there a few weeks earlier. Faced with unusually severe blizzards and storms on the return journey, all five men perished. Scott was the last to die and wrote a number of letters and notes before his death. Previous pages: (left) The *Terra Nova* in the ice; (top right) unloading stores in January and (bottom right) fodder for the ill-fated ponies being dragged to store. Right: One of Ponting's most famous photos of the *Terra Nova*. Below: Scott and his team at the South Pole. Facing page top: Scott at work in his tiny study. Facing page bottom left: The cairn of ice and cross of skis erected over the bodies of Scott, Bowers and Wilson.

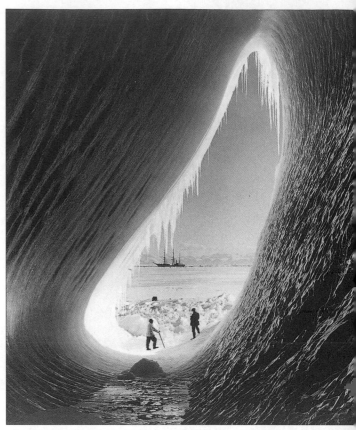

The last message to the public written by Scott as he waited to die in March 1912.

"Had we lived I should have had a tale to tell of the hardihood, endurance and courage of many companions which would have stirred the heart of every Englishman. These rough notes and our dead bodies must tell the tale, but surely, surely a great rich country like ours will see that those who are dependent on us are properly provided for."

THE WRECK OF THE TITANIC

On 10th April, amid much celebration and publicity the magnificent new liner RMS Titanic set out from Southampton bound for New York on her maiden voyage. The new ship was fully equipped with all the latest luxuries. She also had 16 watertight compartments and so far exceeded flotation requirements of the day as to be regarded as virtually unsinkable. At 11.40pm on the 14th she was steaming off the Newfoundland Grand Banks when the lookout reported an iceberg, the First Officer ordered a turn to port, and the ship missed the berg. However, an underwater projection of ice struck the ship below the waterline, ripping open several of the watertight compartments. Within minutes it was clear to Captain Smith

that the ship was sinking and he ordered distress rockets to be fired an radio signals to be sent before giving the fateful order to abandon ship. Du to inadequate safety regulations, the Titanic carried only enough lifeboa for 1,178, although a total of 2,201 passengers and crew were aboard. Du to some confusion and an inability to accept that the Titanic was doome only around 800 actually left by lifeboat, and one boat was sucked under b the ship as she sank. The remainder, including the captain and most of th crew, stayed aboard as the ship plunged beneath the icy waves at 2.20 an The liner Carpathia arrived on the scene at 4am to find only 712 survivor New safety regulations were introduced within weeks.

Left: Lord Joseph Lister who died on 12th February after a lifetime devoted to medical research and improvement. Born in Essex in 1827, Lister took a medical degree when aged 25 before moving to first Edinburgh and then Glasgow to practise. In 1862 he announced his theory that the infection of wounds was due to newly discovered bacteria. The remainder of his life was devoted to finding methods by which bacterial infection could be prevented. Such a process would reduce the appalling death rate then common after surgery and enable doctors to undertake operations with some certainty of the patient surviving. He produced new methods of ensuring bandages and other dressings were sterile, carbolic acid being his preferred medium, and introduced important new techniques for draining wounds. He was raised to the peerage in 1897 as recognition for his work.

The Balkan War

On 8th October the long feared Balkan War finally erupted when the tiny state of Montenegro declared war on Turkey. The small mountain kingdom of Montenegro stood between the sprawling Turkish territories and the Adriatic Coast. She was allied to Serbia, Bulgaria and Greece in the Balkan League of 1912. All four nations had gained independence from the Turkish Empire during the 19th century and wished to free the Serbs, Greeks and Bulgars whose territories lay within the Ottoman Empire. Throughout 1912 the Balkan nations made increasingly loud demands of Turkey, culminating in a call for self government for the Christian peoples in European Turkey. When the Ottoman government refused war was declared. Within a few weeks of campaigning, the Balkan League had driven Turkish troops back almost to the gates of Constantinople. Winter closed down the major warfare and Turkey did not accept defeat until May, granting hugely expanded realms to all four members of the Balkan League.

Above right: King George V and Queen Mary meet local dignitaries while on a visit to Silverwood Colliery in Yorkshire's South Riding in July. Right: British politician Enoch Powell, born on 16th June, who went on to become a dominating influence in the Conservative Party. Powell had a commanding personality and intellect, being the youngest Professor of Greek in Britain, but he felt unable to remain within a tight party system and so went his own way. Established as a brilliant, but unorthodox politician, Powell remained in Parliament for many years until his eventual retirement.

Jan 2	Turkey agrees to give up all but one of its European territories
Jan 9	Turkey breaches armistice with attacks on Bulgaria
Jan 9	Birth of US President Richard Nixon
Jan 13	UK: National Insurance Act offers sickness benefit
Jan 13	The Pope bans films of a religious nature
Jan 13	Two people are killed by London's Black Fog
Jan 17	France: Raymond Poincare is elected President of the Republic
Jan 22	Turkey accepts ceasefire ultimatum
Jan 27	Athlete Jim Thorpe is stripped of two Olympic gold medals for his involvement in 'professional' sport
Feb 2	Grand Central station opens in New York
Feb 3	Bulgaria restarts Balkan war
Feb 8	Turkish/Bulgarian battle leaves 5,000 Turks dead
Feb 9	Felix Diaz, nephew of ex-president, seizes Mexico City
Feb 10	The bodies of Captain Scott and his companions found in their tent just eleven miles from a food depot
Feb 22	Deposed president of Mexico, Francisco Madero, shot to death in the streets of Mexico City
Feb 25	US: Federal Income Tax is introduced
Mar 2	Suffragettes attacked by mob in Hyde Park, London
Mar 4	Woodrow Wilson inaugurated
Mar 18	Greek King assassinated in Salonika
Mar 4	UK: Suffragettes lock Labour Party delegates into their conference hall in Manchester
Mar 25	Bulgarians capture Adranople from Turks
Apr 16	Turkey signs armistice with Bulgaria
Apr 8	Peking: Opening of China's first parliament
Apr 20	The two children of Isadora Duncan and their nurse are drowned in the Seine, France
May 20	London: First Chelsea Flower Show
May 23	London: 10mph speed limit set at Hyde Park Corner
May 30	Turks sign Balkan Peace Treaty
Jun 4	Emily Davidson killed by King's horse at the Derby
Jun 29	Norway: Equal electoral rights for men and women are granted in Parliament
Jul 1	Zanzibar incorporated into British East Africa
Jul 1	Greece and Serbia declare war on Bulgaria
Jul 3	Rumania orders mobilisation
Jul 10	Russia declares war on Bulgaria
Jul 14	Birth of US President Gerald Ford
Aug 7	Conscription introduced in France
Aug 10	Balkan Peace Treaty signed in Bucharest
Sep 1	Louis Bleriot loops the loop for the first time
Oct 14	Pit disaster in Wales killed 439
Oct 17	Serbia invades Albania
Oct 21	Royalist rising fails in Portugal
Nov 2	Burt Lancaster born
Nov 5	Vivien Leigh born
Nov 17	First ship passes through Panama Canal
Dec 14	Greece annexes Crete
Dec 23	The Federal Reserve established in US

The Panama Canal

On 10th October a decades old dream became reality when American President Wilson set off charges which opened the final section of the Panama Canal. Within weeks ocean-going ships were able to travel between the Atlantic and Pacific Oceans without the need to travel the long and dangerous route around Cape Horn, notorious for its ferocious storms and dangerous currents. An attempt by the French builders of the Suez Canal to construct a Panama Canal collapsed in the 1870s due to technical difficulties. In 1903 the United States signed a treaty with Panama which allowed the United States to build and operate the Canal as well as to control a 10 mile strip of land on either side of the canal in return for a down payment of $10 million and an annual rent of $250,000. US Army Engineer George Goethals solved the construction problems while Dr Gorgas produced an effective treatment for both malaria and yellow fever, diseases which had threatened to decimate the work gangs. In 1982 administration of the Canal was handed over to Panama, on condition of permanent neutrality, but the United States continued to take a close interest in the region to protect their interests.

Left: Britain's King George V rides with Germany's Kaiser Wilhelm II in Potsdam, a smart town near Berlin, which was fashionable with the German aristocracy. The two men shared Queen Victoria as a grandmother and family ties between the British and German royal families were close. The visit was officially to attend the wed-ding of the Kaiser's daughter, bu the monarchs took the opportun to discuss many problems. Not least of these was the growing instability in the Balkans where Serbia, Montenegro, Greece, Rumania and Bulgaria had diff culties and disputes which threat ened to escalate from minor loca fighting to a widespread war.

Right: British sportsman and aviation inventor Thomas Sopwith in one of his aircraft. Sopwith devoted the research arm of his aircraft company to improving the performance and speed of his models. In 1913 he produced the Sopwith Gordon Bennett Racer, a sleek biplane with a top speed of 105 miles per hour. This research was to pay fine dividends during World War I when Sopwith designed and produced some of the finest aircraft to be used on either side. The most famous creation was, of course, the Sopwith Camel which ended the war with 1,294 kills to the credit of its pilots. The Camel was a highly manoeuvrable aircraft which had a top speed of 122 miles per hour and a ceiling of 23,000 feet. With an armament of twin vickers machine guns and the ability to turn to the right almost in its own length, the Camel was a magnificent dogfighter in the hands of experienced pilots.

Left: King George V (right) with Tsar Nicholas II of Russia at a meeting of the crowned heads in 1913. Above: British actress Vivien Leigh. After a promising stage and screen career in England, Leigh landed the part of Scarlett O'Hara, in the Hollywood movie **Gone with the Wind**, thus ensuring her future success.

Right: In June 1913 the campaign to gain women's suffrage in Britain took a tragic turn when Emily Wilding Davidson leapt from the crowd on Tattenham Corner during the Derby and flung herself at the King's horse. Both horse and rider were brought crashing to the ground, and Miss Davidson was killed by the impact. A few weeks earlier, on 6th May, the House of Commons had rejected a Bill which would have given women the vote, by 266 votes to 219. The Women's Suffrage movement vowed to step up their campaign of civil disobedience and disruption. The tragic events at the Derby caught public notice, but failed to sway the politicians. It was not until women had proved their worth to society during World War I that the British political establishment granted them the right to vote.

Jan 1	First daily scheduled flight service begins from Tampa, Florida to St Petersburg	**Aug 4**	Britian declares war on Germany
Jan 3	Sylvia Pankhurst is rearrested under the 'Cat and Mouse' Act	**Aug 5**	First electric traffic lights are erected in Cleveland, Ohio
Jan 14	France: Actress Sarah Bernhardt receives Legion of Honour	**Aug 8**	British troops land in France
Feb 18	British explorer Captain Campboll Beeley announces discovery of three Inca cities in Peru	**Aug 20**	Death of Pope Pius X
		Aug 23	Japan declares war on Germany
Mar 5	Irish Home Rule Bill is introduced in the Commons	**Sep 2**	Turkey mobilises
Mar 30	UK: 100,000 miners in Yorkshire strike for a minimum wage	**Sep 3**	New Pope, Benedict XV, is elected in Rome
Apr 2	Birth of British actor Sir Alec Guinness	**Sep 10**	South Africa proclaims loyalty to the UK during the war
Apr 17	UK: Yarmouth Pier destroyed by a Suffragette bomb	**Sep 22**	Three British cruisers are sunk in North Sea
May 5	Birth of US actor Tyrone Power	**Sep 23**	British airmen bomb Zeppelin shed at Dusseldorf
May 9	Italy: Over 150 die in an earthquake in Catania	**Sep 27**	Russian troops invade Hungary
May 15	House of Commons reject Scottish Home Rule Bill	**Oct 1**	Turkey closes the Dardanelles
May 25	UK: Irish Home Rule Bill gets third Commons reading	**Oct 4**	First bomb is dropped on London
Jun 1	UK: Suffragettes burn a church near Henley	**Oct 5**	Thor Heyerdahl (Kon Tiki) born
Jun 15	Denmark, Holland, Sweden and Switzerland form a defence league	**Oct 14**	Canadian troops land in Britian
		Oct 17	Royal Navy sinks 4 German destroyers in North Sea
Jun 20	Liner 'Bismarck' is launched, the world's biggest ship	**Nov 1**	British fleet defeated at Battle of Coronel, Chile
Jul 26	Serbia's army is ordered to mobilise	**Nov 5**	Britain annexes Cyprus
Jul 28	Austria declares war on Serbia	**Nov 8**	Admiral Sturdee sinks German squadron off Falklands
Aug 1	Italian government proclaims neutrality	**Dec 17**	A British Protectorate is proclaimed in Egypt
Aug 2	UK: Royal Navy is mobilised	**Dec 17**	Anzac troops occupy Samoa and German New Guinea
Aug 3	Germany declares war on France	**Dec 24**	The first air raid on British soil
Aug 4	German troops invade Belgium	**Dec 29**	The first Zeppelin appears over the British coast

Above: The Archduke Franz Ferdinand, heir to the Imperial Austrian throne, with his family. Left: The Archduke and his wife leaving the Town Hall of Sarajevo moments before they were shot dead by Gavrilo Princip, a Serb nationalist. The murder led to the start of World War 1. Facing page: (top) British soldiers struggle in the autumn mud of northern France where they faced the German army for 4 years; (centre left) A British soldier walks through a heavily shelled French city; (bottom left) Russian prisoners taken into captivity after the Battle of Tannenberg. The five-day German assault under von Bulow began on 26th August and led to the rout of the Russians with 30,000 dead and 90,000 captured.

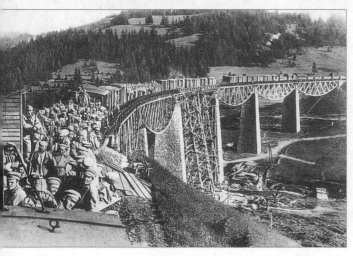

Above: The main artillery workshop at the Krupp Works in Essen. The vast Krupp heavy industry complex was a mainstay of German munitions production throughout the First World War. The Krupp business was founded in 1812 by Friedrich Krupp who developed a secret method of producing fine quality steel. His son, Alfred turned the company towards gun manufacture and rapidly took over rival steel companies in the Essen region. In 1902 Alfred's son, Friedrich, died leaving the business to his daughter and her husband, who took the joint name of Krupp von Bohlen and Holbach. Though threatened by French vengeance after the end of World War I, Krupp's survived unscathed to produce arms for Germany in World War II. Despite allegations of involvement with slave labour, the company survived the collapse of 1945. The industrial giant finally left the hands of the founding family in the 1960s when the heir signed away his inheritance on moral grounds.

Above: King George V with Admiral David Beatty on board the cruiser HMS Queen Elizabeth. Beatty commanded the battle-cruiser squadron of the Home Fleet when war was declared. On 28th August he went to the rescue of a British flotilla off Heligoland. In the fighting Beatty's ships sank 3 German cruisers and one destroyer. Beatty later fought at Jutland and in 1916 was appointed commander of the Grand Fleet. After the war he became Admiral of the Fleet and held the post of First Sea Lord. Above right: Sylvia Pankhurst addresses a crowd in Trafalgar Square. Her flirting with Communism and the birth of an illegitimate son put her on the periphery of political life in Britain. Right: Flora Drummond, known as the General, was arrested in Hyde Park, London, on Ulster Day for loudly proclaiming her views on women's suffrage.

Jan 1	German submarine torpedoes HMS Formidable	Aug 29	UK sends £55,000,000 in gold to pay for US munitions
Jan 12	US Congress defeats Bill for Womens Suffrage	Sep 11	The Women's Institute is founded in England
Feb 1	Birth of British footballer Stanley Matthews	Sep 18	London: Government reveals that the war is costing £3.5 million daily
Feb 1	Passport photographs are first required in Great Britain	Sep 22	Bulgaria mobilises its army
Feb 17	German army captures Polish port of Memel	Sep 23	Greek King Constantine gives the order to mobilise
Feb 26	UK: Clydeside armament workers strike for more pay	Sep 26	Death of British politician James Keir Hardie
Mar 11	British impose naval blockade of Germany	Oct 12	Edith Cavell, English nurse, executed by German firing squad for helping allied prisoners to escape
Mar 11	HMS Bayano is sunk off Scotland, 200 casualties	Oct 12	UK breaks off relations with Bulgaria
Mar 14	Royal Navy sinks German battleship Dresden	Oct 17	Birth of US playwright Arthur Miller
Apr 20	President Wilson says US is strictly neutral	Oct 23	Death of British cricketer W.G. Grace
Apr 22	Germans first use poison gas at Ypres on Western front	Oct 28	The first performance of Richard Strauss's 'Alpine Symphony' is heard in Berlin
Apr 23	Rupert Brooke, poet, dies of blood poisoning	Nov 8	Over 200 die when Italian liner 'Ancona' is torpedoed off Sardinia
Apr 25	British and French forces land at Gallipoli	Nov 9	Birth of US actress Hedy Lamarr
May 1	US ship Gulflight is sunk without warning by U-boat	Nov 13	Churchill resigns from cabinet over Dardanelles
May 7	Lusitania torpedoed by German submarine,1198 killed	Nov 14	Death of US black leader Booker T. Washington
May 22	Britain's worst train disaster at Gretna Green kills 158	Nov 19	London: Allies ask China to join the Entente
May 23	Italy enters war on allied side	Dec 4	US: The state of Georgia recognises the Ku Klux Klan
Jun 9	British troops are issued with hand grenades	Dec 12	Birth of US singer and actor Frank Sinatra
Jul 9	All German forces in SW Africa surrender to Botha	Dec 12	Germany: First all metal aeroplane is built
Jul 15	200,000 Welsh miners strike for more pay	Dec 19	Allied troops pull out from Gallipoli
Jul 27	Revolution in Haiti	Dec 30	Liner Persia sunk by U-Boat, 400 drowned
Aug 5	German army takes Warsaw		
Aug 6	New Allied landings in Gallipoli		
Aug 21	Italy declares war on Turkey		
Aug 29	Birth of Swedish actress Ingrid Bergman		

When the year 1915 opened the attention of the world was concentrated on the conflict which was tearing Europe apart. Non-combatant nations, such as Italy and the United States watched as their economies suffered and long-time friends fell into chaos. Throughout the world colonial troops were fighting their own wars for local superiority. In East Africa the German troops and settlers formed a disciplined force, backed up by well trained guerrilla troops. A few islands in the Pacific remained ignorant of the war, the settlers merely wondered why the infrequent ships had stopped calling. In Europe the bleak horror of war was becoming apparent. After the swift and decisive campaigns of recent wars, most people expected the Great War to be over within months. Instead it looked like stalemate. On the Western Front all major movements stopped in November. The combatants were installed in a series of sieges stretching from the Channel to Switzerland. The trenches, wire entanglements and dugouts had been intended for temporary use only, but they became home to armies for nearly 4 years. On the Eastern Front the Russians had recovered from their defeats and were preparing a winter offensive against East Prussia with 800,000 men. The crack Serb army was holding the much larger Austrian forces at bay. It was becoming depressingly clear to the generals and the public that the hoped for lightning victories would not materialise. As the professional soldiers were killed or spread thinly, vast new armies of civilians were raised to plug the gaps. For the first time in a century Europe found itself embroiled in total war.

Left: The young poet, Rupert Brooke, who died on active service on 23rd April 1915. Brooke's works, first published in 1911, reveal an intense love of life and zest for enjoy- *ment. He returned from an extended tour of the Pacific islands to take up a commission in the RND. He died after a bout of sunstroke at Lemnos in the eastern Mediterranean.*

Facing page, top: German seamen escape from the burning
wreck of the battlecruiser Blucher
during the Battle of Dogger
Bank, on 24th January. A
German flotilla en route to bom-
bard British coastal towns was
sighted at dawn by a British
squadron. Admiral Beatty
ordered an immediate attack.
Although the Blucher was the only
ship sunk, 2 other German ships
and the British flagship were put
out of action. On 25th April the
Allied troops stormed ashore at
Gallipoli in Turkey in an attempt
to capture Constantinople. The
campaign became a stalemate
and the troops were withdrawn
in December after heavy losses.
Facing page, bottom and above:
Australian troops in Anzac Cove.
Right: A British post in Suvla Bay.

24 800

The stalemate on land led the warring countries to adopt desperate measures to secure victory. On 18th May the Germans declared they would sink any ship in British waters without warning in an attempt to starve Britain into surrender and cut off her industries from raw materials. On 7th May U-boat 20 torpedoed the luxury liner *Lusitania* as she headed for Liverpool. The liner sank in just 18 minutes, taking 1,198 people with her. The Germans claimed the Lusitania had been carrying arms, but world opinion was outraged and the U-boats were ordered to issue warnings before sinking merchant ships in future. Top: The *Lusitania* a few weeks before she was sunk. Above: A German medal issued to commemorate the sinking, the figure of Death is shown selling ship tickets.

Facing page, bottom right: Professor Schrefeld at work in his Berlin laboratory. Schrefeld produced the poison gas which the Germans unleashed for the first time on 22nd April. The new weapon caused high casualties, but the Germans failed to exploit the situation properly. Gas continued to be used by both sides for the rest of the war, but was banned in later conflicts. Above left: With men away at the front, many jobs opened up to women for the first time. This woman is working as a omnibus conductress. Above right: Early anti-German propaganda was crude but later techniques became highly sophisticated. Right: A postcard distributed to British troops to write home.

Top left: The footballer Stanley Matthews was born on 1st February. Top right: Scottish novelist John Buchan whose classic spy novel The 39 Steps was published in 1915. Buchan went on to write a number of novels, as well as serve as an MP. Left: Frank Sinatra, born 12th Decembe Above: Film star Ingrid Bergman, born 29th August.

1916

Jan 5	Washington: War debate starts in the Senate
Jan 15	Zuider Zee dam in Holland collapses
Jan 17	Russia begins offensive against the Turks
Jan 29	First Zeppelin raid on Paris
Jan 31	President Wilson says US Navy is ready for war
Feb 4	The Crown Prince of Turkey is assassinated
Feb 6	Death of South African poet Ruben Dario
Feb 8	German food shortages cause riots in Berlin
Feb 9	Military conscription is introduced in Britain
Feb 19	National Savings certificates go on sale in Britain
Feb 28	Death of US Author Henry James
Mar 9	Pancho Villa leads attack into New Mexico
Mar 9	Germany declares war on Portugal
Mar 12	Birth of British Prime Minister Sir Harold Wilson
Mar 15	US Army invades Mexico on punitive expedition
Mar 20	Rationing in Germany as food becomes scarce
Mar 22	Death of Yuan Shi-kai, China
Apr 5	Gregory Peck born
Apr 8	Norway: Women win the right to vote in national elections
Apr 14	Allies bomb Constantinople
Apr 22	British violinist Yehudi Menuhin born
Apr 24	Easter Rising in Dublin
Apr 25	The first Anzac Day is celebrated
May 8	Australian and New Zealand troops arrive in France

May 9	UK Government says no conscription in Ireland
May 12	Irish rebels are executed after the Easter Rising
May 21	Daylight saving is introduced in Britain
May 26	Battle of Jutland (British and German fleets)
Jun 9	Sherif Hussein of Mecca leads revolt against Turks
Jul 1	Beginning of Somme offensive
Jul 1	US: Alcohol is prohibited in Michigan, Montana, Nebraska and South Dakota, bringing the total of dry states to 24
Jul 1	US: The Coca-Cola Co. introduces its new contoured bottle to discourage imitation
Jul 2	Hundreds die in race riots in St. Louis
Jul 9	Edward Heath born
Aug 19	German warships bombard English coast
Aug 28	Italy declares war on Germany
Sep 29	Trevor Howard born
Oct 16	Allies occupy Athens
Oct 26	Francois Mitterand born
Nov 7	Janet Rankin is first woman member of US Congress
Nov 7	Woodrow Wilson is re-elected as President of US
Nov 21	Emperor Franz Joseph of Austria-Hungary dies
Nov 22	Death of US author Jack London
Dec 7	David Lloyd George becomes head of wartime coalition government
Dec 18	Betty Grable born

On 21st April Roger Casement was caught landing 20,000 German rifles in Ireland. The weapons were intended for use in a rising by various Irish nationalist groups. The British promised Home Rule after the defeat of Germany. However, despite the promise and the lack of weapons and men the Rising took place as planned on Easter Monday when 2,000 confirmed patriots rebelled in Dublin. A number of strategic buildings were seized, but the hoped-for general rising failed to materialise. By Wednesday the rebels were surrounded and outnumbered. Severe fighting raged through Dublin city centre, laying waste to large areas. The last rebels surrendered on Saturday and executions followed. Public opinion, at first against the rebels, softened as the executions continued. Facing page, top: British troops guard a makeshift barricade in Talbot Street. Facing page, bottom: Troops guard shops against looting. Left: Relatives visit prisoners in June. Below: Dublin burns on the night of Easter Monday. Bottom left: A tank batters down a door in the hunt for snipers. Bottom right: Sackville Street after the fighting. Previous page: Liberty Hall after the uprising.

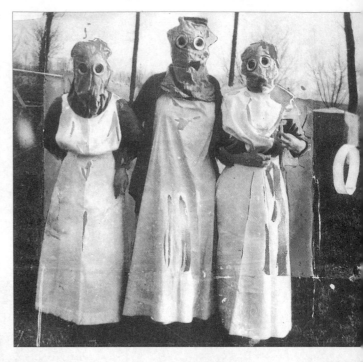

FIELD MARSHAL HAIG

Field Marshal the Earl Haig took command of the British forces in France in December 1915 and held that post to the end of the War. As a dashing young cavalry officer, Haig achieved much in the Sudan, India and South Africa. During the early days of World War I his eye for fast movement and rapid action brought many successes to the 1st Corps, which he commanded. Once trench warfare began his cavalry training was of little use and it may be that he accepted needless casualties. Haig was, however, a superb administrator who ensured plentiful supplies of food, ammunition and post for his men. In the sweeping advances and retreats of 1918, Haig's skills again came to the fore. After the war he devoted himself to helping veterans and the crippled.

Top right: British nurses in their anti-gas suits. Nurses and other medical staff were expected to work in forward positions, close to the reserve trenches. Gas was a much hated weapon among soldiers. It was at the mercy of the wind, and frequently blew back on those who had released it. Likewise it might drift to rear areas, threatening hospitals, civilians and others generally considered non-combatants. Right: Benito Mussolini, later dictator of Italy, photographed when serving on the mountainous Carso Front in northern Italy.

Left: German troops of the 31st Regiment at Verdun. This bloody battle opened on 21st February with a massive German assault on the city. French national pride insisted on Verdun being retained and troops were asked to hold virtually indefensible positions. The Germans made the most of the situation and inflicted huge casualties. The battle ended in December after nearly 1 million men fell. The French army turned mutinous soon after. Below left: A German soldier captured at Ancre on 13th November. Below right: An unknown British steamer torpedoed by a U-boat, the photograph was taken by the German captain. Bottom left: A dog, trained to carry messages, leaps over the barbed wire on the Western Front.

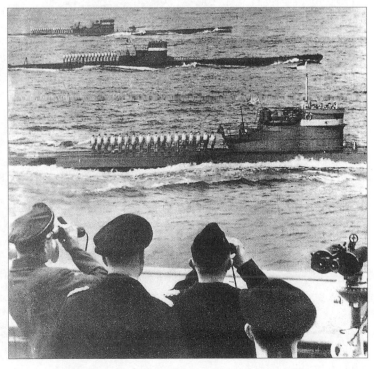

The year 1916 saw two massive battles for British arms. On 1st July 18 divisions attacked along a 15 mile front in the Somme Valley of northern France. Despite a heavy artillery barrage, the German defences were almost intact and 60,000 British troops were killed on the first day. Within a few days Haig realised the German defences were too strong for a breakthrough, but he was compelled to continue attacking in order to relieve the pressure on French forces at Verdun further south. The Battle of the Somme ended on 18th November with 418,000 British casualties. Below left: British troops go over the top from a saphead. Below right: A battery of British 8 inch howitzers. Bottom: A forward British field dressing station. On 31st May the German High Seas Fleet put to sea on a raid, but was located by British cruisers under Beatty. Signalling for help, Beatty dashed to the attack. Admiral Hood's battlecruisers were first to arrive, followed by the entire British Grand Fleet. After a fierce battle the German fleet raced back to port and never dared put to sea again. Facing page top: The Rostock, a German ship which fought at Jutland. Facing page bottom: At 6.20pm Admiral Hood brings his battlecruisers into the firing line. Minutes later HMS *Invincible* blew up, killing Hood and over 700 crew.

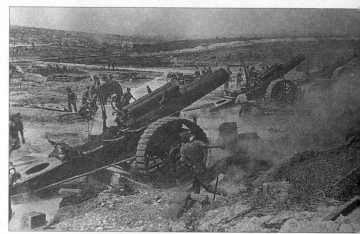

1917

Jan 25	US purchases Virgin Islands for 25 million dollars from Denmark
Jan 29	US: New law passed requiring all immigrants to know over 30 English words and banning all Asians except Japanese
Feb 7	Germany: All US citizens are held as hostages
Feb 25	Birth of British writer Anthony Burgess
Mar 2	Puerto Rico becomes US territory
Mar 11	British capture Baghdad
Mar 20	Dame Vera Lynn born
Mar 27	Cyrus Vance born
Apr 1	Death of US composer and pianist Scott Joplin
Apr 6	US officially enters the war
Apr 7	Cuba declares war on Germany
Apr 20	US severs relations with Turkey
May 18	Selective conscription is introduced in US
May 29	Birth of US President John Fitzgerald Kennedy
Jun 3	Italy declares protectorate over Albania
Jun 4	Brazil declares war on Germany
Jun 7	Dean Martin born
Jun 10	Sinn Fein uprising in Dublin
Jun 14	First bombing of London by German aircraft
Jun 14	Prisoners held since Easter Rising are released
Jun 16	First Congress of Soviets meet in Russia
Jun 19	British Royal Family renounce all German titles
Jul 2	75 blacks are murdered during race riots in Illinois
Jul 11	Yul Brynner born
Jul 11	Ireland: Eamon de Valera wins East Clare by-election
Jul 15	Bolsheviks fail to take over Petrograd
Jul 17	British Royal Family adopts 'House of Windsor' title
Jul 19	German Reichstag passes motion to end war
Aug 4	US: The administration says avoiding conscription can be punishable by execution
Aug 6	Birth of US actor Robert Mitchum
Sep 15	China offers 300,000 soldiers to aid the Allies on the Western Front
Sep 15	Russia proclaims a Republic with provisional government
Sep 26	Death of US painter Edgar Degas
Oct 15	Mata Hari is executed in Paris
Oct 21	Birth of US jazz trumpeter Dizzy Gillespie
Oct 25	Start of Bolshevik Revolution led by Lenin
Oct 26	First shots are fired by US in France
Oct 28	Vittorio Orlando becomes Italian Premier
Nov 5	London: The War Office agrees to supply British troops in France with Christmas puddings
Nov 6	British and Canadian troops capture Passchendaele
Nov 16	Georges Clemenceau heads new French Government
Nov 16	Russia: Bolsheviks take Moscow
Nov 17	Death of French sculptor Auguste Rodin
Nov 18	Palestine: British troops take Jaffa
Nov 18	Indira Gandhi born
Nov 26	Lenin offers an armistice to Germany and Austria
Dec 1	German East Africa is cleared of German troops
Dec 3	The Quebec Bridge over St. Lawrence River is opened
Dec 7	Finland proclaims independence from Russian rule
Dec 7	US: President Wilson declares war on Austria
Dec 12	World's worst train accident occurs in France, 543 killed
Dec 17	Death of Britain's first woman doctor, Elizabeth Garrett Anderson
Dec 17	William Frederick Cody 'Buffalo Bill' dies

By early 1917 the Russian Empire was on its knees, both militari and economically. On 8th March protests in Petrograd turned calls for the Tsar to dismiss the government and install honest mini ters. Soldiers sent to put down the protest joined it instead. On th 12th the Duma, or elected advisory body, set up a provisional gover ment and three days later forced the Tsar to abdicate. It was notic able that outside the capital events had been watched with apath and resignation. The new Republic was governed by the modera Socialist Alexander Kerensky, who tried to hold together an unea alliance of political interests. In July the Bolsheviks tried to sei power, but were defeated by troops loyal to Kerensky. In Septemb the tough Cossack general Lavr Korniloff lost patience with th dithering civilian government and tried to organise a coup. This to failed and Korniloff was arrested. The government, meanwhile, ha lost the support of the people as food shortages became acute and w casualties mounted. On 25th October the Bolsheviks, led by Leni launched a second revolt. This time they were better armed and ha a better plan. Key buildings in Petrograd and Moscow were capture and government ministers bundled into prison in what was a class and precisely managed coup. The bulk of Russia watched events wit the same fatalism as it had in the spring. Most considered th Bolshevik government to be a transitory affair. Korniloff escape from prison and raised the southern Cossacks in revolt.

Facing page: Tsar Nicholas II under arrest following his abdication. Left: The first Bolshevik propaganda cartoon on a post card. The banner reads "Long Live the Revolution!" Below left: Leon Trotsky addresses a group of Red Army soldiers in Moscow after the October Revolution. Below: Street fighting during the October Revolution. Bottom left: Lenin speaking to a Moscow crowd in October. Bottom right: Cossacks demonstrate their military might in Petrograd during the confused days of Revolution.

Above: The men and transports of the British 7th Division marching through Thielt Market Place on their way to the Front on 12th October. The 3rd Battle of Ypres had been under way since June and the 7th Division was heading for the muddiest and bloodiest battlefield of the war. On 6th November Canadian troops finally captured the Passchendaele Ridge, thus ending the battle.
Right: King George, Queen Mary, the Prince of Wales and General Haig with French President Poincare on a visit to the Front. Facing page, top left: Artillery shells being manufactured in England. Facing page, centre left: A strike of workers calls for peace. Facing page, bottom: London factory workers, exempted from conscription, march from Horse Guards Parade after volunteering. Facing page, centre and centre right: Newspaper billboards shout the news.

WOMEN AT WORK

During the War there was a continual demand for fit young men to join the forces, creating a problem at home. Factories were retooling for essential war work and they too needed fit and active workers by the thousand. The solution found was to hire women. Instead of entering service or caring for a home, hundreds of thousands of women found themselves working in factories, often for the first time. Munitions work was the best paid, but the occasional explosion made it too dangerous for many. After the war the proven economic importance and value of women played a large part in their winning the vote.

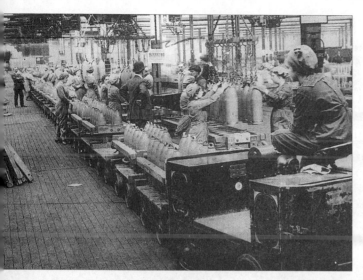

AMERICA ENTERS THE WAR

In 1916 President Wilson fought a campaign on the proud boast that he had kept America at peace. On 6th April, 1917 he took it to war. Germany had resumed unrestricted U-boat warfare on 1st February and outraged American public opinion. On the 25th February the liner Laconia was torpedoed and many Americans drowned. On 1st March the infamous Zimmermann Telegram in which Germany proposed an alliance with Mexico was intercepted. Four American merchant ships were then sunk in rapid succession, and Wilson was left with no alternative. He declared war. Above: A recruiting parade in New York. Right: President Wilson with his War Cabinet.

Left: Exotic Indonesian dancer Mata Hari at the height of her prewar career. During the war she worked as a German spy, gaining secrets from the officers and diplomats she seduced, and was shot by the French on 15th October. Much debate surrounds her spying and its efficacy, but Sir Basil Thomson who interviewed her for British intelligence was under no illusions. "Of all the people that I examined during the War she was the quickest on the uptake". The execution of the dancer created a sensation.

Left: Buffalo Bill, Colonel William Cody, died on 17th December after a colourful career which included buffalo hunting, Indian fighting and running a circus which entertained large crowds in America and Europe to displays of trick riding and recreated battles of the Indian wars. Above: The 20th March saw the birth of Vera Lynn, destined to be a favourite entertainer in the Second World War. Far above: Actor Yul Brynner on the set of the movie *The Magnificent Seven*. He was born on 11th July.

1918

Jan 8	President Wilson starts his 14 points
Jan 8	Recruiting begins in Britain for the WRNS
Jan 28	Germany: Workers strike begins in Berlin
Feb 5	A parliamentary candidature deposit of £150 is introduced in Britain
Feb 6	Women receive right to vote in British general elections
Feb 9	Ukraine signs separate peace treaty with Germany
Feb 21	Australian troops take Jericho from Turks
Feb 22	Robert Wadlow - the world's tallest man - born weighing 8.5 lbs, died in 1940 weighing 31st 5lb, 8 foot 11 1/10 inches tall
Feb 26	604 people are killed when the stands at the Hong Kong Jockey Club collapse and catch fire
Mar 3	Germans and Russians sign Treaty of Brest-Litovsk
Mar 22	German gun 'Big Bertha' shells Paris from 75 miles
Mar 23	Lithuania declares itself an independent Republic
Mar 25	Death of French composer Claude Debussy
Mar 29	Paris: 75 die when a German shell hits a church during a Good Friday service
Apr 1	The Royal Air Force is formed
Apr 1	US: The first day of daylight saving
Apr 9	Latvia declares itself an independent Republic
Apr 16	Spike Milligan born
Apr 21	Manfred von Richthofen, 'The Red Baron' is shot down
Apr 25	Birth of US jazz singer Ella Fitzgerald
Apr 26	Fanny Blankers-Koen, Dutch athlete, born
May 7	Rumania signs peace treaty with Germany
May 23	Georgia proclaims independence from Russia
Jul 8	National Savings stamps go on sale in Britain
Jul 14	Birth of Swedish film director Ingmar Bergman
Jul 16	Execution of Tsar Nicholas and family
Aug 13	UK: The government recognises the state of Czechoslovakia
Aug 15	US breaks off relations with Bolshevik government
Aug 25	Hungary: Government expels Jews and confiscates their assets
Aug 25	Birth of US conductor and composer Leonard Bernstein
Sep 13	US: 14 million men register for conscription
Sep 29	Bulgaria signs armistice with Allies
Oct 1	British and Arab armies take Damascus
Oct 17	Yugoslavia gains independence from Austria-Hungary
Oct 17	Rita Hayworth born
Oct 20	Germany stops U-Boat warfare
Nov 1	Anglo-French troops take Constantinople
Nov 3	Austria signs an armistice with the Allies
Nov 6	Republic is proclaimed in Poland
Nov 7	Billy Graham born
Nov 9	Kaiser Wilhelm II abdicates
Nov 11	The Armistice signed in Marshal Foch's railway coach, France, marking the end of the war
Nov 11	Birth of Russian writer Alexander Solzhenitsyn
Nov 14	German fleet surrenders
Nov 21	The German High Seas Fleet is interned at Scapa Flow
Nov 29	Austrian Government says it will try those responsible for starting the war
Dec 1	Iceland becomes independent of Denmark
Dec 6	Allied troops occupy Cologne
Dec 9	Kirk Douglas born
Dec 14	Women vote in a British General Election for the first time

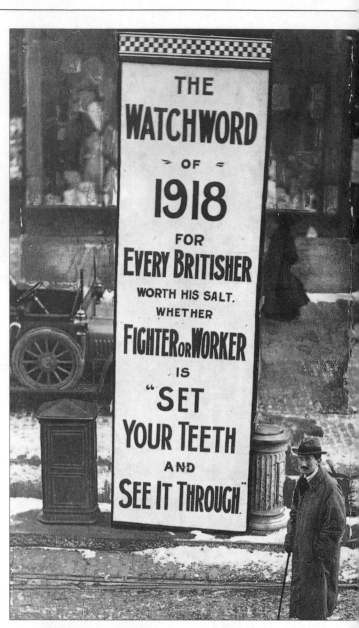

THE ROYAL FAMILY AT WAR

By 1918 Britain had been at war for three years and was becoming wear
The propaganda poster (*above*) in London reflects the mood. The Roy
Family took a decisive role in holding the nation together and creating
feeling of grim determination. King George visited numerous regimen
ships and factories (*facing page, bottom right*) to encourage his people an
spent much time with the wounded. Queen Mary (*facing page, top*) help
organise women workers on farms and in factories and devoted muc
effort to encouraging women to become nurses (*facing page, bottom le,*
and to send clothing to men at the Front. Young Prince Albert, lat
George VI, served in the navy and fought at the Battle of Jutland in 191
only narrowly escaping with his life. In 1917 he transferred to the RF
serving as a pilot on the Western Front during the closing months of th
war. More controversy surrounded Edward, Prince of Wales. He joine
the army and served as a staff officer, but continually asked to make fora
to the Front. When he complained about his role, stating that if he we
killed he had brothers to take over, Kitchener put him firmly in his plac
"If I were sure you would be killed," said the old general, "I wou
not restrain you. But I cannot take the chance of the enemy takir
you prisoner."

The Red Baron

During the war conflict in the air was a new, romantic and extremely dangerous pastime. In the early days of the war aircraft were used to reconnoitre behind enemy lines. This remained an important task. Soon, however, larger bombers came into use as did fast-single seater scouts. It was the scout pilots who won the headlines with their daring exploits. The most successful were called aces and the best known was the Red Baron, Manfred von Richthofen of Germany. In his year of active flying he downed 80 Allied aircraft and developed new tactics before being shot down on 21st April. Britain's Albert Ball downed 40 enemy planes before vanishing on patrol in 1917. The fictional pilot Biggles keeps the air fights of the First World War alive for modern children.

Facing page, top: No.1 Squadron at its base in France. In 1918 Britain amalgamated its aerial units into the Royal Air Force. Facing page, bottom: Damage wrought at Etaples by German bombers. Top left: Exhausted British infantry with German prisoners rest at Bouzincourt on 26th March. Five days earlier the Germans had launched their last great offensive. At one point the line broke at Albert, but the gap was plugged before German reinforcements arrived. Top right: Cambrai after the German troops pulled out. Left: Josephus Daniels, Secretary of the Navy, and F.D. Roosevelt, Assistant Secretary, in Washington. Above: Four American submarines in port. The influx of American military might tipped the balance in the West.

On 8th August a well-planned attack by British tanks and Imperial troops cracked open the German front line at Amiens. General Ludendorff called it the "Black Day of the German Army". German morale collapsed quickly in the face of new tactics and new troops. German troops began to surrender by the battalion and even to desert, unheard of until then. By the end of September the German High Command realised that it was only a matter of time before their army vanished and Germany lay open to a victorious foreign army. On 3rd October Germany asked for "Peace with Honour". The Allies refused. The Armistice unconditionally surrendering German forces was signed in a railway carriage in Compiegne Forest on 11th November. Left: British and French officers, led by Admiral Wemyss and Marshal Foch, leave the Armistice carriage. Below: The Armistice carriage was turned into a museum, but was destroyed by Hitler in 1940. Bottom: WRAFs celebrate the Armistice in London.

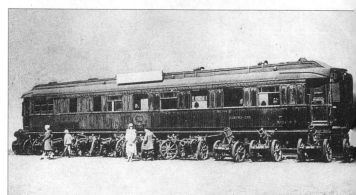

MURDER OF THE TSAR AND HIS FAMILY

The Tsar of Russia had held absolute power, conferred by divine right, over his empire. But on 16th July he and his entire family were shot by a group of revolutionaries in an obscure village. After his abdication on 15th March 1917, Tsar Nicholas II had been promised that his private position would be respected and he retired to his summer palace in the Crimea. As the summer passed and the political situation destabilised he was arrested and moved to the palace at Tsarkoe Selo near Petrograd. When the Bolsheviks seized power he was put under close arrest and moved to Ekaterinburg in Siberia. There the Imperial family was forced to adopt peasant dress and the little prince Alexis was given a Red Army uniform. By July 1918 the Communist regime was coming under severe pressure. The Ukraine had declared independence and signed a separate peace with Germany. The Cossacks were in open rebellion and were pillaging their way across the southern steppes. Many of these disparate forces legitimised their activities by claiming loyalty to the Tsar and opposition to Lenin. The Communists therefore took the decision to eliminate the Tsar. He and his family were butchered with methodical brutality. The Romanov dynasty, which had ruled Russia for over 300 years was gone. It was unclear at the time, and remains so, whether the local Soviet officials carried out the executions or if the deaths were ordered by central Communist authority. Bones, thought to be those of the Imperial family, were discovered in 1992.

VOTES FOR WOMEN

In 1918 women were allowed to vote in Britain for the first tim
Throughout the 19th century the franchise had been gradually exten
ed to all men, but women had been excluded. The important role
women in winning the War could not, however, be ignored and th
claims of suffragettes took on new respectability. In the 1918 electio
only women over 30 were allowed to vote, but within a few yea
women gained the same rights as men. A famous cartoon in the sati
cal magazine Punch showed a crowd of women clamouring to be l
back into the polling station so that they could change their min
Such male prejudice did not last long, however, and soon women we
playing an active role in all areas of politics.

Top right: Ella Fitzgerald singing at a Jazz Festival in Antibes, France. She was born on 25th April and is considered by many to be the finest female jazz singer of her time. Above: Spike Milligan arriving at London's Criterion Theatre with Peter Sellers in 1970. Milligan was born on 16th April and went on to lead an amazing career which included manic comedy and bouts of depression. Right: The American actor Kirk Douglas, born on 9th December, photographed in 1972. Douglas made a speciality of tough, macho roles in a succession of films including the Dark Age epic **Vikings** *and a number of westerns.*

Jan 1 UK: Over 200 sailors drown when the yacht Stornoway is wrecked off Scotland

Jan 1 Birth of US writer J.D.Salinger

Jan 5 The National Socialist (Nazi) Party is formed in Germany

Jan 6 Death of Theodore Roosevelt

Jan 11 Rumania annexes Transylvania

Jan 22 Socialists win German election

Jan 25 Peace conference adopts principle of League of Nations

Feb 4 President Wilson presides at first League of Nations

Feb 5 Germany: First public air service is introduced

Feb 11 Friedrich Ebert is elected President of Germany

Feb 23 Benito Mussolini founds the Fascist Party in Italy

Mar 14 France: Emile Cottin is sentenced to death for attempting to murder the prime minister

Mar 15 Birth of Nat King Cole

Mar 22 Bela Jun declares Hungary a Soviet Republic

Apr 5 Eamon de Valera is elected President of Sinn Fein

Apr 8 Red Army invades Crimea

Apr 14 The Amritsar Massacre: British troops kill 380 Gandhi followers

May 3 Fighting breaks out between Britain and Afghanistan

May 6 Peace conference shares out German colonies

May 14 Henry John Heinz dies

May 16 Liberace born

May 18 Margot Fonteyn born

Jun 6 Finland declares war on Russia

Jun 15 First non-stop Atlantic flight, a Vickers-Vimy biplane piloted by Captain John Alcock and navigated by Lieutenant Arthur Whitten Brown

Jun 21 72 German warships are scuttled in Scapa Flow

Jun 22 US: 200 die when a tornado strikes in Minnesota

Jun 28 Peace treaty between Germany and Allies is signed at Versailles

Jul 4 Jack Dempsey beats Jess Willard in the world heavy-weight boxing championship

Jul 4 France: Demobilisation comes into force

Jul 6 British airship R34 becomes first to cross Atlantic

Jul 15 Birth of British writer Iris Murdoch

Jul 27 Large-scale race riots in Chicago

Aug 25 Daily air service between London and Paris begins

Aug 27 Death of South African leader General Louis Botha

Aug 31 US Communist party is founded

Sep 22 UK: 50,000 iron foundry workers go on strike

Sep 25 Spitzbergen is given to Norway by Paris Peace Conference

Oct 5 Donald Pleasance born

Oct 6 Norway adopts alcohol prohibition

Oct 7 The world's oldest airline KLM is established

Oct 13 Dock strikes in New York

Oct 18 Pierre Trudeau born

Oct 25 UK: Six Sinn Fein prisoners escape from prison

Nov 2 US: 500,000 coal miners go on strike

Nov 28 UK: Nancy Astor is elected as Britian's first woman MP

Nov 28 Latvia declares war on Germany

Nov 30 France: Women vote for the first time in general elections

Dec 3 Death of French impressionist Auguste Renoir

Dec 10 Australia: The Smith brothers become the first to fly from the UK to Australia

Dec 16 German troops leave Latvia and Lithuania

Dec 18 John Alcock, English aviator, dies of injuries received in a plane crash

ALCOCK & BROWN

On 15th June air history was made when a giant biplane crash-landed in an Irish bog. The aircraft had flown non-stop from Newfoundland, demonstrating that long-distance flight was possible and winning a £10,000 prize put up by a British newspaper. The feat showed the enormous strides in aircraft design during the war. Before 1914 a short hop across the Channel was considered daring. The aircraft used in the Atlantic crossing was a converted Vickers Vimy bomber fitted with extra fuel tanks and stripped of all unnecessary weight. The two pilots were both war veterans, Alcock having gained fame by bombing Constantinople in September 1917. The intrepid pair took off on 14th June and despite problems with icing and poor visibility made the crossing safely. Soon after the flight both men were knighted by King George V. Alcock was killed in December in an air crash. Above: Alcock and Brown (in uniform) a few days after the flight.

The German High Seas Fleet surrendered on 21st November. The immediate problem of what to do with the ships was solved by sending them to Scapa Flow in the Shetlands. In June the following year they were still there, awaiting the outcome of the Versailles Peace Conference. On 21st June German officers took matters into their own hands and scuttled the entire fleet rather than allow Britain to use it. Left: Sailors from the cruiser Nurnberg, sinking in the background, surrender. Bottom left: The capsized battleship Derfflinger under tow to the breakers yard. Below: The battlecruiser Moltke being towed into Rosyth. Bottom right: British marines prepare to board a German destroyer in an attempt to stop it sinking.

Left: Lady Nancy Astor. On 28th November 1919 she became the first lady MP in Britain when she won the by-election for the seat of Plymouth Sutton. Below: The declaration of the result outside Plymouth town hall. The by-election was caused by the resignation of Nancy Astor's husband when he succeeded to his father's Viscountcy and ownership of the *Observer* newspaper. She took her seat for the first time on 1st December and quickly established a reputation as a hard worker and fine speaker. In her Parliamentary career, which lasted into the 1930s, Lady Astor concentrated her efforts on child welfare, temperance reform and other social issues. Her husband, meanwhile, continued his ministerial career from the House of Lords and spoke out on agricultural and health issues.

Left: Benito Mussolini espoused socialism before the War, but his experiences in the trenches and contacts with Bolshevism during his recuperation from wounds, turned him into a bitter opponent of communism. In 1919 he founded the movement Fascio di Combattimento *to oppose the Bolshevist revolution. The movement grew into the Fascist Party which swept him to supreme power. Above: Alfred Dreyfus being created an officer of the Legion of Honour for his services in the War.*

THE TREATY OF VERSAILLES

The Treaty of Versailles was signed on 28th June and imposed harsh conditions on the defeated empires. Facing page: The Victory Parade of 19th July passes up Whitehall to Trafalgar Square. Top: Lloyd George, British Prime Minister, leaves the Palace of Versailles after signing the Treaty. Left: The German delegation to the Versailles Conference on 28th June. Above: A room during the conference.

1920-1929

1920

Jan 5	The Radio Corporation of America forms for world broadcasting
Jan 5	US: Yankees pay a record $125,000 for Red Sox baseballer Babe Ruth
Jan 10	Treaty of Versailles takes effect
Jan 15	Prohibition becomes law in US
Jan 25	Death of Italian painter Modigliani
Feb 2	Estonia signs peace treaty and claims independence
Feb 4	Birth of Norman Wisdom
Feb 7	Bolsheviks execute white Admiral Kolchak
Feb 8	Bolsheviks capture Odessa
Feb 8	Birth of Lana Turner
Feb 11	Birth of Farouk, the last King of Egypt
Feb 20	Death of Robert Peary, first man to reach the North Pole
Feb 24	Viscountess Astor becomes first woman to speak in British parliament
Feb 27	Russian peace offer is rejected by US
Mar 16	Constantinople is occupied by Allies
Mar 19	US Senate definitively rejects Treaty of Versailles
Mar 20	Assassination of the Mayor of Cork, Thomas MacCurtain
Mar 29	Mary Pickford marries Douglas Fairbanks, the World's most eligible bachelor
Apr 1	Birth of Nazi party in Germany
Apr 30	Britain abolishes conscription
May 8	Poles and Ukrainians capture Kiev
May 17	KLM, national airline of Netherlands, starts its first scheduled service
May 18	Birth of Pope John Paul II
May 21	London: A car tax is proposed of £1 per horse power
Jun 24	Riots in Londonderry put down by British Army
Jun 25	The Hague becomes permanent seat of International Court of Justice
Jul 6	Russia opens big offensive against Poland
Jul 10	Canada: Arthur Meighen becomes PM
Jul 12	Panama Canal is opened by President Wilson
Jul 21	Sinn Fein and Ulster Unionists riot in Belfast
Jul 23	Poland seeks peace with Russia
Aug 1	Communist Party of Great Britain is founded in London
Aug 19	Russian Army is defeated by Poles at Warsaw
Aug 28	19th Amendment gives women the right to vote in US
Sep 1	Lebanon wins independence from France
Oct 1	Birth of Walter Matthau
Oct 16	US Marines kill Haitian rebel leader
Oct 18	Britain's miners strike over a claim for two shillings more per week
Nov 2	Warren Harding becomes President of US
Nov 29	The IRA kills 15 army cadets
Dec 23	North and South Ireland to have own parliaments

Facing page: The unfortunate Warren Harding, elected President of the United States on 2nd November, and his wife Florence. Harding was selected for the job by his pushy wife and a clique of corrupt backers. His sudden death in 1923 may have saved him from impeachment for corruption. Top left: The 29th March saw the Hollywood wedding of Douglas Fairbanks and Mary Pickford. Top right: Dame Nellie Melba, possibly the best soprano of the century, retired from the stage. Left: Karol Wojtyla was born in Poland on 18th May. Young Karol became a priest in 1946. He was elected Pope on 16th October 1978. Above: King George V, Queen Mary and the Prince of Wales leaving Westminster Abbey in July after a Thanksgiving Service for the king who had recovered from a long illness.

Jan 2	Spain: The ship Santa Isabel sinks with the loss of 160 lives		**Jul 11**	British government and Sinn Fein agree truce
Jan 3	India's first parliament meets		**Jul 27**	Insulin is first isolated, thus providing treatment for diabetes
Feb 8	South Africa: General Jan Smuts is elected Prime Minster		**Jul 29**	Hitler becomes President of National Socialist Party
Mar 1	Australia sets a record by winning each match of the cricket series against England		**Jul 31**	Belgium is divided into French and Flemish provinces
Apr 3	Coal rationing starts in the UK		**Sep 8**	Birth of Harry Secombe

Jan 2 Spain: The ship Santa Isabel sinks with the loss of 160 lives
Jan 3 India's first parliament meets
Feb 8 South Africa: General Jan Smuts is elected Prime Minster
Mar 1 Australia sets a record by winning each match of the cricket series against England
Apr 3 Coal rationing starts in the UK
Apr 16 Birth of British actor Peter Ustinov
Apr 27 German reparations are fixed at £6,650 million
May 5 China: Dr Sun Yat-sen becomes president
May 8 Sweden abolishes capital punishment
May 14 The British Legion is founded in London
May 14 Fascists win seats in Italian elections
May 22 US: The city of Chicago plans to fine women for wearing short skirts and exposed arms
May 25 Sinn Fein burns down Dublin Customs House
Jun 1 US: Race riots result in over 80 deaths
Jun 4 US: Floods kill 500 in Eastern Colorado
Jun 5 First Northern Ireland Parliament sits
Jun 10 Birth of the Duke of Edinburgh
Jun 12 Last Sunday delivery by British postmen
Jun 21 Birth of Jane Russell
Jul 8 Ireland: Eamon de Valera agrees to talks with Lloyd George on an Irish truce

Jul 11 British government and Sinn Fein agree truce
Jul 27 Insulin is first isolated, thus providing treatment for diabetes
Jul 29 Hitler becomes President of National Socialist Party
Jul 31 Belgium is divided into French and Flemish provinces
Sep 8 Birth of Harry Secombe
Sep 21 Germany: An explosion at a chemical plant kills over 55
Sep 27 Death of German composer Engelbert Humperdinck
Oct 11 London: Irish Treaty Conference begins
Oct 18 Russia grants Crimea its independence
Oct 19 PM Antonio Granjo assassinated in Portugal
Oct 23 Death of John Boyd Dunlop, British inventor of the pneumatic tyre
Nov 11 British Legion holds its first Poppy Day
Nov 23 US: President Harding bans doctors from prescribing beer to patients
Nov 25 Hirohito becomes Regent in Japan
Nov 27 Alexander Dubcek, Czech politician, born
Dec 2 South Africa: After 125 years of service, the British Arm hands over to the Union's forces
Dec 6 Irish Free State is established after independence from U
Dec 10 Albert Einstein is awarded a Nobel Prize for physics
Dec 16 Death of French composer Camille Saint-Saens
Dec 29 Liberal Mackenzie King becomes PM of Canada

REVOLUTION IN TURMOIL

The Russian Revolution, which began with the Bolshevist Coup of 1917 came to an end in November when the last of the anti-Communist armies, led by Count Wrangel in the Crimea, was defeated by Soviet forces. One month earlier, the Soviet regime had accepted a border with Poland after a long war. With the ending of external threats to their power, the Communists turned against internal enemies. The picture (below) shows a squad of the Red Army marching out on a Punishment Tour. Such a "Tour" involved the arbitrary beating of those suspected of anti-Communist views, and the looting of their property. Particular targets were made of landowners or peasants who were better off than their neighbours. The brutal nature of the Punishment Tours ensured a servile population while the Communist Party tightened its grip on power and gradually excluded even the workers' soviets from any real place in the decision making process.

Facing page: State troopers impound crates of alcoholic drinks as the Volstead Act, the 18th Amendment, comes into force on the 16th January. The Act banned spirits, wine and all but the weakest beers from the entire United States. Within a few months the impossibility of enforcing the law became clear as large scale organised crime became involved in producing and supplying illegal alcohol to the thirsty folk of America. Right and above right: French troops in the Rhineland. The French army marched into Germany in April to stop alleged breaches of the Versailles Treaty, but soon came under heavy international pressure to retire. The occupation sparked off large scale demonstrations in Germany which left about a dozen civilians dead when the French opened fire. Such bloody incidents led to the withdrawal of the troops.

acing page: (top) Irish volunteers splay their military might and bottom) Dublin women protest against the British execution of 6 inn Fein men. Below: The agagement photograph of the uke of Edinburgh and Princess Elizabeth. The Duke was born in June into the Greek royal family on Corfu, but served in the British Royal Navy with distinction during World War II and was naturalised a Briton. Right: The actress Jane Russell was born in Minnesota.

The Mothers' Clinic Scandal

Dr Maria Stopes *(right)* leapt to public notice in February 1921 when she launched a libel action against a Scottish professor. Although she lost her case, she won much publicity for her controversial cause, that of contraception. After a glittering academic career which won her a PhD in Munich and recognition·in Japan and America, Dr Stopes became interested in contraception and in 1921 set up the Mothers' Clinic in London to distribute free advice and cost-price equipment to poor women. She ran into a storm of abuse and opposition from the Church and from others who believed her action would lead to the spread of immorality. When she sued Dr Sutherland it was with little hope of winning, but the court case allowed Dr Stopes to parade scientific backing for her programme to a fascinated public. Though she had to pay huge costs which nearly crippled her financially, Dr Stopes believed she had scored a major victory for her cause as knowledge of contraception spread rapidly and brought about great changes in the size of families.

Jn 2 Germany: £1 buys over 30,000 German marks as the currency plummets out of control
Jn 5 Death of British explorer Sir Ernest Shackleton
Jn 10 Gold workers strike on South African Rand
Jn 28 The roof of the Knickerbocker Theatre in Washington collapses under the weight of snow, killing 108 people
Fb 2 22 policeman die in Indian riots
Fb 5 First Reader's Digest is published in US
Fb 5 US: Ford buys the Lincoln Motor Company
Fb 9 Birth of Jim Laker, cricketer
Fb 11 Honduras becomes an independent Republic
Mar 6 US bans export to China
Mar 6 South Africa: General strike begins in Johannesburg
Mar 10 Martial law follows strike in Johannesburg
Mar 16 Egypt declares independence under King Fuad
Mar 18 Gandhi jailed for 6 years for civil disobedience
Mar 21 UK: Waterloo station is opened by Queen Mary
Apr 4 Armand Jeanns is sentenced to death for betraying nurse Edith Cavell
Apr 16 Germany restores relations with USSR
Apr 16 Birth of British author Kingsley Amis
May 27 Birth of Christopher Lee
May 30 Dedication of Lincoln Memorial in Washington
Jn 4 Socialists are elected to the Hungarian parliament for the first time

Jun 10 Birth of US actress and singer Judy Garland
Jun 24 German Foreign Minister, Walter Rathenau, murdered by Nationalists
Jul 1 US: The world's first shopping centre opens
Jul 14 France: President Millerand escapes an attempt on his life
Aug 2 Death of Alexander Graham Bell, the inventor of telephone
Aug 6 Freddie Laker born
Aug 28 US: Broadcast of the first advertisement
Sep 9 William Cosgrave is elected President of the Irish Free State
Sep 19 Emil Zatopek born
Sep 27 Constantine I abdicates as King of Greece
Oct 6 Alcohol ban is imposed on all US ships in port
Oct 18 British Broadcasting Company (BBC) is formed
Oct 23 UK : Bonar Law forms Conservative government
Oct 30 Benito Mussolini's Blackshirts seize Rome
Oct 31 Benito Mussolini becomes PM and Dictator of Italy
Nov 1 Licenses for radios introduced in Britain, 50p per annum
Nov 8 Dr Christiaan Bernard born
Nov 13 Charles Bronson born
Nov 14 BBC makes its first broadcast
Nov 26 The Tomb of Tutankhamun is discovered by Howard Carter and Lord Carnarvon
Dec 23 The BBC begins daily news broadcasts
Dec 24 Ava Gardner born as Lucy Johnson

The distinguished nobleman and amateur Egyptologist Lord Carnarvon had his greatest success in November when his professional adviser, Howard Carter stumbled across the only known intact royal tomb of ancient Egypt. For years Carter had worked in Egypt, turning up much of minor scientific value and in 1923 Carnarvon was due to withdraw his funding. But when digging in an unexcavated section of the Valley of the Kings near Luxor, Carter found a buried door sealed with the name of Pharaoh Tutankhamen. Carnarvon hurried to Egypt and on 26th November the doors were opened for the first time in 3,300 years. Vast treasures were revealed, including gold jewellery and gilded furniture. Even the king's war chariot was present. Facing page: Lord Carnarvon (hand on hip) and Howard Carter (to Carnarvon's left) pose with a group of visitors outside the nondescript doorway which leads to the tomb. Left: The magnificent, solid gold funerary mask of Tutankhamen.

Birth of an Institution

On 18th October the BBC was formed under general manager John Reith. Originally the British Broadcasting Company, the organisation did not become a Corporation until 1927, by which time it had already established a reputation for broadcasting excellence. The first radio broadcast was made on 14th November using equipment which was then the best and most sophisticated available, though it would today appear incredibly primitive and liable to malfunction. Reith was intent on creating a model for all other broadcasters, and went to extraordinary lengths to get what he wanted. Those employed to read the news on the radio were required to dress in evening wear, even though the listeners could not see them. Reith firmly believed that wearing more formal clothes would encourage the broadcasters to take their role more seriously and act with the required demeanour.

Below: Stephen Donoghue riding Captain Cuttle to victory in the 1922 Derby, a race which he won 6 times. Donoghue won all the classic flat races during his extraordinary career which began in 1909 and lasted over 20 years.

Right: The actress Judy Garland in perhaps her most famous role, in the film Wizard of Oz. She was born on 10th June. Bottom right: The Hollywood star Ava Gardner, who was born plain Lucy Johnson on Christmas Eve.

THE TELEPHONE MAN

On 2nd August Alexander Graham Bell died. He was born in Edinburgh in 1847, but at an early age moved to America. There he established himself as a noted authority on the medical study of vocal physiology. In 1872 he moved to Boston University and there began to study the mechanics of the voice and tried to study methods of reproducing the human voice by electrical means. In 1876 he succeeded and patented equipment which could convert the human voice to an electrical signal, transmit it along a wire and reproduce the sound through an electric speaker. After several years of work, Bell produced a two way apparatus which became the basis of the telephone. Facing page: Alexander Graham Bell in later life. Above: Bell making the first ever telephone call from New York to Chicago in 1892.

1923

The big Royal story of 1923 was the marriage of Prince Albert George, second son of King George V, to the demure Lady Elizabeth Bowes Lyon, a daughter of the prestigious Scottish baronial family of the Earls of Strathmore and Kinghorne. The marriage service on 26th April was held in Westminster Abbey and the streets of London were packed with vast crowds, tens of thousands strong. As with all royal brides, the dress was an all important decision for fashion watchers were sure to note every detail. In the event, Lady Elizabeth produced a dress which epitomised the fashions of the time and went a long way to popularising what has become thought of as typically 1920s lines. The new Duke and Duchess settled down quickly to a relatively quiet family life and diligent attention to official duties. Two daughters were born, the future Queen Elizabeth in 1926 and Princess Margaret in 1930. The Duke's liking for technical matters earned him the name in the Press of 'The Industrial Prince'. His marriage and growing family left one question unanswered, when would his elder brother, Prince Edward, find a wife and settle down.

Facing page: The Duke and Duchess of York photographed in Buckingham Palace after their wedding. Above left: Lady Elizabeth Bowes-Lyon, soon to become the Duchess of York. Top right: The Duke and Duchess attend the christening of Prince Peter of Yugoslavia, one of their first official duties as a married couple. The baby's father, King Alexander, stands on the left accompanied by the Queen of Greece and King Ferdinand of Rumania. The baby rests in the arms of his grandmother Queen Marie of Rumania. Above: Lady Elizabeth leaving her parents Mayfair home for her wedding. Left: The Duchess of York enjoying one of the robust country sporting days, a favourite of hers from her early days on the family's Scottish estates.

Facing page, top: Central Tokyo after the earthquake of 1st September. The massive quake was the strongest recorded in Japan and flattened not only Tokyo but also Yokohama and several smaller towns. It was estimated that about 300,000 died in the quake and the subsequent fires and cholera epidemic. Facing page, bottom: Adolf Hitler with Ludendorf on his right and Rohm on his left, and other sympathisers of the Munich Putsch. The attempted coup began on 8th November when Hitler kidnapped the entire Bavarian State Government and forced them to declare a dictatorship at gunpoint. Hitler made the mistake of allowing the statesmen to escape, whereupon they fled Munich and renounced their earlier promises. The rising ended in a bloody fiasco when Nazis tried to storm a police roadblock. The police opened fire, killing a number of Nazis, Hitler himself sustaining a slight graze in the rush to escape the gunfire. Four days later Hitler was arrested at the home of a friend and later sent to prison. Below: Calvin Coolidge, became President of the United States on the death of President Harding on 2nd August. His taciturnity and honesty became legendary and he easily held on to office in the elections of 1924. Right: Women in London hurrying to enjoy their right to vote in British elections.

The End of the Revolution

Pancho Villa, the flamboyant and blood-thirsty Mexican revolutionary was gunned down on 20th July, bringing to an end the chaotic bloodletting which had plagued Mexico for a generation. Outlawed at age 16 for killing a man who molested his sister, Villa built up a notorious bandit gang. During the Mexican Revolution, Villa recruited a huge army of dispossessed peasants and used this military might to put first Madero, then Carranza and finally, in 1914, himself into power. In 1920, after further civil war, Villa came to an arrangement with Carranza under which Villa disbanded his army in return for a huge bribe and a ranch to which he retired. But Villa had reckoned without the Herrera family, four of whom he had personally executed during the civil wars. On 20th July the Herreras killed Villa and his three bodyguards. With Villa's death the worst of the civil disorder ended and Mexico settled down to the peaceful years.

Right: the actress Sarah Bernhardt who died on 26th March after a glittering stage career which stretched from 1862 to the time of her death. Her real fame began in 1874 when experience had taught her to control her strong and dominating stage presence and use it to best effect.

Jan 21	Death of Vladimir Lenin, founder of Soviet Russia
Jan 22	Ramsay MacDonald takes office as Britain's first Labour Prime Minister
Jan 22	Moscow: A council is appointed to succeed Lenin, consisting of Grigori Zinoviev, Leon Kamenev and Joseph Stalin
Jan 22	USSR: Petrograd is renamed Leningrad
Jan 25	First Winter Olympics are held at Chamonix, France
Jan 28	Moscow: It is announced that Lenin's embalmed body will be on permanent public display
Feb 1	London: The government recognises the USSR
Feb 3	Death of ex-US President Woodrow Wilson
Feb 4	Mahatma Gandhi is freed from prison
Feb 5	BBC pips are heard for the first time
Feb 8	US: Gas chamber is used for first time as capital punishment
Mar 15	Cairo: King Fuad opens first Egyptian parliament
Apr 1	Hitler is sentenced to 5 years imprisonment
Apr 3	Birth of US actor Marlon Brando
Apr 3	Birth of Doris Day
Apr 6	Italy: Fascists win overwhelming victory in election
Apr 13	US: President Coolidge wins the Republican presidential nomination
May 26	US : Bill signed to limit immigration and bar Japanese
Jun 2	US grants full citizenship to American Indians
Jun 9	Mountaineer George Mallory and a young climber, Andrew Irvine, die attempting to reach the unconquered summit of Mount Everest
Jun 17	South Africa: Nationalists, led by Hertzog, win election
Jun 23	UK: The seeding system is introduced for competitors at Wimbledon
Jul 5	Paris: The Olympic Games open but Germany is not represented
Aug 3	Death of Polish-born British author Joseph Conrad
Aug 13	50,000 are feared dead following severe flooding in China
Sep 16	Birth of US actress Lauren Bacall
Sep 18	Mahatma Gandhi fasts in bid to end riots in India
Oct 1	Birth of US President Jimmy Carter
Oct 4	Birth of Charlton Heston
Oct 10	Washington Senators win World Series
Oct 12	Death of French writer Anatole France
Oct 29	UK: Conservative victory in General Election
Nov 1	Ireland: Eamon de Valera is sentenced to prison for entering Ulster illegally
Nov 4	Calvin Coolidge is elected US president
Nov 4	US: Texas elects the first woman state governor
Nov 6	UK: Prime Minister Baldwin names Winston Churchill as the new Chancellor of the Exchequer
Nov 26	Trotsky is denounced by Communist Party
Nov 29	Giacomo Puccini, composer of Madame Butterfly, dies of throat cancer
Nov 29	John D. Rockefeller Jr makes a gift of one million dollars to the Metropolitan Museum of Art
Dec 2	Birth of US politician and soldier General Alexander Haig
Dec 5	Mussolini introduces widespread press censorship
Dec 20	Adolf Hitler is released from jail on parole
Dec 24	Albania is declared a Republic
Dec 24	Death of Russian artist Leon Bakst
Dec 24	UK: 8 people die in Britain's worst air disaster

TURMOIL IN RUSSIA

Lenin, *(right)*, the architect of the Revolution and its chief intellectual asset died on 21st January aged just 54. Lenin's assumption of power had been the culmination of a remarkable life. His highly personal style and philosophy was firmly imprinted on the Soviet system and made the task of finding a successor all the more difficult. He began publishing *Pravda* in 1912, a publication which was to become the official newspaper of the Revolution, and was instrumental in setting up the elitist party structure which came to rule the Soviet Union in place of the more democratic workers' soviets. His sudden death left the Soviet hierarchy in confusion as to who should assume power. Among Lenin's last actions was to indicate that he wanted Leon Trotsky to play a leading role and that Joseph Stalin should be removed from his post as Secretary General of the Communist Party. The naked ambition of Stalin made Lenin's wishes unworkable and for a full year the Soviet system was plunged into clandestine intrigue and secret factional dealings. In January 1925 Trotsky was ousted from the War Council, an action which marked his loss of any chance of power. Stalin, meanwhile, worked secretly to discredit all his friends and allies in turn until, by 1927, he was the only powerful figure left and was the virtual dictator of the Soviet Union. Trotsky was murdered soon afterwards.

Facing page: Adolf Hitler in prison in the fortress of Landsberg-am-Lech. Hitler was sentenced to five years in prison for organising the failed Bavarian coup of November 1923. Throughout the trial he was treated leniently by the judges who allowed him to heckle witnesses and put forward his Nazi views. He was released after only 6 months in prison. Top left: Ramsay MacDonald who formed the first British Labour Government on 22nd January. In 1900 MacDonald had been instrumental in persuading the Trades Unions to set up a political party to represent the interests of working men. His elevation to the premiership was seen as a vindication of his vision. Above: President Calvin Coolidge who saw his son die of blood poisoning on 7th July and gained enormous public sympathy for his family.

Assault on Everest

Mystery surrounds the British expedition to scale Mount Everest in June. The expedition was led by George Mallory, a highly experienced mountaineer who had climbed in the Himalayas before. The climb ended with the tragic death of Mallory and his companion Andrew Irvine, and with a mystery which remains unsolved. By 9th June the expedition had scaled the lower and middle slopes and had established a camp high on the flanks of Mount Everest. Early that morning Mallory and Irvine set out to climb the final stretch to the summit itself. The anxious team in camp watched the two men depart, and later saw the weather close in dangerously. After several hours a gap opened in the clouds to reveal Mallory and Irvine only a few hundred feet from the summit and climbing steadily. Then the clouds closed again. The two men were never seen again and must have succumbed to the biting cold winds of the bad weather. Argument has raged ever since as to whether or not they could have reached the summit. It is most likely that the truth shall never be known.

Above right: Queen Mary walking with the Duke and Duchess of York at Balmoral. Right: Lauren Bacall, who was born on 16th September. Below right: Marlon Brando, who achieved fame as the archetypal method actor, was born on 3rd April. Below: Eric Liddell breasts the tape to take the 400 metre gold medal at the Paris Olympics. The running track was dominated by rivalry between Britons Liddell and Abrahams and the Americans Paddock and Scholz. The intense rivalry was later made the subject of a movie entitled **Chariots of Fire.**

Jan 1   Norway's capital Christiana is renamed Oslo
Jan 2   Australia scores 600 runs in its first innings against England
Jan 3   Mussolini assumes full dictatorial control
Jan 11 Peking is seized by Chi Hsieh-yuan and Sun Chuan-fang
Jan 16 Leon Trotsky is ousted from leadership in the Soviet Communist Party by Stalin
Jan 20 UK and China make Treaty of Peking
Jan 25 Paul Newman born
Feb 11 The Portuguese government is overthrown
Feb 14 Ban on Nazi Party is lifted in Bavaria
Mar 2   The schilling is introduced as the new Austrian currency
Mar 18 Two floors of Madame Tussaud's waxworks museum are destroyed by fire
Mar 23 US: Tennessee law prohibits teaching of evolution
Mar 28 UK: The Oxford boat sinks in the University boat race
Mar 29 Japan passes Bill for universal male suffrage
Apr 3   Tony Benn born
Apr 6   First in-flight movie ("The Lost World")
Apr 10 Paul Painleve succeeds Herriot as Premier of France
Apr 14 Birth of US actor Rod Steiger
Apr 14 Death of US painter John Singer Sargent
Apr 16 Turkey: End of the Kurdish Uprising
Apr 26 Germany: Paul von Hindenburg is elected President
May 1   Cyprus is declared a British colony
May 8   South Africa: Afrikaans becomes official language of the Union
May 19 Birth of US black leader Malcolm X

May 23 Death of British publisher Sir Edward Hulton
Jun 2   The Canadian government claims all land between Alaska and Greenland up to the North Pole
Jun 3   Tony Curtis born
Jun 20 The invention of a wireless telephone for cars is demonstrated in Germany
Jun 22 Hong Kong: A general strike begins
Jun 29 US: A serious earthquake hits Santa Barbara
Aug 7   UK: Daylight saving becomes a permanent fixture in Britian
Aug 12 Birth of Norris and Ross McWhirter, Guiness Book of Records
Sep 8   Birth of British actor Peter Sellers
Sep 16 Birth of US musician B.B. King
Oct 13 Birth of Britain's first woman Prime Minister Margaret Thatcher
Nov 5   Mussolini bans all left-wing parties
Nov 10 Birth of Richard Burton
Nov 17 Birth of Rock Hudson
Nov 20 Death of Danish-born Queen Alexandra
Nov 27 Birth of British comedian Ernie Wise
Dec 3   The border is settled between Northern Ireland and the Irish Free State
Dec 8   Sammy Davis Jnr born
Dec 10 George Bernard Shaw wins the Nobel prize for literature
Dec 12 World's first motel opens in California
Dec 18 USSR adopts policy of 'socialism in one country'

The Tennessee Monkey Trial

The most famous trial of the year took place in Tennessee and centred on the legality of science. It was a classic confrontation between science and religion which went down in history as a success for the former. In March the Tennessee state legislature passed a law banning the teaching of any except the Biblical account of human origins. In May a high school teacher named John Scopes taught his class about Darwinian evolution theories and was at once indicted under the new law. The trial, held in the little town of Dayton, attracted prestigious figures as both witnesses and counsel. Charles Darrow appeared for the defence while William Bryan aided the prosecution. After a lengthy trial in which the fundamentalist prosecutors were made to look rather silly and bigoted the jury found Scopes guilty, as indeed he was under the law. However, the scientists had made their point and the law was soon repealed.

On 26th April Paul von Hindenberg (right) was elected President of Germany, the first man to hold that office through popular election. Recalled from retirement in 1914 to take command of the Imperial German armies, Hindenberg proved himself to be a highly capable commander-in-chief who was extremely popular with his men and idolised at home. Even his eventual defeat could not destroy the respect in which he was held. It was only natural that Germany would turn to Hindenberg when anarchy seemed close, and he took up his task as his duty to the nation. Hindenberg behaved as a constitutional monarch, frequently expressing his view and steering the nation, but never ignoring the wishes of the people. In 1932 he was re-elected, defeating Adolf Hitler by a narrow margin. However, the venerable soldier was quite unable to thwart the Nazis adroit manipulation of the constitution which brought them to supreme power in 1933.

Top left: The sensual singer
Josephine Baker who hit the
headlines in October with her
exotic, near nude appearances
on the Paris stage in The Negro
Review. Her dancing was
described by a leading critic as
decadent wriggling, but the
audience loved it. The american had scored a minor success
on Broadway as a dancer, but
her Parisian appearances
assured her of stardom, and no
a little notoriety. Top right:
Paul Newman; (left) Peter
Sellers and (above) Tony
Curtis, three film stars who
were born in this year.

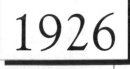

THE BIRTH OF A QUEEN

Above: The Duke and Duchess of York with their first baby, Princess Elizabeth, born on 21st April 1926. The birth took place at the London home of the Duchess's family in Bruton Street and mother and baby stayed there for some time. There was an almost permanent crowd outside the smart home as people hoped to catch a glimpse of the new royal baby. Within a few months, the Yorks were scheduled to leave for Australia on an Imperial state visit and, in line with tradition, Princess Elizabeth was left behind. By all accounts this caused much distress to the Duchess. At the time of her birth few believed that the new princess would ever occupy the British throne. A contemporary account of the birth described the baby as being "the fourth lady in the land and, for the time being, third in succession to the throne." It was still confidently expected that Edward, Prince of Wales, would marry soon and produce heirs which would deny the crown to the Yorks. However, the dramatic events of 1936 were to ensure that the Princess Elizabeth would ascend the throne as Queen Elizabeth II and embark on a long and memorable reign.

Jan 5	UK : Widows pension is issued for first time at Post Office
Jan 6	Germany: The airline Lufthansa is formed
Jan 8	New King Ibn Saud renames Hejaz, Saudi Arabia
Jan 12	Pasteur Institute says it has found anti-tetanus serum
Jan 27	UK: Logie Baird demonstrates television for the first time
Feb 2	Birth of Giscard d'Estaing, French president
Feb 3	Czech becomes the official language of Czecholslovakia
Feb 8	Germany applies to join the League of Nations
Feb 12	Italy: Strikes are made illegal
Feb 18	Mexico: Five Mayan cities are discovered in the Yucatan
Apr 7	Italy: Mussolini survives assassination attempt
Apr 21	Birth of Queen Elizabeth II
Apr 25	Riza Khan crowned Shah of Persia
Mar 29	UK: Cash on delivery parcel post is introduced
Mar 5	London: Four paintings by Constable are stolen from the Royal Academy
Mar 20	Scotland beats England in the Calcutta Cup
Apr 4	India: Martial law is declared in Calcutta following Hindu-Moslem riots
May 4	UK: General Strike begins
May 7	US troops arrive in Nicaragua following coup
May 8	David Attenborough born
May 9	Richard Byrd makes first flight over North Pole
May 12	General Strike ends
May 12	Military coup in Poland led by Joseph Pilsudski
May 13	Polish President Wojciechowski is arrested by Pilsudski
May 14	Eric Morecombe born
May 23	France declares Lebanon a Republic
May 25	Birth of US jazz musician Miles Davis
May 31	Coup in Portugal led by Comes da Costa
Jun 1	Poland: Joseph Pilsudski assumes dictatorial powers
Jun 1	Birth of US actress Marilyn Monroe
Jun 3	Birth of US poet Allen Ginsburg
Jun 28	Canada: Liberal Premier Mackenzie King resigns following a customs scandal
Jul 10	US: An explosion is caused when lightning strikes a US Navy munitions dump
Jun 29	Mussolini increases the working day in Italy by one hour
Jul 24	UK: The first greyhound racing track opens in Manchester
Aug 3	London: Traffic lights come into operation at Piccadilly Circus
Aug 6	US woman is first to swim the English Channel
Aug 7	The first British Grand Prix takes place at Brooklands
Aug 23	Death of US film star Rudolph Valentino
Sep 7	Spain: The government decides to leave the League of Nations
Oct 1	Alan Cobham makes the round-the-world flight in 58 days
Oct 7	Italy: All political opposition to fascism is banned
Oct 18	Birth of US rock musician Chuck Berry
Oct 31	Death of Harry Houdini, Hungarian-born escape artist
Oct 31	Birth of Jimmy Savile
Nov 3	Death of Annie Oakley
Nov 19	6 month miners strike ends in UK
Nov 27	Mount Vesuvius erupts
Dec 3	Agatha Christie goes missing
Dec 5	Claude Monet dies a recluse
Dec 25	Hirohito becomes Emperor of Japan
Dec 28	Australia: Victoria scored 1107 against NSW, highest recorded cricket innings

In the spring a potentially damaging strike by British miners turned into a General Strike and some worried about the possibility of a Communist revolution. The dispute began when the Government withdrew cash subsidies paid to the coal industry. Mine owners, anxious to protect profits, cut the miners wages and so sparked off a bitter dispute. On 3rd May the Trades Union Congress decided to back the miners in what seemed to be an intractable dispute. Iron and steel, press and transportation workers were all called out on strike and the nation was paralysed. In the event volunteers manned all vital services and within days the country was showing signs of struggling through. A compromise deal was negotiated with the mine owners under severe pressure from the government and TUC. When the miners refused to accept the deal, the TUC withdrew support on 12th May and the General Strike ended.

Above left:City workers make their way to work by foot and in a wide variety of motorised transport in the Aldgate, London.
Above: Stanley Baldwin arrives to chair a meeting between mine owners and miners. Left: The First Guards parade through the streets of London on their way back to barracks after being stationed in the London docks area during the General Strike.
Facing page: (top left) Rudolph Valentino, who died on 23rd August; (top right) Anita Loos, author of the classic **Gentlemen Prefer Blondes***; (bottom left) Logie Baird who demonstrated his television invention to the Royal Institution on 27th January and (bottom right) Harry Houdini about to perform one of his famous escape stunts. Houdini died of peritonitis after he ignored doctors' warnings and continued with a stunt.*

Jan 1	BBC broadcasts its first programmes	**May 9**	Canberra inaugurated as new capital of Australia
Jan 7	Harlem Globetrotters are founded	**May 21**	Charles Lindbergh becomes first pilot to fly the Atlantic solo
Jan 7	Transatlantic telephone service begins, £15 for three minutes	**Jun 1**	Lizzie Borden dies
Jan 9	Canada: 77 children die while fleeing a burning theatre	**Jun 18**	Germany: The Nurburgring motor racing circuit opens
Jan 15	Italy: Winston Churchill meets Mussolini	**Jul 7**	Christopher Stone becomes first DJ on British radio
Jan 21	Telly Savalas born	**Jul 10**	Death of Irish statesman Kevin O'Higgins
Jan 28	UK: A hurricane hits Glasgow killing 8	**Jul 21**	Bucharest: Prince Mihai succeeds to the throne at the age of 5
Jan 29	UK: The Park Lane Hotel opens, the first with en suite bathrooms	**Aug 13**	Birth of Cuban leader Fidel Castro
Feb 4	Malcolm Campbell breaks the world land speed record reaching 174 mph along the Pendine Sands, Wales	**Sep 14**	Isadora Duncan accidentally strangled when her scarf catches in the wheel spokes of her Bugatti sportscar
Feb 8	UK: Sex equality is introduced into the wedding service in the revised Book of Common Prayer	**Sep 14**	Japan: 3,000 are killed by a tidal wave
Feb 20	Birth of French fashion designer Hubert Taffin de Givenchy	**Oct 18**	Germany: Dancing bears are banned from the streets of Berlin
Mar 29	Major Henry Seagrave takes the world land speed record from Campbell, achieving 203 mph on the Daytona Beach racetrack, Florida	**Nov 5**	UK: First automatic traffic lights begin operating
		Nov 10	US: General Motors announces the largest dividend in US history - $62 million
Apr 2	France beats England at Rugby for the first time	**Nov 12**	First London to Brighton veteran car rally
Apr 23	UK: Cardiff City win the FA Cup Final when Arsenal's goal keeper scores an own goal	**Nov 18**	Head of the International Football Association announces the creation of a 'World Cup'
May 1	Adolf Hitler holds his first Nazi meeting in Berlin	**Dec 27**	Leon Trotsky is expelled from the Communist Party

Trouble in China

As 1927 opened the turmoil in China was descending into chaos and anarchy. In various sections of the Celestial Empire warlords held territory in their grip and fought each with a ferocity unknown in China for centuries. The chaotic conditions threatened trade while the violent anti-foreigner riots stirred memories of the Boxer Rebellion of 1900. Western powers decided to intervene to protect their interests and troops were sent to Shanghai and other European-dominated ports. The civil war and disorder necessitated the stationing of Western troops until the Japanese invasion. Left: A large "Down with Foreigners" demonstration in Shanghai. Below left: The Gloucester Regiment marches through Shanghai in March after disembarking. Below: Barbed wire defences around French property in Shanghai erected in February as a temporary measure to keep out antagonistic Chinese. Bottom: The public executioner of Shanghai parades through the streets with his drawn sword in an effort to intimidate potential rioters.

Facing page: Stanley Baldwin, whose record as a Prime Minister was patchy by any standards. First taking office in 1923 on the resignation of Bonar Law, Baldwin quickly called an election which he lost in spectacular fashion. Returned to office in the election of October 1924, Baldwin won praise for his firm handling of the General Strike, but in almost every other issue tried to compromise and ended up by pleasing virtually nobody. He lost the election of 1929, but was called back to the cabinet in the National Coalition Government formed during the depths of the Depression. In 1935 he became Prime Minister yet again, and held that office during the Abdication Crisis in which he again acted with firmness, though the supporters of King Edward VIII did not appreciate Baldwin's efforts to hold the Empire together.

On 20th May American airman Charles Lindbergh set off from New York in a specially adapted aircraft named *The Spirit of St Louis*, to complete the first solo flight across the Atlantic. After stops in Ireland and England he arrived in Paris the following day to find himself a national hero. Facing page, top: Charles Lindbergh lands at Croydon Airfield, 21st May. Facing page, bottom: *The Spirit of St Louis* at Curtis Field. Left: Lindbergh poses with wife Anne before a flight. Below: Sir Malcolm Campbell seated in the cockpit of his record-breaking car *Bluebird*, before leaving Surrey for Daytona Beach, Florida where he would attempt to break Major Henry Seagrave's land speed record of 203 mph.

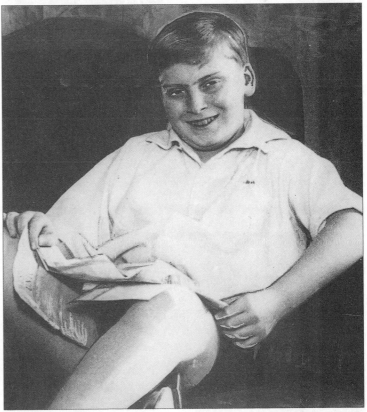

Left: The great dancer Isadora Duncan who was killed in a motor accident outside Nice, France on 14th September. Beginning her career in 1899, Duncan gained almost as much fame from her tangled private life as from her formidable ballet skills. Above: Yehudi Menuhin, who leapt to fame as a violinist, aged 7 in Paris.

Below: The Duke and Duchess of York attend the State Opening of the Australian Parliament in Canberra, a city built from scratch to be the new capital of Australia. Prior to the building of Canberra, Sydney and Melbourne had argued bitterly over the prestige of being the seat of government. The new city, located in a specially cre-ated autonomous territory, solved the argument. Right: King George V confers a knighthood on Vice Admiral Pakenham on board HMS Princess Royal. Bottom left: Photographed on her return from Australia, the Duchess of York and her daughter, Princess Elizabeth. Bottom right: Princess Elizabeth, aged 1.

Jan 2	Pan American Airlines use the world's first male stewards
Jan 11	Death of British author Thomas Hardy
Jan 14	Libya: Clashes with Italian troops result in the deaths of 100 tribesmen
Feb 1	US: Dr Herbert Evans discovers Vitamin E
Feb 6	China: 50,000 flee as Communists raid Peking
Feb 12	British colony of Malta gets Dominion status
Feb 15	Death of Herbert Henry Asquith, leader of Liberals and Prime Minister
Feb 19	US: Campbell sets new land speed record of over 206 mph
Feb 26	Birth of Fats Domino
Mar 13	Over 400 die as Los Angeles dam bursts
Mar 27	US: Record trading on the New York Stock Exchange
Mar 28	France: Military service shortened to one year
Mar 30	Birth of French film director Agnes Varda
Apr 22	Earthquake in Corinth leaves 50,000 homeless
Apr 23	Shirley Temple born
May 7	UK: Voting age for women reduced from 30 to 21
May 15	Flying Doctor Service is inaugurated in Australia
May 21	Italy: Catholics are instructed to disassociate themselves from Fascism
May 29	US: Chrysler and Dodge motor companies merge
Jun 14	Death of British women's rights campaigner Emmeline Pankhurst
Jun 14	Birth of Argentine revolutionary Che Guevara
Jun 15	Scotland: Race from London to Edinburgh between the 'Flying Scotsman' and a plane is won by the train
Jun 18	Death of Roald Amundsen, first man to reach South Pole
Jun 17	Amelia Earhart is first woman to fly Atlantic
Jul 1	Mexico: General Alvaro Obregon is the new president
Jul 3	TV sets go on sale for the first time to the public at $75
Jul 3	First TV transmission in colour by John Logie Baird
Jul 4	Gina Lollobrigida born
Jul 6	First all talking feature film shown in NY
Jul 17	President Obregon of Mexico is assassinated while celebrating his recent election
Jul 21	Death of British actress Dame Ellen Terry
Jul 22	Japan severs relations with China
Aug 2	Italy and Ethiopia sign 20 year friendship treaty
Aug 6	Birth of US artist Andy Warhol
Aug 9	Dutch East Indies: Volcano erupts killing 1000
Aug 25	Anfield's famous Kop is opened
Aug 27	Fifteen countries sign the anti-war Kellogg-Briand pact in Paris
Sep 1	Albania is declared a Kingdom with Zog I as monarch
Sep 15	Alexander Fleming reports discovery of penicillin
Sep 18	US: Hurricane kills over 100 in Florida
Oct 9	New York Yankees' second consecutive World Series
Oct 12	US: First iron lung is used at Boston Childrens Hospital
Oct 14	Roger Moore born
Oct 20	China: Chiang Kai-shek invites Henry Ford to become an honorary economic advisor
Oct 30	Graf Zeppelin makes first commercial transatlantic trip
Nov 5	Sicily: Mount Etna erupts
Nov 7	Republican Herbert Hoover is elected President
Nov 30	Mexico: Emilio Portes Gil is sworn in as President

Sir Alexander Fleming in his laboratory. It was in 1928 that Fleming discovered penicillin, a drug which was capable of killing many types of germ without damaging the human patient. The discovery was made by accident when Fleming neglected to clean culture dishes in which he had been growing and studying various types of germ. On his return to the laboratory he noticed that several of the germs had been killed, or their growth impeded, by a type of mould which had found its way into the trays. Fleming guessed that the fungus was responsible. After lengthy research he managed to isolate the chemical which the fungus was producing. The announcement of the discovery was made to a grateful world on 15th September. The resulting drug has been responsible for saving the lives of many millions of people over the years since it came on to the market. Fleming received the Nobel Prize for Science in 1945.

EARHART FLIES THE ATLANTIC

On 17th June Amelia Earhart became the first woman to fly across the Atlantic Ocean, then still very much an adventurous and risky undertaking. The flight was made in a three engined Fokker, one of the more reliable aircraft of the day. Although Earhart was almost a passenger, playing little part in flying the aircraft, the flight made her name a household term for feminine daring. As a university graduate and master of several languages, Earhart was already well known. Her love of flying, and innate skill, promised great adventures for the future. She did not disappoint the world and over the next few years went on to complete several daring and headline-worthy flights both alone and in the company of others. Right: Earhart in a favourite aircraft. Below: Earhart presented with flowers on arrival at Southampton for a demonstration flight.

Left: Herbert Asquith, the Earl of Oxford and Asquith, addressing a meeting shortly before his death on 15th February. After practising as a lawyer, Asquith was elected as a Liberal MP in 1886, reaching cabinet rank just 6 years later. In 1908 he became Prime Minister and though resolute in the early months of the Great War, Asquith resigned in December 1916. He lost his seat at the 1918 election and was created Earl of Oxford and Asquith in 1924. Above: The Japanese Emperor Hirohito. Though his father had died in 1926, it was not until November 1928 that Hirohito formally assumed full power, and the throne.

Below: Lloyd George pictured with Viscount St David and St David's niece Miss Burnett. Lloyd George, once the hero of wartime Britain, watched the Liberal party slip towards anarchy and defeat in this year. Right: A colourful cavalcade declaring the virtues of one of the candidates in the general election. Bottom left: The Earl of Balfour, photographed in July, when he was Lord President of the Council. Bottom right: Christabel and Sylvia Pankhurst in mourning for their mother Emmeline, who died on 14th June.

In August a new era in travel was ushered in with great pomp and luxury. Everyone believed the innovation would revolutionise the way people travelled, none could guess it would be a short lived wonder. On 7th the German airship *Graf Zeppelin* left New Jersey and 22 days later returned having encircled the globe. The giant rigid airships were invented by Count Zeppelin in the years before the Great War as bombing and reconnaissance aircraft for the Imperial German Navy. With the coming of peace, however, the giant craft were converted to passenger uses. The airships could provide luxurious and spacious accommodation far superior to anything available on trains or aeroplanes, and at a cruising speed in excess of that of ships. For those wealthy enough to travel by Zeppelin airship the experience was rewarding and enjoyable. Only 16 passengers were carried on the round the world voyage, but the publicity it generated helped to ensure full bookings for transatlantic and other routes. However, a number of accidents with the highly inflammable hydrogen gas which provided lift ultimately destroyed their popularity.

Left: Fats Domino pounding keyboard in 1957. He was born on 26th February 1928. Below; The English novelist Thomas Hardy who died on 11th January. Below left: The child star Shirley Temple, born on 23rd April. Bottom left: Walt Disney with one of his famous creations, Donald Duck. On 19th September Disney released his fir successful independent cartoon, **Steamboat Willie**. Bottom right: The three Bentley 4.5 litre cars which competed in the 1928 Le Mans classic 24 hour race prepa ing for the start. Car No.4, driven Woolf Barnato and Bernard Rub won the race.

TROTSKY EXILED

Russian Revolutionary Leon Trotsky was exiled from the Soviet Union he had helped to create by the man who beat him in the power struggle following Lenin's death, Joseph Stalin. Trotsky had been one of the chief organisers of the Revolution of 1917, but lost influence. On 23rd January Soviet secret police swooped on 150 friends and associates of Trotsky, arresting them on charges of treason and plotting a civil war. Trotsky evaded capture and fled across the border to Turkey. The Turkish government, alarmed by Soviet hostility, hastily expelled Trotsky who failed to find refuge in a total of nine nations before being allowed to live on the islands first Prinkipio and later Corsica. While in this island exile, Trotsky wrote an autobiography which sold widely throughout the world and further enraged Stalin. The Soviet Union flexed its influence to make life difficult for Trotsky, who was eventually thrown out of France in 1934 after being caught with compromising documents pointing to a Communist plot in France. Thereafter Trotsky wandered with the memory of his former greatness and the implacable animosity of Stalin dogging his steps.

Jan 1	Figures released in England show that there are 3.6 telephones for every 100 people
Jan 6	Yugoslavia: King Alexander declares himself absolute ruler
Jan 10	Belguim: Herge's cartoon character Tintin appears for the first time
Jan 13	US: Western law enforcer Wyatt Earp dies
Jan 15	Birth of US civil rights leader Martin Luther King
Jan 16	The Listener first published
Jan 31	Leon Trotsky is exiled from Russia by Stalin
Feb 5	Eamon de Valera is arrested in Belfast for entering Northern Ireland
Feb 11	Vatican City becomes an Independent Papal State
Feb 11	Mussolini signs treaty with Pope
Feb 12	Death of British actress Lillie Langtry
Feb 14	St. Valentines Day massacre
Feb 14	Germany: Josephine Baker is banned from the stage for indecent behavior
Feb 15	Graham Hill born
Mar 4	US: Herbert Hoover is inaugurated as President
Mar 10	Egypt: Women granted limited rights of divorce
Mar 22	Grand National has a record 66 runners
Mar 23	Roger Bannister - sub 4 minute mile man - born
Apr 4	Death of German engineer Carl Benz
Apr 14	The first Monaco Grand Prix
Apr 24	Socialist government is formed in Denmark
Apr 29	Jeremy Thorpe born
May 16	Film Academy Awards first presented in Hollywood
May 27	Aviator Charles Lindberg weds Ann Morrow
May 30	UK: Labour party win General Election
Jun 3	US: Actor Douglas Fairbanks Jr marries actress Joan Crawford
Jun 10	UK: Margaret Bondfield is first woman cabinet minister
Jun 12	Birth of Anne Frank
Jun 27	First colour TV pictures demonstrated in NY
Jul 1	US cartoon Popeye created by Elzie Segar
Jul 28	Jacqueline Onassis born
Aug 19	Death of ballet impressario Serge Diagilev
Aug 29	Airship Graf Zeppelin completes a round the world trip in 21 days
Sep 3	New York stock exchange reaches high of 381.17
Sep 10	Arnold Palmer born
Sep 13	New traffic light system in UK to be standardised
Sep 17	Stirling Moss born
Sep 24	USSR: Workers are given 2 days off a week
Sep 25	Ronnie Barker born
Oct 3	Britain resumes diplomatic relations with USSR
Oct 14	Maiden flight of Britain's first rigid airship,R101
Oct 24	Wall street crash begins, more than 12 million transactions recorded
Oct 29	New York Stock Exchange crashes on "Black Tuesday"
Nov 1	Pony Club is founded in Britain
Nov 8	Museum of Modern Art opens in New York
Nov 12	Birth of US actress and Princess of Monaco, Grace Kelly
Nov 21	Henry Ford raises workers wages in all plants
Nov 24	Death of Georges Clemenceau, French Statesman and Premier
Nov 29	Richard Byrd makes first flight over South Pole
Dec 2	Britain's first public telephone boxes come into service
Dec 7	Turkey grants vote to women

A Food Revolution

A revolution in the way food is stored and bought got under way on 6th March when Clarence Birdseye put a packet of frozen peas on sale in Springfield, Massachusetts. Up until that time the only way to preserve foods was to change their form radically, such as by drying, pickling or turning into jam. Frozen food is very similar to its original condition when it is thawed. This enormous advantage was first noticed by Birdseye when he was surveying wildlife in Labrador in 1912 and saw how local natives preserved fish by packing them in snow. It took until 1930 for Birdseye to develop a commercially viable method of bulk freezing and to gain the financial backing for his scheme. At first sales were restricted by high price and consumer resistance, but within two years frozen vegetables available out of season and fish available far from the sea had established the popularity of frozen foods. The concept of frozen food was eagerly taken up elsewhere, reaching Europe in 1936. Birdseye sold his company within months for $22 million.

Facing page: President Herbert Hoover with Marie Curie. Hoover presented Curie with a cheque for $50,000 which was to be used to purchase a gram of radium. Top left; Stanley Baldwin and his wife attending the Summer Exhibition at the Royal Academy. Baldwin lost the General Election of 30th May, but retained the leadership of the Conservative Party. Left: Ramsay MacDonald, the Labour leader who defeated Baldwin, strolls with his daughter at Chequers, the official country seat of the Prime Minister. MacDonald made history by making Margaret Bondfield the first woman cabinet minister. Above: John D. Rockefeller II who died on 23rd May.

The gangster wars of Chicago and New York grew steadily in violence and intensity during the 1920s. Chicago was divided between the Italian gangs headed by Al Capone and the Irish mob of Bugs Moran. On 14th February Moran arranged a meeting of his top men to discuss plans to oust the Italians, but Capone heard of the arrangement. He sent four of his best gunmen, two disguised as policemen, to the motor garage venue. In just 8 minutes, t Capone men burst in, slaughtered the entire Moran team and escap The St Valentine's Day Massacre, it was known, led to a crackdown the gangs. Left: George Moran, known to friends and enemies ali was the chief target of the St Valentine's Day Massacre, but wa absent when the gunmen struck. Below: The scene which greeted police on their arrival at the garag

In 1929 the Wall Street Crash ruined thousands and spelled the start of the Great Depression. For years the stock market had been a safe investment, leading to spiralling stock prices and rampant speculation. Several banks had lent recklessly to investors in an effort to cash in. On 24th October the bubble burst and the value of stocks fell. Panic selling set in as investors realised their shares were priced higher than the company stock was worth and feared massive losses. In one day billions of dollars were wiped from share values. Banks intervened and caused a temporary rally, which gave way on the 29th to further mass selling and plummeting values. Right: Anxious investors await news outside the Stock Exchange. Above: A sign which says it all.

Top left: Gary Cooper, born 1929, and Audrey Hepburn star in the movie **Love in the Afternoon.**
Above left: Motor racing ace Graham Hill, born this year, was to achieve great fame in the 1960s. He is shown here being congratulated by Jackie Stewart after his return to racing following a break. Above: Anna Pavlova, one of the greatest dancers to emerge from pre-Revolutionary Russia. She was born in 1885 and debuted in St Petersburg before moving to London in 1909 and America soon after. Returning to England in 1921, she bought a mansion in Hampstead. The pavlova dessert is named in her honour. Left: Black civil rights leader Martin Luther King, born this year, pictured in December 1963 after holding talks with President Johnson.

1930-1939

Jan 3	Stalin collectivises all farms in USSR
Jan 11	Egypt: A new parliament opens after 18 months of dictatorship
Jan 20	Birth of Edwin 'Buzz' Aldrin, 2nd man on moon
Feb 18	New planet is discovered beyond Neptune
Mar 2	Death of English novelist D H Lawrence
Mar 6	Frozen foods, developed by Clarence Birdseye go on sale
Mar 7	Birth of Antony Armstrong-Jones, Earl of Snowdon
Mar 8	Death of former US President Taft
Mar 13	The name 'Pluto' is given to the new planet
Mar 16	Death of Spanish prime minister Miguel Primo de Rivera
Mar 24	Birth of Steve McQueen
Mar 30	Birth of Rolf Harris
Apr 3	Haile Selassie is proclaimed Emperor of Ethiopia
Apr 4	UK: The free discussion of sex is approved by the Archbishop of Canterbury
Apr 11	Daily Express becomes first paper to publish TV programmes
Apr 11	US: Scientists predict that man will have landed on the moon by the year 2050
Apr 12	Wilfred Rhodes becomes oldest man to play in a Test when he plays for England against West Indies aged 52 years, 165 days
Apr 24	Amy Johnson arrives in Darwin, becoming the first woman to fly solo to Australia
Apr 28	UK: John Gielgud stars as Hamlet at the Old Vic
Apr 1	Don Bradman of Australia scores 236 in his first cricket match in the UK
May 4	Gandhi is arrested by British authorities
May 21	Birth of Malcolm Fraser, Australian PM
May 31	Birth of US actor Clint Eastwood
Jun 4	UK: The Aga Khan wins his first Derby
Jun 13	UK: Henry Seagrave is killed when his speedboat achieves a record speed of 98 mph
Jun 13	US: Al Capone is arrested for perjury
Jun 22	British cars take the first four places in the Le Mans race
Jun 30	Britain recognises Iraqi independence
Jul 7	Death of British writer Sir Arthur Conan Doyle
Jul 13	World Cup Football competition first held in Uruguay
Aug 4	Soviet troops kill 200 strikers in Odessa
Aug 5	Birth of US astronaut Neil Armstrong
Aug 7	UK: Unemployment reaches 2 million
Aug 7	Canada: Conservative R B Bennett becomes PM
Aug 13	Charles Greighton and James Hargis arrived in LA having driven the 3,340 miles from NY backwards
Aug 21	Birth of Princess Margaret
Aug 25	Birth of British actor Sean Connery
Aug 25	Poland: Marshal Pilsudski becomes Prime Minister
Aug 26	Death of US actor Lon Chaney
Aug 29	Death of Irish academic the Rev. Dr. William Spooner
Sep 2	China: A rebel government is formed in Peking
Sep 15	Germany: Hitler is denied seat in the elections because he is Austrian, and not German
Sep 29	London: George Bernard Shaw refuses the offer of a peerage
Oct 5	British airship R101 crashes in France, killing 48
Oct 5	Gordon Richards rides his 12th consecutive winner in 3 days
Nov 2	Haile Selassie is crowned Emperor of Ethiopia
Nov 14	Japan: The prime minister is shot dead by an extreme right-wing militant
Dec 3	Birth of Andy Williams

British airwoman Amy Johnson leapt to fame in 1930 with a series of record-breaking flights. She later married aviator James Mollison with whom she made several more pioneering flights. Left: Amy Johnson receiving a cheque for £10,000 from Esmond Harmsworth of the Daily Mail for her record breaking solo flight to Australia. The flight was the first by a woman and was completed in 19 days. Right: Amy Johnson takes off from England at the start of her flight to Australia.

The Depression gripped the world economy in 1930 with a vengeance. Millions were thrown out of work, for many it was their first experience of long term hardship. The causes of the Great Depression were complex, and are still the subject of dispute among economic historians. The Wall Street Crash and the following lack of investment confidence in industry were much blamed at the time, but a fall in money supply and unwisely fixed international exchange rates also played their part. Right: Butlers Wharf in London stands idle as dockers strike in May against redundancies. Below right: Striking dockers gather outside their Union office for news. Below and bottom left: A large crowd of unemployed men protest on Tower Hill, demanding government action to provide jobs and alleviate hardship.

Voices End Movie Careers

The success of the movie *The Jazz Singer*, with its partial sound track, in 1927 pointed to the future and by 1930 nearly all films were accompanied by sound. This posed problems for the film stars. Accustomed to silent movies several lacked the ability to put emotion into their voices for the microphones. Others simply had the wrong type of voice, such as the dashing romantic hero of the silent screen, John Gilbert, who had a squeaky voice. It became a source of much gossip, speculation and real anxiety as to who would prove to "have a voice" and who would not. Some stars, however, were made by the transition. Singing cowboy Gene Autry would never have made his 92 movies in silence. Likewise minor silent slapstick men Laurel and Hardy leapt to fame once their verbal gags could be filmed. Sound brought other changes to the movie world. For the first time the various members of the production crew had to stop chatting during takes and locations free of passing railway trains and other extraneous sounds had to be found. Many movie buffs of the day complained that films would never be the same again, and they never have been.

China Slips into Chaos

The personal rivalry between two of the leading Chinese statesmen set the scene for civil war, administrative breakdown, foreign invasion and the eventual communist revolution. Chiang Kai-Shek was trying to establish the rule of the Nationalist government over the whole of China in the face of Communist agitation and Japanese interference with a large measure of success. In January 1930 he released military control of the northern provinces to General Yen Hsi-Chain while attempting to assert his personal authority over the intricate civil service hierarchy of China. In April Yen Hsi-Chain announced the independence of the Northern provinces under his own military regime and launched his troops south towards Chiang Kai-Shek's home base in Nanking. Hsi-Chain succeeded in pushing his rival south of the Yellow River but failed to obliterate nationalist power in the south. In July the Communists rose in rebellion while six weeks later Hsi-Chain tried to legitimise his power with a facade of civilian government in Peking. Japan watched the turmoil with interest, waiting a chance to invade the rich Manchurian provinces which lay temptingly within reach.

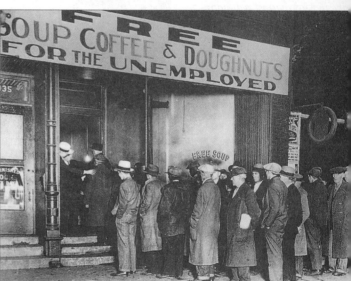

Top right: A mass of unemployed men queue for a Sunday lunch in New York. Above: Al Capone relaxes in his Florida mansion while (above right) the unemployed of Chicago enjoyed free food at his expense. Capone was following in a long tradition among the Sicilian mafia of providing help for the poor from his criminal funds. Right: Russian kulaks, or rich peasants, being evicted from their land on Stalin's orders. Facing page, top: Egyptian police quell riots in Mansurah on 22nd July sparked by the suppression of the nationalist Wafd Party by the pro-Western King Fuad. Facing page, bottom: A procession of Indian women demand the boycotting of British goods to demonstrate support for Gandhi, arrested by the British authorities in May.

Right: Child violinist prodigy Yehudi Menuhin performs at London's Royal Albert Hall in December, aged 10. Below: The outsider Blenheim racing to victory in the Derby. The horse was owned by the Aga Khan and proved to be the first of a long line of successes for the aristocrat. Bottom left: Madge Elliott, a talented Australian dancer who had already scored some film successes, made her stage debut on 24th February at the London Palladium. Bottom right: Bobby Jones powering his way to victory in the British Open golf tournament. Facing page: (top left) The Duchess of York with Princess Margaret, born this year; (bottom left) movie star Clint Eastwood who first emerged in the television series Rawhide and (bottom right) Babe Ruth who set both pitching and batting records during his 21 year professional baseball career.

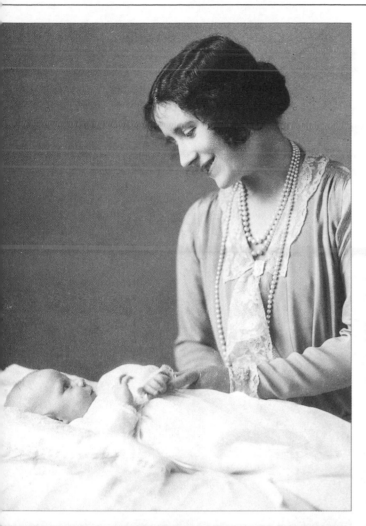

THE EARL OF BALFOUR

Below: The Earl of Balfour, who died on 19th March. Balfour gained fame as a Conservative MP and Prime Minister who worked tirelessly for the principles in which he believed, even when he knew them to be a lost cause. First an MP in 1874, Balfour began slowly with a reputation as a man about town, rather than as a politician. His appointment to an Irish ministerial post in 1887 when land reform unrest was at its height established his reputation for determination and statesmanship. Prime Minister from 1902 to 1905, Balfour was sensible but dull, but this changed to his accustomed vigour and panache during the long years in opposition to the Liberals. Created an Earl in 1925, Balfour played the role of elder statesman to perfection and his death was much mourned.

Jan 1	UK: Road Traffic Act comes into force, introducing traffic policemen and compulsory third party insurance
Jan 23	Death of Russian dancer Anna Pavlova
Jan 26	Gandhi is released from prison
Jan 26	Winston Churchill resigns from Baldwin's shadow cabinet
Jan 27	Pierre Laval becomes French Premier
Feb 1	Gandhi orders continuation of civil disobedience in India
Feb 5	Campbell breaks land speed record in Bluebird
Feb 8	Birth of US actor James Dean
Feb 28	UK: Sir Oswald Mosley forms the 'New Party'
Mar 2	Birth of Soviet leader Mikhail Gorbachev
Mar 3	'The Star-Spangled Banner' designated US National Anthem by Act of Congress
Mar 10	UK: Sir Oswald Mosley is expelled from the Labour Party
Mar 11	Birth of Australian-born media magnate Rupert Murdoch
Mar 23	Dame Nellie Melba, Australian soprano, dies
Apr 1	British aircraft carrier hits French liner 'Florida' resulting in 30 deaths
Apr 14	King Alfonso abdicates, Spain is declared a Republic
Apr 14	UK: The Highway Code is first issued
Apr 19	US: Unemployment reaches seven million
May 1	Official opening of The Empire State Building, the World's tallest building
May 11	Austrian bank failure starts panic in Middle Europe
May 15	Italy: Pope Pius XI condemns Communism
May 23	UK: Whipsnade Zoo opens
May 27	Prof. Auguste Piccard becomes the first man to reach the stratosphere during his balloon flight
Jun 13	Death of British businessman Jesse Boot, founder of Boots the Chemist
Jun 28	Socialists win the Spanish general election
Jul 22	An attempt is made on the life of Sir Ernest Hotson, acting Governor of Bombay
Jul 29	George Bernard Shaw meets Stalin
Aug 7	Death of US jazz musician Bix Beiderbecke
Aug 28	Ramsay MacDonald is sacked as Labour leader
Sep 7	UK: The King takes a £50,000 cut in pay for the duration of the economic crisis
Sep 17	33 1/3 rpm LPs first are launched in New York
Sep 18	Japan seizes Manchuria from China
Sep 20	British sterling currency is taken off the gold standard
Sep 27	Norway, Sweden and Egypt abandon the gold standard
Sep 28	Denmark abandons the gold standard
Oct 16	Spain: The government legalises divorce
Oct 18	Death of US inventor Thomas Alva Edison
Oct 22	US: Al Capone is jailed for eleven years for tax dodging
Oct 23	Diana Dors born
Oct 28	UK: Ramsay MacDonald is returned as Prime Minister in the general election - a landslide victory for the National Government
Nov 8	The element halogen is discovered by US scientist Frederick Allison
Nov 10	US scientists discover the secrets of atomic nucleus
Nov 15	Nazi Party wins state election in Hesse, Germany
Nov 20	Spanish King is charged with high treason
Nov 25	Australia: The Labour government is defeated
Nov 30	EMI is formed through merger of His Master's Voice and Columbia
Dec 11	Japan abandons the gold standard
Dec 30	Nazi party is formed in Holland

NEW ERA IN BRITISH POLITICS

As the economic situation gradually worsened, Ramsay MacDona (*facing page, top left*), acting on advice from the Bank of England an City of London, decided on a radical package of economic measur including drastic cuts to the Government spending plans. He failed gain the support of his Labour cabinet and so turned to King George The King agreed to multi-party coalition with the Conservatives und Baldwin (*facing page, top right*) and the Liberals in a Nation Government. In August the government took office and in October p its programme to the country in a general election. Returned with huge majority the National Government, still headed by MacDona pushed through its policies and, in the opinion of many economis spared Britain the worst of the Depression.

Above: The Empire State Building, opened on 1st May, was the tallest building in the world at 1,472 feet (449 metres), including its 200 foot (60 metres) radio mast. Used principally as offices, the building retained its world record status for 41 years and is still in use today. The fame of the structure ensured its use in guidebooks, tourist outings and even in the classic monster movie King Kong.

THE CAWNPORE RIOTS

In March a young Punjabi terrorist, Bhagat Singh, was executed for the shooting of a British police officer. The Sikh majority in the Punjab protested and called for massive demonstrations and mass strikes as a sign of mourning for Bhagat Singh. In Cawnpore the shopkeepers, who were chiefly Moslem by religion, refused to close. Angry mobs of Sikhs attacked and burnt any shop they found open, butchering the shopkeepers and their families. Moslems responded in kind and for several days Cawnpore was the scene of savage religious violence. The killings stirred dangerous memories for it was in Cawnpore that a massacre of hundreds of British civilians occurred during the Indian Mutiny eighty years earlier. Gandhi tried to intervene to secure peace, but was assaulted by the angry crowds. Left and above: The British authorities cracked down hard on the violence, placing troops and armed police throughout the city. An uneasy peace was imposed, but discontent simmered on.

The Countdown to Civil War

The countdown to civil war in Spain began in 1931, though it would be five years before nation wide fighting would begin in earnest. The crown, which could trace its descent back to the early warriors who fought for Christianity against the Moslem invaders from North Africa in the 8th century, had become weak. In 1923 the ineffective Cortes, or parliament, was overthrown by a military coup led by Primo de Rivera, Marquess of Estalla. Rivera ruled with firmness and efficiency until ill health forced his resignation in 1929. At once uncertainty and inefficiency began to take hold. Efforts by King Alphonso XIII to bring the nation together failed dismally. Spain increasingly divided between Republicans and supporters of the old order, though many people preferred not to take sides. In 1931 a series of elections put the Republicans into power and they turned against the king, who fled precipitously to France. The nation slid slowly towards chaos.

acing page, top: The first epublican government phographed on 15th May with, left to ght, Miguel Maura, Fernando ios, Alvaro Albornoz, Alcala mora, Francisco Caballero and asares Quirega. Facing page, botm: A detachment of the Civil uard anxiously awaits instrucms in a Madrid side street on 8th March in the run up to the eneral Election to the Cortes hich resulted in a sweeping victory r the Republican party. Above: ung women on their way to vote Madrid municipal elections. ove right: A huge Madrid crowd thers outside the Town Hall to ar the Republic proclaimed folwing the flight of King Alphonso II on 14th April. Alphonso headfor Paris where he expected, and ceived a warm welcome. Right: ful crowds surged through adrid on hearing of the absence of ng Alphonso XIII on 15th April.

The fight against organised crime in the United States took a new and dramatic turn when the greatest gangster of all was arrested. Al Capone and fellow gangster Arthur "Dutch Schultz" Flegenheimer were apprehended in June and charged with tax evasion. It had proved too difficult to convict leading mobsters with their true crimes of extortion and murder, but accountancy irregularities were easier to prove. On 24th August Capone was found guilty and sentenced to 11 years in prison for avoiding paying hundreds of thousands of dollars to the Federal authorities. It was estimated that over 800 men had died in the bloody years which brought Capone to the pinnacle of his criminal career. Dutch Schultz was released, but fell victim to internal mob feuding in 1935 when he was shot and mortally wounded at the Palace Chophouse. Schultz gained fame with his dying words. Asked who had shot him Schultz, who probably knew his killer personally, muttered "Who shot me? No one." before expiring. The Mafia code of silence was preserved.

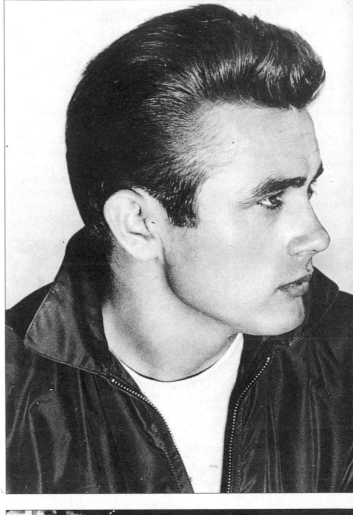

Left: Diana Dors, born on 23rd October as Diana Fluck. She began acting at 15 before becoming billed as Britain's sex symbol film star. Top right: James Dean, the archetypal teenage rebel was born on 8th February. After dropping out of university to act in cola adverts, Dean played in television *before landing star billing Hollywood. He was killed in a motor accident aged just 24, leaving an enduring legend. Boris Karloff, born William Pratt in 1887, starred* **The Criminal Code** *this year, his big break which led such horror movies as Bride of Frankenstein (above) in 1935.*

THOMAS EDISON

Possibly the world's greatest inventor, Thomas Alva Edison (*left and below*) died on 18th October. During the course of his 50 years as an inventor and scientist, Edison took out over 1,000 patents. Though some of these turned out to be of little worth, they also included the electric lightbulb and the phonograph. Born in Ohio in 1847 of Dutch and Scottish parents, Edison scored bottom of his class in school, which he left to be a newsboy when aged 12. He moved to Boston in 1866 and there began to read avidly about electricity. Working first on improving telegraphy, Edison moved to New York and set up a laboratory and works in Newark, New Jersey. There, in 1878, he started work on the electric light and perfected a commercially viable bulb 13 months later. By 1900 he had a full-time staff working with him. He continued his research, later into chemicals, until his death.

Left: Dame Nellie Melba, the famous Australian singer, died on 23rd March. She took her stage name from the city of Melbourne, near which she was brought up, her real name being Helen Porter Mitchell. Above: The seaplane S6B which won the Schneider Trophy outright for Great Britain.

The trophy was set up to test the speed and and manoeuvrability of seaplanes and was won out by three victories. The expertise and research which went into producing the S6B was later used to produce the famous Spitfire fighter plane much used by the British RAF during World War II.

1932

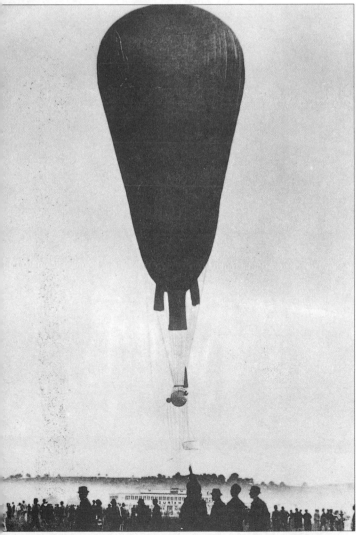

Facing page: Paddington Railway Station in London. It was in December that the first stretches of mainline track in Britain were electrified, the first sign of a threat to the dominance of steam. Top: The Sydney Harbour Bridge, which was opened on 19th March to link the southern and northern suburbs of this, the oldest city in Australia. The bridge has a main span of 1,650 feet (503 metres) and carried 4 tracks of railway and 6 lanes of highway.

Left: Swiss Professor Auguste Piccard taking off in his specially pressurised balloon capsule on 18th August. Piccard broke all altitude records when his balloon reached 10 miles high. Above: Lord Adrian won the Nobel Prize for Medicine in 1932 for his work on electricity in the human brain. His work showed the importance of electrical impulses in passing messages from sense organs to the brain and from the brain to motor neurons in muscles.

Facing page: *Facing page: Franklin D. Roosevelt, Democratic Governor of New York, won a landslide majority in the United States Presidential election. He promised Americans a New Deal which would restore employment, financial security and welfare. Right: Ramsay MacDonald talks to French politician M. Tardieu during international talks at No. 10 Downing Street. Below left: Princess Elizabeth and Princess Margaret photographed on 12th August. Below right: French President Paul Doumer who was gunned down by a fanatic in Paris on 6th May. Doumer was attending a charity function when the gunman, a Russian named Gorguloff, leapt from the crowd, with a gun and pumped bullets into several people. President Doumer died after emergency surgery.*

The Nazi Rise To Power

The Nazi Party continued its rise to power in Germany in 1932. On 25th February Adolf Hitler, born an Austrian, was granted German citizenship which enabled him to stand in the Presidential Elections. Although Hitler was beaten by von Hindenburg the fact that he captured 37% of the votes was counted as a major triumph for his Nazi Party. A further triumph came on 30th August when leading Nazi Herman Goering, the Great War fighter ace, was elected President of the Reichstag, the German parliament. The Nazi conviction that they and leader Adolf Hitler were heading for national power was barely touched when a Nazi newspaper was banned for inciting riots in August and their share of the vote fell in the November elections.

Left: Film star Jayne Mansfield, born on 19th April. Below: Professor Aldous Huxley who published his searing futuristic science fiction novel **Brave New World** in December. Bottom left: Edward Kennedy, born on 22nd February. Bottom right: Film star Elizabeth Taylor, born on 27th February. Facing page: (top) US athlete Babe Didrickson in the Olympic 80 metre hurdles when she set a new record 11.7 seconds; (bottom left) Helen Wills Moody winning her 5th ladies singles at Wimbledon and (bottom right) A crash in the TT races.

The Kidnapped Baby

The great crime of 1932 was the kidnapping of the infant son of Charles Lindbergh, the American airman who gained fame and popularity by becoming the first man to fly solo across the Atlantic. The 20 month old toddler was taken while Lindbergh and his wife ate dinner. The kidnapper left behind a home-made ladder which he used to gain entry to the house. A ransom was paid, but the baby was not returned and in May the body of the toddler was found in a nearby wood. Patient police and forensic work continued until, in 1934, a German immigrant was arrested with $11,000 of the kidnap money in his house. Bruno Hauptmann was convicted when timber in his home was found to match that of the makeshift ladder abandoned at the Lindbergh home. Hauptmann was executed on 3rd April 1936.

Jan 5	Death of Calvin Coolidge, 30th President of US
Jan 10	Spain: Martial law is imposed
Jan 30	Adolf Hitler becomes German Chancellor
Jan 30	France: Edouard Daladier becomes premier
Feb 10	Hitler attacks democracy in a speech in Berlin
Feb 15	Attempted assassination of Roosevelt by Guiseppe Xangara
Mar 1	Germany: Nazis begin mass arrests of political opponents
Mar 4	US: Roosevelt inaugurated as US President
Mar 5	Sir Malcolm Campbell sets a new world land-speed record of 272 mph in 'Bluebird'
Mar 6	US banks close for 4 days because of financial crisis
Mar 14	Germany: Nazis ban kosher meat
Mar 20	Germany: Nazis open first concentration camp at Dachau
Mar 22	Death of British car builder Sir Frederick Henry Royce
Apr 1	Germany: Nazis seize Jewish bank accounts
Apr 3	Two British planes become first to fly over Mount Everest
Apr 10	Italy: An air speed record of 424 mph is set by Francesco Agello
Apr 19	UK bans Soviet imports
Apr 30	Peru: President Luis Sanchez Cerro is assassinated
May 8	US: The gas chamber is used for the first time
May 10	Germany: Burning of Books ceremony in Berlin's Opera House Square
May 21	Britain agrees a ten-year non-aggression pact with Italy, Germany and France
Jun 8	Spain: Manuel Azana is dismissed as premier
Jun 16	US: Roosevelt's New Deal begins
Jun 23	Nazis ban all other political parties in Germany
Jul 4	India: Gandhi is imprisoned for one year
Jul 5	British doctors isolate the influenza virus
Jul 22	Wiley Post becomes first man to fly round the world
Jul 23	Germany: Decree says importing banned books is punishable by death
Jul 25	Leon Trotsky is granted asylum in France
Jul 26	Germany: 'Imperfect' Germans will be forced into sterilisation by Nazis
Aug 2	Nicaragua: Martial law is imposed
Aug 18	Birth of Polish film director Roman Polanski
Aug 22	First boxing match is televised in Britain
Aug 28	BBC made first broadcast appeal on behalf of police
Sep 8	Death of Iraqi King Feisal
Sep 10	Fred Perry becomes the first Briton to win the US Open tennis championship
Oct 20	Mussolini denounces Roosevelt as a dictator
Oct 23	France: Premier Edouard Daladier resigns
Nov 10	Austria: Martial law is declared
Nov 15	The new Reichstag opens excluding women and Jewish members
Dec 5	Prohibition in America is repealed by 21st Amendment
Dec 6	Germany: Nazis plan to abolish women's suffrage
Dec 9	London to Singapore airline service is inaugurated

Facing page: An armoured car in Chicago with its attendant gunmen. The brutality between the gangs of mobsters made such vehicles necessary. Left: British pilots Clydesdale and MacIntyre in their Westland Wallace aircraft on their way to fly over Mount Everest, the first ever to do so. Below left: Wreckage of the American airship Akron floats off New Jersey after crashing on 4th April. Only 4 of the 77 on board were saved when the aircraft plunged into the sea after being struck by lightning. Below: Malcolm Campbell races along Daytona Beach to set a new land speed record of 272 mph on 5th March. Bottom right: The legendary Dixie Dean grasps the FA Cup after leading his team, Everton, to victory.

At 5.32pm on the 5th December the most disastrous experiment in social engineering ever attempted came to an end. It was then that the 21st Amendment to the USA Constitution abolished the 18th and alcohol again became legal in the nation. In fact Congress had jumped ahead of the amendment and legalised beer in March. The nation had celebrated so hard that 1.5 million barrels were drained on the first night of legal beer, and many towns were dry again the next day. The Anheuser-Busch brewery in St Louis, which traditionally proclaimed itself 'beer capital of the world', threw a tremendous party to send their first consignment of legal beer on its way. About 30,000 drinkers attended in a cavalcade over 20 blocks long. But it was 5th December which saw wines and liquors legalised. The British liner *Majestic* waited just offshore with 6,200 cases of gin and whisky in her holds until the captain heard the good news, and then she steamed into New York to a rapturous reception. The Noble Experiment, as it had been heralded at its inception, was over. It had led to a massive rise in organised crime as gangsters supplied the thirsts which could not be slaked legally. It could be argued that America has never really recovered from the 18th Amendment, which had been born out of such fine motives.

HITLER'S RISE TO POWER

n 30th January Adolf Hitler was named Chancellor of Germany. His
azi Party was the largest in the Reichstag, or Parliament, but did not
mmand a majority. Hitler had politicians of other parties in his cabinet
d they believed that they could keep the ambitious, but inexperienced
itler under control. On 27th February the Reichstag Building was burnt
wn and police arrested a young communist. Hitler used this as a pretext
arrest all communist members of the Reichstag, giving his party a
ajority. On 23rd March the Nazi majority gave Hitler and his cabinet
e right to rule by decree. The Nazi grip on power was complete. Facing
ge: Adolf Hitler in characteristic pose. Below: The Reichstag fire.
ght: Sir Oswald Mosley photographed in October. His efforts to emu-
te the success of Hitler in Britain resulted in failure and ignominy.

The brutality and undemocratic
nature of the regime installed by
Stalin since his accession to
supreme political power in the
Soviet Union became increasingly
clear as 1933 wore on. Stalin
ordered the Communist Party to
purge itself of all those who held
unsound ideologies, that is those
who disagreed with Stalin. Left:
A Purge Committee of a local
Soviet interrogates its members
in May. Above: A Comrades
Court of prisoners sits in judgment of a fellow offender who has
applied for remission of sentence.

Above: The novelist John Galsworthy died in 1933. He is best known for his Forsyte Saga trilogy. Top right: Lloyd George produced his memoirs in 1933. He is shown here in July meeting Mary Golding, who had been the first baby to benefit under his National Health Insurance Act. Above right: President Roosevelt and his family set sail on board his yacht Amberjack II on 5th July for a summer vacation. A few weeks earlier Roosevelt had signed what he called "the most important bill ever passed by Congress" into law as the National Industrial Recovery Act. Right: Jazz musicians Duke Ellington and Jack Hylton arrive with their band at London's Waterloo Station on 9th June during their sensational tour of Britain.

Jan 1	Germany: The plan to sterilise 'inferior' citizens becomes law
Jan 26	Germany signs a ten-year non-aggression pact with Poland
Jan 30	All Austrian parties banned except 'Fatherland Front'
Feb 11	Birth of Mary Quant
Feb 23	Death of British composer Sir Edward Elgar
Feb 25	US: Tornadoes hit the Southern States, killing 23
Mar 8	Germany: The new Volkswagen car is unveiled at the Motor Show with a price tag of just £61
Mar 9	Birth of Soviet Yuri Gagarin, the first man in space
Mar 14	El Salvador: An explosion on a train kills 250 people
Mar 26	Driving tests become mandatory in UK
Apr 4	Moscow: Latvia, Estonia and Lithuania renew their pacts of frienship with the USSR
Apr 16	Greece: A bombing raid on Rhodes kills 10 people
Apr 24	Birth of Shirley Maclaine
May 3	Birth of Henry Cooper
May 16	UK: Wimbledon officials allow women to wear shorts
May 23	US: Criminals Bonnie and Clyde killed in an ambush
May 25	Death of British composer Gustav Holst
May 28	Quins born, and survive, in Canada
Jun 10	Death of British composer Frederick Delius
Jun 23	Albania is invaded by Italy
Jun 30	US: A policeman is killed during a bank raid by escaped gangster John Dillinger
Jul 2	John Dillinger is gunned down by the FBI
Jul 4	Death of French physicist Marie Curie
Jul 18	UK: The King opens the Mersey Tunnel, Liverpool
Jul 13	Heinrich Himmler is appointed overlord of Germany's concentration camps
Jul 25	Engelbert Dollfuss, Chancellor of Austria, is assassinated by Austrian Nazis
Aug 2	Death of Paul von Hindenburg, German President
Aug 3	Hitler created 'Der Fuhrer' by German cabinet
Aug 19	Al Capone is moved to Alcatraz jail
Sep 1	US: 400,000 textile workers go on strike
Sep 4	Germany: The opening of the Nazi party conference draws an audience of 750,000
Sep 18	Italy: Mussolini says that Italians from the age of eight must have military training
Sep 20	Birth of Italian actress Sophia Loren
Sep 22	262 miners die in Welsh pit disaster
Sep 26	UK: The Queen Mary is launched at Clydebank
Sep 28	Birth of French actress Brigitte Bardot
Oct 5	Spain: An uprising begins in an attempt to declare Catalonia an independent state
Oct 9	Alexander, King of Yugoslavia, is assassinated during a trip to Marseilles
Oct 16	Mao Tse-Tung's 'Long March' begins
Nov 1	The USSR exiles 12,000 'enemies of the state' to Siberia
Nov 8	France: Gaston Doumergue resigns as premier
Nov 29	UK: Prince George marries Princess Marina of Greece
Dec 2	US: Johnny Weissmuller, Olympic swimming champion, stars for the first time as Tarzan in 'Tarzan of the Apes'
Dec 14	Turkey: Women get the vote

Au Barricades!

Civil unrest spread in several European countries in 1934. First to erupt into violence was France where the traditional revolutionary cry of 'Au Barricades' echoed through Paris on 6th February. A combination of political scandals and resignations drove the Parisians to erect barricades in the Place de la Concorde and around the Hotel de Ville. A total of 17 people were killed and nearly 1,000 injured before order was restored. More bloody was the unrest in Spain where Catalonia declared itself independent and the Asturias collapsed into chaos and riots. The Spanish government reacted fiercely by imposing martial law and calling out the troops. Catalonia was crushed by a pincer movement of army columns and naval forces which bombarded Barcelona and forced the resignation of the self-proclaimed government. The strike of miners in the Asturias sparked off more widespread protests and the Communists called for a national strike. Troops sent to impose law and order in the Asturias found themselves opposed by armed strikers who proclaimed a Workers Commune. Fighting lasted for 12 days before the Commune was quashed. The army officer in charge of operations was named General Francisco Franco, the youngest general in Europe since Napoleon. He had already won fame and respect by his bravery under fire in colonial wars and came to be viewed as a strong and dependable, if intolerant, leader.

Left: Notorious American gangster Bonnie Parker in characteristic pose. She teamed up with her lover Clyde Barrow in 1930. Together the pair robbed shops, petrol stations and banks, shooting anyone who got in their way.

It is thought that some 20 people were killed by Bonnie and Clyde. Their deadly career came to an end on 23rd May when a posse of Louisiana police ambushed them on a remote road, shooting both bandits dead.

Right: German Chancellor Adolf Hitler acknowledges the salutes of workers while visiting a factory on 5th May. Hitler would not achieve supreme power as Fuhrer until August when he became President as well as Chancellor. A dark side of Nazi action was shown on 25th July when Austrian Nazis killed Austrian Chancellor Dr Engelbert Dolfuss. Hitler knew that he could never take over Austria with Dollfuss as Chancellor. It is widely believed that Hitler ordered the local Nazis to carry out the murder. Below: The guard of honour at Dollfuss's funeral. Below right: Stalin helping carry the cremated remains of Sergei Kirov who was shot dead on 1st December. Stalin used this assassination of a close advisor as a pretext to eliminate powerful rivals. Within two weeks a total of 93 leading Communists had been tried and executed.

Bodyline Cricket

Possibly the greatest controversy ever to shake the world of cricket came to an end in 1934. The 'bodyline' dispute had begun in the winter of 1933 when the England team, under Douglas Jardine, toured Australia. Noticing that the formidable Australian batsman Don Bradman, and several others, were unhappy playing on the leg side, Jardine ordered his fast bowlers Larwood and Voce to bowl consistently at the leg stump. Several Australians were hit hard by the fast balls. Oldfield suffered a fractured skull while Woodfull was hit twice over the heart. Australians dubbed the tactic bodyline. Feeling ran so high in Australia that the Imperial diplomatic service had to be called in. When the Australians came to tour England in 1934, the emotional atmosphere was so charged that Jardine and Voce were dropped, while Larwood refused to play. The bodyline controversy fizzled out with Australia claiming victory over what the Australians termed 'Pommy Cheating.'

Top left: Stanley Baldwin at a meeting in December on the India Question. Above: Young Chinese Communist leader Mao Tse-Tung came to the fore in October when he gathered the shattered remnants of the defeated Communist field army and began the Long March. Urging the scattered troops to head northwest to Yenan, for some a 6,000 mile trek, Mao Tse-Tung established himself as the military and ideological leader of the faltering movement. The move to a safe stronghold saved Communism and laid the foundations for future success. Above left: A hunger demonstration in Hyde Park on 26th February. Left: Curious spectators gather around a street corner in Chicago on 2nd July after shots rang out. The shoot out marked the death of notorious bank robber John Dillinger, betrayed to FBI marksmen by his girlfriend.

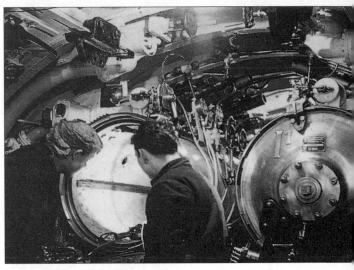

*Above left: British tennis star Fr[ed] Perry winning the Wimbledon men's singles title on 7th July. To[p] right: The SS **Queen Mary**, launched this year, was named [in] honour of the then Queen of England and represented the las[t] word in both luxury and speed o[n] the Atlantic crossing. Above: Th[e] torpedo tubes on the new Frenc[h] submarine **Surcouf**, which enter[ed] service in 1934 as the largest su[b]marine afloat. She was armed with four guns and ten torpedo tubes as well as a seaplane. She escaped to Britain in 1940 to jo[in] the Free French Navy, but was [lost] with all hands in 1942. Left: Th[e] British composer Sir Edward Elgar, who died on 23rd Febru[ary.] Elgar was easily the best loved British composer of the early 20th century and his works continue [to] be performed.*

GLORIA'S STORY

The great society scandal of the year was the custody battle over Gloria Vanderbilt, heiress to the Vanderbilt millions. The court battle involved the wealthy Morgan clan, who had married into the Vanderbilts, and erupted into a catalogue of heated and emotional exchanges between the fantastically rich relatives which kept the Press and public keen for more disclosures. It became clear that Gloria Morgan Vanderbilt, little Gloria's widowed mother, led a life of ostentatious luxury in Europe, mixing with royalty and nobility, while the child was sorely neglected. Gloria's aunt, Mrs Harry Whitney, sister of the girl's dead father, launched a custody battle when she became concerned for the child's health. After a sensational trial which dragged out many scandals the Vanderbilts and Morgans would have preferred to keep secret, Gloria was entrusted to her aunt. Left: The young heiress Gloria Vanderbilt with her mother on 23rd May.

Above: The French-born actress Claudette Colbert achieved her greatest screen triumphs in 1934 with the Cecil B. DeMille epic **Cleopatra**, *playing the title role, and* **It Happened One Night,** *in which she played a runaway heiress. Both films were enormously successful with the public and the critics. Miss Colbert's performances were particularly remarked upon for the two roles were demanding in completely different ways. As Cleopatra, Colbert was called upon to exude sexual magnet-* *ism combined with autocratic power while the runaway heiress needed charm, spirit and considerable comic timing. Before the two films, Colbert had been a stage actress in New York, though she had made a couple of appearances in small movies. Left: Shirley Maclaine, born in Virginia in 1934, is the sister of Warren Beatty. She made her film debut in 1956 in* **The Trouble with Harry** *and went on to scoop various Oscar nominations.*

Jan 1	Africa: Libya is formed by the merger of Italian colonies of Cyreaica, Tripoli and Fezzan	**May 25**	Jesse Owens sets 6 world records within 45 minutes
Jan 1	Turkey: All surnames must be Westernised	**May 30**	India: An earthquake destroys the hill station of Quetta and kills 20,000 people
Jan 4	Birth of Floyd Patterson	**Jun 1**	Driving Tests and 'L' plates introduced
Jan 8	Birth of US rock and roll singer Elvis Presley	**Jun 7**	Stanley Baldwin becomes British PM
Jan 24	Italy: Mussolini dismisses the whole of the Italian cabinet	**Jul 3**	Death of French engineer Andre Citroen
Feb 8	Death of German painter Max Liebermann	**Jul 16**	Parking meters come into service in US
Feb 12	Death of Escoffier, the famous french chef	**Jul 30**	Penguin paperbacks go on sale in Britain
Feb 18	Germany: Two women are beheaded in Berlin for spying	**Aug 14**	President Roosevelt signs Social Security Act
Feb 25	UK: England's greatest batsman, Jack Hobbs, retires from cricket	**Aug 15**	Hitler bans German-Jewish marriages
Feb 26	RADAR first demonstrated by Robert Watson-Watt	**Aug 20**	US: H. McLean Evans reports isolation of Vitamin E
Mar 7	Nine year old Prince Ananda is crowned King of Siam	**Aug 29**	Queen Astrid of Belgium is killed in a car crash
Mar 12	UK: 30mph speed limit introduced in towns and built up areas	**Aug 31**	Roosevelt bans arms sales to warring countries
Mar 15	France: The government increases military service to two years	**Sep 3**	Malcolm Campbell breaks his own speed record at 301 mph
Apr 1	The Japanese government rejects an alliance with Germany	**Sep 15**	Germany legalises anti-Semitism
Apr 7	US: Tornadoes hit Mississippi and kill 26 people	**Oct 1**	Birth of Julie Andrews
Apr 13	London to Australia airline service inaugurated	**Oct 2**	Italy invades Ethiopia
Apr 19	Birth of British comedian and musician Dudley Moore	**Oct 3**	Italy invades Abyssinia
Apr 29	'Cat's Eyes', the glass reflectors used on roads are used in Britain for the first time	**Oct 19**	League of Nations imposes sanctions on Italy
May 12	Alcoholics Anonymous founded in Ohio	**Oct 23**	Canada: Mackenzie King returns as Prime Minister
May 19	Death of British soldier and writer, 'Lawrence of Arabia' following a motor cycle accident	**Nov 1**	Birth of Gary Player
		Nov 5	Birth of Lester Piggott
		Nov 11	US balloonists Anderson and Stevens reach 74,000 fee
		Nov 30	Non belief in Nazism is grounds for divorce in Germany
		Dec 1	Woody Allen born

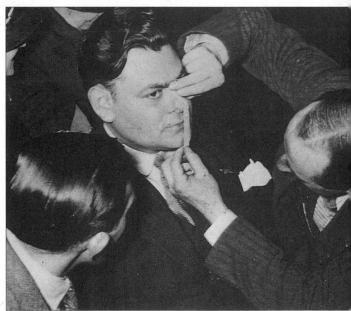

Left: Adolf Hitler, secured in power as Fuhrer, addresses a mass rally of Nazi Party members at Nuremberg. Above: German state officials measure the nasal proportions of a man suspected of having Jewish origins. Such harassment became common-place under Nazi rule. Facing page, top left: British premier *Stanley Baldwin continued to struggle against the Depression and with various colonial and f eign troubles. Facing page, botto right: King Leopold III and Que Astrid of the Belgians. Queen Astrid was killed on 29th Augu when a car the king was drivi went out of control and smashe into a tree near Lucerne.*

In the spring of 1935 Mussolini's Italy began to build up troop and military hardware in its East African colonies. At the same time Italy began to jostle and provoke Ethiopia, the only remaining African state not controlled by a European nation, which Mussolini saw as an ideal candidate for conquest. War began on 2nd October when Italian troops crossed the border from Eritrea. It was thought that the invasion would be a walkover, but rugged landscape, appalling weather and determined guerrilla resistance by the Abyssinian army slowed the Italian columns until the following spring. Airpower and poison gas finally finished off the last pockets of Abyssinian resistance. Below left: Abyssinian troops on training exercise near Addis Ababa on 29th May. The Abyssinian army was woefully short of trained men and modern equipment. Bottom left: Italian Alpine troops at Massawa on 27th August, part of an army which grew to be 650,000 strong.

In 1935 Britain celebrated the Silver Jubilee of King George V. Top left: A London scene. Centre left: The Royal party on the balcony of Buckingham Palace. Top right: The Duke and Duchess of York with Elizabeth and Margaret arriving at St Paul's Cathedral. Left: An official portrait of Queen Mary taken in 1935. Above: Children put up decorations in London. Facing page, top: A street party in Stepney's Heath Street. Facing page, bottom: The Lord Mayor of London presents the king with a pearl sword during the silver jubilee celebrations.

cing page: Colonel T.E. Lawrence photographed during his time in
e RAF as an ordinary airman. Lawrence was an enigmatic figure, con-
ered to be something of an outsider by his contemporaries. His power-
personality and liking for eastern mysticism caused some friction with
lows, be it as a pre-war scholar or a soldier. He gained great fame and
ormous public popularity during the First World War. Sent to gain
ormation about an Arab Revolt in the Arabian desert, Lawrence saw
e possibilities of using the Arab unrest to disrupt the Turkish war effort.
e persuaded the hard-pressed British army in Egypt to supply the Arabs
th guns, armoured cars and even an aircraft or two. With these
wrence led the Arabs in their attacks on strategic railways and per-
ided them to capture the vital town of Aqaba. Thereafter the Arabs
oported British advances through Palestine. Lawrence was furious
en the Arabs were not given the independence they craved in the
ce treaties. He was killed when riding a motorcycle along a country
e in England.

ove: Jesse Owens competing in
long jump at the USA vs.
itish Empire athletic games at
White City stadium in
ndon. Top right: British
ress Julie Andrews, born this
r, who found lasting fame in
the movie **The Sound of Music**.
Right: The British jockey Lester
Piggott was born in this year.
Piggott has won many classic
races and is considered by
many to the finest thorough-
bred rider ever to compete.

1936

Jan 4	US: First 'hit-parade' appears in New York
Jan 18	Death of British poet and writer Rudyard Kipling
Jan 20	UK: Death of King George V
Feb 3	Birth of Bobby Simpson, Australian test cricketer
Feb 6	Hitler opens the Winter Olympic Games in Germany
Feb 11	Birth of Burt Reynolds
Feb 26	The first Volkswagen factory is opened by Hitler
Feb 27	Death of Russian physiologist Ivan Pavlov
Feb 28	Tokyo: The army coup d'etat fails
Mar 3	Mussolini nationalises Italian banks
Mar 3	Birth of Swiss actress Ursula Andress
Mar 5	UK: The Spitfire fighter plane makes its maiden flight
Mar 29	Nazis win 99% of the vote in German elections
Apr 1	Austria brings in conscription
Apr 28	Death of Egyptian King Faud
May 3	Engelbert Humperdinck born
May 5	Abyssinia: Addis Ababa falls to Italian troops
May 9	Birth of Glenda Jackson
Jun 14	Death of Russian writer Maxim Gorky
Jul 6	German airship Hindenburg crosses Atlantic in 46 hours
Jul 11	Hitler recognises Austrian independence
Jul 18	Spanish Civil War begins
Jul 24	UK: The speaking clock is introduced by GPO
Jul 28	Sir Garfield Sobers born
Aug 1	Berlin: Eleventh Olympic Games are opened by Hitler
Aug 1	Birth of French fashion designer Yves Saint-Laurent

Aug 2	Death of French aviator Louis Bleriot
Aug 3	Jesse Owens wins the 100 metres gold medal
Aug 4	Jesse Owens wins the long jump gold medal
Aug 5	Jesse Owens wins the 200 metres gold medal
Aug 25	Stalin executes 16 senior Communists
Aug 26	UK: The BBC broadcasts television programmes with sound for the first time
Aug 26	Leslie Mitchell becomes first television announcer
Sep 7	Buddy Holly born
Sep 10	India: A landslide destroys seven Himalayan villages
Sep 21	Death of British engineer Frank Hornby
Sep 28	Spain: General Franco is appointed head of the rebel forces
Oct 1	General Franco takes office as Head of Nationalist Government
Oct 1	UK: The BBC begins regular broadcasts
Oct 5	UK: The commencement of the Jarrow March to London by the unemployed
Oct 6	UK Labour party refuses affiliation to the Communist party
Oct 8	Major Clement Atlee becomes leader of the Labour party
Oct 11	UK: 100,000 anti-Mosleyites clash with Fascists
Oct 27	Mrs Wallis Simpson divorces her husband, Ernest
Nov 3	King Edward opens his first parliament
Nov 30	UK: The Crystal Palace burns down
Dec 6	Mexico grants asylum to Trotsky
Dec 11	Edward VIII abdicates

In October 1936 200 men set out from Jarrow in County Durham to march to London with a petition. Unemployment in the town ran at 75% after its main shipbuilding business closed down. After covering 300 miles in 16 days the men arrived in London, but Prime Minister Stanley Baldwin refused to meet them. Facing page: The Jarrow Crusade marches through rain sodden streets on its way to London. Top left: The box containing the Jarrow Petition. Above: The men of Jarrow break during their march. Above right: Clement Attlee, leader of the Labour Party, who criticised the government's handling of the situation. Right: Stalin presenting his draft new constitution for the Soviet Union to the Congress of Soviets. Democratic in principle, but autocratic in fact, the constitution was passed unanimously.

The Abdication Crisis of 1936 struck Britain like a thunderbolt. Just eleven months after the death of George V the Empire found itself facing a constitutional crisis like no other. The new king's love was deemed by most to be unsuitable. At 40 Edward was old for a bachelor, but most people expected him to take a wife suitable to be queen at some time. But in 1935 he had fallen in love with a married American woman named Wallis Simpson. When he became king, Edward announced his intention of marrying Mrs Simpson, by then divorced, and so precipitated a full scale row with his governments both in Britain and the Dominions. At issue was the question of whether the nations of the Empire would accept Mrs Simpson as queen. The various governments refused, and Baldwin refused to contemplate a marriage which would leave Wallis Simpson a commoner, thus leaving Edward the choice of abandoning her or abdicating. In the event he abdicated, leaving his younger brother the Duke of York to shoulder the duties of kingship as George VI.

Facing page, top left: A newspaper seller announces the death of King George V on 21st January. Facing page, top right: The funeral train bearing the body of King George V on its way from London to Windsor. Facing page, bottom left: King Edward VIII on an official visit to South Wales in November is accompanied by Ernest Brown, Minister for Labour and Sir Kingsley Wood. Facing page, bottom right: The new Queen Elizabeth and Princess Elizabeth a few days after the abdication. Left: King Edward and Wallis Simpson photographed at Tregir, near Split during their infamous Balkan holiday. Centre left: The King and Mrs Simpson at a social function in the summer. Bottom left: The former King Edward VIII arrives at Portsmouth Dock just after midnight to begin his voluntary exile. Below: The Instrument of Abdication signed by King Edward VIII and witnessed by his brothers. Edward made an emotional farewell broadcast to the nation from Windsor Castle during which he said that he had "found it impossible to carry the heavy burden of responsibility and discharge my duties as King as I would wish to do without the help and support of the woman I love." Following his accession to the throne George VI's first act as King was to bestow the title of the Duke of Windsor upon Edward.

INSTRUMENT OF ABDICATION

I, Edward the Eighth, of Great Britain, Ireland, and the British Dominions beyond the Seas, King, Emperor of India, do hereby declare My irrevocable determination to renounce the Throne for Myself and for My descendants, and My desire that effect should be given to this Instrument of Abdication immediately.

In token whereof I have hereunto set My hand this tenth day of December, nineteen hundred and thirty six, in the presence of the witnesses whose signatures are subscribed.

SIGNED AT
FORT BELVEDERE
IN THE PRESENCE
OF

Edward RI

Albert

Henry.

George.

Top left: Adolf Hitler, accompanied by members of the International Olympic Committee, enters the Berlin Olympic Stadium to officially open the 1936 Olympic Games. Above left: Hitler and Goering congratulate German athlete Tilly Fleischer who took the women's javelin gold medal on the first day. Germany also won the men's shot put on the first day. Above: American athlete Jesse Owens who won four gold medals, putting an end to the supposed triumph of the Aryan race which had begun on the first day with German victories. Owens was snubbed by Hitler, who ostentatiously left the stadium rather than present the gold medal to a Negro. Left: A Nazi parade marches through the Brandenburg Gate, the emotional heart of Prussia.

Last Of The Victorian Romantics

When Rudyard Kipling died on 18th January, the English language lost one of its most inventive storytellers and poets. Kipling had been, in 1907, the first Briton to win the Nobel Prize for Literature and only missed being Poet Laureate due to some unwise remarks about Queen Victoria. Born in Bombay in 1865, Kipling was educated in England before returning to India as a journalist in 1882. It was India which provided Kipling with some of his most moving influences. During the 80s and 90s he poured out a torrent of short stories and poems of which *Plain Tales from the Hills* and *The Jungle Book* are probably the most widely read today. During and immediately after the Great War, in which his only son was killed, Kipling produced a number of excellent stories and other works concerning the face of modern warfare and its effect on the individuals caught up in it. But with the 1920s his popularity began to wane as he was identified with a somewhat stuffy Edwardian past. Only after his death were his earlier works revived.

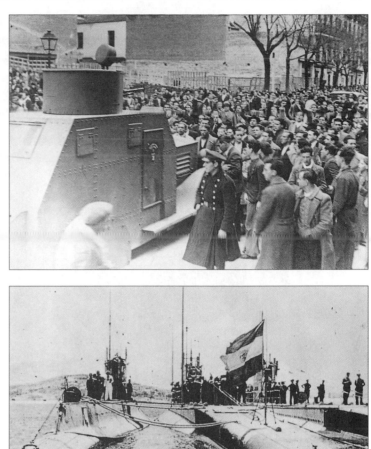

In July the smouldering unrest in Spain erupted into civil war. Growing anarchy culminated on the 17th when a group of senior army officers launched their troops in a coup. Though they failed to take complete control, the rebel Generals, calling themselves nationalists, seized much of the country. Having chosen General Franco as their leader, the Nationalists launched a series of bloody offensives on the Loyalists. Top left: General Franco receives news of the fighting. Top right: An armoured car rumbles through the streets of the Madrid in a vain attempt to quell riots on the 19th February. Above: The submarines, whose captains were loyal to the Republican government, blocked rebel troop ships arriving from North Africa. Left: A gun being loaded on board a Loyalist ship for the assault on Nationalist Majorca, 22nd August.

Top left: Ursula Andress, born this year in Berne, Switzerland, became famous as the love interest in the James Bond movie Dr No in 1962. Top right: Buddy Holly, the innovative rock and roll musician who was born in 1936, achieved massive success with his music-writing skills and died a tragically early death. Above: The clownish Marx Brothers were at the height of their fame in 1936 with 7 movies behind them and 8 more to be made. Right: Glenda Jackson born into a Cheshire building family, became an actress with a stage appearance in 1964 and went on to take two Oscars.

Jan 1	UK: Public Order Act comes into force banning political processions when there is a risk of disorder. Effectively puts an end to the provocative marches of Sir Oswald Mosley's British Union of Fascists	Jun 21	First televised lawn tennis at Wimbledon
Jan 8	Birth of Shirley Bassey	Jun 19	Death of British author JM Barrie
Jan 10	London: Government bans volunteers from fighting in Spain	Jun 22	Joe Louis wins the world heavyweight boxing title
		Jul 1	999 Emergency Service comes into operation in Britain
		Jul 2	Amelia Earhart dies during attempted circumnavigation of the world
Jan 14	First ever Gallup opinion poll in Britain	Jul 9	Birth of British artist David Hockney
Jan 30	Birth of British actress Vanessa Redgrave	Jul 11	Death of US composer George Gershwin
Jan 26	US: The Ohio River floods, killing 15 and leaving 150,000 homeless	Jul 19	Death of Italian engineer Guglielmo Marconi
Feb 16	Nylon is patented in America	Jul 21	Ireland: Eammon de Valera is re-elected president
Mar 15	America sets up its first blood bank at Cook County Hospital, Chicago	Jul 28	UK: Ex-rector Harold Davidson is fatally mauled by a lion at an amusement ground
Mar 16	Death of British statesman Sir Austen Chamberlain	Aug 8	Birth of Dustin Hoffman
Mar 18	US: 500 die in Texas school fire	Aug 14	1,000 people die when Chinese aircraft accidentally bombs Shanghai
Mar 24	UK: Oxford wins the boat race after losing 13 consecutive times to Cambridge	Sep 2	Pierre de Courbertin, reviver of Olympic Games, dies
May 3	US: Margaret Mitchell wins a Pullitzer Prize for her novel 'Gone with the Wind'	Sep 4	Birth of Dawn Fraser, Australian Olympic swimmer
		Oct 11	Bobby Charlton born
May 6	German airship Hindenburg explodes in New Jersey	Oct 13	Germany: Hitler pledges to defend Belgium
May 12	King George VI and his wife Queen Elizabeth are crowned	Nov 9	British statesman Ramsay Macdonald dies at sea while taking a cruise for his health
May 23	Death of US capitalist J D Rockefeller	Nov 9	China: The Japanese take Shanghai
May 27	US: The Golden Gate Bridge, the world's longest suspension bridge, is opened in San Francisco	Dec 8	London: Joseph Kennedy is made US ambassador
May 28	UK: Neville Chamberlain becomes PM	Dec 10	Scotland: A train crashes in a blizzard, killing 34
Jun 3	Duke of Windsor marries Wallis Simpson in France	Dec 14	Brazil bans all political parties
		Dec 21	Jane Fonda born
		Dec 29	Irish Free State becomes Eire

The Horror Of Modern War

The potential for barbarity in modern warfare was revealed to an awestruck world at Guernica on 27th April. The Basque region of northeastern Spain was a major target for the Nationalist forces as the campaigning season opened. Guernica stood in the way and needed to be captured. Franco ordered the Condor Wing, made up of German pilots and aircraft lent by Hitler, to soften up the target. It is thought that 43 Heinkel and Junkers bombers took part in the raid which occurred without warning in the middle of the day. The attacking aircraft rained high explosives and incendiaries on to the undefended town on a market day. Nearly 1,000 people, mostly civilians, were killed without the loss of a single aircraft. Guernica was rapidly abandoned and left to burn by the terrified inhabitants. The event shocked international opinion, which was being increasingly revolted by the slaughter of the Civil War. The sheer destructiveness of this raid, and other assaults on more military targets reinforced the reputation of strategic bombing as a weapon of horrific war. This played no small part in Hitler's ability to bully his neighbours in the succeeding months. Indeed, when Britain declared war on Germany in 1939 it was confidently predicted that German bombers would flatten London within days.

On 27th May the Golden Gate Bridge spanning the entrance to San Francisco Bay was opened, and some 200,000 people walked across the huge structure to celebrate. At 4,200 feet long the bridge had the longest span in the world, and the adjacent approach arches stretched the length to a total of over 8 miles. The upper deck carried six lanes of highway while the lower deck had four lanes, but two railway lines. Together the road and rail links connected San Francisco with Oakland and the main routes to the East. The total cost was in excess of $77,200,000.

Left: The German airship Hindenburg over New York on 6th May. Below: Just hours later the airship exploded when landing at Lakehurst, New Jersey, at 7.23pm. About a third of the 97 crew and passengers were killed. Facing page: (top left) George Gershwin died on 11th July after a lifetime of composing popular tunes; (top right) John D. Rockefeller, American multimillionaire and philanthropist, who died on 23rd May; (bottom right) Amelia Earhart who vanished while flying across the Pacific on 2nd July amid rumours of an illicit Japanese military build up; (bottom right) The former Reverend Harold Davidson, Vicar of Stiffkey, was defrocked after a scandal involving various women and church funds and took up lion taming and was mauled to death on 28th July.

On 12th May hundreds of thousands of people packed the processional route from Buckingham Palace to Westminster Abbey to watch the Coronation Procession of King George VI. The ceremony attracted heads of state from around the world while troops from every corner of the Empire added colour to the London streets. Facing page, top: King George passes Admiralty Arch on his return from the Abbey. Facing page, bottom: The new King and Queen with their ceremonial attendants on the balcony at Buckingham Palace. Left: The official photograph of the new royal family. Below: King George in the Abbey. Centre left: The Royal Family, including the dowager Queen Mary, on the balcony at Buckingham Palace. Centre right: Some of the many people who camped out the night before the ceremony to be sure of a good spot. Bottom left: A children's race at a London street party. Bottom right: The procession in the Mall on its way to the Abbey.

Below: King George VI leaves Downing Street after private talks with Neville Chamberlain (right) who took over as Prime Minister on 28th May. Bottom left: The former King Edward VIII and Mrs Simpson marry to become the Duke and Duchess of Windsor together with their best man Major E.D. Metcalfe. Bottom right: The Duke and Duchess outside the chapel at the Chateau of Conde, Tours, where they were married. After the abdication, the ex-King caused much disquiet and concern in London by frequent telephone calls to his brother giving advice on political and royal matters. Eventually the Palace switchboard was given instructions not to put such calls through, the beginning of a rift which would never heal.

The year of 1937 saw the continued rise of Adolf Hitler. He played host to many notable people including (bottom left) the Duke and Duchess of Windsor. The Windsors visit to Germany was, to say the least, controversial. They were entertained at length by Hitler and other Nazi leaders in Berlin and at the Berghof, Hitler's villa at Berchtesgaden in Bavaria. Bottom right: The Duke and Duchess during a tour of Berlin's industrial centres. Below: A Nazi rally in Berlin in May. Left: Mussolini and Hitler reviewing the German Army in action during manoeuvres in Mecklenburg and Pomerania, on the Baltic coast.

War In China

The continuing anarchy in China took a fatal new turn in 1937. Ever since the collapse of the Imperial Manchu Dynasty in 1912 the Celestial Empire had been wracked by civil wars. By 1937 the conflict had settled down to a contest between the Communists led by Mao Tse-Tung and the Nationalists under Chiang Kai-Shek, though several independent warlords retained power over isolated areas. Taking advantage of the chaos, Japan had been gradually expanding its power in Korea and Manchuria in the north. This turned into an outright war of aggression and on 23rd February Mao Tse-Tung suggested to Kai-Shek that they bury their differences to resist Japan. The Nationalist leader refused. In August, however, Peking fell to Japanese troops and Shanghai was pounded by co-ordinated air and naval attacks. On 29th September the two Chinese factions united against Japan, but the advance of the Japanese forces continued unabated. International pressure began to build up against Japan for their aggressive policies. On 5th October President Roosevelt made a speech calling on the nations of the world to quarantine Japan, and others followed suit.

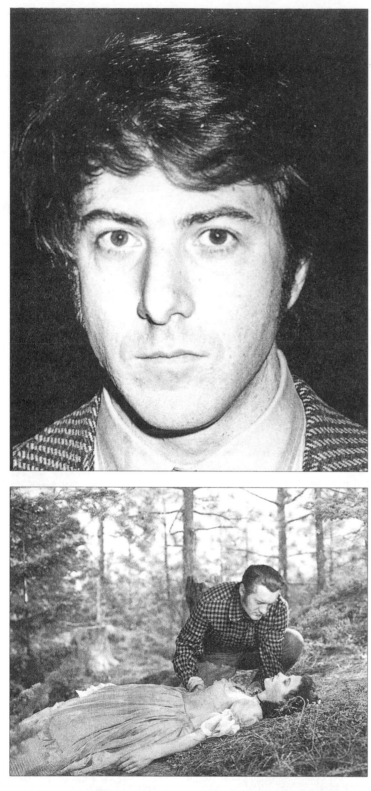

Top left: Dustin Hoffman, born this year in Los Angeles, hit stardom in **The Graduate** in 1967. Top right: Jean Harlow blazed a startling, but all too brief career in films which began with a Laurel and Hardy comedy in 1928, progressed through major movies like **Dinner at Eight** and **Public Enemy** . She died a trag- ically early death in 1937. Above: Hedy Lamarr, the Austrian screen beauty who came to Hollywood in 1937, starring opposite George Sanders, an English import to the USA. Right: Boxer Joe Louis who beat James Braddock in 9 rounds on 22nd June to become world heavyweight champion.

Jan 3	UK: The government announces that all school children will be issued with gas masks	**Jul 14**	Howard Hughes and 4 companions land in New York after a record-breaking around the world flight lasting 3 days, 19 hours and 17 minutes
Jan 5	Birth of King Juan Carlos of Spain	**Jul 14**	Italy officially adopts anti-semitism
Jan 14	France: Premier Chautemps resigns, Leon Blum is to form a new government	**Jul 18**	US pilot Douglas Corrigan lands in Dublin - he thought he was on his way to California
Jan 18	Leon Blum fails to establish a new government and Chautemps is back in office	**Aug 9**	Birth of Rod Laver, Australian tennis player
Feb 19	Austria: Austrian Jews are told they have nothing to fear	**Aug 15**	Birth of British author Frederick Forsyth
Mar 10	France: Premier Chautemps resigns	**Aug 17**	Henry Armstrong wins Lightweight boxing title, only man to hold 3 titles at different weights at the same time
Mar 13	France: Leon Blum becomes premier	**Aug 22**	UK: The first 'automatic' car is tested
Mar 13	Nazi Germany invades Austria	**Sep 27**	The liner Queen Elizabeth is launched by Queen Mother
Mar 17	Rudolf Nureyev, ballet dancer, is born on a train in Siberia	**Sep 27**	UK: Royal Navy mobilises
Mar 30	Birth of Warren Beatty	**Oct 3**	Birth of US rock and roll singer Eddie Cochran
Mar 31	Birth of UK politician David Steele	**Oct 17**	Evel Knievel born
Apr 7	Austria: Rothschilds' Bank is seized by Nazis and Baron Rothschild is arrested	**Oct 21**	Tokyo: A typhoon kills over 200 people
Apr 30	UK: Live coverage of FA Cup Final for first time	**Oct 21**	China: Japanese occupy Canton
May 3	Italy: Hitler and Mussolini meet in Rome	**Oct 25**	Libya is incorporated into Italy
May 4	Protestant Douglas Hyde becomes first President of Eire	**Oct 31**	Orson Welles sends thousands of radio listeners into panic when they mistake his reading from H G Well's "The War of the Worlds" for a real account of a Martian landing
May 17	UK: A tube crashes at Charing Cross station, killing six	**Nov 10**	Death of Turkish president Mustafa Kemal Ataturk
Jun 2	Regents Park Zoo is opened by Robert and Edward Kennedy	**Nov 11**	Turkey: Ismet Onu becomes President
Jun 27	All Austrian Jews are given two week's notice by employers	**Nov 14**	Germany: Jews are expelled from colleges
Jun 30	US: The comic strip 'Superman' appears for the first time	**Dec 10**	US: Pearl Buck receives the Nobel Prize for Literature
Jul 2	All five Wimbledon titles are won by Americans	**Dec 25**	Death of Czech writer Karel Capek
Jul 3	The 'Mallard' achieves speed of 126 mph, world record for a steam locomotive	**Dec 29**	Birth of British horseman Harvey Smith
		Dec 31	Indianapolis PD begin official breath testing of drunken drivers

Left: The **Queen Elizabeth** was launched in 1938 for the lucrative North Atlantic crossing. Before she could enter service, however, the government commandeered her as a troopship, a role she played to perfection throughout the Second World War. She actually entered service as a liner in 1946, and was destroyed by fire in 1972. Below: Sylvia Pankhurst speaking to a Peace Meeting on 29th May. The speech followed a demonstration march from Victoria Embankment to Hyde Park. Bottom right: Tom Smith leads his Preston North End team down from the Royal Box at Wembley after winning the F.A. Cup. The winning goal came in the last minute of extra-time, ending possibly the most thrilling final ever played.

The Spitfire (above) was introduced to service in Britain's RAF in August 1938, and over 1,200 were delivered before war broke out. The fighter was designed by Reginald Mitchell at Supermarine. Much loved by pilots, the Spitfire was fast, manoeuvrable, had a good rate of climb and was heavily armed with eight machine guns. The aircraft was also relatively easy to fly and had graceful lines which appealed greatly to the public. When war broke out, spitfires formed the front line of defence for Britain against the massed bomber raids of the German Luftwaffe and gained enduring fame in the Battle of Britain. Previous page: The 200 mph Ensign entered service with Britain's Imperial Airways on 25th March. The technology used to produce such large airliners would soon be turned to producing bombers.

Wrong Way Corrigan

On 17th July a young American airman named Douglas Corrigan took off from Roosevelt Airfield in New York, heading for California. Soon after takeoff he lost sight of land in thick clouds, checked his course by compass and settled down for the long flight. Some hours later the clouds broke to reveal he was over water. Not unduly worried, Corrigan guessed he was over the Great Lakes. Only when no land appeared did Corrigan realise that he had been following a reciprocal compass bearing and was now over mid-Atlantic. He landed near Dublin after a completing the ocean crossing. Though he had completed the flight without obtaining either permits or a passport, Corrigan was not charged, but allowed to return home. His feat earned him the name in the Press of Wrong Way Corrigan.

Top left: Queen Mary visiting Willy Lot's Cottage in Flatford, Suffolk. Above: King George VI, Queen Elizabeth, Princess Elizabeth and Princess Margaret arrive at Olympia for the Royal Tournament on 25th June. This showpiece for Britain's military was primarily a public entertainment, but also served to emphasise technical advances in weaponry. Left: The King and Queen, Prime Minister Neville Chamberlain and Mrs Chamberlain meet in September. As international tension grew the Prime Minister increasingly called on the King to advise and inform him as to the progress of events. Under British constitutional etiquette the monarch has the right to be informed, and to advise politicians. King George made full use of these rights in the growing crisis. The support of the King and his support among ordinary people would prove to be vital.

German aggression reached new heights in 1938. In February Hitler took the command of the German army and established an inner foreign policy cabinet which met in secret. On 12th March German troops marched into Austria to force a union between the two nations, helped by Austrian Nazis. A subsequent referendum in Austria approved the move, but since all opponents of the Nazis were under arrest most other nations did not accept the decision. Hitler next agitated for the German-speaking Sudetenland, part of Czechoslovakia, to be joined to Germany. Amid growing fears of an invasion, an international conference in Munich attended by Britain and France, agreed to German claims in return for a promise from Hitler of an end to his claims. Chamberlain called the agreement 'peace in our time'. After the horrors of the Great War, many fervently hoped that he was right and greeted the announcement enthusiastically. However, the realities of German aggression argued that war was inevitable and military build ups were begun in France and Britain.

Facing page: (top left) British Prime Minister Neville Chamberlain is met by Herr Ribbentrop at Munich airport on 29th September; (centre left) Chamberlain inspects a guard of honour at Munich airport; (bottom) Chamberlain at Heston Airport on his return from Munich following his agreement with Hitler; (top right) German troops march through Kufstein on the Austrian border on 13th March. This page: (top right) Hitler Youth members in Vienna; (above left) Nazis guard the home of Dr von Schuschnigg, Chancellor of Austria; (above) German troops in Kufstein being greeted by enthusiastic crowds; (left) Hitler and Mussolini visiting the Tomb of the Unknown Warrior in Rome during their meetings in May.

Top left: Shirley Temple dances with George Murphy in the movie Little Miss Broadway, which was released this year. Top right: Orson Welles, who broadcast a radio play on 30th October which many Americans took to be news of a real invasion from Mars. Above: Rudolph Nureyev, Russian ballet dancer, born this year. Right: Warren Beatty, born this year in Richmond, Virginia.

an 4	Tokyo: Fascist Baron Hiranuma becomes premier
an 11	Neville Chamberlain visits Mussolini
an 17	Germany: Jews are banned from driving
an 24	Chile: A massive earthquake destroys two Chilean cities, killing 30,000
an 26	Franco captures Barcelona with help of the Italians
an 28	Death of Irish poet W. B. Yeats
eb 10	Death of Pope Pius XI
eb 14	Germany launches the battleship Bismarck
eb 20	London: The first washing machine goes on show at the British Industries Fair
eb 20	US: Nylon stockings go on sale for the first time
eb 23	Germany: Nazis confiscate precious stones and metals from Jews
Mar 1	US: The government recognises Franco's government
Mar 12	Rome: Coronation of Pope Pius XII
Mar 28	Surrender of Madrid to France ends Spanish Civil War
pr 4	The Iraqi King is killed in an accident and succeeded by the four year old Emir Faisal
pr 8	King Zog flees Albania
pr 27	Britain calls up all men of 20 and 21
pr 30	US: World Fair opens in New York
May 7	Spain leaves the League of Nations
un 11	Birth of British motor racing driver Jackie Stewart
Jun 17	Multiple murderer Eugen Wiedmann publicly guillotined in Paris
Aug 23	British driver John Cobb breaks a new land speed record at 368.85 mph
Sep 1	BBC Home Service begins
Sep 1	Hitler declares war on and invades Poland, starting WW II
Sep 3	Great Britain and France declare war on Germany
Sep 4	British liner 'Athenia' is sunk by a German submarine
Sep 6	First air raid of the war on England
Sep 19	RAF begins leaflet raids on Germany
Sep 23	Death of Austrian psychoanalyst Sigmund Freud
Sep 30	Identity cards are first issued in Britain
Oct 6	Britain and France reject Hitler's peace bid
Oct 8	Nazis incorporate Western Poland into Germany
Oct 14	Royal Navy ship 'Royal Oak' is sunk in Scapa Flow by Germans, 810 die
Oct 27	Birth of British actor John Cleese
Oct 28	Germany: All Jews will wear a yellow Star of David
Nov 30	USSR invades Finland
Dec 1	Lee Trevino born
Dec 13	The Battle of the River Plate
Dec 14	USSR is expelled from the League of Nations
Dec 15	Nylon is first produced commercially
Dec 17	German ship Graf Spee is scuttled in Montevideo harbour

THE SLIDE TO WAR

The year 1939 saw the opening of the second pan-European war in just 40 years. The countdown began on 9th March when the Czechoslovak President Hacha sacked his pro-German Prime Minister. Just 6 days later Hitler sent his troops into Czechoslovakia to impose a protectorate. The legal government was suppressed and the Gestapo began rounding up any who might oppose the invasion. There was international outrage but no positive moves to block the enlargement of Germany. Britain and France accepted the inevitable and began a massive rearmament. On 1st April a treaty of mutual protection was signed between Britain and Poland, widely expected to be Hitler's next victim. On 22nd May Germany and Italy agreed the Pact of Steel, a military and economic alliance, which left few in any doubt of their bellicose intentions. The 23rd August saw the surprise non-aggression pact between Germany and the Soviet Union, which effectively isolated Poland. Europe had become a powder keg. The actual spark which ignited the conflict was the German invasion of Poland on 1st September. Britain and France were allied to Poland and so declared war while the Soviet Union joined Germany in taking territory from the hapless Poles. However, the underlying causes of the struggle were many and complex. Many blamed Hitler's outright aggression. Others blamed the harsh peace terms imposed on Germany in 1919 for instilling a lust for revenge. Still others found the underlying cause to be the unification of Germany in 1870 and the consequent search for a role for a powerful and wealthy nation in the centre of Europe. It was this latter supposition which was accepted in diplomatic circles and much of the history of post-1945 European diplomacy has been concerned with finding a suitable role for Germany.

Left: Queen Elizabeth and her daughters, Elizabeth (left) and Margaret, photographed in the early months of 1939. As Britain moved slowly towards war with Germany the nation came to look to the Royal Family for inspiration and for an example.

DRUMMING UP SUPPORT

As the possibility of war grew to become a probability, both sides in the coming conflict set about trying to win international support. The attitude of the United States of America was considered vital. Facing page, top: President Roosevelt discusses the situation with Secretary of State Cordell Hull on 29th August. Hitler knew he could never gain active American help, but instead played on the loyalties of German settlers and general fears of unnecessary bloodletting in an attempt to ensure neutrality. The British, by contrast, represented the war as a struggle of democracy against dictatorship with a view to gaining material aid, and eventually American involvement. The British had the added advantage of the Empire and in May King George and Queen Elizabeth embarked on a tour of Canada (facing page, bottom) to gauge feelings in the Dominion and to help rally support for the mother country.

Top left: As Europe slipped towards war, Britain still had around 1 million unemployed workers. Protests and marches such as this one took place, though with decreasing regularity. The Ernie Brown referred to was the then Minister for Labour. Top right: Sir Oswald Mosley inspects the women's section of the British Union of Fascists on 7th May. Mosley's movement had attracted followers in the 30s when European fascism seemed on the rise, but when war broke out support for Mosley evaporated as the war effort took over. Left: Veteran Liberal politician Lloyd George arrives at the House of Commons to hear a statement from the Prime Minister on 24th August. Above: The body of poet W.B. Yeats is guarded by French sailors on its journey from Mentone to Sligo.

READY FOR WAR

The outbreak of war in September found the belligerent nations in very different states of readiness. Germany was probably the best prepared of all the nations which went to war. Under Hitler, Germany had been getting ready for years. Modern theories of Blitzkrieg, or lightning war, had been developed together with the devastating weapons which made it possible. Heavy tanks and motorised troops were trained to punch a hole in an opposing army through which lighter, faster units could flood. The Luftwaffe was trained in close ground support to smash resistance and the will to fight. Hitler had the best military force in the world at his command in 1939. Britain had begun preparations later and her forces were less well equipped. However, some world class machines such as the Spitfire fighter aircraft and the Cromwell tank were in production. Given time, Britain would produce some of the finest fighting units of the war. France waited behind her obsolete Maginot Line, thinking herself safe from attack. Poland was totally unprepared for modern war as her leaders had deliberately avoided re-arming with modern weapons so as not to provoke her powerful neighbours.

Facing page, top: British newspaper boards announce the invasion of Poland. Facing page, bottom: British Prime Minister Neville Chamberlain (centre in wing collar) with his first war cabinet. Top left: German military scientists producing poison gas. The threat of gas attacks was present throughout the 2nd World War, but it was not used even when Germany was collapsing. Above left: German troops march through Prague. The subjugation of Czechoslovakia and other conquered territories tied up many German troops. Above: A squadron of Polish light tanks on manoeuvres in August. Left: French North African troops, drafted in from the desert colonies arrive in Paris in November before taking their places on the Western Front.

Britain at War

On 3rd September Britain and France declared war on Germany following the invasion of Poland. In Britain long prepared plans went into operation. Stock-piled gas masks were distributed to every citizen in case of poison gas attacks from German aircraft. Left: On 5th September Queen Elizabeth set an example by carrying her gas mask on an official visit to the Red Cross in London. The move was much needed as many people preferred not to carry the cumbersome masks with them. Below: King George VI tirelessly visited troops to raise morale. He is shown here leaving a trench in a forward area of northern France in December. Bottom left: Even before war was declared children were being evacuated from London because of the fear of aerial bombardment from the Luftwaffe. This picture shows the scene at Victoria Station on 1st September. Children wore labels giving their name, address and personal details. Bottom right: The King and Queen leave an air raid shelter in south London while on a tour of ARP units in the capital. Air raid shelters were hurriedly constructed all over the country, while the people of central London relied on the underground railway system for shelter from bombs.

Left: Among the first British men to be called up were railway workers who were recruited into the Railway Reserves to run trains for the military. Below: A Heinkel 111 which was brought down on a Scottish moor on 29th October. Bottom left: British reservists training on 25th September. During the first months of warfare men were schooled in rifle fire from behind entrenched positions. Such tactics dated from 1918, and were easily swept aside by the German Blitzkrieg. New tactics were hastily devised after the disasters of spring 1940. Bottom right: Prefabricated air raid shelters are delivered to householders in South London. Such shelters were protection against shrapnel but could not survive a direct hit.

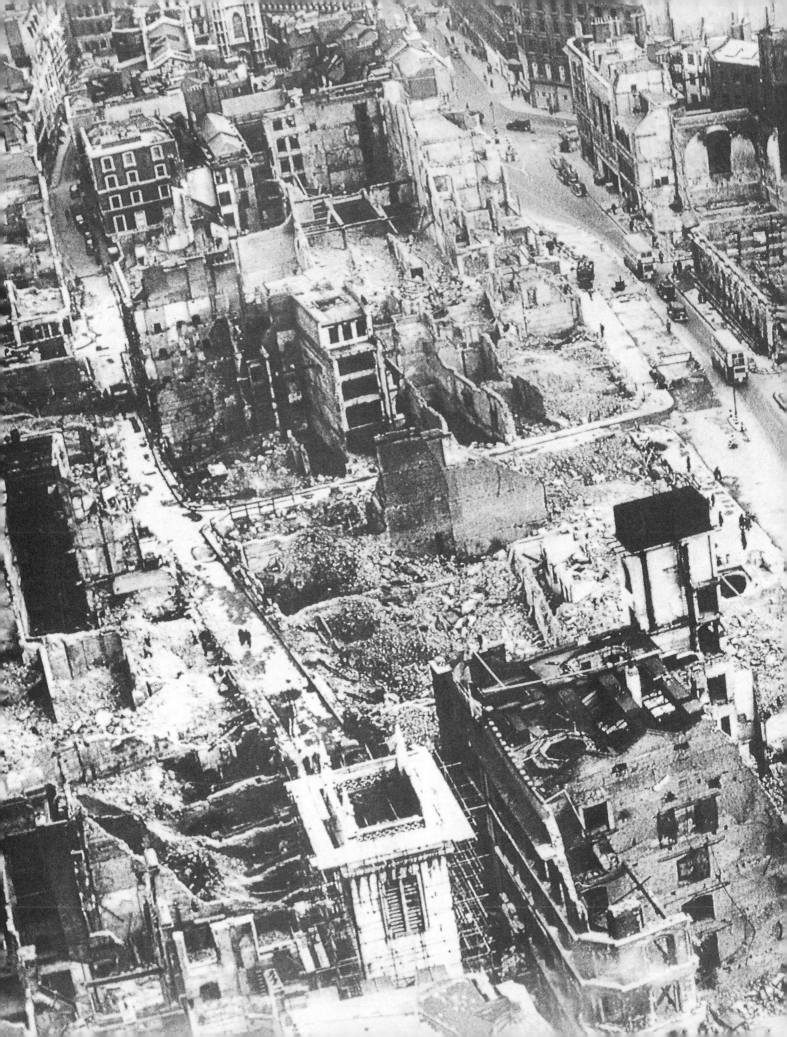

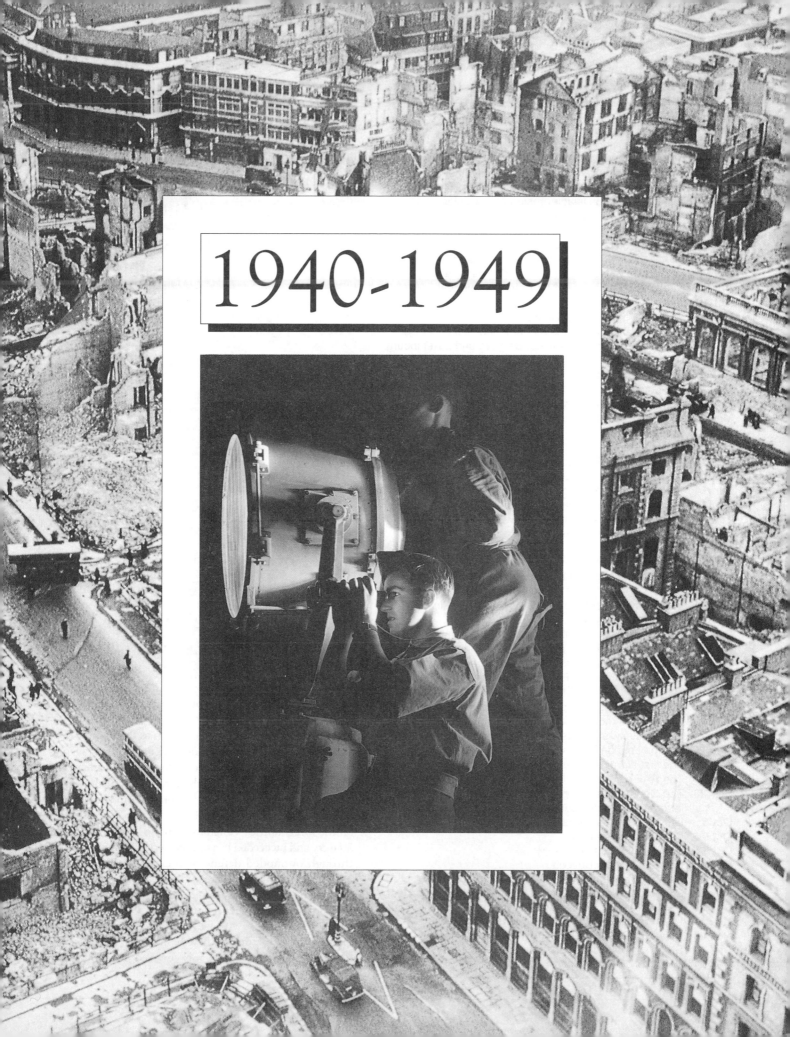

1940-1949

1940

Jan 8	Sugar, butter and bacon are rationed in Britain
Jan 21	Jack Nicklaus born
Feb 1	Death of British writer John Buchan
Feb 24	Birth of Dennis Law, footballer
Mar 8	Martial law is declared throughout the Netherlands
Mar 16	The first British civilian dies in an air raid
Mar 20	France: Edouard Daladier resigns as premier
Mar 22	France: Paul Reynaud becomes premier
Mar 23	UK: IRA prisoners riot in Dartmoor prison
Mar 29	UK: Metal strips are introduced in £1 bank notes
Apr 2	All Italians over the age of 14 are mobilised
Apr 9	Denmark and Norway are invaded by Germany
Apr 9	Death of British actress Mrs Patrick Campbell
Apr 10	Sweden insists on its neutrality
Apr 14	British naval forces land in Norway
May 7	UK: Chamberlain resigns as Prime Minister
May 10	German army enters Holland, Belgium and Luxembourg
May 10	UK: Winston Churchill becomes head of wartime coalition government
May 14	UK: Local Defence Volunteers 'Home Guard' is formed
May 15	Dutch army surrenders
May 27	The evacuation of British and French troops from Dunkirk begins
May 28	Belgian King Leopold III surrenders to Germany
Jun 5	UK: Strikes are banned by the government
Jun 10	Italy declares war on Britain and France
Jun 14	Paris is captured and occupied by Germany
Jun 17	British troopship Lancastria sinks, 2,500 lives are lost
Jun 20	UK: The first Australian and New Zealand troops arrive
Jun 22	French surrender to Germany
Jun 23	Adam Faith born
Jul 2	The Vichy Government is formed
Jul 2	First German daylight bombing raid on London
Jul 3	Royal Navy bombards French Navy at Oran
Jul 5	Vichy Government breaks relations with Britain
Jul 7	Ringo Starr born
Jul 9	RAF begins night bombing raids on Germany
Jul 10	UK: The British Union of Fascists is banned
Jul 20	Singles charts are first published in America
Jul 21	Lithuania, Latvia and Estonia vote to become part of the USSR
Aug 18	UK: The first German plane is shot down over London
Aug 18	Death of US motor tycoon Walter Chrysler
Aug 21	Leon Trotsky is assassinated in Mexico
Aug 23	Blitz on London begins
Aug 25	The first air raid on Berlin by allies
Sep 9	The RAF carries out a three hour raid on Hamburg
Sep 23	The George Cross, highest civilian award for courage, is introduced by King George VI
Oct 3	UK: Neville Chamberlain resigns from the government
Oct 9	Birth of John Lennon
Oct 14	Birth of Cliff Richard
Oct 21	Birth of Geoffrey Boycott
Oct 23	Birth of Brazilian footballer Pele
Nov 5	US: Roosevelt is returned for another term as President
Nov 9	Death of former Prime Minister Neville Chamberlain
Nov 13	US: Walt Disney's 'Fantasia' opens in New York
Nov 14	Coventry Cathedral is destroyed by enemy action
Dec 10	Stockholm: No Nobel Prizes are awarded
Dec 21	Death of US writer Scott Fitzgerald

Above: Big Ben seen through barbed wire which festoone
Parliament Square and other London thoroughfares in 1940. Th
year opened with what became known as the Phoney War. No maj
attacks were made by either side after Poland had fallen as both sid
prepared themselves. American diplomats made attempts to negotia
a peace, but to no avail. On 9th April the war began in earnest whe
German troops overran neutral Denmark and swept on to Norwa
On 10th May the full force of the German Blitzkrieg was unleashe
on the low countries. Columns of massed tanks, backed by motoris
infantry and preceded by accurate aerial bombing smashed their wa
through outmoded defences to capture Antwerp, Brussels ar
Nivelles. After just four days of the meticulously planned and viole
assault, the Netherlands surrendered. Two weeks later Belgium fo
lowed suit. The German units had a clear run to France ar
advanced at speed. By the close of the year only Britain remaine
undefeated by Germany, though she had taken a severe batterir
from the Luftwaffe. Britain only survived due to the efforts of RA
Fighter Command during the Battle of Britain.

Top left: London firemen tackle a blaze in Newgate Street. Top right: George VI visits bombed homes in Bristol after a raid in December. Above centre: Firemen fighting a ferocious blaze with their backs to St Paul's Cathedral in the heart of the City of London. Above: Hop-pickers in Kent shelter nervously while watching an aerial dogfight taking place overhead. Left: Rescue workers drag wounded civilians from the rubble of a London home in October.

When war broke out, Britain was led by Neville Chamberlain who had proved to be a capable peace-time premier. In forming a war government, Chamberlain called in many talents including that of Winston Churchill, who served as First Lord of the Admiralty as he had done during the early days of World War I. Churchill's opposition to appeasement and his administrative genius won him many friends during the first winter of war. When German troops overran Denmark, Norway and Holland, Chamberlain lost much of his support and resigned on 7th May. King George turned to Churchill as the only man able to pull the nation together in adversity. On 10th May Churchill entered the House of Commons for the first time as Prime Minister and made the first of many memorable speeches when he said "I have nothing to offer, but blood, toil, tears and sweat". Right: Churchill in bulldog mood visits defences in northeast England.

Top left: Wartime singer Vera Lynn entertains British troops in September at a base 'somewhere in England'. Left: Roosevelt addressing the Democratic Convention from the White House on 25th July. In his speech he promised that war material would be sent to nations resisting the aggression of dictators. Above: King George VI fires a Bren gun while on a visit to an arms factory. Armament factories were kept busy 24 hours a day and 7 days a week during 1940 in an attempt to produce enough modern equipment to face the onslaught of the German army and Luftwaffe.

...low: A rare success for the Allies ...the bitter fighting as a damaged ...rman panzer crew surrenders ...British infantry. Below right: A ...ge crowd of young girls of the ...tler Youth attend a rally at ...uremberg in January to hear ...tler speak of the progress of the ...r to date. Bottom left: An anti-...craft gun and its crew scan the ...es above the Ruhr for British ...mbers. The Ruhr contained the ...artland of Germany's industrial ...ight and a heavy concentration ...armament works. German war ...inners worried constantly for ...e safety of the Ruhr. In fact ...ritish bombing forays were large-...restricted to coastal towns dur-...g 1940. It was not until long-...nge heavy bombers entered ser-...ce in 1941 that Harris, in ...arge of RAF Bomber ...ommand, could take the war to ...e enemy.

THE GERMANS IN PARIS

The swift German victories in the Low Countries brought their armoured columns around the northern flank of the main French defences by late May. By the 28th May the Germans were on the Aisne, punching a gap through the Allied lines and sweeping all before them. By 4th June, the British army had pulled back to Dunkirk and a massive naval and aerial operation was under way to evacuate 340,000 troops from the beaches to safety in Britain. On 10th June the French government abandoned Paris and declared the city to be 'open'. In effect the capital would not be defended so as to spare the citizens and buildings the destruction wrought by seige and street fighting. German advance units arrived on 14th June and the city was fully occupied within hours. Top right: German horse artillery, marching through Paris, pass the Arc de Triomphe.

Backs to the Wall

With German troops marching virtually unopposed across northern France; Paris and Versailles in Nazi hands and the British army evacuated to England, France surrendered on 22nd June. Hitler insisted that the surrender was signed in the same railway car in which Germany had surrendered in 1918, and then the carriage was destroyed. Under the surrender terms northern France was to be occupied and all military equipment handed over to the Germans. In Britain Churchill announced gravely that "The Battle of France is over. The Battle of Britain is about to begin." Within days German bombers were attacking RAF bases in an attempt to destroy British air power and clear the way for a naval force to transport the German army across the Channel to invade England. British fighters struggled against great odds, but managed to stave off defeat. Meanwhile, British defences were bolstered by hurriedly constructed concrete strongpoints at strategic points and by the arrival of thousands of Empire troops. The Home Guard was formed to help the army defend Britain from the invasion which, in the event, never came.

*acing page, top: British air min-
ter Sir Archibald Sinclair visits
squadron manned by Polish
'lots. Facing page, bottom: HMS
xeter arrives in England in
ebruary. Her crew took part in a
rade to celebrate their ship's vic-
ry over the German pocket bat-
ship Graf Spee in December
939. Top left: British troops meet*

*Belgian soldiers in the days before
the Blitzkrieg knocked Belgium
out of the war. Above right: A
British night pilot takes to his cockpit. Above: A ship carrying
Australian troops arrives in
England in June. Right: Australian
troops training in southern
England on 25th June to repulse
the expected German invasion.*

Jan 3	Italy: Australian troops take 5,000 prisoners at Bardia	**Jul 4**	UK: Coal rationing begins
Jan 4	German actress Marlene Dietrich becomes a US citizen	**Jul 7**	US forces land in Iceland
Jan 5	Amy Johnson disappears and is feared drowned	**Aug 8**	The Soviet air force raids Berlin for the first time
Jan 8	Death of Boy Scouts founder Robert Baden-Powell	**Aug 30**	Seige of Leningrad by German forces begins
Jan 9	Birth of Joan Baez	**Sep 16**	The Shah of Iran abdicates
Jan 13	Death of Irish author James Joyce	**Sep 17**	UK: Government orders potatoes to be sold at 1p so people will eat more of them
Jan 20	US: Roosevelt is inaugurated for his third term as President	**Oct 8**	Birth of US black civil rights leader Jesse Jackson
Feb 1	Libya: The RAF raids Tripoli	**Oct 30**	A German U-boat attacks USS Reuben James, resulting in the loss of 70 American sailors
Feb 10	Iceland is bombed by the Luftwaffe	**Nov 3**	President Roosevelt is warned of a possible attack on the US by the Japanese
Feb 28	Death of Spanish ex-King Alfonso XIII	**Nov 14**	HMS Ark Royal is sunk
Mar 17	UK: Minister of Labour, Ernest Bevin, calls for women to fill vital jobs	**Nov 25**	HMS Barham is sunk
Mar 28	Death of British authoress Virginia Woolf	**Dec 6**	President Roosevelt appeals to Emperor Hirohito to avoid a war with the US
May 10	Luftwaffe damages House of Commons, London	**Dec 7**	Japanese attack US base at Pearl Harbour
May 10	Rudolf Hess, Hitler's deputy, parachutes into Scotland	**Dec 8**	Britain and US declare war on Japan
May 15	UK: The first aircraft with a jet engine makes its maiden flight	**Dec 8**	Britain declares war on Finland, Rumania and Hungary
May 20	Crete is invaded by Germany	**Dec 10**	British battleships Repulse and Prince of Wales are sunk by Japan
May 23	King George II of Greece flees from Crete	**Dec 10**	Japanese invade Malaya
May 24	HMS Hood sunk by the Bismarck	**Dec 11**	US declares war on Germany and Italy
May 24	Birth of US singer Bob Dylan	**Dec 19**	Germany: Hitler becomes Commander in Chief of the army
May 27	German battleship Bismarck sunk by Royal Navy	**Dec 22**	Churchill arrives in Washington for talks with Roosevelt
Jun 2	Clothes rationing starts in Britain	**Dec 25**	Hong Kong surrenders to Japanese forces
Jun 6	Death of US motor engineer Louis Chevrolet		
Jun 19	Germany and Italy expel US consuls		
Jun 22	German army invades Russia		
Jun 27	Hungary declares war on Russia		

The year 1941 saw what had for two years been a European war spread to become a World War. On 21st June Hitler launched his magnificent army into the Soviet Union to meet little resistance in their drive across the Steppes. On 7th December Japan launched a surprise attack on Pearl Harbour with the object of destroying the United States Pacific Fleet, so leaving that ocean open for Japanese aggression. Facing page: St Paul's Cathedral surrounded by smoke and flames as London burns beneath the impact of German bombs. Top: An American battleship settles into the waters of Pearl Harbour during the surprise attack by Japanese carrier-bourne aircraft on 7th December. Above left: HMS *Ark Royal* listing badly on 13th November after being struck by a German torpedo in the Mediterranean. She sank a few hours later. Above: Dockside wreckage at Pearl Harbour. Left: The Japanese battleship *Idzuma* steams into Shanghai on 8th December to take possession of the city.

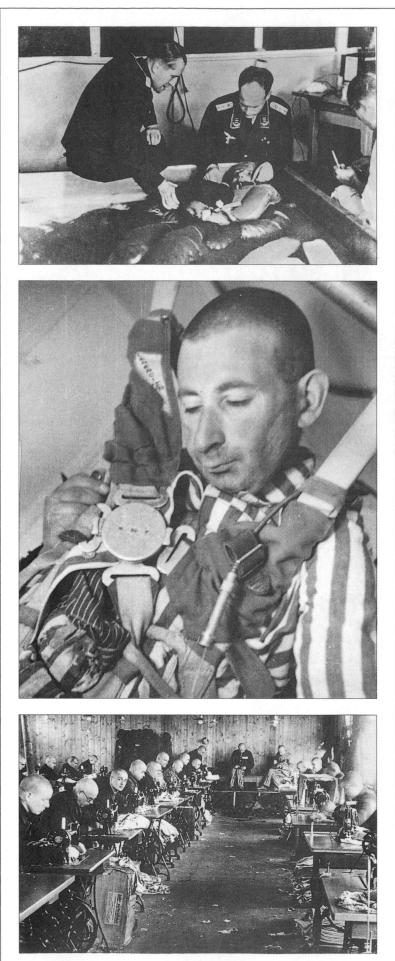

The Concentration Camps

The Nazis opened their first concentration camps for political opponents in March 1933, just a few weeks after coming to power. Conditions were tough from the start, but became increasingly brutal as time passed and the Nazi grip on power increased. The death rate grew alarmingly as conditions worsened. The history of the camps became increasingly identified with the persecution of the Jews, though others such as gypsies suffered too. Systematic persecution gathered pace after the outbreak of war. In September 1941 all Jews in German occupied countries were forced to wear a badge proclaiming their race. On 20th January 1942 senior Nazis met to discuss the fate of the Jews and decided on a Final Solution, the extermination of the race. New death camps were built in which millions met their deaths. Top left: The notorious Dr Holzloehner (left) conducting experiments on an inmate at Dachau Camp to determine how long sailors can stay alive in freezing water if their ship sinks. Centre left: Another inmate of Dachau is forced to test parachute harnesses. Bottom left: The tailoring workshop at Sachsenhausen Camp.

Above: Rudolf Hess, Hitler's Deputy Fuhrer, and his son. On 10th May Hess flew to Scotland, reportedly in an effort to persuade Britain to make peace by dividing the world into British and German spheres of influence.

German radio at once denounce Hess as insane and disassociate Hitler from the flight. Churchill ordered Hess to be imprisoned, and after the war he remained i Spandau Prison in Berlin until his death.

Above: Hitler at a mass Nazi rally on 30th January. Left: Australian infantry at Tobruk on 20th April. The largely Australian garrison of Tobruk held out for 240 days against Rommel until relieved on 29th November. Below left: A British light tank passes a burning German counterpart during the Allied autumn advance on Gambut. Below: German survivors from the Bismarck are landed in Britain. The powerful German battleship sailed on a raid on 18th May and successfully broke through into the Atlantic by sinking the British battlecruiser HMS Hood on 24th, but was intercepted and sunk by a British fleet on 27th May.

Left: One of 700 dogs trained by
the British to carry messages.
Below: British paratroopers on a
practice jump. Below left: British
paratroopers board a Wellington
aircraft. Below centre: Carrier
pigeons were carried by paratroopers in case of radio failure. Below
bottom: British paratroopers in

full kit. Facing page top: Flight
Sergeant K.B. Chisolm describes
how he shot down a German fighter in September. Facing page bottom: Pilots of the RAF's Eagle
Squadron, made up of American
volunteer pilots, race for their
Hurricane fighters on 25th
March.

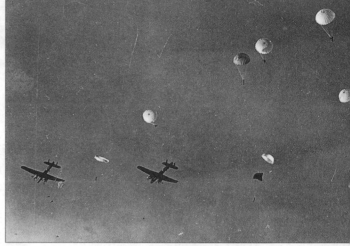

THE NEW WEAPON

Paratroopers were widely viewed as a new weapon of devastating importance. In May 1941 paratroopers gained their greatest ever victory when
Germany invaded Crete. The island was held by 27,000 British,
Commonwealth and Greek troops, though they had few guns or tanks. On
19th May the Luftwaffe pounded the few RAF bases out of service. Next
day General Lohr led thousands of German paratroopers to Crete, landing
at carefully selected strategic centres. On 21st Maleme Airfield was captured and German transport aircraft flew in more troops and guns while
bombers struck at Allied troop positions. On 28th May the Royal Navy
evacuated 15,000 Allied survivors. However, paratroopers generally failed
to live up to this early promise. It was found that the light weapons that
they could carry were only effective in surprise assaults and could not stand
up to sustained battle, as the debacle at Arnhem in 1944 was to show.

1942

Jan 2	Japanese take Manila in Philippines
Jan 10	Japanese invade Dutch East Indies
Jan 15	India: Gandhi names Nehru as his successor
Jan 17	Birth of US boxer Muhammed Ali
Jan 17	US actess Carole Lombard is killed in a plane crash
Jan 19	Birth of Michael Crawford
Jan 26	Northern Ireland: First US troops land in Europe
Jan 29	Desert Island Discs begins with Roy Plomley
Feb 9	Soap rationing begins in Britain
Feb 10	Glenn Miller is awarded first ever gold disc for Chattanooga Choo Choo
Feb 15	Singapore falls to Japanese
Feb 23	Austrian author Stefan Zweig kills himself
Mar 25	Birth of US singer Aretha Franklin
Apr 15	Island of Malta is awarded the George Cross
Apr 24	Barbra Streisand born
Apr 25	UK: Princess Elizabeth registers for war service
Apr 26	World's worst mining disaster in China, 1572 die
May 5	Battle of Coral Sea in the Pacific
May 26	Britain and Russia sign a twenty year peace pact of alliance
May 29	Bing Crosby records White Christmas, biggest selling record of all time
May 29	Death of US actor John Barrymore
Jun 6	Czechoslovakia: Village of Lidice massacred by Nazis

Jun 8	Australia: Sydney is bombed by the Japanese
Jun 8	Winston Churchill arrives in Washington for talks with President Roosevelt
Jun 18	Birth of ex-Beatle Paul McCartney
Jul 4	US Air Force bombs German air bases in Holland
Jul 16	Birth of Australian tennis player Margaret Court
Aug 22	Brazil declares war on Germany and Italy
Aug 25	Duke of Kent, son of George V, dies on active service
Sep 5	Raquel Welch born
Sep 10	RAF drops 100,000 bombs on Dusseldorf in under one hour
Sep 12	A German U boat torpedoes British ship 'Laconia' killing over 1,000 Italian prisoners of war
Oct 2	'Curacao' a British cruiser sinks after colliding with Queer Mary - 358 die
Oct 3	New US price law freezes wages, rents and farm prices
Nov 8	British and American troops invade North Africa
Nov 13	British army recapture Tobruk
Nov 21	James Hertzog, SA soldier and statesman, dies
Nov 27	French fleet is scuttled in Toulon harbour when German forces enter
Nov 29	US: Coffee rationing begins
Dec 20	First nuclear power station to produce electricity opens in the USA
Dec 21	British army take Benghazi in Libya

Dit is een foto, zoals ik me zou wensen, altijd zo te zijn. Dan had ik nog wel een kans om naar Holywood te komen.

Anne Frank.
10 Oct. 1942

(translation)
"This is a photo as I would wish myself to look all the time. Then I would maybe have a chance to come to Hollywood."
Anne Frank, 10 Oct. 1942

Facing page: The view from the wheelhouse of a British destroyer on station at the rear of a convoy crossing the Atlantic. It was vital for Britain to keep the supply routes open, but 1942 was a crisis year with 1,664 ships being lost to U-boat and aircraft attack. Above: Anne Frank with an excerpt from her famous diary. The Jewish Frank family lived in hiding for years to escape Nazi persecution, but were discovered and executed before the war ended. Right: Nazi troopers interrogate Jews in the Warsaw Ghetto in January 1942. The brutal treatment was taken to new levels in March when train-loads of Jews began being sent to the extermination camp at Belsen. During the spring of 1943 the surviving Polish Jews rose in rebellion against the German oppression.

Left: An RAF pilot takes a nap next to his Spitfire on a base in southern England. Below: The pilots at 'ready' await the order to scramble on the same base. Though the immediate danger of invasion was gone, the RAF stayed alert to attack bombers which continued to pound British cities. Facing page, top left: The firing pin being fitted to a grenade. Women worked long hours in munitions factories to supply the army. Facing page, above right: A battery of anti-aircraft rockets guard the outskirts of Liverpool. Facing page, bottom right: Land Army girls at work bringing in the harvest on a Hertfordshire farm. The Land Army supplied much of the muscle power for British agriculture, but the girls could have a hard time on a non-mechanised farm miles from any town and out of touch with home.

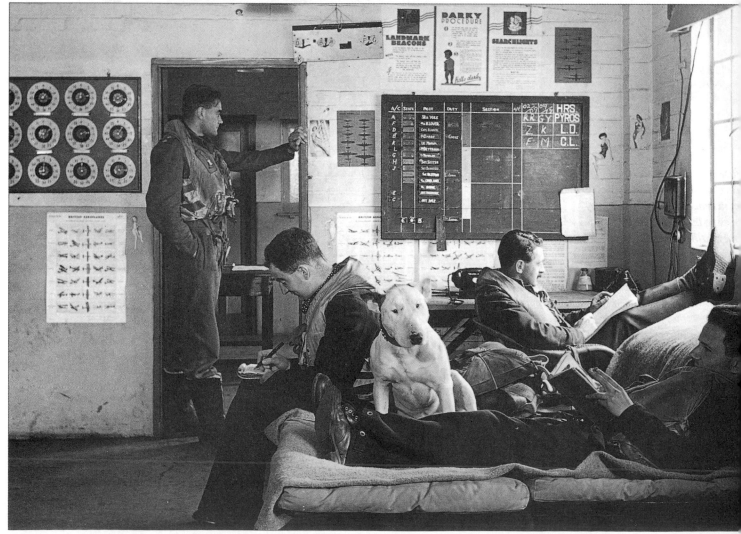

The Bomber Offensive

Bottom left: King George VI inspecting an American squadron equipped with Flying Fortress heavy bombers at a base in central England in November. Until 1942 Britain had been subjected to intense bombing without being able to respond. The Wellington and Blenheim bombers of the RAF were essentially designed for mine laying and tactical strikes and so were unable to undertake long-range work with heavy loads. In 1942, however, the situation changed dramatically. Not only were American squadrons equipped with Flying Fortress and Liberator aircraft, but the RAF was re-equipped with heavy bombers such as the Lancaster and Stirling. These aircraft could carry heavy bomb loads the long distances needed to reach the industrial heart of Germany and make the return journey. March 28th saw the first heavy RAF raid of Germany when Lancasters bombed Lubeck at night, destroying around 1,000 buildings. On 30th May 1,000 RAF aircraft attacked Cologne, destroying many factories and causing heavy civilian casualties. The bomber offensive had begun.

The year opened with a modest Russian assault which stopped German troops within sight of Moscow. As spring released the Steppes from winter, new German advances scored major victories. A major push through the Ukraine engulfed vast territories and led to the capture of Sebastopol. A Russian counterattack at Kharkov was bungled and the Germans encircled and captured 200,000 men. In August the Germans reached Stalingrad, but were unable to capture the vital city. By autumn the production of the T34 tank in large numbers and a new command structure gave the Russians new hope. By the end of the year the German 6th Army, 300,000 strong, was trapped in Stalingrad. Right: Red Army ski troops launched winter raids behind German lines. Below: Red Army troops follow retreating Germans out of Moscow in January. Below right: The Red Army, with ski-mounted armour, attack in October. Bottom: Russian gunners defend a bridge near Stalingrad.

Top left: John Barrymore, who died in 1942. He played not only handsome leading men, but also specialised in dark villains, such as Svengali. Top right: Bing Crosby who made the first of his famous 'Road' movies in 1942 when he starred opposite Bob Hope in **Road to Singapore**. Left: Carole Lombard was killed in an aircrash while selling warbonds in 1942. Above: Barbra Streisand, born this year in New York, became a successful actress and singer during the 1970s.

1943

Left: Stalin, Roosevelt and Churchill take a break during their arduous talks at Teheran in November. The meeting was called as differences between the Allies became increasingly clear over the summer. United only by their war against Hitler and his allies, the Big Three leaders had many differences. The Teheran Conference was called to try to resolve these. It was agreed that the war against Germany would be pushed to its conclusion before major forces were moved to the Pacific to deal with Japan. Churchill and Roosevelt agreed to open up a second European Front to relieve pressure on the Soviet Union. However, the thorny problem of future borders in the Balkans was left unresolved. Though it was agreed that Russia could take a large section of eastern Poland, the final fate of that nation was left obscure.

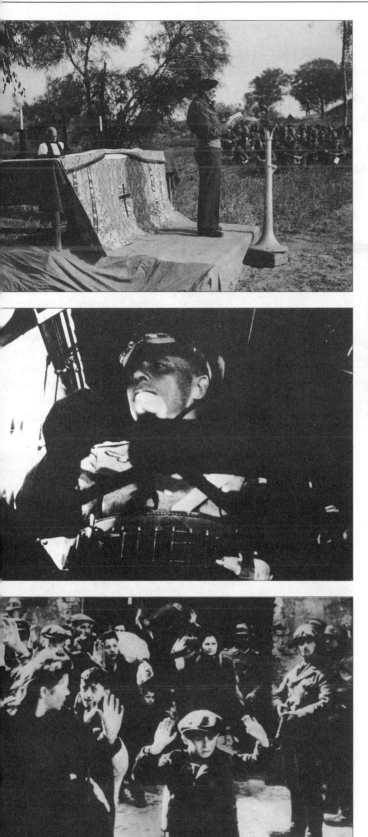

The war in North Africa, long a saga of rapid advances and equally fast retreats, finally ended in an Allied victory in May. The previous July the British Eighth Army under Auchinleck halted a massive German assault masterminded by Field Marshal Rommel deep inside Egypt. In October the Eighth Army, now under Montgomery, launched its own attack and, after two weeks fierce fighting, broke through the German lines. The retreat begun at El Alamein continued, interrupted only by a few rearguard actions, for months. In March Rommel was flown to hospital to recover from exhaustion and in May the 150,000 German troops left in North Africa surrendered to Montgomery. In July the Allies pursued the enemy north when they invaded Sicily. Top left: General Montgomery reading the lesson during the Eighth Army Thanksgiving Service on reaching Tripoli in March. Above: Montgomery addressing the men of the Eighth Army who took part in the invasion of Sicily in July. Above left: Field Marshal Rommel, the Desert Fox. In April the battered and oppressed Jews of Warsaw rose in armed rebellion against their German masters. Faced with the choice between fighting or death in the extermination camps, the Jews hoarded small arms and home-made bombs. The fighting lasted nearly a month, ending on 16th May with some 56,000 Jews dead and only a few hundred prisoners. Left: Polish Jews are led under armed guard from the Warsaw Ghetto to their fate in extermination camps.

Left: The headquarters of RAF Coastal Command with Air Marshal Sir John Slessor (right), Air Vice-Marshal Durston (left) and naval Captain Peyton-Ward (centre). Together these three men masterminded the air campaign in the Western Approaches which helped secure Britain's supply route. In 1943 Coastal Command bombers and patrol aircraft sank 84 U-boats. The summer marked the turning point in the Battle of the Atlantic with the Germans putting 250 U-boats to sea to sink 500,000 tons of shipping, but by the autumn German losses were so high the campaign was cut back. Below: A battery of searchlights ready to probe the night sky for German bombers over East Anglia. Once an aircraft was picked up by a searchlight beam, anti-aircraft batteries within range would fire in an effort to bring the enemy aircraft down.

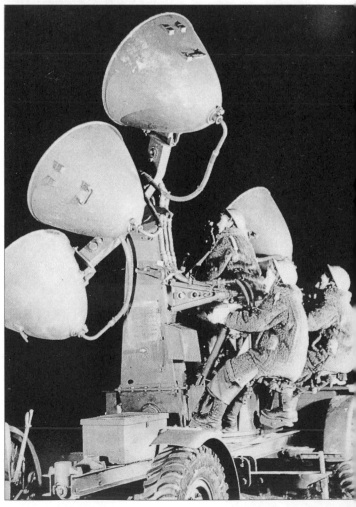

THE EASTERN FRONT

The year opened with a savage blow to Germany on the Eastern Front. On 31st January Field Marshal von Paulus surrendered the remnants of the 6th Army after weeks of starvation, bitter cold and fighting had cost him 150,000 men. Above: A Soviet soldier waves the Red Flag over central Stalingrad. By the end of February Leningrad and Kursk had also been retaken. By July, however, the Soviets had pushed forward into a vulnerable salient west of Kursk and German General von Kluge was determined to take advantage. He launched a massive attack on 5th July of 37 divisions, backed by 3,000 tanks, in an effort to encircle the Soviets under General Rokossovski. At first the attack went to plan, but on 12th July the Soviets counterattacked. The largest tank battle of history followed in which the German armour was annihilated, but at frightful cost. The Germans called off the attack, which proved to be their last major effort on the Eastern Front.

USAAF In Europe

During 1943 the immense power of the USAAF began to be felt in Europe. The men and machines had begun to arrive in Britain in 1942, but not until 1943 were they present in large numbers. The main aircraft of the USAAF were the B-17 Flying Fortress and the 51 Mustang. The American pilots were trained to fly at high altitude in formations allowing each bomber to cover its companions with machine gun fire as protection against German fighters. Mustang fighters accompanied the massed formations for the first section of the flight. The huge American formations flew by day to allow more accurate navigation than the RAF could achieve at night. Inevitably losses were huge, but the Americans were able to replace losses in men and machines with ease. Right: Mustang pilots await the order to take off. Centre right: A B-17 crew blessed by the station padre before take-off for Germany. Bottom right: The famous *Memphis Belle* returns to America.

ove: General Dwight D. senhower who was appointed to e key command of Allied forces the planned invasion of western urope. Taking up his post on th December, Eisenhower was *chosen for his superb grasp of strategy which was deemed vital for the campaign. He was also the only man capable of handling the brilliant but difficult subordinates, Generals Montgomery and Patton.*

Above Barnes Wallis, possibly the greatest British engineer of the war. His first contribution was the Vickers Wellesley light bomber which entered service in 1937. His chief contribution was the unique geodetic, or cross-lattice, construction of the hull and wings which allowed great strength for weight. Next came the medium bomber the Wellington which was the mainstay of RAF Bomber Command from 1939 to 1942. In 1943 Wallis perfected the bouncing bomb which allowed the RAF to destroy the vital Ruhr Dams and thereafter Wallis concentrated on bomb design. His new bombs allowed the RAF to attack targets previously thought impervious to aerial assault. Above right: British Labour politician Ernest Bevin. Right: Hitler takes a break with Eva Braun at their Bavarian retreat. The holiday snap was found among Hitler's personal effects after his death.

*Left: Ingrid Bergman, the powerful Swedish actress, who won an Oscar for the film **Casablanca** this year. Below: Betty Grable whose bouncy personality and impressive ability to display her legs to good effect made her a favourite pin-up with American troops. Bottom left: British movie star Leslie Howard was killed when his aircraft was shot down by German fighters while flying from Lisbon to London.*

Fall Of Mussolini

In July Allied forces landed on Sicily and within two weeks had captured the capital Palermo. Within days of this success, bombers raided Rome. Seeing their nation on the brink of collapse, high ranking Italians turned to dictator Mussolini in an appeal for peace before the nation endured too much destruction. Mussolini, after talks with Hitler, refused. On 25th July King Victor Emmanuel dismissed Mussolini and ordered the highly respected general Pietro Badoglio to form a new government. On 8th September the new government surrendered to the Allies, and declared Rome to be an open city. On 13th October, the Italians declared war on Germany. Mussolini fled to Hitler, who used him as a pawn to legitimise his campaigns in Italy. In January Mussolini ordered the execution of his son-in-law Count Ciano, who had defected to the Allies. On 28th April, 1945, Mussolini was captured by Italian guerrillas and shot, his body then hung in Milan.

1944

Jan 1	Oswald T Avery makes a breakthrough in DNA research
Jan 1	Death of British architect Sir Edwin Lutyens
Jan 3	Germany: An RAF raid hits Hitler's Chancellery
Jan 4	Hitler mobilises all children over the age of ten
Jan 10	Mussolini's son-in-law is sentenced to death for treason
Jan 22	Allied Army landings at Anzio in Italy begin
Jan 23	Death of Norwegian artist Edvard Munch
Jan 27	Seige of Leningrad ends after 2 years
Jan 29	The USS Missouri, world's biggest warship, is launched
Feb 18	Eisenhower is awarded the USSR's highest military honour
Mar 8	9,000 Welsh miners go on strike over pay differentials. They remain out until the government meets their demands
Mar 13	Diplomatic relations are restored between Italy and the USSR
Apr 6	UK: PAYE (Pay As You Earn) income tax comes into operation
Apr 30	UK: The first of half a million pre-fabricated houses goes on display
May 9	The first eye bank opens in the US
May 12	Death of British author Sir Arthur Quiller-Couch
May 23	Birth of John Newcombe, Australian tennis player
May 25	Yugoslavia: Tito flees from the Germans
Jun 4	Allied forces enter and liberate Rome
Jun 6	D-Day. Start of the allied landings on coast of Normandy
Jun 7	Belgium: King Leopold III is arrested
Jun 12	First flying bomb falls in England
Jun 17	Iceland becomes an independent Republic
Jul 20	German Generals make attempt on Hitler's life
Jul 20	US: Roosevelt wins nomination for a fourth term
Aug 1	Post codes are first introduced, in Germany
Aug 1	Uprising in Warsaw, Poland begins
Aug 2	Germany breaks off relations with Turkey
Aug 19	Death of Sir Henry Wood, co-founder of the Proms
Aug 22	Italy: Allies take Florence
Aug 23	Paris is liberated
Aug 28	Birth of David Soul
Aug 31	Birth of Clive Lloyd, cricketer
Sep 4	Belgium: Allies capture Brussels and Antwerp
Sep 6	Bulgaria declares war on Germany
Sep 8	First German V2 flying bombs fall in Britain
Sep 11	US troops enter Germany
Sep 13	Death of British humorist Heath Robinson
Sep 17	British airbourne invasion of Arnhem and Eindhoven
Oct 2	British troops land on Crete
Oct 14	Rommel is forced to commit suicide
Nov 7	Franklin D. Roosevelt is re-elected for record 4th time
Nov 10	Birth of Tim Rice
Nov 12	German battleship 'Tirpitz' sunk by RAF
Nov 12	Paris: Churchill is given the Freedom of the City
Nov 20	Paris: P.G.Wodehouse is arrested
Nov 30	HMS Vanguard, Britian's largest ever battle ship, is launched
Dec 15	Glenn Miller disappears in mysterious circumstances
Dec 16	Germans begin Battle of the Bulge in the Ardennes

Left: Captain Don Gentile of the USAAF marks up another kill on the side of his machine to bring his total to 22. He also won the Air Medal with three bars. The Americans favoured giving publicity to individuals to help boost morale. Facing page: Dr Joseph Goebbels, Hitler's Minister of Propaganda. Many regard Goebbels as being one of the finest publicists and propagandists of all time. His total mastery of mediums as diverse as posters, newspaper columns and film documentaries made him invaluable to the Third Reich. One of his innovations was to give each leading personality within the Third Reich a theme tune which was played before any speech be it on radio or in person. His deft manipulation of the truth helped keep German morale high during 1943 and 1944. Only the increasing disasters of 1945 proved too much for him. He committed suicide on 1 May 1945.

THE ANZIO WHALE

"We thought we would throw a tiger ashore, but we got a beached whale" was Churchill's rather harsh comment on the Anzio Landings. The daring plan was to land 50,000 Allied troops at Anzio, 70 miles behind German lines, cut enemy lines of communication and capture Rome. The landing took place on 22nd January, achieving complete surprise and laying central Italy open to attack. The commanding officer, US General Lucas, however, decided to dig in and safeguard his supply port first, thus giving the German 14th Army time to arrive and blockade the landing force. It was not until the major assault in Italy was successful in taking the fortress Monte Casino that the Anzio force managed to break out of the German stranglehold. The delay meant that much savage fighting was needed, and large casualties sustained, before the Allies could move into Rome, the first enemy capital to be captured. Left: American troops wade ashore at Anzio on 22nd January. The original American troops would later be strengthened by heavy reinforcements of both American and British regiments complete with armoured back up.

Above: Glenn Miller, the popular American band leader, met a mysterious fate. On 15th December he ignored RAF weather news and took off for France to arrange a special Christmas Concert in the newly liberated Paris. He never arrived and his fate remains unknown. No German squadrons reported downing an Allied aircraft that day and no wreckage was ever found. Above right: A young child is rescued from her bombed London home on 23rd June by a woman rescue worker. Though the worst days of the Blitz were over, German bombers continued to assault Britain until their bases in France were overrun. Right: Winston Churchill surveys bomb damage in London.

The V Weapons

For some months in 1943 and 1944 Hitler had been boasting about possession of a secret weapon which would win the war for Germany. On 13th June 1944 the first secret weapon was fired at England. Witnesses at first thought it was a small aircraft in trouble which crashed on wasteground near Swanscombe in Kent. Only when the wreckage was inspected was the craft identified as being a small, pilotless aircraft powered by a ram jet. Soon to be dubbed Doodle Bugs by the British, the V1 was capable of flying on a predetermined course to deliver a high explosive warhead of frightening power. RAF fighter pilots tried to intercept, but often suffered damage to their own planes when the Doodle Bugs exploded. Not until sophisticated anti-aircraft guns were deployed along the coast did the V1 cease to be a threat. The V2 (above left) carried a heavier warhead and, because it flew faster than the speed of sound, was impossible to intercept. The damage they inflicted, not only to London but also to civilian morale, was immense. Only the capture of their bases in northern France averted severe consequences in Britain.

Top right: Squadron Leader the Hon. Max Aitkin poses before leading his formation of Mosquito aircraft on a raid against shipping off Norway. The Mosquito was a successful aircraft. Its light wooden construction and powerful engines allowed high speed and great altitudes to be achieved. The pilots specialised in daring, pinpoint raids. Left: An X-Craft or miniature submarine in service with the Royal Navy in the spring of 1944. These tiny craft were used in successful attacks on the battleship Tirpitz and on the port of Bergen.

D-DAY

On 6th June the long awaited Allied assault on Hitler's Europe was unleashed. Years of careful planning had gone into selecting beaches with the correct characteristics to take a major mechanised landing. An elaborate misinformation campaign was undertaken to convince the Germans that the landing would take place at Calais, and much German armour was in fact placed there. The invasion began with predawn assaults by paratroopers on vital inland targets, such as bridges and rail links the capture of which would disrupt German troop movements. At dawn the entire Allied invasion fleet of 3,000 ships arrived off Normandy and landed tens of thousands of men on open beaches, codenamed Utah, Omaha, Gold, Sword and Juno. The Germans were caught by surprise, but fought with tenacity, inflicting heavy casualties especially on Omaha where the American troops landed in the wrong places. Within 24 hours, however, all five beach forces had linked up and by 12th June a heavily defended perimeter 80 miles long and 10 miles deep was firmly established behind which a military build up could take place.

The March Across France

With the bridgehead established in Normandy the first priority for the Allies was to secure a deep water port. This was achieved on 27th June with the capture of Cherbourg, though the dock facilities were destroyed by the Germans before their surrender. On 10th June the British, under Montgomery, began determined assaults toward Caen. These tied down large numbers of German troops, and persuaded Hitler to commit his crack Panzer troops. On 25th July a co-ordinated American attack at St. Lo smashed through the weakened German defences and drove deep into France. As one column marched on Brittany, a second ploughed south to loop around the Germans facing Montgomery. Much German armour was trapped in the Falaise Pocket, and forced to surrender. The German retreat was swift and on 25th August, Allied troops marched into Paris. On 15th August a new landing was launched in Provence, with troops breaking out to liberate southern France. On 3rd September British troops reached Brussels and on 20th October the Allies entered Germany at Aachen. Everything seemed set for the final assault on the Reich.

Jan 17	Soviets capture Warsaw
Jan 27	Soviet troops enter Auschwitz
Jan 30	German liner Wilhelm Gustloft is torpedoed by Russian submarine killing c.7700 people
Feb 12	Churchill, Stalin and Roosevelt conclude their discussions at the Crimean resort of Yalta
Feb 16	US Air Force begins heavy raids on Tokyo
Mar 7	Allied troops cross the Rhine at Remagen
Mar 26	David Lloyd George dies
Apr 11	US troops enter Buchenwald concentration camp
Apr 12	US: Roosevelt dies, Truman succeeds as President
Apr 22	Allies capture Bologna in Italy
Apr 23	Germany: American and Soviet troops meet up
Apr 28	Mussolini is executed after the German collapse
Apr 29	Allies take Venice
Apr 30	Hitler and Eva Braun commit suicide in Berlin
May 1	Germans surrender on Italian front
May 1	Joseph Goebbels kills wife and 6 children and then commits suicide
May 2	Soviets take Berlin
May 7	Germany surrenders unconditionally
May 8	War in Europe officially ends
May 9	Soviets capture Prague
May 23	Heinrich Himmler commits suicide
Jun 15	Family allowance payments are first made in Britain

Jun 26	The United Nations Charter is succeeded by the League of Nations
Jul 10	Virginia Wade born
Jul 16	First atomic bomb is detonated in New Mexico
Jul 17	The Potsdam conference of Allied Leaders begins
Aug 6	US drops atomic bomb on Hiroshima
Aug 9	Atom bomb is dropped on Nagasaki
Aug 14	Japanese surrender ending World War II
Aug 28	American forces land in Japan
Aug 30	Hong Kong is re-occupied by British after four years of Japanese occupation
Sep 2	Japanese surrender is signed on board USS Missouri
Sep 10	Vidkun Quisling 'Puppet' Premier of Norway is sentenced to death
Oct 9	French statesman Pierre Laval is sentenced to death
Oct 15	Peirre Laval, leader of Vichy Government who collaborated with the Germans, is executed for treason
Oct 24	United Nations formally comes into existence
Oct 24	Vidkun Quisling, Norwegian premier, is executed for collaboration
Nov 13	De Gaulle is elected as French president
Nov 20	The Nuremburg war crimes tribunal begins
Nov 29	Yugoslavia is proclaimed a communistic Republic with Tito as President
Dec 27	International Monetary Fund is established

VICTORY IN EUROPE

The early months of 1945 saw the collapse of Hitler's Third Reich. On 27th January Soviet troops captured Auschwitz in Poland and discovered the grim facts about Nazi attempts to destroy the Jewish race. In March the western Allies crossed the Rhine and began the final drive to victory. With Allied success assured 13 nations, as diverse as Ecuador and Saudi Arabia, belatedly declared war on Germany. On 30th April Hitler committed suicide, leaving Admiral Doenitz in control. On 7th May Doenitz ordered the unconditional surrender of all German forces. Facing page: The Royal Family and Churchill appear on the balcony of Buckingham Palace. Top left: crowds in Trafalgar Square. Above: A scene in Piccadilly Circus. Above right: A street party in Chelsea on 6th July. Right: cheering crowds outside Buckingham Palace.

MEETING IN YALTA

n 4th February Churchill, Stalin and Roosevelt met at Yalta (*facing page,
ttom*) to discuss the fate of Europe following the expected rapid defeat of
ermany. Each of the three had very different aims. Roosevelt wanted to
sengage American troops from Europe to concentrate on the defeat of
pan; Stalin wanted to extend Soviet influence and control over as much
Europe as possible, while Churchill was determined to build a democra-
from the ruins of the Third Reich. In the event it was Stalin who came
t as the clear winner. The ailing Roosevelt, he died in April, trusted
alin saying "he will work to build a peaceful and democratic world", and
agreed that most of Eastern Europe, including Poland, would fall under
viet administration and control. Greece was excluded only because
hurchill insisted that it be given a Western-style democracy. Stalin also
ined the Kurile Islands and Sakhalin in the Pacific in return for war effort
ainst Japan which was never given. It was at Yalta that the world order
hich would last for over forty years was established.

*Facing page, top: The British 7th
Armoured Division, the 'Desert
Rats', enter Berlin on 7th July
watched by silent German crowds.
Top left: Jews in the Dachau concentration camp cheer Allied
troops as they arrive to free them
on 12th May. Top right: German*
*troops captured on 4th May cross
the Rhine. Left: The corpses of
Mussolini (centre), his mistress
Clara Petacci and government officials were displayed in Milan on
28th April. Above: The shattered
Reichstag in Berlin, scene of a desperate last stand by SS troops.*

With Germany defeated, the true scale of the disaster for Europe and America was revealed. The appalling discoveries in the concentration camps shocked world opinion. There was a growing desire to see those responsible severely punished. The Allies took the unprecedented, and legally doubtful, step of setting up a war crimes trial. The Nazis on trial included Hess, Goering, von Ribbentrop, Speer and Streicher. *Above:* A gaunt Hess photographed during the Nuremburg Trials. He was found guilty and sentenced to life imprisonment. *Top right:* Hitler's air force chief Hermann Goering during his trial, he later committed suicide. *Centre right:* An American soldier inspects part of Goering's huge store of looted art treasures which was uncovered in May. *Right:* The courtroom in November.

While the war in Europe was ending, the conflict in the Far East was still in full swing. Showing with fanatical loyalty to their Emperor, the Japanese refused to accept defeat and fighting continued. In Burma the British and dominion armies pushed the Japanese back from the borders of India while in the Pacific the Americans cleared island after island of occupying Japanese. One of the bloodiest battles fought was for Okinawa, an island in the Ryuku archipelago. The 100,000 Japanese defenders held out from 1st April to 2nd July despite heavy aerial and naval bombardment and inflicted some 43,000 casualties before they were defeated. Left: British nurses attend to newly released prisoners. Below: Lord Louis Mountbatten, Supreme Commander in S.E. Asia, speaks to Australian troops in Burma in February. Bottom: An American pilot leaps to safety as his damaged Hellcat fighter bursts into flames while landing on USS *Lexington*.

THE POST WAR WORLD

By 16th August the world was at peace. Statesmen turned their minds to setting up a new world in which such destructive warfare as the world had suffered could be made a thing of the past. The United Nations was established in June to act as a forum for international discussions and the resolution of disputes. It was widely hoped that through this organisation, the countries of the world would be able to co-operate to restrain any future aggressor by use of economic sanctions and concerted military activity. In December top finance ministers signed the Bretton Woods agreement which established the International Monetary Fund and World Bank, as well as tying currencies together in an attempt to stabilise exchange rates and aid economic recovery. In many parts of the world international borders were redrawn with Korea being partitioned and Poland grabbing parts of Germany, but relinquishing some land to Russia. The hopes that these arrangements would lead to lasting peace did not last more than a few years.

With savage fighting continuing throughout the Pacific the decision was taken to drop the new atomic bomb on Japan in an attempt to force surrender. The first bomb fell on Hiroshima and the second on Nagasaki. The immediate death toll was around 70,000, but many more died from burns and radioactive poisoning. Japan surrendered just hours later. Top left: A child walks through the ruins of Hiroshima after the atomic bomb blast. Above: The crew of the B-29 Superfortress which dropped the atomic bomb on Hiroshima. Above right: Troops and civilians in Singapore cheer the news of the Japanese surrender. Right: US Fleet Admiral Chester Nimitz signs the Japanese surrender document on board the battleship USS Missouri in Tokyo Bay.

KING ZOG OF ALBANIA

One of the more colourful monarchs of the Balkans lost his kingdom permanently in 1946 when Albania fell beneath the Communist yoke. Zog had been born Ahmed Bey Zogu, a member of the Zogolli family. The Zogolli led a powerful Moslem faction in mountainous Albania so when, in 1912, Zog joined the anti-Turkish independence movement many Moslems abandoned their traditional religious loyalties to push for national freedom. Under the new King William, Zog achieved high office and in 1922 he became Prime Minister, but was forced to flee abroad in 1924. After the overthrow of King William, Zog returned in 1925 to become President of the newly created republic. By carefully playing off factions within his religiously divided nation, Zog slowly gathered personal power and had himself declared king in 1928. As king, Zog introduced many liberalising measures, but was unable to withstand pressure from Mussolini's Italy and in 1939 he had to allow Italian troops to land in Albania for the invasion of Greece. His credibility ruined, Zog was easily ousted by the Communists.

Jan 2	King Zog of Albania is deposed
Jan 3	William Joyce "Lord Haw Haw" is hanged for treason
Jan 7	The West recognises the Austrian Republic
Jan 8	The trial of Goering and von Ribbentrop starts
Jan 19	Birth of US Country Western singer, Dolly Parton
Jan 20	France: De Gaulle resigns
Jan 30	Hungary is declared a Republic
Feb 1	First civilian test flights from Heathrow Airport
Feb 7	Hess on trial at Nuremberg for war crimes
Feb 14	It is announced that the next Olympic Games will be held in London
Feb 21	Egypt: Twelve people are killed in riots in Cairo
Feb 24	Juan Peron is elected President of Argentina
Mar 1	Bank of England passes to public ownership by Act of Parliament
Mar 2	North Vietnam: Ho Chi Minh is elected President
Mar 21	Goering denies that he knew anything of the Final Solution
Mar 12	Birth of Liza Minnelli
Apr 1	Hawaii: 300 people are killed by tidal waves
Apr 2	Royal Military Academy is established at Sandhurst
Apr 17	Birth of Clare Francis
Apr 18	The US recognises the People's Republic of Yugoslavia
Apr 18	The League of Nations is dissolved
May 17	France: The coal mines are nationalised
May 25	Jordan becomes independent with Emir Abdullah as King
May 26	Czechoslovakia: The Communists come into power
Jun 1	UK: The milkmen go on strike
Jun 1	First TV licenses in Britain
Jun 9	Thailand: King Ananda Mahidol is assassinated
Jun 13	Italy: After 35 days on the throne, King Umberto II abdicates allowing the establishment of a republic
Jun 14	Death of John Logie Baird, the pioneer of television
Jul 1	Pacific: An atomic bomb is exploded, sinking three ships
Jul 4	The Phillippine Islands are given independence by US
Jul 8	UK: Margaret Roberts (later, Margaret Thatcher) is elected president of Oxford University Conservatives
Jul 22	Bread rationing begins in Britain
Jul 22	Jerusalem: The HQ of the British Palestine Army Command at the King David Hotel is destroyed by a terrorist bomb, killing over 40 people
Jul 25	Pacific: An atomic explosion is detonated at Bikini Atoll
Jul 27	US author Gertrude Stein dies in Paris
Aug 1	UK: British European Airways is formed
Aug 13	Death of British author H G Wells
Sep 8	Communists take power in Bulgaria
Oct 15	Hermann Goerring poisons himself hours before he is due to be hanged
Oct 15	Cardinals win World Series in St. Louis
Oct 16	Nuremburg executions take place, including that of von Ribbentrop
Oct 31	Italy: Terrorist bombs wreck Britain's embassy in Rome
Nov 4	United Nations Educational, Scientific and Cultural Organisation established, UNESCO
Nov 6	British National Health Act comes into force
Nov 11	UK: Stevenage in Hertfordshire becomes first 'New Town' to be designated in Britain
Dec 5	New York is chosen as the permanent site for UN
Dec 12	Birth of Emerson Fittipaldi
Dec 20	Birth of Uri Geller

VIVA PERON

The Peron family starred as one of the most important political dynasties in South America in the post war years. Juan Domingo Peron, was a soldier who turned to politics late in life. During the later 1930s, the career army officer, Peron, joined an officers' club at which many political discussions were held, and he became interested in the chaotic politics of Argentina. When premier Castillo fell in 1943, Peron became a minister in the new government. Peron backed policies which appealed strongly to the working classes making him a popular figure. In 1946 he was elected President of Argentina. In his rise to power, and his subsequent tight hold on Presidential office, Peron was aided by his wife Eva. Rising from the squalor of the back streets, the strikingly beautiful Eva Peron proved herself an astute and powerful politician. She organised women's causes, winning them the vote and substantial welfare payments among other concessions. Together Eva and Juan were unbeatable. Juan Peron was re-elected President in 1951 and survived an attempted army coup in November to establish a seemingly invincible grip on power. However, in August 1952 Eva died taking with her much of the charismatic appeal which secured the Perons in power. Despite Eva's death, Peron was re-elected in 1954 but not without difficulty. His first act was to arrest opposition leaders and then he turned on the Catholic Church. In June 1955 the Pope excommunicated Peron and on the 18th the army, navy and air force staged a revolt which tore him from power. Peron fled into exile. In September 1973 Peron and his new wife, Maria, were elected to the Presidency and Vice-Presidency on a policy of social reform. Just one year later Peron died. Though Maria tried to hold on to power, she was ousted by the military in 1976.

Above: The War Crimes Trials at Nuremburg came to an end in 1946. The trials had begun after the true enormities of Nazi barbarity had come to light. As the months progressed evidence of mass murder was paraded before the court.

Eventually, on 1st October 1946, the court pronounced the death penalty on nine Nazi chiefs. Above: Two men who escaped the noose, Goering, who committed suicide and Hess who was sentenced to life imprisonment.

In 1946 the British Government worked towards granting independence to the Indian Empire. Prominent in the negotiations on the Indian side was Pandit Jawaharlal Nehru, seen *(below)* broadcasting to the world on 7th September and *(right)* with his wife Kamla. Nehru eventually became the first prime minister of India in 1947, but during 1946 was only one of several leading politicians. The most difficult problem facing those working on the independence arrangements was that of religion. The Moslems, who dominated the northeast and northwest of the territories of the British Raj, feared that they would lose civil rights under the Hindu majority and demanded separate independence. Nehru resisted, but eventually gave way and so allowed the birth of Pakistan.

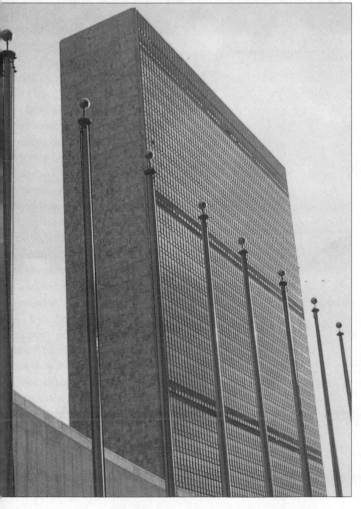

The Bikini

In the summer of 1946 the bikini hit the headlines for two very different reasons. The more frivolous fame of the bikini was based on its use as a fashion item. The two piece swimming costume for women, which daringly left the midriff bare, was named the bikini and sold in large numbers. More sombrely, Bikini Atoll, in the Pacific Marshall Islands, was chosen by the United States as the test site for their nuclear weapons programme. The first test took place on 25th July when an atom bomb was detonated on the seabed a short distance from the atoll. A number of obsolete warships, including the infamous German cruiser *Prinz Eugen,* were anchored around the blast point for the effects to be measured. Eleven of the ships were sunk and six seriously damaged, providing valuable data for the scientists. The nuclear weapons tests continued until 1958 and in 1969 the island's original inhabitants were allowed to return. They were evacuated again in 1978 after new radiation scares.

Left: The headquarters building of the United Nations in New York. The United Nations was created out of the carnage of the Second World War as a forum for the peaceful settlement of disputes and the enforcement of international security. In addition to the formal meetings of national representatives the United Nations is also sponsor of a number of specialist divisions including UNICEF, the United Nations Children's Fund which was founded in 1946 to help provide medical care, food and relief to children in disaster hit regions. The United Nations has grown to have about 170 members.

The British Royal Family emerged from the Second World War as a focus of national pride and resilience. King George VI had overcome the circumstances of his accession and his shyness to become a popular and effective king. Above left: King George VI and Queen Elizabeth entertained General Eisenhower and his family at Balmoral in the autumn. Top right: The king and queen with their daughters, Elizabeth and Margaret, on the lawns of Royal Lodge, Windsor in July. Above: The king and his daughters at Windsor in July. Left: A formal portrait of the two princesses. Facing page, top left: Liza Minnelli was born this year to film director Vincente Minnelli and his wife Judy Garland. Liza went on to establish herself as a talented singer and dancer in such films as Charlie Bubbles in 1968 and Stepping Out in 1991. Facing page bottom left: British yachtswoman Clare Francis, born in 1946.

THE BROWN BOMBER

Below: Joe Louis, the famed Brown Bomber, who defended his heavy-weight world boxing championship against Tami Mauriello in September. Louis won the title in 1937 when he defeated James Braddock and held it until he retired undefeated in 1949, a record for holding the title which has never been surpassed. The Braddock fight was a classic. Before the bout many claimed Louis had been barred from a title fight because of his colour. In the first round Braddock floored Louis, but from the 2nd round the fight went increasingly Louis's way. It finished in the 8th when Louis landed a right hook on Braddock's jaw and knocked him out. Louis defended his title for the first time on 30th August, beating Tom Farr. Thereafter title fights continued to be won with ease, in 1939 Louis knocked out his opponent in the first round.

The Business Of Murder

On 26th May was guillotined one of France's most notorious criminals. Dr Marcel Petiot made a business of murder, using the circumstances of the war as a cover for his crimes. Petiot was a wealthy and highly respected doctor who had served as Mayor of his home town before moving to Paris to pursue a more lucrative medical clientele. During the German occupation Petiot posed as a member of the Resistance with access to an escape route to Spain. Wealthy Jews and others with reason to fear the Germans were lured to Petiot's practice, fleeced of their wealth and then murdered, the bodies being disposed of in a number of ways. In March 1944 police visited the Petiot home after complaints about a smoky chimney. They found parts of 27 bodies in the cellar. Petiot fled, but was caught in December and confessed to a total of 63 killings, but claimed his victims were Nazis. The evidence was against him and he was executed.

With the end of the war the youth of the combative nations let their hair down with a vengeance. Fashions scorned the severe functionalism of style demanded by cloth rationing and instead concentrated on flowing lines and graceful sweeps not seen for years. Music and dance similarly reflected the prevailing joy and thrill of release from the threat of sudden death. In short succession two dance crazes swept the western world - the Jitterbug and the Bebop. Right: Ronald Ali shows his partner the steps of the Jitterbug. Below: The more energetic Bebop on display at the Feldman Club in London.

With the end of war, factories could return to their peacetime roles. The Ford factories around the world abandoned the manufacture of tanks and armoured vehicles for civilian motoring. The first vehicles were merely updated pre-war designs, but in 1946 the exciting new range appeared to be eagerly snapped up by the public. Above: A publicity shot of the new Ford Anglia. Right: A British-built Ford Prefect snapped beneath the Athens Acropolis. Such exotic foreign travel remained a rarity for British people in 1946.

Jan 1	Britain nationalises its coal mines
Jan 3	US: Congress is broadcast on television for the first time
Jan 8	UK: A shortage of coal causes closure of steel works
Jan 23	Death of French artist Pierre Bonnard
Jan 25	US: Criminal Al Capone dies in Miami
Feb 2	The RAF begins evacuating Britons from Palestine
Feb 20	Lord Louis Mountbatten is appointed the last Viceroy of India
Feb 24	Germany: Ex-chancellor Franz von Papen is jailed for eight years
Mar 1	The British Officers' Club is bombed in Jerusalem
Mar 1	International Monetary Fund begins operating
Mar 2	Martial law is imposed on five Jewish areas
Mar 4	Britain and France sign a 50 year alliance
Mar 1	UK: Artificial insemination is put down as illegal and adulterous
Mar 1	Death of Greek King George II
Mar 3	UK: BUPA, the private medical company, is founded
Mar 15	Floods in England are the worst ever recorded
Mar 25	Birth of Elton John
Apr 1	School leaving age in Britain is raised to 15
Apr 7	Death of US car maker Henry Ford
Apr 19	Explosions in Texas City kill 377
Apr 20	Death of Danish King Christian X
Apr 22	UK: A photo-finish camera is used for the first time, at Epsom race course
Apr 25	Birth of Johann Cruyff
May 7	UK: An explosion in a pit in Barnsley kills nine miners
May 8	Death of department store founder Henry Gordon Selfridge
May 29	US: A United Airlines plane crashes on take off at La Guardia airport, killing 38
Jun 5	American Secretary of State, George Marshall, offers aid to Europe
Jun 10	Truman becomes the first US president to make a state visit to Canada
Jun 11	UK: Princess Elizabeth is made a Freeman of the City of London
Jun 24	UK: Clement Atlee meets with US officials for further talks on the Marshall Plan
Jun 30	UK: Post war food rations are cut further in the midst of an economic crisis
Jul 19	The Burmese premier, U Aung San, is assassinated
Aug 15	India gains independence
Aug 15	Britain's first atomic reactor begins operation in Harwell
Aug 21	Death of Italian car designer Ettore Bugatti
Aug 29	Birth of James Hunt
Sep 21	American 'Skymaster' flys across Atlantic without a crew
Oct 1	US: Rita Hayworth files for divorce from Orson Welles
Oct 5	US: President Truman urges Americans to give up meat on Tuesdays and poultry and eggs on Thursdays to aid Europe
Oct 14	First supersonic flight is achieved
Oct 24	UK: 24 people are killed in a train crash at Croydon
Oct 26	UK: 26 people are killed in a train crash in Berwick-upon-Tweed
Nov 11	Rodney Marsh, cricketer, born
Nov 20	Princess Elizabeth marries Philip Mountbatten
Dec 30	King Michael of Romania abdicates in favour of a Communist Republic

With austerity gripping Britain, few could afford foreign travel and the best most could expect as a holiday was a few days at the seaside in Britain. The nationalised railways rose to the challenge by laying on special services which attempted to reproduce, at less cost, the glamorous continental express services such as the Orient Express and the Silver Arrow. Left: The Devon Belle express run by Southern Railways. The service featured a non-stop service from London Waterloo to Devon in which both 1st Class and 3rd Class passengers were treated to all restaurant seat carriages and prestige service not available on ordinary trains. The distinctive name plates and headboards of the engine were painted in a smart red livery, part of a long tradition of special decor for top class services.

Top: Earl Mountbatten of
Burma speaks at Government
House, New Delhi, during his
inauguration as Governor
General of India. Left: British soldiers escort Indian politician
Pandit Nehru, marked with an x,
through the streets of the Punja[b]
past buildings destroyed in rioting. Above: A peaceful crowd
gathers around a Congress flag
on the beach at Bombay. Minu[tes]
later the crowd turned violent
and attacked police.

NEW NATIONS BORN IN BLOODSHED

In 1947 India and Pakistan became independent of the British Raj which had ruled them for nearly a century. The actual date of legal independence was the 15th August, and the negotiations leading to the sovereignty were long and complex. The major problem was one of religion. The Hindu majority desired a united India, but the Moslems, concentrated around the deltas of the Indus and Ganges rivers, feared they would be swamped. Bitter riots and revenge attacks left thousands dead as the two factions fought in the streets. Added complications were the legal status of the hereditary princes who had not lost their realms to Britain. Some princes relinquished political power for private wealth, but others preferred to keep some form of autonomy within the new state. The pre-independence violence continued after 15th August with intercommunal bloodshed continuing to claim lives. The newly formed nations of India and Pakistan themselves came to blows over the status of Kashmir, a border territory with a largely Moslem population but a Hindu ruling caste.

Right: British Prime Minister Clement Attlee, who led the Labour Party from 1935 until 1955. Below: Harold Wilson, who was created President of the Board of Trade by Attlee in 1947 and went on to lead the Labour Party becoming Prime Minister in 1964 and again in 1974. Below right: Anthony Eden who held the foreign secretary brief for the Conservatives both in and out of government from 1939 to 1955.

The Marshall Plan

As Europe suffered from the effects of the Second World War, many diplomats saw signs that a new order was emerging. The Soviet Union was forcing east European nations to accept Communist governments and civil discontent in many western and southern European nations seemed to be creating conditions favourable to Communist takeovers. The United States Secretary of State, George Marshall, realised the dangers this posed to America and in 1947 proposed a massive financial aid package to ease the economies of Europe. Dubbed the Marshall Plan, the scheme eventually passed Congress as the European Recovery Act in 1948. A total of $14 billion was earmarked for the plan which was initially open to all European nations. The Soviet Union, however, refused to accept the cash, as did its Communist satellite states. The majority of free nations accepted Marshall Aid to get their economies moving again and within a decade Europe was once again a prosperous continent.

On 20th November vast crowds packed the streets of London to watch the ceremonial surrounding the royal wedding of the young heiress to the throne, Princess Elizabeth, to a dashing young naval officer, Prince Philip, who had served with some distinction during World War II. The wedding took place at Westminster Abbey and was both preceded and followed by the traditional parades of troops and bands through the streets. Right: The bride and groom together with the king and queen and queen dowager on the balcony of Buckingham Palace after the service. Facing page: Princess Elizabeth and Prince Philip leaving Westminster Abbey.

FROZEN BRITAIN

The first winter of peace proved to be the harshest for years. The season began rather mildly and Christmas passed with barely a frost. Late in January, however, the first snows fell. Days later, with the snow still lying deep and unthawed, more snow fell and froze on top of that already causing problems. In February more heavy falls and bitter frosts brought stagnation to the country with many roads and railways being completely impassable. The snow continued to be a problem, and several smaller communities remained isolated, until the thaw began in April. Above: A bulldozer is pressed into service to help clear Yorkshire's Scarborough-Bridlington road on 1st March. Above right: Snow is cleared from the ground of London soccer team Chelsea in preparation for a match on 8th March. The goalposts are being painted red to make them more conspicuous in the snow. Right: A squad from the RAF Arctic Team based at RAF Topcliffe form part of a rescue mission which pushed through deep snow on Bransdale Moor to bring food and fuel to 25 remote farms in Yorkshire which had been cut off for over three weeks.

The Kontiki Expedition

In 1947 the unorthodox historian and ethnologist Thor Heyerdahl hit the headlines when he attempted to prove one of his theories in spectacular fashion. Heyerdahl scorned the traditional theory that the Polynesians were of Asian origin and believed instead they came from South America and pointed to various cultural similarities between the two groups. In order to prove that such a lengthy voyage would be possible, Heyerdahl constructed a raft made of balsa wood to a traditional South American design and set off for Polynesia. In the raft, which he named *Kontiki*, Heyerdahl set sail with a crew of five friends from the coast of Peru. Taking advantage of ocean currents and prevailing winds, Heyerdahl succeeded in reaching the nearer Polynesian islands. Despite this triumph, few ethnologists took his claims seriously and orthodox science still accepts an Asian origin for the island peoples. Undaunted Heyerdahl continued his researches into Polynesian origins and spent much time on Easter Island trying to solve the riddle of the giant stone statues on that island. He later made a second epic voyage from Africa to America in an attempt to prove cultural links between ancient Egypt and early Meso-American civilisations.

*Above: The great Dutch football star Johann Cruyff who helped his national team to numerous sports successes, was born this year. Above right: British pop star Elton John, born in 1947, on stage at a concert in Leningrad in 1979. Elton John proved himself to be a performer of enduring popularity, though he rarely captured the coveted No.1 slot for a single. Right: Susan Hayward and Lee Bowman starring in the movie **Smash Up**, made in 1947. The film was Hayward's first big break and won her an Oscar nomination. She had begun as a model from a poor New York area and slowly fought her way through B-pictures and bit parts to star roles by sheer hard work and determination. After eleven years at the top, Hayward won an Oscar and thereafter stuck to less demanding roles and cameo appearances.*

Jan 1	British railways are nationalised	**Jun 10**	Field Marshall Smuts is made chancellor of Cambridge University
Jan 4	Burma gains independence from Commonwealth	**Jun 19**	Selective Service Bill in US for men aged 19 to 25 years
Jan 12	First full size supermarket in Britain opens, the Co-op	**Jun 24**	The Berlin Airlift begins
Jan 12	US: A law school in Oklahoma is ordered to admit a black girl	**Jul 1**	UK: The first Oxfam shop opens
Jan 30	Death of US aviator Orville Wright	**Jul 5**	UK: The National Health Service comes into operation
Jan 30	Mahatma Gandhi is assassinated in India	**Jul 6**	The Young Conservatives are formed
Jan 31	Riots break out in Bombay, following the death of Gandhi	**Jul 15**	Alcoholics Anonymous begins in Britain
Feb 18	Ireland: John A. Costello is the new Prime Minister as de Valera is voted out of office	**Jul 23**	Death of US film director David Wark Griffith
Feb 28	The last British troops leave India	**Jul 24**	France: New French premier is Andre Marie
Mar 10	Czecholslovakia: Foreign Minister, Jan Masaryk is found dead, having fallen from a window - it is not known if he jumped or was pushed	**Jul 29**	14th Olympic Games are declared open by King George VI
		Jul 29	Bread rationing ends in Britain
Mar 11	Offices of Jewish agency in Jerusalem are blown up	**Jul 30**	The World's first radar station opens at Liverpool
Mar 22	Andrew Lloyd Webber born	**Aug 8**	A gale hits Britain killing 12
Mar 27	Egypt: The foundation stone of the Aswan Dam is laid by King Farouk	**Aug 16**	Death of US baseballer Babe Ruth
		Sep 4	Wilhelmina abdicates from throne of Netherlands in favour of daughter Juliana
Apr 1	UK: The electricity industry is nationalised		
Apr 7	World Health Organisation is established	**Sep 9**	North Korea becomes a Republic
Apr 19	Bobby Charlton makes debut for England	**Sep 17**	Counte Folke Bernadotte, Swedish diplomat and UN mediator for Palestine, is killed by terrorists in Jerusalem
Apr 26	UK: It is announced that the new GCE (General Certificate of Education) is to replace School Certificates		
		Sep 28	The First Grand Prix to be held at Silverstone
May 3	US: 'A Streetcar Named Desire', by Tennessee Williams, wins the Pulitzer Prize for best US play	**Oct 12**	First Morris Minor comes off the production line
		Nov 2	Harry S Truman wins US Presidential elections
May 11	Italy: Luigi Einaudi (Liberal) becomes president	**Nov 14**	Birth of Prince Charles, Prince of Wales
May 14	Israel is established as a Jewish state	**Dec 1**	UK: National Service is increased from 12 to 18 months
May 16	Israel: Dr Chaim Weizmann is first president	**Dec 10**	T S Eliot wins Nobel Prize for Literature
		Dec 15	France's first atomic reactor begins operation

The Growth Of Communism

As the aftermath of war rumbled across Europe, the intentions of Stalin's Soviet Union became increasingly clear. The wish was to impose by force dependencies in the states of eastern Europe to guard the Soviet Union's western frontier and to gain valuable allies. In Czechoslovakia the Soviet-funded Communist Party organised mass demonstrations and had thousands of armed men at its command. Communist leader Klement Gottwald demanded, and got, extensive concessions from the democratic government. In February tension came to a head when senior government ministers demanded Gottwald be stripped of his powers. Armed Communists moved quickly to capture key government buildings, newspaper offices and radio transmitters. Faced by naked aggression President Benes reluctantly extended Gottwald's powers into a 'Government of the Workers'. Leaders of non-Communist parties were hounded from office or fled abroad. Moderate Jan Masaryk at first joined the Communists, hoping to temper their demands but on 10th March he fell to his death from a government office block. Whether his death was murder or suicide was never clear, but his death gave the Communists undisputed power.

Right: Queen Mary, widow of Britain's King George V holds her great-grandson, Charles, Duke of Cornwall, at his christening in Buckingham Palace. The baptism took place on 15th December, some four weeks after the birth. The choice of name excited comment as the last king to be named Charles was a notoriously 'merry monarch' much given to riotous living and who had a string of mistresses, while his predecessor had lost both his crown and his head in civil war.

THE BERLIN AIRLIFT

On 21st March the Soviet representatives stormed out of the joint control meetings at which British, American, French and Russians determined policy in occupied Germany. On 24th April the Soviets imposed a blockade on the Allied zones of Berlin, cutting them off from the West. It soon became clear that Stalin wanted to starve Berlin into surrendering to a Communist takeover. The British and Americans responded by flying provisions into Berlin in any aircraft that could take to the air. The blockade lasted until May 1949 when the Soviets opened road links. Below: A group of German workers watch an aircraft coming in to land in Berlin. Right: A 7,000 pound consignment of tinned meat is unloaded from a British Sunderland transport aircraft on to a barge which will carry the food from the Havel Lake to the city centre. Bottom left: USAAF air traffic controllers at work in the control tower of Templehof Airport in July. Bottom right: Airmen check in at the Operation Desk at Templehof Airport on 30th June.

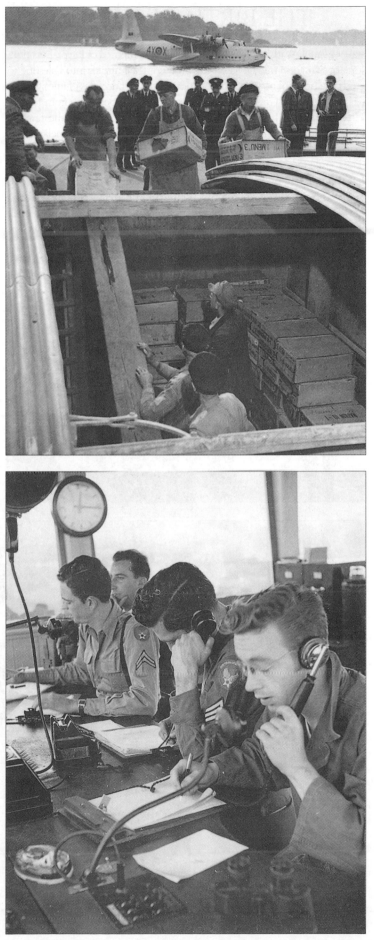

THE BIRTH OF ISRAEL

On 14th April Jews in Palestine proclaimed their nationhood as the new state of Israel. Within days the Arab League, composed of Egypt, Lebanon, Jordan, Syria and Iraq declared war and sent their armies into Palestine to crush the new country. The declaration came after decades of immigration to Palestine which raised the Jewish section of the population from 11% in 1920 to 32% in 1947. The horrific genocide attempted on the Jews by Hitler gave moral credibility to the demand for a Jewish homeland and many nations were prepared to accept this. Britain, however, held a mandate to rule Palestine and were intent on trying to keep the peace between Jewish and Arab militias. After the British withdrawal civil war broke out, followed by the Arab invasion. Despite being heavily outnumbered the Jewish militia fought back savagely and within months had pushed back their enemies. An uneasy peace was agreed in February 1949.

Above left: Police help civilians flee from the bomb blast of 24th February which tore through the Jewish quarter of Jerusalem. A total of 51 people were killed in Ben Yehuda Street, many of them women and children. The Jews blamed British soldiers and murdered nine in reprisal, but it was later revealed Arab terrorists were responsible.
Above: David Ben-Gurion making the radio broadcast in which he proclaimed the independence of Israel on 24th May. Ben-Gurion was born in Poland but moved to Palestine in 1906 and led the call for Jewish settlers in the region during the 1920s and later campaigned for a Jewish homeland. He was to become the new state's first prime minister. Left: Britain lowers the Union Jack over Haifa on 14th May as the last troops leave troubled Palestine.

On 30th January Gandhi, the hero of Indian independence, was shot dead by a Hindu fanatic. Riots broke out in Bombay and other major cities as the homes and offices of extremist Hindus were ransacked. It was Gandhi's moral authority and leadership which gave Indians their belief in the possibility of independence. Gandhi concentrated on passive resistance to taxation, laws and the courts though his actions sometimes led to bitter violence. The eventual freedom for India was credited by many to his leadership, though he refused to take office. Right: Mahatma Gandhi outside No.10 Downing Street during his visit to the seat of Imperial Power in 1931. An Indian Prince who witnessed King George V welcome Gandhi to Buckingham Palace remarked prophetically "That handshake will cost you India." Far right: Gandhi in later life.

POLITICAL SHOCKS

Both America and Germany suffered political surprises this year. In November President Truman (*above*) pulled off one of the great election victories when he defeated Republican Thomas Dewey to regain the White House. Early newspapers had even been printed declaring Dewey the victor, before late results gave the election to Truman. The Truman campaign had been hindered by break away Southern Democrats who took much support from him in the crucial last weeks of campaigning. In Germany the summer of 1948 brought shock news out of East Germany that the Russians had taken over Hitler's Concentration Camps and were using them to intern political opponents. It was estimated that around 16,000 were held in Sachsenhausen Camp in brutal conditions which claimed many lives each day. Above left: A grim sign warns any who get too close to Sachsenhausen Concentration Camp that they will be shot on sight. Left: Bodies strewn outside Schwabmunchen Camp.

The 1948 Olympic Games were held amid post-war austerity and were possibly the lowest key ever held. Despite this, the Games did much to restore the Olympic reputation, badly tarnished by the politicised nature of the 1936 Games held in Nazi Germany. America swept the board with 38 medals. The Games were notorious for the number of defections of East European athletes who refused to return home. Left: Wembley Stadium, in west London, where the main events of the 1948 Olympic Games took place. Bottom left: The crowd applauds athlete John Mark as he carries the Olympic Torch into Wembley Stadium at the opening ceremony. Below: The 800 metre final. Bottom right: The 100 metres sprint leg of the men's decathlon. The event was won by Robert Mathias shown in the centre of this picture.

THE IMPORTANT THING IN THE OLYMPIC GAMES IS NOT WINNING BUT TAKING PART. THE ESSENTIAL THING IN LIFE IS NOT CONQUERING BUT FIGHTING WELL.
BARON de COUBERTIN

Top left: The playwright Tennessee Williams whose classic **A Streetcar named Desire** first appeared this year. Top right: T.S. Eliot who won the 1948 Nobel Prize for Literature with his continuing output of highly emotive poetry. Left: Fred Astaire who hit the movie headlines with **Easter Parade**, in which he starred opposite Judy Garland. Above: A brooding Laurence Olivier as Hamlet in the movie of that name. He took the Oscar for best actor, though he preferred stage work.

Jan 3	US: Tornadoes hit Arkansas, killing 41
Jan 9	Death of British comedian Tommy Handley
Jan 10	US introduces 45 and 33.1/3 rpm records
Jan 10	Birth of George Foreman, boxer
Jan 12	Britain hangs Margaret Allen, first woman to be hung for 12 years
Jan 19	US: President Truman is inaugurated
Feb 1	Clothes rationing ends in Britain
Feb 9	US: Actor Robert Mitchum is jailed for smoking marijuana
Feb 18	Argentina: Army leaders try to force Eva Peron to retire and leave the country
Feb 22	Birth of Nicki Lauda
Mar 1	US: Joe Louis retires as world heavyweight champion
Mar 2	Capt. James Gallagher flies around the world non-stop
Mar 18	Alex 'Hurricane' Higgins born
Mar 25	Denmark agrees to join NATO
Mar 31	Newfoundland becomes Canada's 10th Province
Apr 4	NATO Treaty is signed in Washington DC
Apr 18	Eire becomes a republic
Apr 18	Start of first 'Bob-a-job' week by Scouts in Britain
Apr 20	The first 3 day Badminton Horse Trials
Apr 24	UK: End of chocolate and sweet rationing
May 1	UK: Nationalisation of the gas industry
May 2	US: Pullitzer Prize is awarded to Arthur Miller for his play 'Death of a Salesman'
May 4	Italy's national football team are killed in a plane crash
May 9	Prince Rainier becomes head of state of Monaco
May 9	First self-service launderette opens in London
May 11	Siam renames itself Thailand
May 11	Israel is voted into the UN
May 12	The Soviets lift their blockade of Berlin
May 13	Test flight of Britain's first jet bomber, the Canberra
May 23	German Federal Republic is formed with capital in Bonn
Jun 22	Birth of US actress Meryl Streep
Jun 28	The last US combat troops leave Korea
Jul 19	Birth of Rumanian tennis player Ilie Nastase
Jul 27	Maiden flight of the world's first jet air-liner, the de Havilland Comet
Jul 29	BBC televises the first weather forecast
Aug 6	John Haigh, 'Acid bath murderer' is executed
Aug 16	Margaret Mitchell, author of 'Gone With the Wind', dies after being knocked down by a car
Sep 4	Birth of US golfer Tom Watson
Sep 9	Birth of John Curry
Sep 18	UK Pound is devalued by 30%
Sep 19	Birth of Twiggy
Oct 1	People's Republic is founded in China, Mao Tse-Tung is chairman
Oct 28	French violinist Ginette Neveu is killed when an Air France airliner crashes
Nov 1	US: A fighter plane collides with an airliner killing 55
Nov 15	Nathuram Godse hanged in India for the murder of Gandhi
Dec 26	Einstein's new general theory of relativity announced

Peace And War

The year 1949 saw the world reorganising itself to take account of the new world order which grew out of World War II. Many colonies and protectorates were asserting their independence. In southern Asia the new states of India and Pakistan displayed their freedom by fighting a war over the disputed mountain state of Kashmir. On 1st January the two nations agreed to a ceasefire proposed by United Nations negotiator Charles Nimitz. Hostility smouldered, however, and occasional fighting continued for some years. Elsewhere fighting also subsided, with peace between Israel and the Arabs and the ending of the Chinese civil war. But the coming of peace masked rising tensions between capitalist and Communist power blocs. Rivalry between the Soviet Union and her enemies would dominate diplomacy for decades to come. Many nations would find themselves dragged into the rivalry which earned itself the name of Cold War. Many smaller nations were able to call on super-power help either in local wars or for economic aid and several corrupt regimes survived on such foreign aid. The balance of power between the two power blocs rocked uneasily, but a catastrophic war was avoided. Tensions did not ease until the collapse of the Communist East in the late 1980s and early 1990s.

In 1949 the much detested clothing ration was abolished. Introduced during the war to enforce economy measures, the rationing was continued by the post-war Labour Government as an austerity tool to restrict spending. Fashions had been forced to be economical on cloth to meet rationing requirements, but could now break free. Similar restrictions were lifted on sweets and other items long put under strict control by the government. Right: A delighted Poppie Willmott of Greys in Essex tears up her clothing coupon book on 14th March before going on a spending spree.

COLD WAR STANDOFF

The first great struggle of the developing Cold War ended on 12th May when the Soviet Union lifted its blockade of the western sectors of Berlin. For nearly a year the people living under British, American and French administration had been under siege from Soviet forces intent on incorporating all of the German capital into the newly emerging Communist state of the Democratic Republic of Germany. Supplies were brought into Berlin by air in a massive logistical exercise which saw aircraft arriving in Berlin at the rate of one each minute during peak weeks. Hopes were high at the time that the occupying powers would allow German unification, but such hopes were disappointed and two German states came into being. Below: A bus leaves Berlin across the Elbe Bridge bound for Hanover on the first day that the Soviet Union opened land borders with West Berlin.

Left: Konrad Adenauer, the leading German statesman signs the new constitution of the Federal Republic of Germany into existence on 23rd May. The constitution was the result of nearly nine months of negotiations between a committee of German democrats and the governments of Britain, France and the United States. The constitution allowed for a powerful central state structure but with important powers delegated to regional government based on the traditional kingdoms and duchies of pre-war Germany. Adenauer went on to become the first Chancellor of the Federal Republic, a post he resigned in 1963. As Chancellor he worked hard to rehabilitate Germany in the eyes of the world and to wash away the memory of Nazism. Top left: Mrs Eleanor Roosevelt, US delegate to the United Nations, delivers a keynote speech on human rights in December.

The long civil war in China came to an end in the autumn of 1949. The fighting had begun with the collapse of the Imperial Manchu dynasty in 1912 and by the 1930s the country was divided by the Communists and Nationalists. The Japanese invasion persuaded the two rivals to join forces, but with the defeat of Japan civil war broke out again. The Communists gained the upper hand through skillful use of propaganda and reliance on the peasants. In January Mao Tse-Tung led his Communist forces into the ancient capital of Peking and in May captured the port of Shanghai. By December the Nationalists were totally defeated and took refuge on the offshore island of Taiwan. Right: A Shanghai policeman shoots dead suspected Communist spies as the forces of Mao Tse-Tung advance on the city.

THE BRITISH ECONOMY IN DECLINE

The post war economy of Britain lurched into crisis in 1949 as industr[y] failed to recover from wartime damage and recession seemed a real possibil[it]y. The summer brought large scale industrial unrest with first the Londo[n] dockers coming out on strike to be followed by the railmen. Above lef[t] Police called out to resist violence during the London dock strike in Jul[y] have little to do as the workers contented themselves with peacefu[l] protests. Above: A dockers' picket singles out Canadian ships for action i[n] support of a strike of Canadian seamen. Left: The Flying Scotsma[n] approaching Hatfield. The service was stopped by striking railmen in Jun[e] Facing page: Sir Stafford Cripps speaking in January outlines progress mad[e] on economic recovery, unaware of the crisis he was about to face. Withi[n] a short space of time the economic forces at work would undermine th[e] policy of the Labour government and force an embarrassing devaluation o[f] the pound sterling on the international exchange markets.

Left: Princess Elizabeth and her grandmother Queen Mary watch a military procession from Buckingham Palace in May. Below: Indian prime minister Jawaharlal Nehru meets Dr Albert Einstein at his Princeton home during a formal visit to the United States. Beside Einstein stands Nehru's daughter Mrs Indira Gandhi who would succeed him in the role of India's national leader. Bottom right: Donald Campbell continues his father's quest for speed with the speedboat Blue Bird which he used on Lake Coniston to take the world record for speed on water.

The Comet

The world's first civil jet aircraft took to the skies on 27th July when the De Havilland Comet made its first test flight at Hatfield in Hertfordshire. At the controls was RAF war hero Group Captain John Cunningham, who declared himself delighted with the handling of the aircraft. The design of the aircraft was revolutionary in many ways. Most obvious was its four jet engines, mounted close to the fuselage to allow for light wing construction. But the aircraft was the first to have a pressurised passenger cabin. This allowed the aircraft to reach 40,000 feet at which altitude the jet engines became efficient and powered the aircraft at speeds of around 500 miles per hour. At the time of its construction the Comet was far ahead of any other airliner in service, but it had an unsuspected flaw. After entering service a number of crashes and structural failures caused the Comet to be withdrawn from service. The cause was the previously unknown metal fatigue caused by the stresses of jet power. Above: One of the first Comets to enter regular service.

DEPARTURES FROM THE WORLD STAGE

Left: Top British radio comic Tommy Handley threatening fellow comedian Clarence Wright in a BBC publicity photograph. Handley's tragic early death from a stroke in January brought tributes from the world of showbiz. Below: Handley's coffin leaves a private chapel in London's Westbourne Grove before cremation. Bottom left: Jane Wyman takes the Oscar for best actress for her role as a deaf mute in the movie *Johnny Belinda*, after which she made only a few films before retiring. Bottom right: The boxer Joe Louis (*right*) in his fight with Billy Conn, Louis's 18th successful defence of his world heavyweight championship. Louis had spent 11 years as champion when he announced his retirement from the ring on 1st March.

1950-1959

OE-69-34

Jan 6	Britain officially recognises Communist China	**Jul 18**	Britain bans the sale of oil to China
Jan 12	Death penalty is reintroduced in USSR	**Jul 22**	Canada: Death of ex-PM William Mackenzie King
Jan 21	Death of British author George Orwell	**Jul 26**	Britain sends troops to Korea
Jan 26	India becomes a Democratic Republic within the Commonwealth	**Aug 1**	Australia decides to send troops to Korea
Jan 29	Birth of South African Jody Sheckter, motor racing champion	**Aug 15**	UK: Birth of Princess Anne
		Aug 16	Birth of Jeff Thomson, Australian cricketer
Jan 31	Truman instructs US scientists to make H-bomb	**Sep 3**	A typhoon in Japan kills over 200
Feb 10	Birth of Mark Spitz, American swimmer	**Sep 7**	All religious orders are dissolved in Hungary
Feb 23	Election returns are televised in Britain for the first time	**Sep 11**	Birth of Barry Sheene, motor cycling champion
Feb 26	Death of British comedian Sir Harry Lauder	**Sep 11**	Death of Jan Smuts, Boer War guerila leader and South African Prime Minister
Feb 28	Attlee forms new Labour government in Britain		
Feb 28	France: A bill is passed curbing the sale of Coca-Cola	**Sep 25**	Korea: The Allies recapture Seoul
Mar 12	Wales: 80 Welsh rugby supporters are killed in an aircrash	**Oct 2**	Legal aid becomes effective in Britain
		Oct 6	Lebanon: The world's longest pipeline is completed
Mar 12	Death of German author Heinrich Mann	**Oct 17**	28 are killed in a plane crash in North London
Mar 19	Death of US author Edgar Rice Burroughs	**Oct 21**	Chinese Communist troops invade Tibet
Mar 30	Death of French statesman Leon Blum	**Oct 23**	Death of US singer and actor Al Jolson
Apr 8	Death of Russian ballet dancer Vaslav Nijinsky	**Oct 26**	UK: The House of Commons, damaged in a 1941 air raid, are re-opened
Apr 11	The USSR shoots down a US bomber over Latvia		
Apr 25	First fashion display by Christian Dior in London	**Oct 29**	Death of Swedish King Gustav V
Apr 27	Britain officially recognises the state of Israel	**Nov 1**	President Truman survives an assassination attempt
May 26	Petrol rationing ends in Britain	**Nov 2**	Death of Irish author, playwright and critic, George Bernard Shaw
Jun 8	UK: BBC radio serial 'The Archers' is first broadcast		
Jun 17	US: The first kidney transplant takes place	**Nov 6**	Korea: The first ever combat between jet fighters takes place when a MIG 15 is shot down by a US F86
Jun 25	The Korean War begins		
Jun 26	US: President Truman sends air and naval forces to the aid of South Korea	**Nov 14**	A Canadian plane crashes in the Alps, killing 58
		Nov 26	The Chinese enter the Korean War
Jul 8	Korea: General MacArthur takes over UN forces	**Dec 13**	UK: Marshall Aid is stopped
Jul 10	Soap rationing ends in Britain	**Dec 27**	US and Spain resume diplomatic relations
Jul 11	UK: Children's television programme 'Andy Pandy' first transmitted by BBC	**Dec 27**	Death of German painter Max Beckmann
		Dec 28	The Peak district is designated as first National Park in Britain

With the return of peace the technology developed during the war was put to civilian use. The development of heavy bombers to carry destruction deep into enemy territory was quickly adapted to produce civilian aircraft capable of carrying unprecedented numbers of passengers over long distances. The first such aircraft were simply converted bombers, but in 1947 the Avro Tudor appeared. This four-engined aircraft could carry passengers well over 2,000 miles without refuelling and quickly established itself as a favourite airliner. On 13th March 1950 a Tudor V coming in to land at Cardiff with a cabin packed with 83 Welsh rugby fans and crew, crashed to earth killing all but three on board. Left: The fuselage of the Tudor V lies on its side amid tangled wing wreckage with the village of Sigginston beyond.

THE CRUSADE OF McCARTHY

On 9th February the previously little known US Senator Joseph McCarthy (*below*) launched his crusade against Communist infiltration. In a speech that day he brandished a list of what he claimed were 205 Communist Party members working for the State Department. The accusation struck a chord with many ordinary Americans who were deeply suspicious of Communist designs on the United States. In September the Anti-Communist Act was passed against President Truman's veto and McCarthy could pursue Communists with a will. The campaign gained credibility with the conviction of the Rosenbergs for passing nuclear secrets to Russia. Soon left wingers in all walks of life came under suspicion and the anti-Communist drive eventually became more of a witch hunt than a search for state enemies. McCarthy kept up his crusade until December 1954 when the Senate dismissed him from investigative office.

Top left: South African politician Jan Smuts who died this year. Smuts first rose to prominence as a commando leader during the Boer War of 1899-1902. After the defeat of the Boers he worked for the peaceful integration of Boer and British areas in southern Africa to form the Union of South Africa in 1910. He rose to be Prime Minister in 1939 but was ousted in 1948 by the Nationalist Party which favoured the policy of apartheid over mild segregation of races. Top right: Bertrand Russell, who won the Nobel Prize for Literature in 1950. Born in 1872 Russell concentrated on mathematics before turning to philosophy. He championed the school of constructionalism and campaigned for numerous social causes such as nuclear disarmament.

THE KOREAN WAR

The Korean war was the first 'hot' conflict in the Cold War between Communism and Capitalism. In June 1950 Communist North Korea invaded South Korea in an attempt to reunite the nation by force. By 21st July nearly half of South Korea had been conquered. On that date large numbers of American troops, acting on United Nations orders, began arriving to back up the South Koreans and one month later the Communist advance was halted near Taegu. In September and October the beleaguered United Nations troops, now including units from many countries, broke out of their foothold around Pusan. Co-ordinated amphibious landings at Inchon, Woonsan and elsewhere deep in enemy territory threw the Communists into confusion. The United Nations troops pushed the North Koreans back to the Yalu River, when China intervened. Thousands of Chinese troops flooded into Korea in November and the fortunes of war reversed again. By the end of the year the front line stabilised near the original frontier. Fighting continued until 1953, principally on a small scale with opposing tactical commanders taking advantage of any mistake by the enemy to seize points of importance. No large scale territorial gains were made by either side, however, and the war fizzled out.

Top right: South Korean naval ship No.512 on striking a mine in Wonsan Harbour in December. Above: A US mortar crew in action in June. Above right: North Korean prisoners held in Seoul in October. Right: Unidentified United Nations troops bury their dead on 16th December. Facing page, top: A United States B-26 bomber attacks North Korean supply routes. Facing page bottom: The Canadian destroyer Athabaskan cruises alongside the Australian aircraft carrier Sydney off South Korea.

*Top left: British novelist George Orwell who died on 21st January of tuberculosis. His most popular works include **1984** and **Animal Farm**, both of which warned against totalitarian government. Top right: Irish playwright George Bernard Shaw who died in November after a lifetime of producing popular plays, and outraging society with his cantankerous views. Above: Singing star Frank Sinatra pictured with Grace Kelly. Sinatra's career as a singer and actor was beginning to take off in this year. Right: An armed police guard outside Windscale, Britain's first atomic power station which was constructed this year.*

The Fall Of Tibet

In May the newly secured Chinese Communist government of Mao Tse-Tung turned its attention to Tibet, long a problem for China. At various times over the centuries Tibet had been both a subject of the Celestial Empire and the source of violent raids into settled Chinese lowlands. After 1913 Tibet had been independent on the insistence of Britain who wanted a buffer Himalaya state between British India and both China and the spreading Russian Empire. With the independence of India, Tibet lost its most powerful ally. In May 1950 Mao Tse-Tung sent a message to Tibet's religious god-king the Dalai Lama offering Tibet the chance to join China as an autonomous province. The Dalai Lama refused to sign away his nation's independence and in October Chinese troops poured into the mountain kingdom. India objected, but took no action to help the Tibetans. The nation fell quickly and, after an uprising in 1959, the Dalai Lama was exiled while the monasteries and cultural life of Tibet were systematically destroyed.

* bove: Roger Bannister after winning the mile race at the British Games. Bannister first shone as a undergraduate athlete at xford, but his real glory came in May 1954 when he became the st human ever to run a mile in s than four minutes. Top right: e 14 year old prodigy of the racing world, jockey Lester Piggott, qualifies as a senior jockey with his 40th win on Zina on 20th September. Centre right: Arsenal won the FA Cup for the third time by beating Liverpool. Right: Jim Laker bowls for England against the Rest of the World at Bradford in an historic match.*

Jan 4	Korea: Seoul is captured by the Communists
Jan 10	Death of US writer Sinclair Lewis
Jan 30	Death of German motor car engineer Ferdinand Porsche
Feb 8	Cecil Day Lewis is elected Professor of Poetry at Oxford University
Feb 9	Swedish actress Greta Garbo becomes a US citizen
Feb 14	Tel Aviv: Ben-Gurion resigns
Feb 14	Birth of British footballer, Kevin Keegan
Feb 19	Death of French author Andre Gide
Feb 21	British bomber crosses Atlantic in record 4 hours 40 minutes
Feb 23	UK: Klaus Fuchs, spy, loses his UK citizenship
Feb 26	US: Presidents to be restricted to 2 terms
Mar 4	Kenny Dalglish born
Mar 9	UK: A bill is approved to make separation for seven years grounds for divorce
Mar 15	Martial law is declared in Teheran
Mar 24	UK: The Oxford boat sinks in the University Boat Race
Apr 5	Julius and Ethel Rosenburg are sentenced to death in US for spying
Apr 11	General MacArthur is replaced in Korea
Apr 11	UK: Stone of Scone is found 3 months after theft
Apr 14	Death of British statesman Ernest Bevin
Apr 16	A British submarine disappears with its crew of 75
Apr 19	First Miss World competition
May 3	The Festival of Britain is opened by George VI
May 12	The first H-bomb is successfully tested on Eniwetok Atoll in the mid-Pacific
May 14	South Africa: The 'Coloured' vote is removed from the electoral register
Jun 7	The two British diplomats, Burgess and MacLean disappear in circumstances suggesting they may be Soviet spies
Jun 9	Germany: Execution by hanging of the last Nazis to be convicted of war crimes
Jun 13	Eamon de Valera is once again Irish Premier
Jun 18	The US is given permission for an air base at Greenham Common in Berkshire, UK
Jul 10	UK: Boxer Randolph Turpin surprises the boxing world when he takes the world crown from Sugar Ray Robinson
Jul 13	UK: The Queen lays the foundation stone of the National Theatre
Jul 16	King Leopold III of Belgium abdicates and his son, Baudouin I is the new King
Jul 20	Death of King Abdullah Ibn Hussein of Jordan
Jul 31	Birth of Australian tennis player Evonne Goolagong
Aug 10	Britain and Cuba sign a trade pact
Aug 14	Death of US newspaper tycoon Randolph Hearst
Aug 15	UK: Dartmoor is designated a National Park
Aug 31	West Germans introduce 33 1/3 rpm long-playing records
Sep 5	Maureen Connolly wins US Tennis championship at 16
Sep 13	The UN talks on Palestine break down
Sep 19	UK: Clement Atlee calls a General Election
Oct 6	Death of US breakfast cereal tycoon William Kellogg
Oct 15	Liberal party makes first BBC party political broadcast
Oct 25	UK: At 26, Margaret Roberts (later, Thatcher) becomes the youngest Tory candidate in the General Election
Oct 26	Winston Churchill is British Prime Minister again
Oct 31	Zebra crossings came into effect in Britain
Nov 11	Argentina: Juan Peron is re-elected President
Nov 12	BBC TV's Come Dancing first transmitted

TORIES SLIP HOME

On 26th October Britain held a General Election which saw the last flickerings of an old guard and the first lighting of a torch for the future. The election was called while the Labour Government was beset by economic difficulties of unprecedented scale. The war had so disrupted international trade patterns that attempts to restore the pre-war balance were doomed to failure. At the same time the Labour Government was embarking on a comprehensive nationalisation and socialist programme which was extremely expensive. The combination brought the British economy close to collapse. The Conservative Party, led by war hero Winston Churchill (*above*) took power, though with a narrow majority of just 20 in the House of Commons. It was to be Churchill's last victory before he retired to his Sussex estate. Standing in the election as a Tory candidate in Dartford was the glamorous 26 year old Margaret Roberts (*facing page*). Though she failed to take the seat, she returned later under her married name of Margaret Thatcher to take Finchley and eventually become Prime Minister.

INTRODUCTION OF APARTHEID

The elections of 1948 brought the Nationalist Party under D. Malan to power in South Africa on a platform of White supremacy and anti-British policies. At first the rhetoric was not matched by action, but in 1950 the policy of Apartheid began to be felt in real terms. Meaning 'separate development', Apartheid was based on the concept of allowing the various tribal groups to develop along their own lines in a form of non-integrated multi-ethnic society. The feature that brought international condemnation was the privileges given to Whites over all the native or immigrant groups and tribes. In particular, choice sections of the country were reserved for White ownership. In May 1951 Coloureds, that is non-European immigrants such as Indians and cross-breeds, were put on a separate electoral roll to Whites with the clear intention of depriving them of full voting rights. The dispute about this law, one of the cornerstones of Apartheid, continued for many months before it became enforceable. Above: A Whites-only park bench. Above right: Some typical Cape Town signs.

In the early months of the year increasing economic problems in Britain beset the Labour government and turned its traditional allies, the Trades Unions, against it. Centre, above: London dockers arriving at Bow Street Court on 9th February to show solidarity with seven colleagues charged with organising an illegal strike. Left: Ernest Bevin, the Labour politician who first organised the Dockers Union in 1910 and in 1951 was Foreign Secretary. Above: A mass meeting of 3,000 London dockers vote to return to work on 12th February, but the strike resumed a week later.

286

Left: Aneurin Bevan leaving his home for the House of Commons after announcing his resignation from the Labour Government. He is accompanied by his wife, also a Member of Parliament, Jennie Lee. Bevan was accompanied in his resignation by future Prime Minister Harold Wilson, then President of the Board of Trade, in protest at the way the government policy was changing. Bevan had been Minister of Health since 1945 and it was he who introduced the National Health Service, under which treatment was provided free to all through a system of taxation. His resignation left a gap in the government as Bevan was widely credited as being one of the leading ideologists of the party and had been consistent in his calls for improved welfare ever since his early days as a trade unionist leader in the 1920s.

DISGRACE OF A HERO

General Douglas MacArthur was an American national hero. After fighting in the trenches of World War I, MacArthur served as Chief of Staff before taking command of the Pacific operations against Japan in 1941. When he took command in Korea his troops, and the public, felt confident of success. President Truman, however, was less happy. MacArthur had a habit of issuing political statements without clearing them with the White House. In March 1951 MacArthur threatened to invade China. Truman, intent on containing the conflict, protested and fired MacArthur who returned home to official disgrace, but public adulation. Above: General MacArthur receives a tremendous tickertape reception in New York after his dismissal. Above right: A North Korean captured behind American lines. Right: A battery of American self-propelled 155mm guns, nicknamed Long Toms, pound Chinese positions in April.

BURGESS AND MACLEAN

The greatest spy scandal to hit Britain broke on 25th May, and its reverberations have continued ever since. That morning two high ranking British diplomats vanished. On 7th June it was revealed that one of them, Guy Burgess, was under suspicion of passing atomic secrets to the Soviet Union. It was thought that his friend Donald MacLean, who vanished with him, had tipped Burgess off about the suspicions and that both had fled to Russia. Soon afterwards a third diplomat, Kim Philby, was forced to resign amid suspicion, though the security forces had little evidence against him. Philby fled to Russia some years later and in the 1980s a fourth man, Anthony Blunt, was unmasked as a spy. The crediblity of the British espionage service was compromised and has yet to recover. Left: Guy Burgess. Below: Donald MacLean before suspicion fell on him.

Right: William Randolph Hearst who died on 14th August. Hearst was a flamboyant and popular figure who built his enormous fortune on catering to the mass appeal for sensational and easily understood news. Born in California in 1863, Hearst developed his journalistic talents early in life with the discovery that bold headlines, short articles and lurid language had a mass appeal for the newly literate industrial workers. Building up his empire to encompass a total of eighteen newspapers, nine magazines, a syndicated supplement, a news agency and several radio stations, Hearst became enormously wealthy and loved to flaunt that wealth. He built a huge mansion in California which he called San Simeon and packed with lavish art treasures. His death robbed America of one of her more dynamic talents.

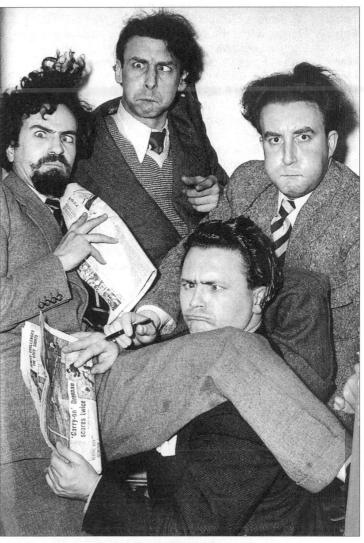

Left: Boxer Sugar Ray Robinson preparing for his 10th July bout with Briton Randy Turpin in defence of his world middleweight championship title. The fight was expected to be an easy victory for Robinson, but Turpin fought with such skill that the battered champion was forced to admit defeat. Below: The crazy quartet of comedians known as The Goons who began their anarchic radio show in March. Left to right are: Michael Bentine, Spike Milligan, Harry Secombe and Peter Sellers.

The Abominable Snowman

In the winter of 1951 the Abominable Snowman leapt into the headlines with a spectacular series of photographs brought back from the Himalayas by a British team led by Eric Shipton who had attempted to scale Mount Everest. The pictures showed a series of footprints running across high snowfields. Each footprint was 13 inches long and was ape-like. Local Sherpa hillmen told Shipton that the tracks were those of the *yeti*, a word which translates into abominable snowman. The beast, they said, was like a giant man some 8 feet tall which was covered in long, reddish hair and lived in high mountain valleys. The hillmen seemed to be frightened of the beast and imbued it with mythical qualities. Over the succeeding years several other expeditions brought back photos of footprints and even hair, but no conclusive evidence as to what the yeti is, or even if it exists. Left: The classic photograph of yeti footprints on the Menlung Glacier brought back by the Shipton Expedition in 1951.

Jan 7	General Dwight D. Eisenhower says he will run for US President
Feb 6	King George VI dies
Feb 8	UK: Elizabeth is proclaimed Queen on her return from Kenya
Feb 15	Funeral of George VI
Feb 21	Identity cards are abolished in Britain
Feb 21	US: Actress Elizabeth Taylor marries Michael Wilding
Feb 29	France: Edgar Faure quits office after 40 days and Paul Reynaud becomes premier
Mar 7	Birth of Isaac Vivian Alexander Richards
Mar 18	Birth of Pat Eddery
Mar 22	Tornadoes hit 5 US States killing 200
Mar 29	Truman pulls out of the US presidential race
Apr 15	Truman signs the peace treaty that officially ends the Pacific war
Apr 21	Death of British statesman Sir Stafford Cripps
May 2	The first scheduled jet flight takes place with a Comet air liner leaving London for Johannesburg
May 6	Death of the nursery education pioneer, Dr Maria Montessori
Jun 15	The Diary of Anne Frank is published
Jul 6	Last London tram runs
Jul 5	American Maureen Connolly, 'Little Mo' wins the Wimbledon singles title at the age of 17
Jul 7	American liner 'United States' makes fastest Atlantic crossing on maiden voyage
Jul 11	US: Eisenhower wins the Republican nomination with Nixon as running mate
Jul 26	King Farouk abdicates in favour of his nine month old so
Jul 26	Eva Peron of Argentina dies
Aug 11	King Hussein becomes King of Jordan due to his father's mental illness
Aug 16	UK: Rivers burst their banks, devastating the resort of Lynmouth and killing 31 people
Sep 2	Jimmy Connors born
Sept 6	Seconds after breaking the sound barrier, a jet aircraft falls apart over the spectators at the Farnborough Air Show, killing 26
Sep 29	John Cobb, land speed record holder, is killed on Loch Ness
Oct 3	Britain detonates her first atomic bomb
Oct 8	Harrow rail disaster, 112 people are killed
Nov 2	Craig and Bentley bungle a robbery and a policeman is killed
Nov 5	Dwight D Eisenhower sweeps to victory in the US Presidential elections with a majority of 6.5 million
Nov 9	South Africa: Seventeen Africans and two Europeans, including an Irish nun, are killed in rioting
Nov 14	NME publishes first singles charts in UK, the Number 1 Record is 'Here in my Heart' by Al Martino
Nov 16	Willie Carson born
Nov 25	Agatha Christie's 'The Mousetrap' opens in London
Nov 30	The US test the first hydrogen bomb on Elugelab in the Pacific
Dec 5	Eisenhower visits the Korean front
Dec 10	Albert Schweitzer wins the Nobel Peace Prize

NEW PRESIDENT ENDS WAR

In 1952 Dwight D. Eisenhower (*above*) was elected President of the United States on a platform which included bringing an end to the Korean War. His landslide victory over Democrat Adlai Stevenson gave him the chance to fulfil his promises, and Eisenhower did exactly that, ably assisted by his Vice President, Richard Nixon. Eisenhower was already well known when he ran for the White House. Born in Texas in 1890, Eisenhower passed West Point in time to fight in World War I but advanced only slowly to be a colonel by 1940. During World War II, however, promotion was rapid and in 1944 he took over Supreme Command of Allied forces in western Europe. The war was followed by a spell as a university president before Eisenhower took command of NATO in 1950. His election in 1952 marked the start of an eight year term which, although not devoid of difficulties, ensured that Eisenhower would be one of the most popular Presidents ever.

The H-Bomb

The year 1952 saw a dramatic new advance in the destructive power available to mankind when the United States tested the H-bomb, or thermonuclear weapon, for the first time. The first blast *(facing page)* took place on the coral atoll of Elugelab in the Marshall Islands. The photograph was taken from a distance of fifty miles and shows the sheer power of the blast. The island of Elugelab vanished utterly, leaving behind only open sea. The thermonuclear device worked by inducing an atomic fission blast, much like an atom bomb, within a shell of lithium deuteride which then produced a fusion blast many times greater than the original. It was estimated that the blast was the equivalent of 15 million tons of TNT and that any combustible material within about ten miles would burst into flames. Death and destruction would be spread over an even greater area. Before long the Soviet Union had also perfected such a weapon and loaded it onto warheads. The fear of total annihilation for the human race began to loom over the world.

Below: On 2nd May the world's first jet air passenger service came into being with BOAC's route from London to Johannesburg. The 7,000 mile route was scheduled to take the unprecedentedly short time of just 23 hours. The first passenger was Mr A. Henshaw, shown here checking in, who had booked his seat on the Comet fifteen months earlier. Bottom right: Jomo Kenyatta arrested in Kenya in October. The arrest followed Mau Mau terrorist outrages and Kenyatta was exiled, though he later returned to be President of Kenya.

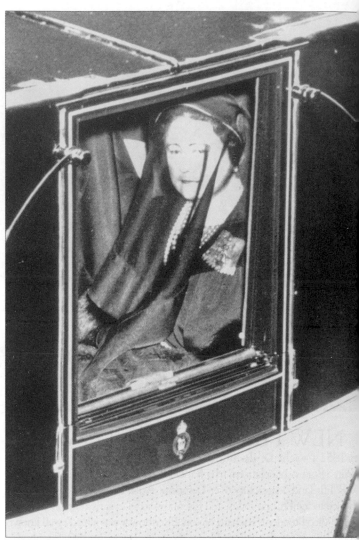

On 6th February Buckingham Palace issued a notice which stated that King George VI had died peacefully in his sleep, and the nation went into mourning. George VI came to the throne because of the abdication, in 1936, of his brother Edward . Though he had been trained as a naval officer, the new king discharged his duties with real skill and great dedication. His sterling behaviour during the war brought him universal admiration and respect. Top left: Three queens in mourning, Queen Elizabeth, Queen Mary and Queen Elizabeth, the Queen Mother. Top right: The widowed Queen Elizabeth drives to her husband's funeral. Above: The Duke and Duchess of Windsor in New York before the Duke embarked on the *Queen Mary* for the funeral. Right: The Queen makes her first Christmas broadcast.

Left: An official informal photograph issued in November to mark the fourth birthday of Prince Charles, heir to the British throne. The Princess Elizabeth had been undertaking a tour of East Africa on behalf of her ailing father when the tragic news of his death reached her. Though in the remote safari location Treetops Hotel, guarded by the redoubtable tiger hunter Jim Corbett, when she received the news, the new queen quickly donned suitable mourning clothing and at once left for Britain, cancelling the remaining parts of her tour. She arrived in time for the funeral which was held on 15th February. Queen Elizabeth II slipped easily into her new role as head of Britain's premier family and though young was able to shoulder the awesome responsibilities which went with the glamour and the wealth.

THE DEVON FLOODS

In August heavy and persistent rain fell on Exmoor, the bleak upland which covers much of northern Devon. The bogs and moss soaked up much of the rainwater, but it fell in such quantities that the moor was quite unable to cope. Sudden and devastating floods swept down from the upland plateau to rush along the normally quiet streams which run down to the sea. In many places the rivers burst their banks without warning and in ferocious manner. Numerous houses had their foundations undercut and collapsed into the roaring waters while many cars and other vehicles were swept out to sea and lost. In all 31 people were killed by the flood waters. Left: Residents in a narrow street in Dulverton begin to clear up the wreckage brought down by the floodwaters. Above: A car washed down through Lynmouth by the powerful rush of the river Lyn and crushed by the strength of the water. Beyond the car can be seen a house torn apart by the floods.

Below: The diminutive but highly popular Maureen Connolly, known as Little Mo, proudly holding the Wimbledon Women's Championship Trophy after winning in 1952 aged just 16. She took the title for the following two years, but was tragically forced to retire after a riding accident.

Right: Film star Humphrey Bogart takes a break from the filming of **The African Queen***, the classic movie released this year. Bottom left: The Czech athlete Emil Zatopek who captured the world's hearts by winning three gold medals in the Helsinki Olympics.*

THE BENTLEY CASE

On 2nd November two London youths, Christopher Craig and Derek Bentley broke into a warehouse intent on robbery. Police arrived while the teenagers were on the roof. Bentley surrendered but shouted "Let him have it, Chris" to Craig who at once opened fire with a pistol. One policeman was killed and others injured before Craig ran out of bullets. At the trial, Craig was convicted of murder but because he was just 16 he could not be hanged. Bentley, however, was 19 and much hinged on the meaning of his words. Were they an incitement to shoot or a plea to hand over the gun? The jury decided on the former and found him guilty. Controversy raged about the case, not least because Bentley was educationally subnormal. Despite pleas for mercy, Bentley hanged on 28th January 1953. Right: Derek Bentley's mother and sister arriving at the Old Bailey to hear sentence passed.

1953

Jan 1	UK: Arthur 'Bomber' Harris is knighted in the New Year Honours list	**May 2**	Stanley Matthews, British football hero, wins his first FA Cup Final
Jan 3	France: Samuel Beckett's play 'Waiting for Godot' has its premiere in Paris	**May 4**	UK: Duke of Edinburgh receives his pilot's wings
Jan 5	Winston Churchill visits President Eisenhower	**May 4**	Ernest Hemingway wins a Pullitzer Prize for 'The Old Man and the Sea' and 'Picnic'
Jan 14	Tito becomes President of Yugoslavia	**May 29**	Everest conquered for the first time, by Edmund Hillary and Sherpa Tensing
Jan 20	US: Eisenhower is inaugurated as President	**Jun 1**	UK: Gordon Richards is the first jockey to be knighted
Jan 31	An Irish car ferry sinks with the loss of 128 lives	**Jun 2**	Coronation of Elizabeth II
Feb 3	Holland: Widespread flooding causes over 1,000 deaths	**Jun 4**	The largest atomic explosion yet is detonated in Nevada
Feb 3	UK: Hurricanes and flooding bring disaster to Britain's East Coast with a death toll of nearly 300 people	**Jun 6**	After 28 attempts Gordon Richards wins the Derby
Feb 5	Sweet rationing ends in Britain	**Jun 7**	UK: Edmund Hillary and Colonel John Hunt are knighted
Feb 23	British WWII deserters granted amnesty	**Jun 18**	Eighteen month old King Faud is deposed and Egypt becomes a Republic
Mar 1	Turkey, Greece and Yugoslavia sign a friendship treaty	**Jun 19**	Atomic spies, Julius and Ethel Rosenberg go to the electric chair in Sing Sing Prison, US
Mar 5	Joseph Stalin, Premier of USSR, dies at the age of 73	**Jul 12**	Martial law is lifted in East Berlin
Mar 5	Death of Russian composer Prokofiev	**Jul 15**	UK: Christie is hanged
Mar 20	USSR: Khruschchev becomes Secretary of Communist Party	**Jul 15**	US: 'Gentlemen Prefer Blondes' starring Marilyn Monroe premieres in New York
Mar 23	Death of French artist Raoul Dufy	**Jul 26**	Fidel Castro is jailed in Cuba
Mar 25	UK: Death of Queen Mary, wife of King George V	**Aug 20**	Morocco: The Sultan is deposed by France
Mar 26	US: Salk vaccine is successful in tests against Polio	**Sep 12**	John Fitzgerald Kennedy marries Jacqueline Lee Bouvier
Mar 28	Death of US athlete Jim Thorpe	**Sep 28**	UK: Ford unveils its new Anglia and Prefect models
Mar 31	UK: John Christie is arrested and charged with murdering his wife following one of London's biggest manhunts	**Nov 9**	Death of British poet Dylan Thomas
		Nov 9	Death of Saudi Arabian King Abd el-Aziz III Ibn Saud
Apr 8	UK: An underground train crashes killing 8 people	**Nov 21**	The 'Piltdown Skull' is found to be a hoax
Apr 15	UK: Christie is charged with the murder of three more women, murders for which a man has already hung	**Nov 27**	Death of US playwright Eugene O'Neill
Apr 16	Royal yacht Britannia launched	**Nov 30**	Iran restores diplomatic relations with Britain
Apr 17	Charlie Chaplin surrenders his re-entry permit to the US under threat of proceedings due to alleged Communist links	**Dec 4**	Australia: A large oilfield is struck
Apr 20	Allied and Communist sick and wounded POWs are swapped in Korea	**Dec 10**	Sir Winston Churchill wins the Nobel Prize for Literature

When Stalin died in March 1953 from a brain haemorrhage, aged 73, many in the Soviet Union heaved a sigh of relief. His later years had been dominated by paranoia and rather odd behaviour. The combination of total power and paranoia led to the infamous purges which took thousands of lives. Before the October Revolution Stalin was involved in various terrorist outrages. He worked ceaselessly to dominate the Bolshevik party system and by the 1920s had an unrivalled grip on the party through patronage and fear. After Lenin's death, Stalin seized supreme power, ousting rivals such as Trotsky who was later murdered. Despite such crimes, Stalin did much to modernise the Soviet Union and his legacy is a mixed one. Left: Stalin's body, surrounded by flowers lies in state in Moscow's Hall of Culture.

295

Khruschchev Takes Over

The death of Soviet dictator Stalin left a power vacuum at the top of the Russian state. For years Stalin had ruled by intimidation and fear. With Stalin gone, the top ranks of the Communist Party were forced to decide on both a new leader and a new direction. On 6th March, the day after Stalin's death, Georgi Malenkov took over as Prime Minister. Malenkov was a trusted aide of Stalin and regarded by many as the natural successor. However, on 20th March Politburo member Nikita Khrushchev *(left)* replaced Malenkov as Secretary of the Communist Party and it was clear a major power struggle was under way. In July secret police chief Beria was charged with being an enemy of the people, stripping Malenkov of his strongest ally. In February 1955 Malenkov himself was ousted and a protege of Khrushchev installed as Prime Minister. Once in power, Khrushchev proved himself an unorthodox Soviet leader by favouring detente with the West, though the Communist grip on power remained absolute.

Top right: A march of petrol tanker drivers on 21st October through East London. The drivers had been on strike for some time and the government was forced to call in troops to make essential deliveries. Above: Gale force winds battered the east coast in February, throwing mountainous seas against coastal defences. The *scene at Felixstow, shown here, is of beach huts, normally in neat rows, flung together by the force of the wind. Right: Two children enjoy the ending of sweet rationing on 5th February. The ration was introduced as a wartime necessity in 1942, lifted in April 1949 but reintroduced as an austerity measure in August 1949.*

Left: A summary execution in the newly formed People's Republic of China. The victim, Huang Chin-Chi was convicted at a local People's Tribunal in Fukang of resisting Mao Tse-Tung's land reform programme. Such brutal and swift justice was meted out to thousands during the early days of Communist rule. Below left: The leading figures of the August conference on the possible strategic use of atomic weapons during wartime. Left to right are: Field-Marshal Viscount Montgomery, General A. Gruenther, Lord Alexander, British Defence Minister, and Sir John Cockroft, the atom bomb scientist. Below: French paratroopers land at Quang-Tri in French Indo-China in one of several military operations against the guerrilla forces working against colonial rule. The unrest was to continue and spread until it engulfed the entire region.

Violence in Kenya

In Kenya violence broke out as native tribesmen tried to oust British rule. Building on traditions of murderous secret societies the leaders of the Kikuyu tribe organised their fighting men into the Mau Mau. Unusual in that it had avowed political aims, the Mau Mau otherwise followed familiar secret society tactics. Cattle were captured or slaughtered, travellers murdered and bush fires started. The aim of driving European farmers off their fertile land in the central highlands led the Mau Mau to concentrate on attacking Whites and dozens were killed. In 1953 the Kikuyu leader Jomo Kenyatta was imprisoned and then exiled for suspected Mau Mau links. Mau Mau, meanwhile, flourished with thousands of followers and British troops had to be brought in to reimpose order on the colony. Self-government was finally achieved in 1963, followed swiftly by full independence. Left: British police and troops of the Devon Regiment search the village of Karoibangi near Nairobi for Mau Mau insurgents.

THE CONQUEST OF EVEREST

In the early 19th century a British surveying team discovered a mountain which they measured to be around 29,000 feet above sea level. They named it Everest after the leading surveyor in India. Ever since teams of mountaineers had tried, sometimes with tragic results, to scale this, the tallest mountain in the world. In February 1953 a team led by Colonel John Hunt left Britain to make yet another attempt. The expedition was planned with meticulous care and great attention was paid to supplies and clothing as well as to actual climbing gear. By the end of May the team had established a string of camps on the mountain, the topmost being only a few thousand feet from the summit. Hunt chose a hardy New Zealand mountaineer Edmund Hillary and a Sherpa, Tensing Norgay, to make the final assault. On 29th May they reached the summit, planted the flags of Britain, Nepal, India and the United Nations and took photographs to commemorate their achievement. A human at last stood on top of the world.

Above left: Sir Edmund Hillary arrives in London accompanied by Khumbo Chumbi a Sherpa elder who guarded jealously what was said to be a yeti scalp. The scalp was later identified as being that of a bear. Above: Edmund Hillary in Bhatgaon before moving off for the high mountains. Left: The expedition's base camp at Thyangboche. Facing page, top: The high base camp at an altitude of 17,500 feet, the highest point which could be reached by pack animals. From here all supplies had to be carried by men. Facing page, bottom left: Sherpa porters carry supplies up the Khumba Glacier with the peak of Everest visible beyond. Facing page, bottom right: A climber crosses a crevasse on his way to Camp 2 using one of the specially constructed ladders.

THE CORONATION OF QUEEN ELIZABETH II

On 2nd June Britain's new Queen Elizabeth II was crowned. Some 2 million people were out on the streets of London that day to watch proceedings. For the first time the ceremony was televised and television sales enjoyed a huge boom in the weeks before the coronation. Facing page, top: The moment of coronation as the Archbishop of Canterbury lowers the crown on to the head of the new queen. Facing page, bottom: The Queen with her maids of honour. Left: The royal coach arrives at Buckingham Palace from the Mall. Below: The Royal Family appears in force on the balcony of Buckingham Palace. Bottom left: Queen Mary, grandmother of Queen Elizabeth II who died before she could attend the ceremony. Bottom right: Queen Elizabeth and Prince Philip photographed after the ceremony.

Jan 6	Ismail Azhari becomes the first prime minister of the Sudan
Jan 11	British Comet jet airliner falls into Mediterranean with the loss of 35 lives
Jan 12	New Zealand: Queen Elizabeth II becomes the first reigning monarch to open the New Zealand parliament
Jan 14	Marilyn Monroe marries ex-baseballer Joe Dimaggio
Jan 21	Launch of Nautilus, first US nuclear submarine
Jan 26	Yugoslavia: Tito is re-elected president
Feb 3	Queen Elizabeth becomes the first reigning monarch to visit Australia
Feb 5	Kingsley Amis's novel 'Lucky Jim' is published
Feb 12	A relationship between smoking and lung cancer is established
Feb 24	American evangelist Billy Graham arrives in Britain for a three month tour
Mar 1	The US tests its second hydrogen bomb and the crew of a fishing boat 70 miles away are seriously ill, suffering from radiation sickness
Apr 3	Oxford wins the 100th University Boat Race
Apr 16	First stock car meeting in Britain
Apr 29	US: J. Robert Oppenheimer, the man who developed the atom bomb is denied security clearance because of alleged links with Communists
May 6	Roger Bannister runs mile in under 4 minutes
May 14	The prototype for the 707 airliner is unveiled by Boeing
May 19	Death of US composer Charles Ives
May 24	IBM announces the development of an 'electronic brain' for office use and plans to rent the 30 models to offices at a cost of $25,000 a month
Jun 2	UK: Lester Piggott becomes the youngest jockey ever to win the Derby, at the age of 18
Jun 21	Australian John Landy beats Bannister's sub-4 minute mile record
Jun 27	First atomic power station goes into service, at Obninsk, Russia
July 3	Food rationing ends in Britain
Jul 10	Gordon Richards rides for last time at Sandown
Jul 15	Maiden flight of Boeing 707
Jul 19	Elvis Presley's first single, 'Thats All Right Mamma' is recorded in the US
Jul 31	Jim Reeves is killed in an air crash
Aug 22	Argentinian Juan Fangio becomes world motor racing champion
Aug 24	US: Eisenhower outlaws the Communist party
Aug 26	J.R.R. Tolkien's 'The Fellowship of the Ring' is published
Aug 29	Roger Bannister wins a gold medal in the 1,500m at the European Games
Sep 3	UK: Fair Isle is bought by the National Trust
Sep 5	Ireland: 28 people are killed when a Dutch KLM airliner crashes into the River Shannon
Sep 9	Algerian earthquake kills 1,500
Sep 17	US: Rocky Marciano achieves his 48th consecutive victory when he beats Ezzard Charles
Oct 13	Chris Chataway breaks the 5,000m record by 5 seconds
Oct 15	William Golding's novel, 'Lord of the Flies' is published
Nov 13	Egypt: Colonel Nasser becomes President after a coup
Nov 22	Death of Andrei Vyshinsky, Soviet Foreign Minister
Dec 10	Ernest Hemingway wins the Nobel Prize for Literature
Dec 21	Birth of tennis player Chris Evert

Above: The launching of the United States Submarine **Nautilus** *on 21st January opened a new era in naval warfare. The submarine's atomic engines did not need oxygen to run and so the ship could remain submerged for weeks at a time. A top speed of 30 knots made her faster than many surface vesse and her array of weapons meant she was a potent instrument of war. Her cost, around $55 millio meant that few sister ships would be built. The use of atomic power for engines led to speculation of nuclear powered merchant ships.*

The Cold War Turns Icy

As 1954 dawned it became increasingly obvious that the rivalry between the Communist states and the western democracies constituted the greatest threat to world peace. The recently finished Korean War had merely revealed the possibilities. The massive growth in the size and numbers of nuclear weapons available to both sides led to growing unease. On 12th January the first of many attempts by the Soviet Union and the United States to reach agreement on arms limitation got off to a shaky start. US Secretary of State John Dulles greeted Soviet Ambassador Georgi Zarubin to the State Department for talks. The Soviet Union had already demanded that the United States stop the testing and production of bombs, a demand rejected out of hand by a US frightened of Soviet capacity for duplicity in its own weapons programme. The talks ended without any meaningful agreement and the arms race continued.

THE FOUR MINUTE MILE

For some years the record time for running a mile had been gradually pushed downwards and by 1954 it stood close to the magic 4 minute barrier. One of the men highly tipped to be the first to break the barrier was British athlete Roger Bannister who held the record for the distance. On 6th May he ran for the Amateur Athletics Association against the University of Oxford in Oxford. Despite a 15 mph crosswind, Bannister set a fast pace and as he crossed the finishing line the crowd thought he may have run in around 4 minutes. When the official announcement was made the crowd roared, Bannister had a time of 3 minutes 59.4 seconds. Below: Roger Bannister breasting the tape after his record-breaking run. Right: Roger Bannister leaves for the British Empire and Commonwealth Games in July together with Chris Brasher (*left*) and Chris Chataway (*right*).

Left: Peter Allis who made golfing history in 1954 when he became the youngest player ever to be picked for the Ryder Cup team. Though only 22 years old, Allis was widely acknowledged to be the finest driver in the business. As son of former Ryder Cup star Percy Allis, Peter had had an early start in golf, taking his first drive at the age of just 18 months. Above: Juan Fangio powers round the Monza circuit in his powerful Mercedes to take first place in the 1954 Italian Grand Prix. Fangio took the World Championship for the second time in 1954, and won it three more times before his retirement in 1958 as the undisputed master of Grand Prix racing.

The highly secretive world of atomic research hit the headlines in April when the leading US atomic scientist was suddenly sacked. It was alleged that J. Robert Oppenheimer was a security risk and could not be trusted on the Atomic Energy Commission. The allegations caused shock and consternation. If he were a spy many secrets were compromised, if not a highly competent scientist was being needlessly persecuted. Oppenheimer had been associated with the atomic research almost from its inception and led the team which produced the war winning atomic bomb for the United States in New Mexico in 1945. Appointed Chairman of the AEC, Oppenheimer attempted to stress peaceful uses for the atomic energy and opposed resources being devoted to the hydrogen bomb. It was probably this which earned him the enmity of the military and led to his disgrace. After his fall from government grace he occupied a post at Princeton University until the year before his death in 1967. Above: President Eisenhower who approved the dismissal of Oppenheimer. Above right: Oppenheimer protests his innocence, but to little effect.

Right: Charlie Chaplin, the star of the silent comedy era, photographed during his much publicised visit to London in October. In the atmosphere of the Cold War, Chaplin's left wing views were regarded with suspicion in Hollywood so he left to live in Switzerland. His visit to England was to hand over a gift of £2,000 to help the poor of London, his native city. Some people expressed the fear that the gift might have an ulterior political motive and dubbed food handouts paid for by the gift 'red soup'. Chaplin denied the charges declaring "I am no Communist. I like peace. I don't understand all these stories."

NASSER TAKES POWER IN EGYPT

On 13th November the world learnt that Egypt had a new master, General Abdel Nasser. The former President Mohammed Naguib had been ousted in a classic coup orchestrated by Nasser as head of the Revolutionary Council. Nasser's climb to power had begun in 1942 when he founded a secret society calling itself the Society of Free Soldiers which aimed at rooting out corruption and foreign influence in Egypt. In 1948 he fought heroically in the war with Israel, and was wounded in action. Four years later he was a leading player in the military coup which pushed King Farouk from power and installed Naguib as President. After taking power in 1954, Nasser showed himself to be a fervent Arab nationalist. In 1956 he nationalised the Suez Canal, causing the brief war with Britain and France, and eleven years later launched a new war against Israel. Domestically, Nasser worked for land reform and showed strong socialist leanings. His dominance in the Arab world was unquestioned and he often spoke for Arabs to the outside world. He was much mourned in Egypt when he died in 1967.

In the early 1950s the increasing ease and cheapness of long distance travel combined with lax immigration laws to make Britain a haven for many Commonwealth citizens looking for work opportunities. First to arrive in large numbers were the West Indians. Below left:

Jamaican immigrants arriving at Paddington Station in October. Some said they had borrowed the £84 fare on the strength of public assistance money they could claim on arrival. Below: Some of the 600 Jamaicans who arrived in Plymouth on 20th October to join the 30,000 already in Britain.

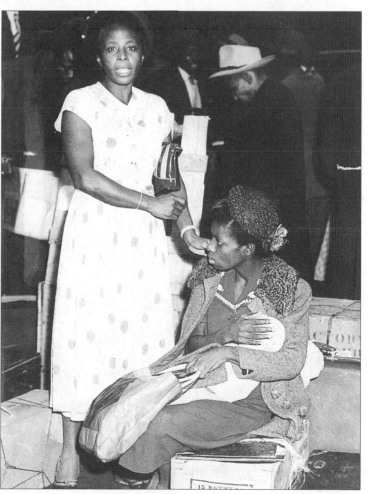

End Of An Empire

The French empire in Indo-China crashed to ruin on 7th May with humiliating military defeat at Dien Bien Phu. The savage fighting followed seven years of largely inconclusive warfare between French troops and the Viet Minh forces working for Communist independence. In November 1953 French General Navarre placed 14,000 men with much artillery into the heavily fortified Dien Bien Phu where they would be in a position to block and disrupt the Viet Minh. Within weeks General Giap had brought up 72,000 Viet Minh and surrounded the French. Navarre found that his much-prized air force was unable to fly in enough payload to keep his men supplied with ammunition and food. In April Giap launched a well co-ordinated assault on the hungry and ill-equipped French. After sustaining heavy casualties, the French surrendered on 7th May. Two months later the French government accepted defeat and pulled out of Southeast Asia.

Top: The legendary Bill Haley and his Comets in typically flamboyant stage poses. The combination of rock beat with country influences produced such early rock and roll classics as **Shake, Rattle and Roll** and **Rock Around the Clock**. Left: Teddy boys at Lowestoft.

The Teddies were a feature of the 50s, with their individual style and long running rivalry with the Mods. Above: The American author Ernest Hemingway who won the Nobel Prize for Literature with his allegory **The Old Man of the Sea**.

an 2	President Jose Remon of Panama is assassinated
an 25	USSR officially ends war with Germany
eb 1	US: Tornadoes hit the state of Mississippi, killing 29
eb 22	Maureen Connolly, 'Little Mo', announces her retirement from competitive tennis
eb 24	Birth of French racing driver Alain Prost
eb 25	HMS Ark Royal, Britain's largest ever aircraft carrier is completed
eb 28	Missing British scientist, Bruno Pontecorvo, says he is working in the USSR
Mar 2	Australia: Severe flooding kills 200 and leaves 40,000 homeless
Mar 11	Death of British biologist Sir Alexander Fleming
Mar 12	Death of US jazz musician Charlie Parker
Mar 24	Tennessee Williams' play, 'Cat on a Hot Tin Roof' has its premiere in New York
Mar 27	Pakistan declares a state of emergency
Mar 28	Lowest test score is recorded-26 by New Zealand against England
Apr 3	Mexico: A train falls into a canyon near Guadalajara, killing over 300 people
Apr 3	The European Cup football contest is set up
Apr 5	Sir Winston Churchill resigns as prime minister and is replaced by Sir Anthony Eden
Apr 7	UK: Harold Macmillan is Eden's new Foreign Secretary
Apr 18	Death of German born US physicist Albert Einstein
Apr 21	Kenya: Two English schoolboys are murdered by Mau Mau terrorists
Apr 28	Ex-model Ruth Ellis is charged with the murder of racing driver David Blakely
May 8	Hiroshoma victims arrive in US for plastic surgery
May 9	West Germany joins NATO
May 14	Warsaw Pact is signed
May 27	Sir Anthony Eden wins the general election
Jun 11	Three cars crash during the Le Mans race and plough into the spectators' grandstand, killing 80
Jun 16	UK: 13 men die when a submarine sinks in Portland Harbour following an explosion
Jun 24	Kenya: Nine Mau Mau activists are sentenced to death for the murder of two schoolboys
Jul 7	UK: A new supersonic plane crashes at the Farnborough Air Show, killing the pilot
Jul 13	Ruth Ellis executed for murder of her 'boyfriend' David Blakely
Jul 17	Stirling Moss wins his first Grand Prix
Jul 18	US: Disneyland is opened at Anaheim, California
Jul 23	Donald Campbell breaks water speed record at 202 mph
Aug 12	Death of German writer Thomas Mann
Sep 19	Juan Peron resigns and leaves Argentina
Sep 22	Commercial TV begins in Britain, with Gibbs SR tooth paste as the first advertisement
Sep 26	Conscription comes into force in East Germany
Sep 30	US actor and teen hero James Dean dies in a car crash
Oct 9	Birth of Steve Ovett
Oct 31	Princess Margaret calls off her wedding to Group Captain Peter Townsend, a divorcee
Nov 5	Death of French painter Maurice Utrillo
Nov 16	US: Donald Campbell sets a new water speed record in his Bluebird speedboat
Nov 24	Birth of British cricketer Ian Botham
Nov 25	'Rock Around the Clock', by Bill Haley and his Comets reaches the number 1 spot in the UK charts
Dec 12	The Hovercraft is patented by Christopher Cockerell
Dec 14	The UN admits 16 new members, but bars Mongolia and Japan
Dec 20	UK: Cardiff becomes the capital of Wales

In July the much awaited Big Four Summit took place in Geneva when the leaders of the United States, Britain, France and the Soviet Union gathered to discuss the tensions and problems which were fuelling the Cold War. For several days the four delegations remained locked in talks remarkable for their openness. On 23rd July the meetings broke up with a joint statement which hailed the talks as a success. Astute observers, however, realised that the most critical issues, such as the future of Germany and the arms race, had not even been discussed. Left: The Soviet delegation await their official vehicles as they leave the first day's talks in Geneva. The leading Soviet representatives include Khrushchev, Prime Minister Bulganin and Foreign Secretary Molotov.

CHANGING FACES OF POLITICS

The year 1955 was a year of change in British politics as both the government and the opposition changed leaders. First to go was Sir Winston Churchill, Conservative Prime Minister, on 5th April. Aged 80, Churchill's last act was to host a formal dinner at No.10 for the Queen. His place was taken by long-standing deputy Sir Anthony Eden. In December Attlee, beset by ideological differences within his Labour Party, resigned. A ballot of Labour MPs resulted in the moderate Hugh Gaitskill taking over as leader of the opposition. Facing page: Sir Anthony Eden arrives at No.10 Downing Street for the first time as Prime Minister. Left: Churchill leaves No.10. Below: Hugh Gaitskill arrives at Transport House, headquarters of the Labour Party, on the evening of his election. Bottom right: Attlee at the press conference called to announce his resignation.

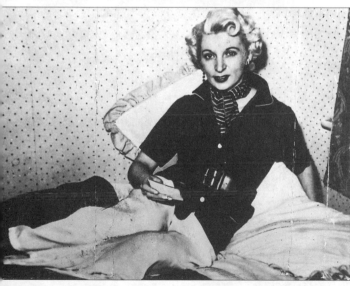

n 10th April Ruth Ellis (above) rode up to her ex-lover David Blakely in a London street and pumped bullets into him, even after he had fallen mortally wounded. An off duty policeman pounced and arrested Ellis. Although there was no doubt of Ellis's guilt, her defence tried to save her from hanging by detailing *extenuating circumstances. The fact that Ellis was recovering from a miscarriage was pointed out, as was the passionate and intense nature of her affair with Blakely and his sudden ending of the relationship. Nevertheless the jury found her guilty and she hanged on 13th July. She was the last woman to be hanged in Britain.*

Death Of A Genius

On 18th April the world's leading physicist, Albert Einstein *(right)*, died in Princeton, New Jersey after some years of heart trouble. Born in 1879 in Ulm, Germany, Einstein did not shine at school. Having worked his way to Zurich University, Einstein showed himself to have a highly inventive mind capable of grasping the fundamentals of particle physics with skill. In 1905 he published his paper on the special theory of relativity and ten years later his general theory of relativity. Together these papers changed humanity's understanding of the universe and made possible both atomic weapons and nuclear power stations. His work won him a Nobel Prize in 1921. In 1933 he left his native Germany due to Nazi persecution of him for his Jewish ancestry and he settled in America. Though his later work lacked the intellectual inventiveness of his early papers, he remained a potent force in the world of physics until his death.

Above left: Albert Schweitzer who won the Nobel Peace Prize this year at the age of 80 for his work as a medical missionary in west Africa. Left: The outstanding hair-dresser 'Teasy Weasy' Raymond who set numerous fashions in hair styling. Above: Princess Margaret with (left) Group Captain Peter Townsend. The romance between the royal princess and dashing war hero pilot first became public when Princess Margaret affectionately brushed a speck of dust from his uniform. However, Townsend was a divorced man and in 1955 Margaret announced she would not marry Townsend.

ight: Possibly the finest right inger ever produced by English ootball, Stanley Matthews pic-red here playing for Blackpool 1955. Matthews was born in 915 and took up professional otball in 1932 when he played r Stoke City. After his transfer to ackpool, Matthews reached ow heights, playing for England no less than 54 matches. His ofessional career ended in *1965 only when he found the arduous training too much to take, his acknowledged skills remaining undiminished. Below: The famous American tennis star Beverly Baker powering her way to victory at Wimbledon in 1955. Below right: French Grand Prix driving star Alain Prost celebrating his winning of the World championship in 1985. He was born in 1955.*

Tragedy At Le Mans

The Le Mans 24 hour race is one of the most famous and popular in the motor racing calendar. It is held on a course largely made up of ordinary roads and is run between two-seater sports cars. Unlike most other races which are won by the driver with the fastest time, Le Mans takes a set 24 hours and the winner is the vehicle which travels furthest. Huge crowds gather for the race which has been held annually since 1923. Their attention is taken not only by the thrilling race but also by a fairground, numerous restaurants and cafes and a host of other entertainments. In 1955 the race came to a tragic end when a Mercedes 300SLR driven by Pierre Levegh collided with an Austin-Healey and spun off the road. It ploughed into the watching crowd at over 180 mph killing the drivers and 83 spectators, and injuring over 100 more. Mercedes at once pulled out of motor sports and did not return to Le Mans until 1988. Left: Some of the 85 victims of the Le Mans crash laid out near the perimeter fence awaiting transport to the local hospital.

1956

STALIN DENOUNCED IN RUSSIA

In the summer of 1956 Soviet leader Nikita Khrushchev made a lengthy speech, the transcript of which ran to fifty pages, which shocked the world. He denounced his predecessor, Joseph Stalin, in terms unheard of in Communist circles. According to Khrushchev, Stalin had been a savage tyrant who was a disgrace to the Communist system. Khrushchev described the purges of 1937 as a totally unnecessary act of brutality against the army. Details of plans by Stalin to arrange the murder of both friends and opponents were revealed for the first time to the outside world. It was said that towards the end of his life Lenin had been worried by Stalin's tendency to repression and execution of opponents but that he had not had time to engineer Stalin's removal from power. On the personal level, Stalin was charged with being rude, arrogant and prone to paranoia and psychotic depression. The outburst staggered the western leaders. Nobody was quite certain how to take the news. Some thought that it showed a genuine desire by Khrushchev to turn against the brutal repression of Stalin and allow more openness. Other commentators suggested Khrushchev was merely showing his power within the Communist state by being able to blacken the name of a past ruler. Such contradictory signals became a regular feature of the Khrushchev regime. Above: Khrushchev (left) and Bulganin on their visit to Britain in April.

In the states of eastern Europe many demonstrations against Soviet repression broke out during the summer, encouraged by Khrushchev's own attack on Stalin. Nowhere was this unrest more determined than in Hungary. The premier Imre Nagy had introduced many reforms, but was thrown out of office by his own party following pressure exerted by the Russians. In October Nagy supporters took to the streets and police opened fire as rioting began. On 23rd October the Hungarian Communist Party agreed to return Nagy to office, on condition that he used Soviet troops and Hungarian police to restore order. Nagy agreed. His capitulation to Soviet force sparked intense anger among those who had been his supporters and civil unrest worsened. In western Hungary rebels declared an independent republic based at Gyor. On 4th November Soviet tanks backed by hordes of troops poured into Hungary while the Soviet air force launched strikes at numerous targets. Nagy turned against such aggression and ordered his army to fight. Resistance against the vast armoured might of the Soviets was short-lived, especially after Hungarian Communists subverted the army. Nagy was arrested, despite a promise of free movement, and Hungary fell beneath a more repressive regime than before. Above: Soviet tanks outside the main Budapest railway station on 30th October. Left: Hungarian soldiers, loyal to the Gyor regime, man a roadblock.

THE INVASION OF SUEZ

Deteriorating relations between Egypt and the West led to war over the Suez Canal in November. Tension began to rise when Anglo-American funding for the Aswan Dam was withdrawn in protest at the policies of President Nasser. In response Nasser seized all revenues from the Suez Canal, owned jointly by France and Britain. British premier Sir Anthony Eden was furious, but was persuaded by the US to lay the case before UN arbitration. By October the talks had got nowhere and Eden, together with French premier Mollet, was clearly losing patience. On 29th October Israel invaded the Sinai Peninsula and headed for Suez. Many suspected that Eden had prompted the invasion. A joint Anglo-French force was dispatched to the eastern Mediterranean and, on 4th November, invaded Egypt. The Egyptian air force was battered and attacks by British ground troops swept all resistance aside. However, United Nations resolutions condemned the move and when it became clear that the US was not backing Britain, the invasion came to a halt. Within weeks all British and French troops were withdrawn. It was an humiliating climbdown for the British and French.

Top left: Earl Attlee, the former Labour Prime Minister talks to Hugh Gaitskill, the current Labour leader at the Party Conference in Blackpool in October. Above: Women workers from Cricklewood protest as they wait to meet their MP in July. The protest was sparked by a slump in the car industry which led to a strike recommendation for the 40,000 BMC workers in July. Above right: Archbishop Makarios who was deported from Cyprus by British authorities who exercised a protectorate over the island state and were concerned about support for terrorists by Greek Cypriot clergy. Right: British soldiers watch a liner pass through the Suez Canal during their occupation of the Canal area in November.

Top left: Film star Marilyn Monroe in London with her new husband, the playwright Arthur Miller, who she married on 29th June. Monroe was met at London Airport by the British acting couple Laurence Olivier and Vivien Leigh. Monroe was in Britain to make the movie **The Sleeping Prince**, in which she starred opposite Olivier. Left: The wedding of the year was without doubt that of Prince Rainier of Monaco to the Hollywood film star Grace Kelly on 19th April. The ceremony was endowed with all the gravity of a state ceremony with the Prince inviting some 1,200 guests from around the world. The couple met when Kelly was in Monaco in 1955 to shoot the movie **To Catch A Thief**, and Kelly eagerly gave up her film career for the life of a royal wife. Top right: Margot Fonteyne dancing **Les Sylphides** with the Festival Ballet in Monte Carlo in January.

Jan 9	UK: Anthony Eden resigns
Jan 9	UK: The Post Office introduces TV detector vans to track down licence dodgers
Jan 10	UK: Harold Macmillan appointed Prime Minister
Jan 14	Death of US actor Humphrey Bogart
Jan 20	US: Eisenhower and Nixon are sworn in for a second term
Jan 23	Monaco: Caroline, the first child of Princess Grace, is born
Feb 21	Israel rejects US and UN demands for withdrawal of her troops from the Gaza Strip
Feb 23	Fidel Castro, believed to have been killed in December of last year, is directing a revolution from hiding
Mar 6	Ghana becomes an independent state in Commonwealth and joins UN
Mar 6	Ireland: De Valera wins the general election at the age of 75
Mar 11	Death of US explorer Admiral Byrd
Mar 17	UK: A plane crashes in Manchester and British European Airways recalls all Viscount turbo-prop airliners
Mar 25	EEC is formed by the Treaty of Rome
Apr 1	West German scientists refuse to work on nuclear weapons
Apr 11	Singapore is granted self-government from Britain
Apr 24	UK: BBC broadcasts Patrick Moore's 'The Sky at Night' for the first time
Apr 25	King Hussein of Jordan proclaims martial law
May 1	UK: A plane crashes at Blackbush airport killing 31
May 2	Death of US politician Senator Joseph McCarthy
May 3	South Africa drops 'God Save the Queen' as its national anthem
May 15	Britain drops her first hydrogen bomb, on Christmas Island in the Pacific
May 15	Billy Graham begins crusade in New York
May 21	France: Premier Guy Mollet resigns
May 31	US: Arthur Miller faces up to a year's imprisonment for refusing to give the names of other allegedly Communist writers
Jun 1	UK: First premium bond winner selected by ERNIE
Jun 3	UK: Sir Anthony Eden says his political career is over
Jun 13	US: Dr Martin Luther King meets with Vice-President Nixon to discuss race issues
Jun 28	Death of German author Alfred Doblin
Jul 6	American Althea Gibson wins Wimbledon final
Jul 12	Prince Karim, aged 20, is declared Aga Khan on the death of his grandfather
Aug 7	Death of US comedian Oliver Hardy
Aug 29	US: An instrument for measuring the amount of alcohol on the breath is tested
Aug 31	Malaya achieves independence
Sep 20	Death of Finnish composer Jean Sibelius
Oct 4	USSR launches first space satellite
Oct 11	Radio telescope at Jodrell Bank goes into operation
Oct 12	Queen Elizabeth visits Canada
Oct 24	Death of French fashion designer Christian Dior
Oct 27	Birth of footballer Glen Hoddle
Nov 3z	The dog "Laika" launched in Sputnik II, the first dog in space
Dec 9	Birth of US singer Donny Osmond
Dec 19	Regular London-Moscow air service is introduced
Dec 25	The Queen makes her first Christmas TV broadcast

THE TREATY OF ROME

In 1957 six nations of Western Europe signed the Treaty of Rome to bring into being the European Economic Community. Representatives of West Germany, France, Italy, Belgium, the Netherlands and Luxembourg had spent many months working on the details of the Treaty. It was eventually agreed that the Treaty would set up an intergovernmental body, with powers of its own, to oversee economic relations and policies. While the overall aim was to establish a common market, or free trade area, the domestic concerns of many politicians led to numerous exemptions, particularly in farming. The Common Agricultural Policy was exceptionally complex and laid itself open to abuse. The structures of the EEC were based around an Assembly of political figures and a powerful bureaucracy known as the Commission, appointed by national governments. From its inception the EEC was a centre for controversy. Some of its founders saw it as a trading body, but others dreamed of European political union. Below: Signor Martino signs the treaty for Italy.

In September racial integration reached a watershed in Little Rock, Arkansas. State Governor Faubus called out the National Guard on 2nd September to stop Negro students attending a whites-only High School. A large crowd of white residents gathered to back up the Guard and some violence broke out. After repeatedly trying to persuade Faubus to change policy, President Eisenhower sent federal troops to Little Rock on 25th September to force the racial integration of schools. Top left: White students watch proceedings. Above: National Guardsmen block the path of a black student. Right: President Eisenhower warns of international Communism on the Voice of America overseas radio service. Facing page: A building crashes to the ground in a scene of London's Burning.

Donald Campbell broke the world water speed record twice in November 1957. Using his specially built craft *Bluebird II*, Campbell raced across the placid waters of Lake Coniston powered by an aircraft jet engine. On 7th November Campbell set a speed record of 225 miles per hour (below right) over the measured kilometre. As laid down in the rules of the Union of International Motorboating, the speed was the average of two runs. Next day Campbell climbed back in to *Bluebird II* to push his two run average speed up to 239 miles per hour. After the run he climbed out (below) to declare that, although happy with his feat, he intended to scrap *Bluebird II* in order to build *Bluebird III*, a craft he estimated would be capable of 300 miles per hour.

Right: Farm workers, watched by Ministry of Agriculture officials, pour hundreds of gallons of milk down the drain. The milk was produced in the vicinity of the Windscale Atomic Power Station where a fire broke out in October, spreading radio-active material across some 200 square miles of surrounding countryside. Milk and crops in the affected area had to be destroyed. Bottom right: The last mail pony in Britain was retired in July. The route across Welsh mountains near Tregaron in Cardiganshire covered some 30 miles. The pony, Mab, was replaced by a land rover. Facing page: The Jodrell Bank telescope was completed in June. It was the world's largest movable telescope with a dish diameter of 250 feet.

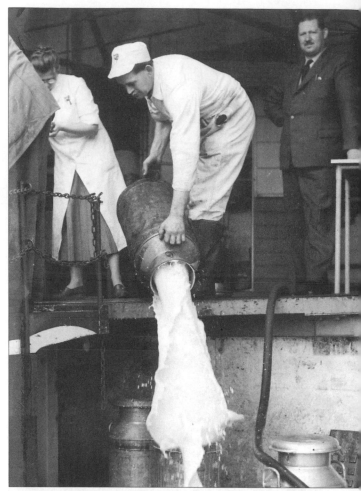

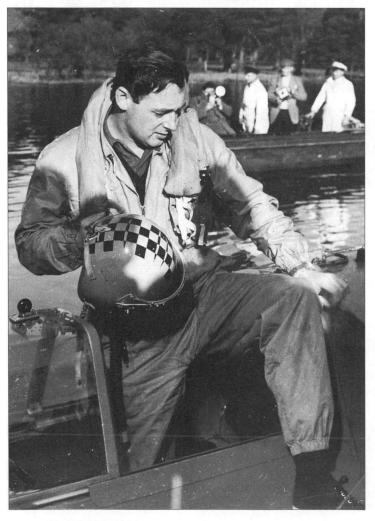

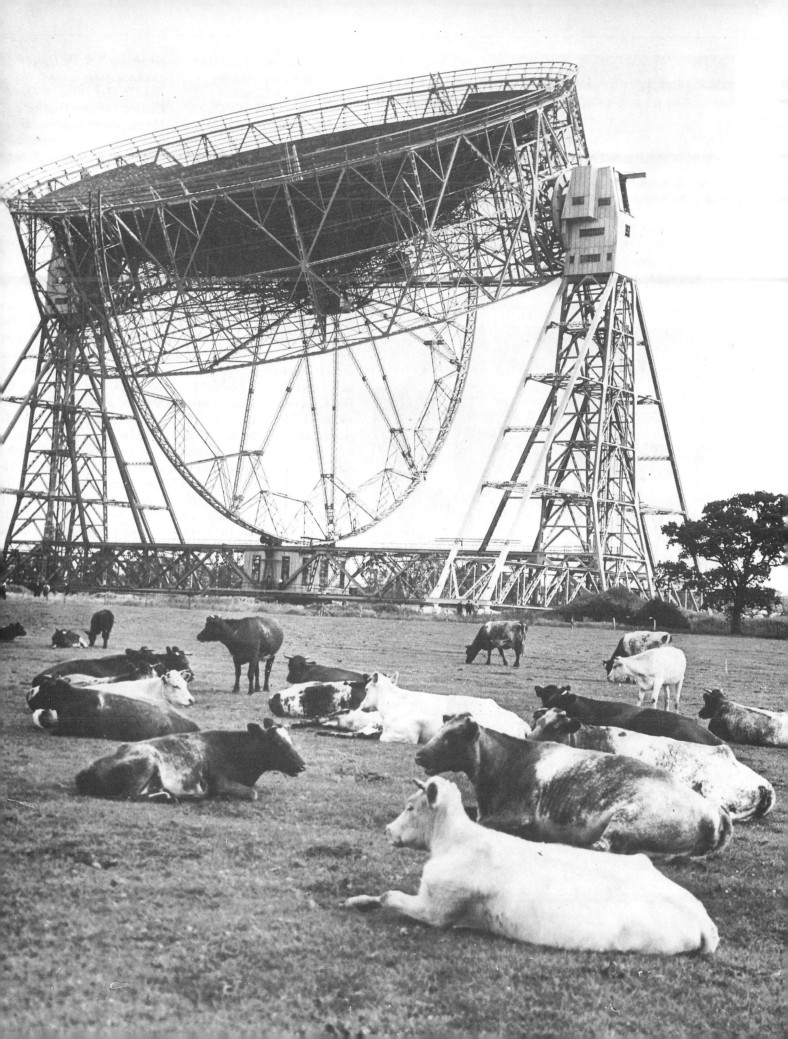

In October Elizabeth II undertook a state visit to North America. After opening the Canadian Parliament in Ottawa the Queen and Prince Philip moved on to Washington to see President Eisenhower. Left: The Queen's cavalcade makes its way to New York City Hall. Below left: Queen Elizabeth welcomes President and Mrs Eisenhower to the British Embassy for a formal state dinner

THE FALL OF EDEN

British politics fell into turmoil in January when premier Anthony Eden was forced to resign by his own Conservative Party. The fall of Eden followed his decision to launch the Suez Invasion the previous November. When, in July Egyptian President Colonel Nasser seized the Anglo-French owned Suez Canal, Eden believed that Britain's vital interests were at stake. He feared that a hostile power in charge of Suez could seriously disrupt British trade during peace and her naval power during times of war. Together with French premier Guy Mollet, Eden planned a joint invasion of Suez to wrest control of the canal away from Egypt. On 29th October the Israelis invaded the Sinai and headed for Suez. Claiming to be acting to safeguard the canal from the growing Egypt-Israeli war, an Anglo-French invasion by amphibious forces backed by paratroops and bombers began on 1st November. It was widely suspected that the Israelis had been encouraged to invade by the British. All military objectives were quickly seized and total success seemed assured. The US, backed by the Soviet Union, then stepped in to demand a peaceful settlement and the withdrawal of all foreign troops from Egyptian soil. Eden was forced into a humiliating climbdown, halting military operations on the 5th November and pulling British troops out in December. His failure to gain American backing, or at least neutrality, was blamed for the mess and the Conservative Party pushed him out. He was replaced on 10th January by Harold MacMillan. Below left: Anthony Eden leaves No.10 Downing Street claiming bad health as the reason for his resignation. Below: Harold MacMillan, the new Prime Minister enters No.10.

320

The Year Of Missiles

Major advances in the technology of missiles were made in 1957. First was the installation of guided missiles around New York in April. Dubbed the Nike Hercules system, the ring of missiles was designed to destroy incoming Soviet Nuclear weapons. The fact that the Nike Hercules missiles themselves had nuclear warheads was dismissed by the Pentagon as unimportant as the risk of fallout from an air blast was "next to nothing". In June the first US intercontinental ballistic missile named the Atlas exploded during its maiden test launch. Scientists were, however, confident they knew the fault and work continued. In August the Soviets outdid the Americans by successfully testing a missile which flew thousands of miles before landing in the target area. The testing of fusion warheads capable of being carried by the missile alarmed American strategists. In December the Atlas finally flew successfully and the world entered a new stage of Cold War standoff.

Top left: Boxer Floyd Patterson celebrates his knockout victory over Tommy Jackson in the 12th round to retain the world heavyweight title. Top centre: Sir Laurence Olivier starred in John Osbourne's **The Entertainer** *to wide critical acclaim. Top right: Alec Guinness shows the award he received from the Variety Club as Actor of the Year on 8th April. Left: Buddy Holly (right) and the Crickets who stormed to success in the world of rock and roll music this year with a string of hits written by Holly. Above: The classic movie comedy duo of the 1920s and 1930s, Laurel and Hardy. Oliver Hardy died of stroke on 7th August, finally breaking up the partnership.*

1958

Jan 1	West Germany joins NATO
Jan 3	Holland: The banks are nationalised
Jan 10	'Great Balls of Fire', by Jerry Lee Lewis reaches the number 1 spot in the charts
Jan 20	In a race to the South Pole, Sir Edmund Hillary arrives 17 days ahead of Dr Vivian Fuchs of Britain
Jan 24	Elvis Presley's 'Jailhouse Rock' goes straight in at number 1 in the charts
Jan 30	23 year old Yves St Laurent is recognised as an extraordinary talent in the design world
Feb 1	US puts its first satellite into space
Feb 7	Most of the Manchester United football team are killed in the Munich air disaster
Feb 9	Birth of Sandy Lyle
Feb 17	UK: CND (Campaign for Nuclear Disarmament) is founded
Feb 28	US: A school bus plunges into a river, killing 28
Mar 2	Vivian Fuchs completes 1st overland crossing of Antarctica
Mar 14	Death of British suffragette Dame Christabel Pankhurst
Mar 16	UK: Mothers who work full-time are condemned as the enemy of family life by the Bishop of Woolwich
Mar 21	London Planetarium opens
Mar 24	Elvis Presley begins his National Service in the US Army
Apr 2	US embargo on arms shipments to Cuba
Apr 5	Castro begins 'total war' against Cuban dictator Batista
Apr 17	South Africa: The Nationalist Party wins the general election for the third time successive time
May 27	State of Emergency declared in Ceylon
Jun 1	Iceland extends fishing limits to 12 miles
Jun 4	First Duke of Edinburgh awards are presented
Jun 9	UK: New £7 million facilities at Gatwick Airport are opened
Jun 16	Hungary: Former Prime Minister Ferenc Nagy is hanged
Jul 6	Alaska becomes 49th State of US
Jul 10	UK: Parking meters come into operation
Jul 14	Iraq: King Feisal is murdered during a coup
Jul 24	First life peerage awarded in Britain
Jul 30	Birth of British athlete Daley Thompson
Aug 7	UK: The Litter Act comes into force
Aug 24	Death of Johannes Strijdom, South African prime minister and enforcer of apartheid
Aug 26	Death of British composer Vaughan Williams
Aug 29	Birth of US pop star Michael Jackson
Sep 2	South Africa: Dr Hendrik Verwoerd succeeds Strijdom as premier
Sep 3	Martin Luther King arrested for loitering in Alabama
Sep 9	UK: Race riots in Notting Hill Gate, London
Sep 12	US: The governor of Arkansas closes all high schools in Little Rock
Oct 9	Death of Pope Pius XII
Oct 9	Yankees defeat Braves to win World Series
Oct 25	UK: Albert E. Mundy of Aldershot scores a goal wiithin six seconds of the start of a match against Hartlepool United
Oct 28	Vatican City: Cardinal Roncalli is elected Pope John XXIII
Oct 31	Stockholm: The first internal heart pacemaker is implanted
Nov 15	Death of US actor Tyrone Power
Nov 21	Work begins on Forth Road Bridge, the longest suspension bridge in Europe
Dec 5	First STD telephone service inaugurated in Britain
Dec 5	First motorway opens in Britain (8 1/2 miles of the M6)
Dec 16	NATO rejects Soviet plans for Berlin
Dec 21	France: General de Gaulle is elected President

In December the United States made history when they launched a squirrel monkey into space on board a Jupiter rocket and then brought it safely back to Earth. The success showed clearly that no phsiological damage occurred in weightless conditions as had been feared. The headline grabbing flight of dog Laika on a Soviet craft the previous year had ended with the unfortunate death of the dog. Above: The Jupiter missile preparing to blast off from Cape Canaveral on her 1,700 mile flight into space carrying her special passenger.

The First Hovercraft

It was in 1958 that the first hovercraft capable of carrying a human was produced. The craft was built on the Isle of Wight by the aircraft company Saunders-Roe and this ancestry was to have a great influence on the hovercraft. Journeys have always been termed 'flights' and the crew on commercial hovercraft bear ranks on a par with civil airline staff although the skills needed usually have more in common with naval pilots. The man behind the new machine was inventor Christopher Cockerell who had produced a working model with his own money. The model so impressed the National Research Development Corporation, a government body, that they put up the money to produce the SR-N1. The subsequent development of the hovercraft was not so straightforward with failures and successes vying with each other for the headlines. Within only a few years, though, hovercraft were being built for civil sea crossings, especially in the English Channel, and for inshore naval work.

On 7th February the bright stars of English football were killed in an horrific crash at Munich's Rhiem Airport. The Manchester United team, known by its fans as Busby's Babes after the manager Matt Busby, were returning from a match with Red Star Belgrade when their aircraft crashed in a snow storm when attempting to take off. Eight of the team were killed, including three England internationals, and others were severely injured. Left: The wreckage of the BEA Elizabethan at Munich. Below: The Manchester Team pose for a photo before leaving for their tour. Below left: Albert Scanlon is visited in Munich Hospital by the Manchester United Deputy Manager. Bottom right: Bobby Charlton back at his home in Beatrice Street, Ashington, on 24th February kicks his first football since the crash.

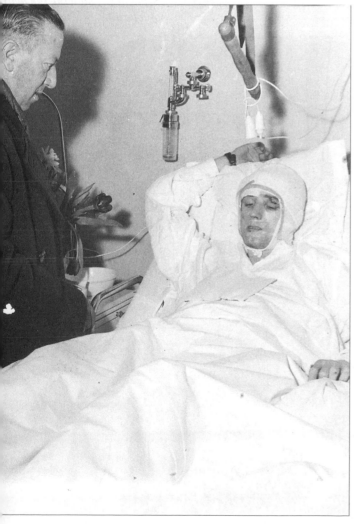

THE VOODOO DICTATOR

In 1958 Francois Duvalier secured his dictatorial hold on Haiti after being elected President the previous year. Duvalier first rose to prominence as a public health specialist who campaigned for proper drainage and sanitation, earning himself the sobriquet 'Papa Doc'. He became active in politics and was embroiled in the tortuous events following the military coup of 1950. Once in power he turned the indiginous Voodoo religion into an instrument of terror backed up by his infamously violent secret police the Tonton Macoute, who were arch practitioners of Voodoo. Duvalier retained his absolute grip on power until his death in 1971. His son Jean Claude, known as 'Baby Doc', continued his policy of rule by Voodoo until he was ousted by an internal rising in 1986. Right: Francois Duvalier backed by Lucien Cahuvet, the sinister Interior Minister, at a press conference.

Top left: Julie Andrews surrounded by bouquets from well wishers after the first night of the musical **My Fair Lady** at the Drury Lane Theatre in London. Top right: British film stars John Mills and Sylvia Syms pictured in their roles for the classic World War II movie drama **Ice Cold in Alex**, set in the arduous North Africa desert campaign. Above: A scene from Dr. Zhivago, made by David Lean. The realistically chilly Moscow winter scene was actually shot in sultry Madrid. Right: The great rock star Elvis Presley has his famous black locks clipped off as he joins the US Army after being drafted in March. Presley won much praise for being prepared to pull his weight and not attempting to gain special privileges.

Jan 1	Batista, director of Cuba, flees to Dominica
Jan 1	Fidel Castro seizes power in Cuba
Jan 1	UK: Alec Guinness is knighted in New Year's Honours
Jan 21	Death of American film director Cecil B. de Mille
Jan 22	British racing driver Mike Hawthorn is killed in a car crash just after becoming world champion
Feb 1	Swiss referendum turns down votes for women
Feb 3	Death of US singer Buddy Holly
Feb 7	Death of Daniel Francois Malan, creator of apartheid in South Africa
Feb 16	Birth of US tennis player John McEnroe
Mar 3	Death of US comedian Lou Costello
Mar 18	Hawaii becomes 50th State of US
Mar 26	Death of American author Raymond Chandler
Mar 27	A hurricane devastates Madagascar, killing over 3,300
Mar 28	Two monkeys return alive from a space trip
Apr 9	Death of US architect Frank Lloyd Wright
Apr 21	A great white shark is caught at Denial Bay, S. Australia, using a rod and line. It weighs in at 2664 lb, and measures 16 feet 10 inches
May 14	UK: Donald Campbell sets a new water speed record of 260.35 mph
May 24	Empire Day is re-named Commonwealth Day
May 24	Death of US statesman John Foster Dulles
May 30	Auckland Harbour Bridge is officially opened
Jun 17	UK: Liberace successfully sues the Daily Mirror for implying he is homosexual
Jun 26	Canada: Queen Elizabeth II opens St. Lawrence Seaway
Jul 3	Number 1 record is Dream Lover by Bobby Darin
Jul 6	German artist George Grosz dies
Jul 17	Death of US singer Billie Holliday
Jul 21	First nuclear merchant ship is launched in US
Jul 31	'Living Doll', by Cliff Richard reaches number 1 in the charts
Aug 4	UK: Barclays Bank becomes the first to use a computer for its branch accounts
Aug 18	UK: The new mini-car is revealed
Aug 24	UK: The House of Fraser is set to take over Harrods of Knightsbridge
Sep 20	Soviet Premier Khrushchev is denied a visit to Disneyland for security reasons
Sep 22	China is refused entry into the United Nations
Sep 25	Solomon Bandaranaike, Prime Minister of Sri Lanka, is fatally shot
Sep 26	UK: Manny Mercer, the jockey, is killed in a parade prior to a race at Ascot
Oct 3	UK: Post codes are introduced
Oct 4	USSR: Lunik III is launched
Oct 9	UK: Macmillan's Tory party win the general election
Oct 9	Margaret Thatcher is elected a Tory MP
Oct 14	Death of British actor Errol Flynn
Oct 16	France: Francois Mitterrand narrowly escapes assassination
Nov 2	UK: The first motorway service station, The Watford Gap, opens on the M1
Nov 19	The government announces the re-introduction of £10 notes with the Queen's head on them
Nov 28	The dockyard in Hong Kong closes after 80 years
Dec 3	France: A dam collapses and 300 people are feared dead on the French Riviera
Dec 14	Cyprus: Archbishop Makarios is elected country's 1st President

THE TRIUMPH OF DE GAULLE

On 8th January Charles de Gaulle returned triumphant to the Elysee Palace as the new President of France. His rise to power followed months of hectic, and at times dangerous, power play between rival factions within France and her colonies. After leading the Free French forces throughout World War II, de Gaulle played a leading role in establishing the new French consitution before retiring from public life in 1946. In 1958 the bitter struggle between French forces in Algeria and indiginous Arabs wanting independence was reaching crisis point. Warfare was endemic but the many thousands of French settlers saw no reason to abandon their homes and businesses and were a potent political force. In May the settlers rioted and the army was given special powers to restore order. The army, however, was on the settlers' side and called on war hero de Gaulle to take charge. On 1st June de Gaulle was appointed French prime minister and three days later visited Algiers. Using all his powers of persuasion and relying heavily on his reputation, de Gaulle persuaded the settlers to accept a free election to decide the future of Algeria. Back in France in September he organised the constitution of the 5th Republic and in the first elections held in January became President with 78% of the vote. Above: The official portrait of de Gaulle released after his installation as President.

CASTRO TAKES CUBA

On 1st January Cuba's President Fulgencio Batista fled to the Dominican Republic. The shock move brought to an end six years of unrest and civil war against the revolutionary movement led by Fidel Castro, backed by expert guerrilla Che Guevara. On the 8th January Castro marched into the capital Havana amid great rejoicing by the ordinary people who rushed out into the streets to greet him. Castro began by freeing the press and declaring the full return of human rights and democracy. Within a few months, however, Castro had strengthened his position and no longer needed the help of other political movements. A more authoritarian regime was introduced by Castro and former Batista supporters were rounded up and shot. In 1961 he declared himself committed to the Marxist-Leninist doctrine, moving closer to the Soviet Union. Right: Fidel Castro during his inaugural speech as Prime Minister on 16th February. Below: Castro and his guerillas in the days of his struggle against the Batista regime.

In February British premier Harold MacMillan travelled on what he called a 'voyage of discovery' to visit both the Soviet Union and the United States. MacMillan was met by Khrushchev at Moscow Airport. The two later visited the Bolshoi Ballet and Leningrad. Though progress on arms talks was limited MacMillan was pleased with agreements on increased trade. The visit to the United States was much more relaxed with Britain and America being in 'complete agreement'. Left: Soviet leader Nikita Khrushchev welcomes British premier Harold MacMillan to Moscow on 21st February. Facing page: Pandit Nehru together with his daughter Indira Gandhi and her children. In February Mrs Gandhi was elected to lead the Congress Party which she managed to unite after months of discord and lead back to power in India.

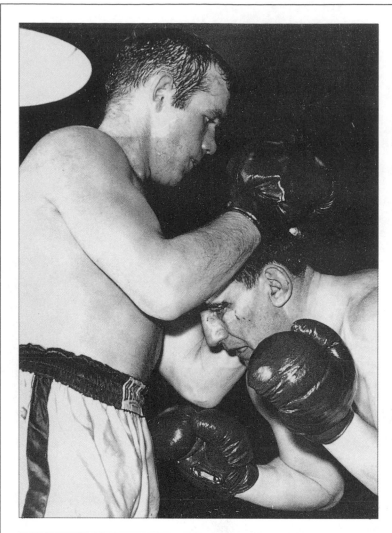

Top left: The British boxer Joe Erskine ducks to avoid a powerful blow from Swedish boxer Ingemar Johansson during the 21st February bout to decide the European heavyweight Championship. Johansson won by a technical knockout in the 13th round.
Top right: Stirling Moss roars to victory in the Italian Grand Prix on 15th September. Moss came close to taking the World Championship, but just missed the ultimate prize.
Above: The crash of Hans Harmann during the Berlin Grand Prix. The track was abandoned for Formula 1 racing soon afterwards. Left: The Morris Mini-Cooper which first entered production this year and became the most popular British small car of all time.

The Enduring Cliff

A young pop prodigy hit the British music charts this year as Cliff Richard emerged as a home-grown rival to the American stars. At first basing his act and image on Elvis Presley, Cliff Richard quickly established himself as a personality in his own right. The movie *Expresso Bongo,* made in 1959, launched him to a wider audience and was followed by a string of light romantic leads in musicals, the most famous of which was *Summer Holiday.* His enduring partnership with musical group The Shadows ensured huge success with the record buying public. Retaining his good looks and youthful charm, Cliff Richard continued to score No.1 record hits into the 1990s. Right: Cliff Richard and The Shadows.

Top left: Charlton Heston and Stephen Boyd don their costumes in the film **Ben Hur** *to shoot the famous chariot race scene watched by 6,000 extras. Heston won the Oscar for best actor for his role in this movie, widely recognised as one of the finest epics of the era. Above: Frank Lloyd Wright, the rebellious architect who preached that form should follow function rather be based on aesthetic considerations. His ego was notorious and he more than once described himself as the greatest liv-* *ing architect. In October his last great building, New York's Guggenheim Museum, was completed. Left: The enduring comedy team Bud Abbott and Lou Costello pose for a publicity shot with actresses Frances Rafferty and Jean Porter. The duo broke up amid acrimony this year and never worked together again. Abbott and Costello had first performed together on the stage in 1931 before moving on to radio and, in 1940, the movies. They made over 15 films together before the split.*

1960-1969

Jan 9	Work begins on Aswan High Dam
Jan 12	Death of British author Nevil Shute
Jan 29	Racial policy causes riots in Johannesburg
Jan 31	US: John Kennedy announces that he will run for president
Feb 19	Queen Elizabeth gives birth to Prince Andrew
Feb 27	US: The magazine 'Playboy' is banned in the state of Connecticut
Feb 29	Agadir, Morocco is devastated by earthquake leaving 12,000 dead
Mar 21	South Africa: 56 killed in the Sharpeville shootings
Mar 30	State of emergency declared in South Africa following violence
Mar 31	Lonnie Donegan's 'My Old Mans a Dustman' reaches number 1 in the charts
Apr 1	US: Tiros I, the first meteorological satellite is launched
Apr 13	British racing driver Stirling Moss loses his driving licence for a year for dangerous driving
May 1	US: U-2 aircraft shot down by USSR
May 1	Elvis Presley marries Priscilla Beaulieu
May 4	The French existentialist novelist Albert Camus is killed in a car crash
May 6	Princess Margaret marries Antony Armstrong-Jones
May 17	Kariba Dam on the Zambesi is opened by Queen Mother
May 30	Death of Soviet writer Boris Pasternak
Jun 9	Hong Kong is struck by typhoon
Jun 23	Eddie Cochran's record ' Three Steps to Heaven' reaches number 1 in the charts
Jul 6	Death of British statesman Aneurin Bevan, responsible for the National Health Service
Jul 8	U-2 pilot Gary Powers indicted as spy by USSR
Jul 18	Malcolm Campbell's Bluebird car has first UK test
Jul 21	Mrs Sirimavo Bandaranaike became PM of Ceylon, first woman to hold such a position
Aug 7	Castro nationalises all US-owned property in Cuba
Aug 16	Cyprus becomes a republic as British rule ends
Aug 19	UK: Penguin Books are summonsed for plans to publish 'Lady Chatterley's Lover'
Aug 22	Two dogs return to Earth from Soviet space trip
Aug 25	Olympic Games open in Rome
Aug 31	East Germans close border with West Berlin
Sep 10	First English Football League match televised
Sep 12	MOTs introduced in Britain
Sep 15	Traffic wardens first introduced in London
Sep 24	First nuclear powered aircraft carrier, USS Enterprise, launched
Sep 26	US: The first presidential debate is televised with Nixon and Kennedy attracting an audience of millions
Sep 27	Death of British suffragette Estelle Sylvia Pankhurst
Nov 3	'Its Now Or Never', by Elvis Presley, goes straight in to the charts at number 1
Nov 7	Moscow : Missiles first appear in Red Square parade
Nov 9	John F. Kennedy is elected US president
Nov 10	UK: 200,000 copies of 'Lady Chatterley's Lover' are sold on the first day of publication
Nov 16	Gilbert Harding, British TV broadcaster, dies on steps of BBC studios
Nov 16	Death of US actor Clark Gable
Dec 9	UK: First episode of Coronation Street screened
Dec 31	British Farthing ceases to be legal tender

THE BEECHING AXE

When Dr Beeching was appointed Chairman of the Transport Commission few can have imagined how his name would be remembered. The increasing use of motor cars and buses were proving a major competitor to the railways, especially on the less frequently used rural lines. Beeching decided to cut the losses being made by the railways by a combination of modernisation and rationalisation. The remaining steam locomotives were replaced with more modern and efficient diesel and electric trains. The rationalisation took the form of closing numerous smaller stations and tearing up the tracks on many rural lines as services were axed completely. The programme became known as the Beeching Axe. Many jobs were lost and hundreds of small villages felt cut off from the outside world. One unforseen result was that the abandoned embankments and cuttings became havens for wildlife and provided green routes along which foxes and other rural creatures could penetrate towns and cities. Above: Dr Beeching (*right*) with Lord Robens, head of the Coal Board at Victoria Station for talks on the railways' use of coal. The bear cub was a publicity mascot for the coal utilisation programme.

KENNEDY SQUEAKS INTO WHITE HOUSE

In 1960 the United States chose Massachusetts Senator John F. Kennedy to be its President. The young President was widely acclaimed as the new leader for the new age of the 1960s. His race for power began in earnest in July when the Democrats chose him to be their Presidnetial candidate with Texan Lyndon B. Johnson as his running mate. The following months of hard campaigning included a live television debate with Vice-President Richard Nixon on 26th September and arduous tours of all parts of the country. The indefatigable Kennedy's youthful vigour and style paid off at the elections in November when he was elected to the supreme office in a knife-edge ballot which ended with Kennedy only 120,000 popular votes ahead of Nixon. In the vital electoral college, however, Kennedy won by 303 to 219. He seemed set for a glorious future. Left: Kennedy speaks to an adoring crowd decked out with campaign hats during the election. Below left: Kennedy in unusually formal dress for a state occasion. The headline grabbing fashions of his wife at such events once caused him to joke "Everyone knows me, I'm Jackie Kennedy's husband". Below: John Kennedy and his wife arrive in New York to a tickertape welcome as they campaign for the state's 45 electoral votes on 19th October.

The Soviet Outburst

In October Soviet leader Nikita Khrushchev visited the United States to take part in a meeting of the United Nations General Assembly. The meeting, which drew many heads of government, followed months of high tension between the two super powers and was widely predicted to be a stormy meeting. Just how turbulent the meeting would become nobody could possibly have predicted. The various speakers were taking a decidedly anti-Soviet line throughout the morning of the 12th and Khrushchev was becoming visibly annoyed. When Philippino diplomat Lorenzo Sumulong accused the Soviets of depriving the states of eastern Europe of democracy and human rights, Khrushchev leapt to his feet and shouted across at Sumulong that he was a western lackey. Khrushchev went on to interrupt US representative Francis Wilcox and the Secretary General Dag Hammarskjold. He reserved his greatest outburst for British Premier Harold MacMillan. As MacMillan outlined British attitudes, again anti-Soviet, Khrushchev stormed and blustered from the Soviet desk. When he realised nobody was paying much attention, Khrushchev whipped off his shoe and began pounding it on his desk in exasperation. MacMillan paused, glanced at the shoe banging and asked "Could somebody translate that for me please?" The whole meeting collapsed in laughter and the Soviets resorted to sulking.

Above: Mrs Bandaranaika, who became the Prime Minister of Ceylon on 21st July. Her surprise elevation to high office followed a turbulent year in Ceylonese politics. The previous September her husband, leader of the socialist Freedom Party, was murdered by a Buddhist monk angered over his anti-religious policies. Mrs Bandaranaika, aged 44, emerged as the new party leader and proved herself to be a tough campaigner. The Freedom Party won the election of 1960 and Mrs Bandaranaika appointed herself Foreign Minister and Defence Minister as well as Prime Minister. Above right: Soviet politician Leonid Brezhnev in unusually jovial mood tries on a Lap hat. Brezhnev took over as Soviet President on 7th May, though Khrushchev retained his firm grip on power. Right: Malta's Labour Party leader Dom Mintoff arriving at Heathrow Airport on 23rd August to appear in a television programme about Malta. His pointed refusal to meet British government officials was taken as confirmation of his anti-British stance.

MASSACRE AT SHARPEVILLE

On 21st March what had been billed as a peaceful protest in South Africa got out of hand and ended with 56 deaths (*above*). The day of action was planned by a section of the African National Congress as a protest against the pass laws which required blacks to carry identification cards at all times. It was proposed that thousands of blacks should leave their cards at home and then march to police stations to be arrested. It was hoped the mass action would prove too much for the administration of justice and point out the folly of the laws. In many towns these protests passed off peacefully. But in Sharpeville, a black industrial suburb of Vereeninging, things turned nasty. About 20,000 blacks marched on the police station. The police were heavily outnumbered and nervous about the protesters intentions. Suddenly the police, believing they were being attacked, opened fire. The unarmed demonstrators scattered, but not before 56 had been killed. Condemnation of the police and government was universal. Prime Minister Verwoerd responded by relaxing the pass laws, but renewed protests and marches forced him to proclaim a national emergency and impose special powers.

On 1st May the Soviet Air Force shot down a United States U-2 aircraft over Soviet territory. The pilot, Gary Powers, was captured and paraded before the world's press by Soviet officials who accused him of being a spy. The Americans responded by stating that the U-2 was a weather research aircraft and President Eisenhower announced an inquiry into the mission. On 7th May the US admitted Powers had been on a mission to photograph a Soviet military base, but claimed the mission was necessary for security. In August a Soviet court found Powers guilty of spying and sentenced him to 10 years in prison. In February 1962 the Soviet Union released Powers in exchange for their agent Rudolf Abel, held in America. Above left: The wreckage of the U-2 aircraft. Left: Gary Powers after his return to America.

The year 1960 was an eventful one for the Royal Family. Left: The marriage of Princess Margaret to Anthony Armstrong Jones which took place in Westminster Abbey on 6th May amid great rejoicing. It was hoped that the princess had found lasting happiness after her tragic romance with Group Captain Peter Townsend. Below: The official portrait of Queen Elizabeth the Queen Mother who celebrated her 60th birthday on 4th August. Bottom right: The Queen Mother with her three grandchildren, Prince Charles, Princess Anne and Prince Andrew, who was born on 19th February. Bottom left: Earl Alexander of Tunis being installed as Constable of the Tower of London in October.

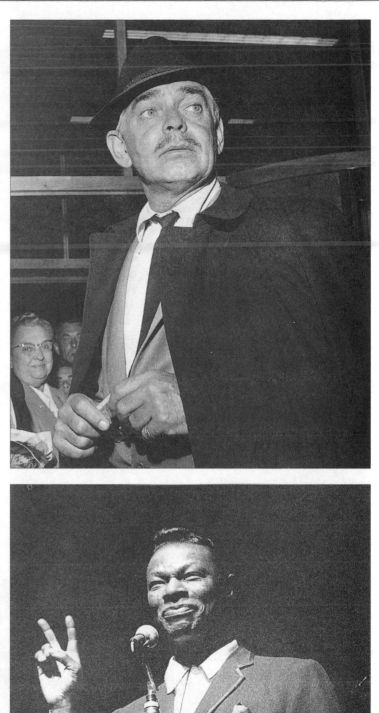

Top left: The Everley Brothers. Their harmonising voices and inspired guitar skills launched the brothers into pop stardom. Top right: Clark Gable, one time 'King of Hollywood' died of a weak heart on 16th November aged 59. His film career began in 1931 with The Painted Desert and he played a succession of heroes and heavies until he left Hollywood to fly bombers during World War II, returning to films with such classics as Mogambo. His finest performance, however, was undoubtedly in Gone with the Wind. Above: Dirk Bogarde at the premier of his film Song without End, released in September. Right: The jazz musician Nat King Cole, photographed in October when his singing career was at its height.

Above left: Australian athlete Herb Elliot crossing the finishing line to take the gold medal in the 1500 metres race at the Rome Olympics. He finished a full 15 metres ahead of his nearest rival and outstripped all the world's best middle distance runners. Above: The Brazilian tennis star Maria Bueno powering her way to victory in the Wimbledon ladies singles final which she won in 1960 for the second of three times. Bueno was famed for her grace and power with which she dominated the court. Left: Australian tennis player Neale Fraser celebrating his win in the men's singles final at Wimbledon on 2nd July. Fraser had already won the US Championship and dominated the Davis Cup.

Jan 17	Ex premier Lumumba of Congo murdered at Katanga	**Jul 1**	Birth of Carl Lewis
Jan 20	John F Kennedy becomes President of the US	**Jul 2**	US author Ernest Hemingway shoots himself
Jan 31	Tel Aviv: Ben-Gurion resigns from his post of prime minister	**Jul 8**	Wimbledon: The all British women's final is won by Angela Mortimer
Feb 15	A US skating team is killed in a plane crash near Brussels	**Aug 10**	Britain applies for membership of the EEC
Mar 1	US: President Kennedy announces formation of the Peace Corps	**Aug 13**	Border between East and West Berlin closed
		Aug 17	Construction of the Berlin Wall begins
Mar 6	Death of British comedian George Formby	**Aug 22**	100 metre no-man's land is created either side of Berlin Wall
Mar 6	Minicabs first introduced in London	**Sep 10**	Italy: Two cars veer off the Monza race track during the Italian Grand Prix, killing 13 spectators
Mar 27	UK: First women traffic wardens go on duty in Leicester		
Apr 11	Trial of Adolf Eichmann opens in Jerusalem	**Sep 18**	Dag Hammarskjold, UN Secretary General, is killed in a plane crash
Apr 12	Soviet Cosmonaut Yuri Gagarin is 1st man in space		
Apr 17	Bay of Pigs - US forces and Cuban exiles unsuccessfully try to invade Cuba	**Sep 21**	Yves Saint Laurent announces that he will start his own fashion business
Apr 21	Adolf Eichmann admits he played a part in the Final Solution	**Sep 29**	Syria secedes from United Arab Republic
May 1	Cuba: Castro abolishes elections and proclaims a socialist nation	**Oct 9**	NY Yankees win World Series for 26th time
		Oct 9	UK: Margaret Thatcher gets her first government job
May 1	Betting shops open in Britain	**Oct 12**	New Zealand MPs vote to abolish the death penalty
May 8	British spy George Blake is sentenced to 42 years	**Oct 24**	Malta becomes independent from Britain
May 13	Death of US actor Gary Cooper	**Oct 30**	Russia: The body of Joseph Stalin is removed from the mausoleum in Red Square and dumped in a nearby plot
May 28	Last journey of Paris-Bucharest Orient Express		
May 31	South Africa becomes a Republic	**Nov 10**	Russia: Stalingrad is renamed Volgograd
Jun 6	Death of Swiss psychoanalyst Carl Jung	**Dec 10**	Dag Hammarskjold is awarded the Nobel Peace Prize posthumously
Jun 16	Soviet ballet dancer Rudolf Nureyev defects to West		
Jun 27	UK: Dr Ramsey becomes 100th Archbishop of Canterbury	**Nov 16**	UK: Commonwealth Immigration Bill is introduced
		Dec 15	Adolf Eichmann sentenced to death in Jerusalem
Jul 1	British troops arrive in Kuwait in case of an attack by Iraq	**Dec 19**	India takes Goa from Portugal after 400 years
Jul 1	Birth of Princess Diana		

On the night of 13th August the Cold War took a turn for the worse. At midnight the East German border guards suddenly and without warning stopped people crossing from East Berlin into the western sectors of the city. Barbed wire was hastily strung around the border, forming a barrier left open only at a few crossing points. When American officials arrived to learn more, the guards repeated orders that only accredited officials were allowed to pass. Next day thousands of prefabricated concrete blocks were delivered and the Berlin Wall was completed on 20th November. The East German guards were given orders to shoot on sight anyone attempting to scale it. The Wall was built to stop the exodus of East Germans fleeing to the West which had reached about 2,000 a day. Left: East German workers constructing the section of the Berlin Wall beside the Brandenburg Gate on 20th November, closing the last gap in the concrete barrier.

THE SPACE RACE

The competition in space achievements reached new limits in 1961 when both America and the Soviet Union put men into orbit. First to leave the Earth's atmosphere was Soviet cosmonaut Yuri Gagarin who was aged 27 when he climbed on board the capsule Vostock 1 for his flight. The lift off on 12th April went according to plan, and Vostock 1 was put into orbit 187 miles above the ground. After completing one orbit, Gagarin steered his craft to a soft landing in a remote area of Russia. He at once became a Soviet hero and media celebrity. The Americans were clearly behind in the space race, as they did not even launch a human until the following year. Above left: John Glenn, fully equipped for a test of the Freedom 7 capsule which was to take astronaut Alan Shepherd into orbit atop a Redstone rocket. Glenn later became the first American to orbit Earth in February the following year. Above: Yuri Gagarin visiting the West in July

Africa was in turmoil during 1961. In South Africa the imposition of apartheid was leading to unrest among the black majority, particularly in urban areas, and violent protests were common. In many European colonies demands for home rule were becoming increasingly vociferous and demonstrations were seen in many cities. But most troubled was the Congo where the Belgian with-

drawal had left a power vacuum and warring factions. Prominent in attempts to find peaceful solutions for Africa was Dag Hammarskjold, Secretary General of the United Nations. It was during a visit to negotiate terms that Hammarskjold was killed in an air crash in Northern Rhodesia. Left: Hammarskjold during the Security Council's debate on the situation in the Congo.

A SPY ESCAPES

In 1960 the Soviet defector Goleniewski revealed that the Soviets had a spy, codenamed Diamond, in the British Secret Service. After the Burgess and Maclean defection of 1951 it came as a blow to learn that another top level spy was at work. Goleniewski refused point blank to be interviewed by the British in case the man sent to question him was really Diamond intent on murder. He did, however, answer British questions. It soon became obvious that Diamond had had access to a variety of top secret documents and that great damage had been done. Only one man fitted the profile of Diamond, George Blake. He was closely questioned and finally broke down and confessed all, including betraying over 40 agents to the Soviets. Put before a court in May 1961 he was sentenced to 42 years in prison, a record for peacetime espionage. The public were outraged at another spy scandal, but satisfied justice had been done. On 22nd October 1966 Blake escaped from Wormwood Scrubs prison. One month later he turned up in East Berlin and soon after moved to Moscow. His mother joined him there two years later. Left: Sean Bourke, the Irishman who helped Blake escape. Below: Blake with his mother in Moscow.

Left: Michael Ramsey who was appointed Archbishop of Canterbury in 1961. His tenure in office was remarkable for its leanings towards ecumenicalism, with Ramsey visiting both the Pope and the Orthodox patriarch, and the introduction of government by synod. Above: Philosopher Lord Bertrand Russell and his wife who were both imprisoned for seven days in September after taking part in a nuclear protest.

Facing page, top: An anti-aircraft battery in Havana prepares for an expected invasion from the United States in January. The invasion came on 17th April and was made by exiled anti-Castro Cubans (above) trained by America's CIA and backed by American hardware. American marines (left) waited nearby in case they were needed to exploit the expected successful invasion. Landing in the Bay of Pigs, the invasion was easily beaten off by Castro and President Kennedy was left embarrassed. Facing page, bottom: A platoon of Belgian troops captured in January by local tyrant Kashamura in Bkavu, the Congo. The captives were severely beaten before being released. Top: US Army helicopters land at Phuoug Vinh in South Vietnam where US advisors were helping the government counter Communist infiltrators from North Vietnam.

SPEND, SPEND, SPEND

In September a Yorkshire miner and his wife hit the football pools jackpot and won a record £152,319 18/6d. Asked what she would do with the money, Vivian Nicholson replied "I'm going to spend, spend, spend". Scorning the advice of financial experts called in by the pools company to advise on investments, the Nicholsons did indeed spend their money. The pair began in Harrods, the exclusive London store, and continued by purchasing a smart house far better than could ever have been afforded on a miner's wage. Disaster struck when Keith crashed a new sports car and was killed. The money then ran out and Vivian returned to her modest origins. Below: Keith and Vivian Nicholson being given their cheque by television celebrity Bruce Forsyth.

Riots In Belgium

January was a month of turmoil in Belgium with some politicians hourly expecting the outbreak of revolution. The trouble had begun in December when the government, incensed by tax dodging, passed a law which allowed tax inspectors to deduct payments from wage packets before they were given to the workers. Opposition members and the trades unions were outraged at what was widely perceived to be an attack on civil liberties, even by those who paid their taxes honestly. When the new law was being debated in the National Assembly tempers became so frayed that one objector launched a fist at a speaker in favour of the law and had to be dragged out of the chamber. Unions called their members out on strike and the nation's industry ground to a halt. Power strikes plunged the country into darkness. Communists began demanding that the workers unite to overthrow the government, and some ministers went in fear of their safety. Tensions were raised again in the second week of January when Liege was subjected to violent riots and police were attacked in the street. But the Left wingers had overplayed their hand and many workers, happy enough to protest against the new tax law, drew back from violent revolution. The protests died down and the new law was passed.

Top left: Large scale archaeological excavations of the ancient Roman city of Pompeii, buried by a volcanic eruption in AD 79 were continued this year. This picture taken in May shows the remains of a family killed while fleeing with young children. Right: Gary Player, the South African golfer who this year took the Masters Tournament for the first time. He went on to win 60 major tournaments and continued to work hard on improving his technique and equipment.

*Left: Gary Cooper as he appeared in his 1952 classic western **High Noon**. The Hollywood actor, who died in this year, specialised in playing honest loners up against evil in the form of violence or deceit. He also took on other roles, managing to stay in the star billing from 1926 until his death. Below: The American folk song legend Bob Dylan whose songs of protest against nuclear weapons and other modern iniquities made him a household name. Bottom left: Liz Taylor being presented with her Oscar for best actress in the movie **Butterfield 8** by fellow star Yul Brynner. Bottom right: The Lancashire comedian singer, George Formby, who specialised in saucy songs accompanied by his ukelele. After a successful music hall career he took to movies in the 1930s, returning to the stage for pantomimes in the 1950s before retiring. He died in 1961.*

1962

Jan 1	400 are arrested in Lebanon for plotting to overthrow the government
Jan 11	"The Young Ones" by Cliff Richard, goes straight in to the charts at Number 1
Jan 27	New Zealander Peter Snell breaks the world mile record
Feb 4	Sunday Times becomes first paper to issue a colour supplement
Feb 17	UK: James Hanratty is sentenced to death for the 'A6' murder
Feb 20	John Glenn becomes first American in orbit
Mar 1	93 are killed in a New York plane crash
Apr 2	Prince Charles begins at Gordonstoun School, Scotland
Apr 8	Cuba: Over 1,000 Bay of Pigs invaders are sentenced to 30 years in jail
May 8	Trolleybuses run for last time in London
May 17	A barbed wire fence is erected on the border of Hong Kong and China to prevent Chinese immigrants
May 25	UK: Coventry Cathedral is consecrated
May 31	Adolf Eichmann is executed for his part in the holocaust
Jun 21	Brazil beats Czechoslovakia 3-1 in Chile to retain the World Cup Trophy
Jul 3	Algeria proclaims independence after 132 years of French rule
Jul 10	US: Martin Luther King is jailed for leading an illegal march
Jul 10	Telstar I is the first TV satellite launched by US
Jul 11	US Fred Baldasare becomes the first swimmer to cross the English Channel underwater
Jul 18	President Prado is arrested by the army in Peru
Jul 20	The world's first passenger hovercraft begins service
Aug 1	President Nkrumah of Ghana escapes an assassination attempt
Aug 5	Death of US actress Marilyn Monroe
Aug 6	Jamaica becomes independent
Aug 6	Death of US writer William Faulkner
Aug 9	Death of German-born Swiss writer Hermann Hesse
Aug 14	Italy: The Mont Blanc tunnel is completed
Aug 20	An 18 year old is shot by East German guards while trying to climb the Berlin Wall
Aug 22	President de Gaulle escapes assassination attempt
Aug 31	Trinidad and Tobago gain independence
Aug 31	Chris Bonnington and Ian Clough become the first Briton to conquer the north face of the Eiger
Sep 3	20,000 are feared dead in Iran's worst earthquake
Sep 26	Spain: Over 300 are killed in floods in Barcelona
Oct 1	US: Mississippi University's first black student attends classes and 200 are arrested in riots
Oct 8	UK: Judge Elizabeth Lane becomes the first female judge to sit in the High Court
Oct 9	Uganda declares independence after 62 years of British rule
Oct 17	King Saud names Prince Feisal as the new premier of Saudi Arabia
Oct 22	Kennedy says USSR has missile bases in Cuba
Oct 22	British Admiralty clerk, William Vassall, is sentenced to 1 years imprisonment for spying for the Soviet Union
Nov 7	Nelson Mandela is jailed for 5 years
Nov 10	Death of Eleanor Roosevelt
Nov 28	Death of Queen Wilhelmina of the Netherlands

The Edge Of War

In 1962 the world came closer to a third World War than at any time before or since. Cuba's leader Fidel Castro was smarting from the US supported Bay of Pigs invasion of 1961 and agreed to a suggestion from Khrushchev that Soviet nuclear missiles be based on Cuban soil. Such a move would have placed almost the entire USA within range of Soviet nuclear weapons for the first time, while Soviet cities remained beyond the reach of American missiles. President Kennedy reacted quickly to the news. On 22nd October he sent the US Navy to blockade Cuba and stop any Soviet ships from approaching the island state. Fearing a full scale invasion was likely, Castro mobilised his nation for war on the 23rd. On the 24th the Soviet ships in the Atlantic halted before encountering American ships, but Khrushchev threatened "retaliation" for the blockade. Two days later American scout aircraft brought back photos which showed work on missile launch sites was being speeded up and the following day a U-2 scout was shot down over Cuba. Khrushchev raised the stakes by linking the Cuban missiles to US missiles in Turkey. War seemed very near. Tension eased on the 28th when the Soviet ships turned back and Khrushchev agreed not to ship any missiles to Cuba. One month later the blockade ended when Soviet air bases on Cuba were closed.

Left: The BBC's most popular show was the satirical That was the Week That Was which reached an audience of millions with its wit and irreverent side glances at current affairs. The young cast included several who went on to become comedy stars i their own right. Left to right the original line up was: Lance Percival, David Kernan, David Frost, Roy Kinnear, Kenneth Cope, Willie Rushton and Millicent Martin.

Left: The anxious features of Greville Wynne, the British businessman arrested in Budapest and flown to Moscow to face charges of espionage in 1962. He was finally released in April 1964. Bottom: George Pompidou who became Prime Minister of France in this year. By profession a teacher he served in de Gaulle's government in 1945, leaving to become a banker when de Gaulle resigned. Later he was instrumental in formulating the constitution of the 5th Republic and was largely responsible for arranging the ceasefire in Algeria which led eventually to its independence from France. As PM he spent much time trying to solve France's economic and social problems including the student riots of 1968. He followed de Gaulle as President in 1969, a post he held until his death in 1974.

The Vietnam War, which lasted for over a decade, gathered momentum in 1962. The origins of the conflict came when France abandoned its rule of Indo-China in 1950. The Western nations recognised the monarch Bao Dai as the ruler in Vietnam, but he only controlled the southern territories. The North was controlled by the Communist guerrilla Ho Chi Minh. In 1955 Bao Dai was replaced by military leader Diem and the regime in the south became increasingly repressive. Soon Ho Chi Minh was sending men called Viet Cong south to spread the Communist message. The US, worried about Communist expansion, sent military advisors to help Diem who, in November 1961, declared war on the Viet Cong. President Kennedy also announced a massive aid package to Vietnam to pay for hospitals, schools and to boost the economy so that the Viet Cong would find fewer peasants willing to listen to their promises of better conditions under the Communists. Kennedy also sent US troops to the region, the start of the long US military intervention in Vietnam. Above: South Vietnamese troops move cautiously through the Mekong Delta in search of Communist Viet Cong.

Trouble In Mississippi

In September President Kennedy's stand against racial segregation in the United States was tested once again, this time by the State of Mississippi. The Board of Trustees of the University of Mississippi decided that they would comply with the Federal law, but State Governor Ross Barnett believed that public opinion in the state was opposed to the move. When Negro James Meredith qualified for admission to the University, Barnett made it quite clear he would block the move. When Meredith arrived to register, his path was blocked by state troopers. A hurried telephone conversation between Kennedy and Barnett resulted only in impasse. In desperation, on 30th September, Kennedy sent federal troops to Mississippi to escort Meredith into the University. Meredith successfully registered, but in the subsequent rioting between whites and troops three people were killed and fifty injured. Right: James Meredith leaves the Registrar's Office of the University of Mississippi after entering his name.

Above left: Police prepare to remove the body of Mafia leader Bugsy Siegel from the Beverly Hills mansion where he was shot by a professional assassin. Siegel was an inventive and ambitious Mafia chief who was largely responsible for the development of Las Vegas as a gambling city. He was murdered on the orders of other Mafia bosses, probably led by Charles 'Lucky' Luciano, after Siegel had welched on a number of underworld deals. Above: John Steinbeck, receiving the Nobel Prize for Literature. Left: British Minister of Aviation, Julian Amery signing a model of Concorde. The agreement by BOAC to buy the airliner for its fleet secured the future of the £10 million project which was being jointly constructed by British and French governments.

Below: Famous British crime writer Agatha Christie cuts a cake during a party at the exclusive Savoy Hotel in London to celebrate the 10th anniversary of the play **The Mousetrap** which was still playing to packed houses. Right: Bob Hope teams up with British Open gold champion Arnold Palmer for a comic scene in the movie **Call me Bwana** which was filmed in October. Bottom left: Two of the greatest ballet dancers in the world, Rudolf Nureyev and Margot Fonteyn join forces for **Le Corsaire** staged at Covent Garden in November. Bottom right: Hollywood sex symbol Marilyn Monroe who died this year aged 36. Her death was officially put down to suicide, but darker rumours have since circulated and her name has been linked to that of President Kennedy. Her screen persona of a sexy but innocent girl was played to perfection and for many she remains the archetypal screen goddess.

Jan 8	US: The Mona Lisa goes on show at the National Gallery
Jan 18	Death of British Labour Party leader Hugh Gaitskill
Jan 29	Death of US poet Robert Frost
Jan 30	Death of French composer Francis Poulenc
Feb 1	Turkey: 67 die when a plane crashes into a market square
Feb 4	UK: A learner driver is fined for driving on after her instructor had jumped out of the car for fear of his life
Feb 5	James R Dick pays £63,000 for an Aberdeen Angus bull which later fails a fertility test!
Feb 9	US: FIrst test flight of the Boeing 727
Feb 14	UK: Harold Wilson is named as Labour's new leader
Feb 22	Death of British businessman John Lewis
Feb 22	The first metal tennis raquet is patented
Mar 17	Volcano erupts in Bali, killing 11,000
Mar 21	Alcatraz Prison is closed
Apr 2	Black civil rights campaign begins in US
Apr 9	Winston Churchill is given honorary US citizenship
Apr 10	US atomic sub 'Thresher' sinks with the loss of 129 lives
Apr 24	UK: Princess Alexandra marries Angus Ogilvy
May 3	President Duvalier of Haiti declares martial law
May 5	US: 1,000 are arrested on a civil rights march in Alabama
May 8	Death of British comedian Max Miller
May 18	US: Kennedy visits the south and praises civil rights demonstrators
May 27	Kenya: Jomo Kenyatta is elected premier in the first general election
May 29	10,000 are killed when a cyclone hits East Pakistan
Jun 4	US: Pan Am places an order for Concorde
Jun 4	John Profumo resigns from his parliamentary seat following the scandal that almost brought down the government
Jun 16	Valentina Tereshkova becomes the first woman in space
Jun 20	US and USSR agree on 'hotline' link
Jun 27	Ireland: President Kennedy visits Wexford County
Jul 1	Kim Philby, British spy, revealed as third man
Jul 8	Margaret Smith becomes the first Australian woman to win the Wimbledon singles title
Jul 26	Earthquakes in Yugoslavia kill 1100
Aug 3	UK: Dr Stephen Ward dies from a drug overdose following his vice trial where he stood accused of living on immoral earnings
Aug 8	UK: The Great Train Robbery takes place
Aug 22	Lord Nuffield, founder of Morris Motors, dies
Aug 28	200,000 US blacks demonstrate for civil rights
Aug 31	Death of French cubist painter Georges Braque
Sep 5	UK: Christine Keeler is charged with perjury
Sep 16	Asia: A new nation is formed named Malaysia
Sep 19	Channel Tunnel is agreed to in Anglo-French report
Oct 1	Nigeria becomes a republic
Oct 3	Army takes control in Honduras
Oct 6	Los Angeles Dodgers win World Series
Oct 11	Death of French writer and poet Jean Cocteau
Oct 11	Death of French singer Edith Piaf
Nov 5	Birth of Tatum O'Neal
Nov 14	Birth of island of Surtsey caused by an eruption of underwater volcano
Nov 18	UK: Dartford Tunnel opens
Nov 22	President John F Kennedy is assassinated
Nov 25	Funeral of President Kennedy
Dec 12	Kenya attains independence

THE PROFUMO AFFAIR

In 1963 the British political establishment was sent reeling by a sex scandal which broadened and deepened to include not only politicians but peers of the realm, East End gangs and even Soviet spies. The scandal first came to light when a West Indian gang member fired a fusillade of shots into a smart London property where his ex-lover Christine Keeler was hiding with her friend Mandy Rice-Davies. The flat was owned by society osteopath Dr Stephen Ward, which caused a mild sensation. But then it was learnt that John Profumo, the Minister for War, had visited Keeler at the flat, as had Soviet attache Ivanov. Profumo made a statement to Parliament on 22nd March stating that nothing improper had occured. Then, amid rising scandal, Profumo resigned on 4th June and admitted that he had had an affair with Keeler. By that time even more lurid facts had come to light. Keeler was known to have frequented underground West Indian clubs and taken drugs while Rice-Davies had been the mistress of notorious slum owner Peter Rachman and both had been linked to Lord Astor. The Press attention centred on Keeler and Rice-Davies for both were extremely attractive and had explosive stories to tell. The police, however, centred attention on Dr Ward and in July brought him to trial for allegedly living on the immoral earnings of the girls. At the trial the evidence against Ward was scandalous and revealed a lifestyle of considerable debauchery, but actual crime was hard to prove. Nevertheless he committed suicide rather than wait for the verdict. Many lives had been ruined by the affair, perhaps the greatest sex scandal in British history. Above: John Profumo and his wife, photographed at a Conservative dance in March. Facing page, top left: Christine Keeler. Facing page, top right: Mandy Rice-Davies.

*ight: The Flying Scotsman which
ent into retirement in January
ter forty years of continual service.
he engine succumbed to the
placement of steam power with
ectric and diesel engines. In its
orking life the engine had trav-
led some 2 million miles and held
veral records, including that of 2
urs 31 minutes for the London to
eds run. The engine was bought
a Nottinghamshire businessman
nd placed in a museum in
oncaster where it was built.*

The Great Train Robbery

One of the greatest British crimes was staged on 8th August. The regular Glasgow-London night mail train was laden with over a million pounds in used bank notes and an equally valuable collection of gems, postal orders and other goods. As the train approached Cheddington in Buckinghamshire the signals turned against it. When the engine stopped armed men leapt aboard and forced the driver to take them to a siding. There over a dozen men smashed open the mail cars and stole their contents. Some two and a half million pounds was lifted in just 15 minutes. At first the police had no clues, but a few days later they discovered the house where the gang had divided up the booty and found fingerprints. These were identified as belonging to a number of notorious London crooks and soon the police knew the names of the gang who pulled off the Great Train Robbery. It took many months to track down the bandits, some evaded capture for years. The most famous, Ronnie Biggs, was captured but escaped and remains free in South America. Left: Detective Superintendent Fewtrell inspects one of the plundered mail coaches.

THE KENNEDY ASSASSINATION

More has been written about the Kennedy Assassination than about any other political murder in history. Yet uncertainties remain and many believe the truth will never come out. On 22nd November Kennedy was paying an official visit to Dallas, Texas. As he drove through the city centre in an open topped limousine three shots rang out from a warehouse. The President slumped forward, his skull smashed by a bullet. He died minutes later. Police, meanwhile, had arrested a 24 year old ex-Marine named Lee Harvey Oswald. He was alleged to have fired the fatal shots. Just two days later a night club owner shot Oswald dead when he burst through a police cordon. The official theory, that Oswald acted alone and that Ruby shot him for revenge, has frequently been criticised. Most often it is alleged that shots other than those fired by Oswald were heard and seen as the President died, and that Ruby shot Oswald to ensure his silence. Certainly Ruby had Mafia connections and there are indications of a second gunman. Who would have been responsible for the conspiracy to kill Kennedy, and how they covered their tracks has never been satisfactorily explained. The assassination remains an enigma, but one which changed the world. Left: Kennedy proclaims his unswerving support for Berlin with the words "Ich bin ein Berliner" in June. Below: Kennedy drives through Dallas on the fatal day. Bottom left: The Kennedy family stands in mourning as the coffin of the President is carried from St Matthew's Cathedral. Bottom right: The murder of Lee Harvey Oswald by Jack Ruby.

Below: The Mayor of Nairobi addresses a formal reception for the Duke of Edinburgh and Prime Minister Jomo Kenyatta on the first day of Kenya's independence on 12th December. Right: Kim Philby. In 1962 evidence was found to prove he was the 'Third Man' in the Burgess and MacClean spy scandal. An agent was sent to interrogate Philby in Beirut, where he then worked as a journalist. Philby promptly vanished and some months later reappeared in Moscow where he happily confessed his treachery.

UNREST IN VIETNAM

In 1963 the government of South Vietnam was led by dictator Ngo Diem. Faced by Communist infiltration from North Vietnam and unrest at home, the Catholic Diem cracked down on Buddhism and civil rights. The Buddhist hierarchy responded by mounting an effective opposition campaign. On 13th June the first of several ritual suicides by devout Buddhist monks was staged. The fourth was particularly gruesome as he doused himself with petrol and set fire to himself in a Saigon street in October (*above*). A workers demonstration in favour of Diem was staged in September by the government (*right*) but its obviously stage managed nature did not fool many observers. On 2nd November a powerful coalition of army and air force officers moved on Saigon and forced Diem to resign. He later committed suicide and a more liberal regime which aimed at winning over its own people was installed. The unrest, however, continued to grow.

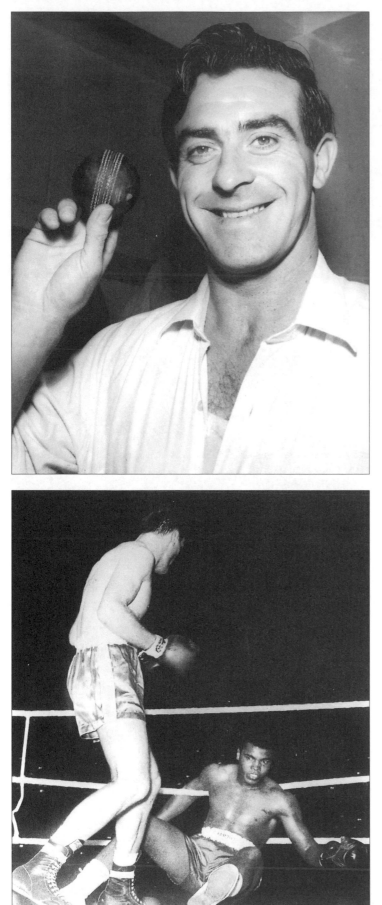

*Top left: English fast bowling crick-
eter Freddy Trueman of Yorkshire
photographed demonstrating his
famous grip on the day he broke all
previous records to take his 243rd
Test wicket in March 1963 during
a tour of New Zealand. Trueman
went on to take a total of 307 Test
wickets before his retirement in
1965. Top right: Film stars Liz
Taylor and Richard Burton dancing at a reception at the British
Embassy in Paris on 18th March.*

*Burton had just split from wife
Sybil Williams and married
Taylor the following year. Left:
American world heavyweight
champion Cassius Clay lies on the
canvas after being floored by
Britain's Henry Cooper. Clay
recovered and won the fight held
on 19th June in London. Above:
The newly elected Labour Party
leader, Harold Wilson, meets the
Beatles at the Variety Club Award
Show in 1963.*

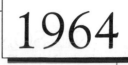

BIRTH OF ZAMBIA

On 1st January the colony of northern Rhodesia was separated from Nyasaland and granted limited self-government. On 24th October the colony became fully independent as Zambia. The move came after nearly a century of British rule, which had begun after the defeat of the dominant military tribe, the Matabele. Some of the more educated blacks in Northern Rhodesia had been agitating for independence for decades. The United National Independence Party was led by Kenneth Kaunda who had first spoken out against British rule in 1949. When freedom came, Kaunda was appointed President and his party took power in the legislature. Kaunda is shown here taking the salute as Commander in Chief of the army as motorised units sweep past the Presidential Podium. Soon after independence he nationalised the copper mines, Zambia's principal source of foreign trade which account for about 90% of exports. In 1972 he outlawed all political parties, except for his own United National, and gave the Party constitutional power over the legislature. His grip on power remained total, being elected President for five year terms no less than six times. In 1990 small opposition parties were allowed for the first time.

Jan 13	Calcutta: 200 are killed in Hindu-Moslem riots
Jan 20	UK: The Great Train Robbery trial begins
Jan 30	Death of American film star Alan Ladd
Feb 10	Australia: The destroyer Voyager sinks and 85 are feared dead
Feb 19	UK: Actor Peter Sellers weds actress Britt Ekland
Mar 7	US: The two men that kidnapped Frank Sinatra's son are jailed for life
Mar 10	Prince Edward born
Mar 15	US: Actress Elizabeth Taylor weds actor Richard Burton
Mar 21	The Beatles 'Can't buy me love' is released with advance world wide sales of 2.1 million
Apr 5	Death of US General Douglas MacArthur
Apr 5	Premier Jigme Dorji of Bhutan is assassinated
Apr 13	Ian Smith becomes PM of Rhodesia
Apr 16	Great Train Robbers sentenced
Apr 16	Geraldine Mock becomes the first woman to fly around the world solo
Apr 21	BBC 2 begins transmission
Apr 22	Greville Wynne is freed in the USSR in a spy swap
May 2	Death of Lady Astor, first woman MP
May 4	US: It is announced that there will be no Pullitzer awards for fiction, music or drama
May 24	Over 135 people are killed during riots at an Argentina v Peru football match following an unpopular decision by the referee
May 24	Liz McColgan born
May 27	Death of Nehru, Indian prime minister
Jun 2	Jerusalem: The Palestine Liberation Organisation is created
Jun 5	Britain's first flight in space with 'Blue Streak' rocket
Jun 8	UK: Christine Keeler is released from prison
Jun 9	Death of British newspaper tycoon Lord Beaverbrook
Jun 9	India: Lai Shastri is new prime minister
Jun 12	South Africa: Nelson Mandela is sentenced to life imprisonment for sabotage and plotting to overthrow the government
Jul 2	US: President Lyndon Johnson signs the Civil Rights Act which bans most racial discrimination
Jul 17	Donald Campbell attains a world speed record of 403mph
Jul 27	Winston Churchill makes his last appearance in parliament
Jul 31	US satellite Ranger 7 returns first close up pictures of the moon's surface
Aug 12	Death of British novelist Ian Fleming
Aug 13	The last hangings in Britain take place
Sep 4	The Forth Road Bridge is opened by the Queen
Sep 21	Malta achieves independence
Sep 28	Death of US comedian Harpo Marx
Oct 10	18th Olympic Games open in Tokyo
Oct 14	Martin Luther King receives Nobel Peace Prize
Oct 14	Harold Wilson becomes Prime Minister
Oct 15	Death of US composer Cole Porter
Oct 24	Northern Rhodesia becomes Republic of Zambia, with Kenneth Kaunda as the first President
Nov 4	Lyndon B Johnson wins Presidential election
Nov 25	Martial law is declared in Saigon following student riots
Dec 10	Sam Cooke, soul singer, shot dead by manageress of a motel
Dec 12	Kenya becomes a republic
Dec 21	UK: Commons vote to end Capital Punishment
Dec 30	500 arrested in India, suspected of being Chinese spies

NELSON MANDELA IN PRISON

Right: Nelson Rolihlahla Mandela who was convicted this year of attempting to overthrow the government of South Africa and given a life sentence. Mandela was at the time already in prison for leaving the country illegally to attempt to raise international support for his political campaign. Mandela was born in 1918 and studied law at the University of Witwatersrand before becoming involved in political activity. With his business partner Oliver Tambo, Mandela found the Youth League of the African National Congress in 1944. When the ANC was banned as a subversive organisation by the government in 1960 Mandela continued with his calls for an end to apartheid and white rule. His arrest in 1962 came as no surprise, though the tough life sentence imposed in 1964 was considered by some to be unnecessarily harsh. During his time in prison, Mandela continued to call for black rule and became a hero of the Xhosa tribe.

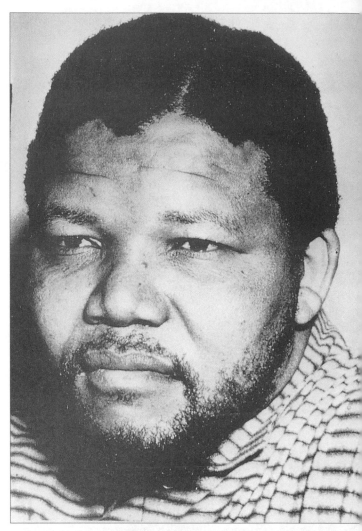

Above: Martin Luther King who was awarded the Nobel Peace Prize in 1964 for his campaign against racial segregation in the United States. Born in 1929 in Atlanta, Georgia, King became a clergyman at a young age. In 1955 he organised a peaceful protest against the segregated public transport in Montgomery, Alabama, which centred around organising a boycott of the buses by Blacks. When this proved successful national recognition came his way and he used the Southern Christian Leadership Conference to push for similar passive resistance tactics to be used elsewhere. It was his famous March on Washington which brought him the international fame which led to the Nobel award. Right: Lyndon B. Johnson, the man elevated to the Presidency by the assassination of Kennedy in 1963, was re-elected in a landslide victory over Republican candidate Barry Goldwater.

Right: Lord Beaverbrook, the newspaper magnate who died in 1964. Born in Canada in 1879 Beaverbrook amassed an early fortune and by 1907 had acquired a formidable reputation as a financier with a gift for picking successful ventures in which to invest. In that year he moved to Britain. In 1916 he bought the Daily Express, founding its sister paper the Sunday Express two years later, and in 1923 acquired the Evening Standard. By 1936 he was a major influence in government and Press circles and worked hard to suppress news of the impending Abdication crisis which engulfed his friend Edward VIII. With his dominion origins, Beaverbrook believed strongly in the ties of friendship within the English-speaking world and loudly opposed those who tried to take Britain into the European Economic Community.

SOCIALISTS WIN POWER IN BRITAIN

On 16th October Britain went to the polls in a General Election held amid general discontent. The economy was not performing as well as some expected and the Conservative government had been discredited by the Profumo Scandal and various minor embarrassments. After thirteen years of control by the Conservative Party, Labour's return to power was something of a surprise. It gave the opportunity for fresh ideas and vigour. The new Prime Minister, Harold Wilson, was aged just 48, making him the youngest premier of the century. The narrow majority of just four MPs which Labour secured was evidence of the divided nature of the nation. Left: James Callaghan who was appointed Chancellor of the Exchequer in the new government. Above: The new Prime Minister is congratulated by former Labour leader Lord Attlee. The new Labour government was committed to socialist principles and embarked on ambitious plans to turn Britain into a caring community by harnessing the white heat of technology to socialist ideals.

COLD WAR BLOODSHED

The continuing ideological differences between the Communist and capitalist systems spread into vicious bloodshed in several parts of the world. Most notable among these was Vietnam where Communist infiltrators of South Vietnam were escalating the conflict into a full scale guerrilla war. In retaliation, conventional warfare between the two Vietnams loomed closer. The United States was already involved in propping up the regime of South Vietnam and President Lyndon B. Johnson had the unenviable task of organising the survival of a government with few virtues. In August a US naval ship was attacked by North Vietnamese gunboats and President Johnson used this as a justification for increased US military involvement. The US air force bombed targets in North Vietnam linked to guerrilla activity and US training and supervision of the South Vietnamese army was stepped up. Top left: A Viet Cong terrorist is prepared for execution in October. Top right: Viet Cong prisoners being led to captivity by US troops. In the Congo Communist terrorists, allegedly Chinese trained, formed just one of several regional groupings struggling for power after the Belgian withdrawal of colonial government. The death toll rose alarmingly as civil war spread throughout the new state and the capital Leopoldville was the scene of bitter street fighting between the factions. Right: Dead Communists lined up for burial by troops loyal to the post-colonial government after fighting in Bakavu and Kampala. Centre right: A Communist band is caught in the open by American reconnaissance aircraft as they advance to take part in the fighting around Kampala in February.

The Aswan Dam

In May Soviet President Nikita Khrushchev visited Egypt to help President Nasser initiate the construction of the Aswan Dam. At an impressive ceremony the two leaders jointly set off charges which altered the flow of the Nile into an artificial canal to allow work on the dam to proceed. The Soviet funding of the project marked the move away from western influences in Egypt and confirmed the pro-Communist bias of Nasser. Khrushchev was, however, in difficulties at home with Communist party hardliners who objected to his policy of detente with the West. In October they organised a peaceful coup by unexpectedly packing a meeting of the supreme Soviet committees with their supporters, specially flown in for the event, and ousting Khrushchev from office. He was replaced by Leonid Brezhnev, who returned the Soviet Union to strict Leninist policies and kept dissent under tight suppression.

Above: Actors Harry Belafonte and Sidney Poitier who began collaborations on all-Black films aimed at a Negro audience which avoided the stereotyping of racial and class groups which sometimes occurred in other movies. Above right: Two great French products which celebrated their 75th birthday this year, the Eiffel Tower and Maurice Chevalier. The Tower was a leading tourist attraction, while Chevalier was celebrating a life long career as a singer and film star. Right: Two of the people honoured at the Variety Club Awards in London on 9th October. Cilla Black was voted top female singer and Jimmy Savile was awarded the title of top disc jockey.

1965

Jan 1	UK: Stanley Matthews becomes the first professional footballer to be knighted
Jan 4	Death of US poet and dramatist T.S. Eliot
Jan 16	US: A US Air Force jet crashes into a house in Kansas, killing 30 people
Jan 20	Lyndon B Johnson is sworn is as 36th President of the US
Jan 24	Death of British Prime Minister Winston Churchill
Jan 30	A state funeral is held for Winston Churchill
Feb 7	US aircraft bomb North Vietnam
Feb 15	Death of American singer Nat King Cole
Feb 18	Independence for Gambia
Feb 21	Black moslem leader Malcolm X is shot dead in US
Feb 23	Death of US comedian Stan Laurel
Mar 18	Alexsei Leonov becomes the first man to walk in space
Mar 28	Death of former US President Dwight D. Eisenhower
Mar 31	US: President Johnson sends Marines into Vietnam
Mar 31	IBM file patent for a computer
Apr 4	US jets are shot down by North Vietnamese
Apr 23	250 mile Pennine Way opens
Jun 2	UK: MPs approve a Corporation Tax on company profits
Jun 3	Major Edward White becomes the first American to walk in space
Jul 14	Madame Vaucher becomes the first woman to climb the Matterhorn
Jul 16	Apollo II is launched with Neil Armstrong, Edwin Aldrin and M Collins on board
Jul 27	UK: Edward Heath becomes the leader of the Conservative Party
Jul 31	Advertising on TV of cigarettes is banned
Aug 11	US: Race riots in Los Angeles
Aug 20	Clive Inman scores 50 runs in 8 minutes

Aug 27	Death of Swiss-born French architect Le Corbusier
Sep 2	Ben-Gurion is expelled from the Mapai party in Israel
Sep 4	Death of German-born French doctor and missionary, Dr Albert Schweitzer
Sep 10	US: Yale University announces the discovery of a map that proves the Vikings discovered North America
Oct 8	The 620 foot Post Office Tower opens in London
Oct 26	The four members of the Beatles receive their MBEs
Oct 28	UK: Ian Brady and Myra Hindley are charged with the 'Moors Murders'
Nov 6	Death of US composer Edgar Varese
Nov 9	Death penalty is abolished in Britain
Nov 9	New York City is blacked out in the biggest power cut in American history
Nov 11	Ian Smith, Prime Minister of Rhodesia, announces UDI (Unilateral Declaration of Independence)
Nov 16	Death of Cosgrave, the first president of the Irish Free State
Nov 23	Muhammed Ali defeats Floyd Patterson to retain his title of Heavyweight Champion of the World
Dec 15	Two American Gemini spacecraft become the first to rendezvous in space
Dec 16	Death of British novelist Somerset Maugham
Dec 19	France: De Gaulle is re-elected as President but with the lowest majority ever
Dec 22	70 mph speed limit introduced in Britain
Dec 22	Death of British journalist and broadcaster Richard Dimbleby
Dec 27	North Sea oil-rig 'Sea Gem' collapses with the loss of 13 lives
Dec 29	Ho Chi Minh declines invitation to peace talks on Vietnam
Dec 30	Philippines: Ferdinand E. Marcos becomes President

Left: The famous British broadcasting journalist Richard Dimbleby who became established as the face of television died in this year. Facing page: The sombre scene at St Paul's Cathedral, London, during the funeral of Winston Churchill. The coffin is carried by a squad of guards officers while close relatives and friends descend the main steps. A procession carried the coffin, loaded on a gun carriage, to the river whence it was taken to Waterloo station by boat. Churchill had long been a maverick politician, but he achieved lasting greatness as a war leader during the Second World War when his grim determination epitomised the nation. The occasion of his death led the Queen to grant him the unique honour of his portrait appearing on a coin of the realm, the only commoner ever to achieve that distinction.

UDI FOR RHODESIA

On 11th November the ruling politicians of the British colony of Rhodesia finally lost patience with the British government and issued a Unilateral Declaration of Independence. At issue was the future of Rhodesia and how the nation should be governed. Britain was following a policy of handing political control over to the black majority in its African colonies and several had already gained independence under such arrangements. In Rhodesia, however, the white minority was much larger and more strongly entrenched than elsewhere. The White Rhodesians, several of whose families had lived in the country for generations, refused to accept government at the whim of an uneducated majority and greatly feared the mass expulsions and nationalisations seen elsewhere in Black Africa. When Britain insisted, Rhodesia refused and declared itself independent saying that "the Rhodesian people who have demonstrated their loyalty to Britain in two world wars now see all that they have cherished about to be shattered on the rocks of expediency". Left: Rhodesian premier Ian Smith, watched by his cabinet, signs the instrument of UDI.

In March the civil rights movement led by Martin Luther King achieved a victory in Alabama. The Alabama state governor, George Wallace, had ruthlessly stamped out black demands in the past, but King succeeded in organising a mass demonstration. Above: Dr King celebrates the decision on 17th March by a Federal Judge to give permission for the Freedom March. Above left: The Freedom Marchers make their way through the pouring rain towards Montgomery, Alabama, on 23rd March. When they reached the State Capitol Martin Luther King declared "We are on the move and no wave of racism will stop us." Left: Ronnie Biggs, a Great Train Robber, leaves Aylesbury Police Station under guard on his way to trial. Found guilty, Biggs was sent to prison but he later escaped and fled to South America.

The Beatles

The official seal of approval was set on the pop music phenomenon The Beatles in October when the four members of the band were awarded the MBE in the Queen's Birthday Honours List. The band came together in Liverpool in the late 1950s, cutting its first record in 1962. The Liverpudlian group became an instant success. Early hits such as *Please Please Me, Love Me Do* and *Do You Want To Know a Secret* powered them to international stardom. In 1964 came the record and film of *Hard Day's Night*. The MBEs awarded to the group merely confirmed what everybody already knew, that the Beatles were the greatest pop music sensation of a generation. The Beatles later went on to lead the pop world into a variety of phases from semi-mystical devotion to Indian religion to psychedelic culture. The band split in 1971 and its members, John Lennon, Paul McCartney, Ringo Starr and George Harrison followed independent careers.

Top left: American Black nationalist Malcolm X after his controversial television interview in which he urged Negroes who face segregation to "have a shotgun with which to retaliate". The remarks put him in direct confrontation with Dr Martin Luther King who advocated peaceful opposition. Top right: David Steele who was elected to the British Parliament for the first time. Steele was an ardent member of the Liberal Party and became its leader in 1976 at a time when the Liberals were in alliance with Labour. Right: Colonel Alexei Leonov a member of the two man crew of the Voshod 2, launched by the Soviet Union on 18th March.

In 1965 the conflict in Vietnam escalated as Viet Cong infiltration of South Vietnam reached the proportions of an invasion. US back up to South Vietnamese forces progressed from air strikes to regular ground attacks and large numbers of US troops were deployed. Top left: US Marines storm ashore at Da Nang to dislodge Viet Cong forces threatening a USAAF base. Centre left: A South Vietnamese soldier interrogates a suspected Viet Cong infiltrator. Top right: A Viet Cong guerrilla is held for trial by men of South Vietnam's 4th Marine Battalion. Right: US Marines hand out rations to a civilian family caught up in the fighting. Facing page, top: US Paratroops prepare to climb aboard their helicopters to take part in a raid deep into enemy held territory. Facing page, bottom: US Marines travel aboard an M-48 tank towards a fire-fight with the Viet Cong.

Top left: Gary Sobers, captain of the West Indies cricket team, accepts the Frank Worrell Trophy from Australian captain Bobby Simpson at the end of the Test Match series on 17th May. Top right: French sex bombshell Brigitte Bardot takes a break from filming her 1965 box-office smash **Viva** **Maria**, shot in Mexico. Left: David Attenborough who became Director of BBC Television in March. He was already famous for his natural history documentaries. Above: The Drifters, whose melodic voices and inspired stage show made them popular performers in 1965.

Jan 8	US launches biggest offensive ever in Vietnam War
Jan 11	Death of Indian Prime Minister Lai Shastri
Jan 17	US H-bomb accidentally dropped over Spanish coast
Jan 19	Indira Gandhi takes over as Indian Prime Minister
Jan 19	Australia: Prime Minister Menzies resigns after 16 years
Jan 26	Dr. Martin Luther King lives in a slum apartment in Chicago to experience the problems of slum life first hand
Feb 1	Death of US actor and director Buster Keaton
Feb 4	An airliner crashes in Tokyo Bay, killing 133
Feb 8	Freddy Laker forms cut-price transatlantic airline
Feb 24	Ghana: President Nkrumah overthrown by army coup
Mar 8	Ireland: An IRA bomb destroys Nelson's Column, Dublin
Mar 17	US astronauts dock in space
Mar 27	A dog finds the stolen 'World Cup'
Mar 31	Labour wins landslide victory in British election
Apr 2	Death of British author C S Forester
Apr 4	Soviet spacecraft orbits the moon
Apr 7	Missing H-bomb is found on the Atlantic sea-bed
Apr 10	Death of British author Evelyn Waugh
Apr 19	Australia sends 4,500 soldiers to fight in Vietnam
Apr 21	The opening of parliament is televised live for first time
Apr 30	First regular English Channel hovercraft service begins
May 6	'Moors Murderers' Brady and Hindley are jailed for life
Jun 2	Ireland: de Valera is once again President, aged 83
Jun 6	Unmanned US spacecraft lands on moon
Jun 11	UK: Peter Sellers and Mary Quant are awarded OBEs
Jun 30	France formally leaves NATO
Jul 19	US: Richard Speck is arrested for the murder of eight student nurses in Chicago

Jul 20	Harold Wilson, British PM, imposes freeze on earnings
Jul 30	England defeats West Germany 4-2 to win the World Cup
Aug 1	US: Charles Whitman murders 12 people at Texas University, Austin before being shot by a policeman
Aug 13	Chairman Mao announces the Cultural Revolution
Sep 3	Captain Ridgway and Sergeant Blyth become first Britons to row Atlantic
Sep 6	Hendrik Verwoerd, South African Prime Minister, is assassinated in parliament
Sep 8	UK: Severn Bridge opens
Sep 13	Johannes Vorster sworn in as PM of South Africa
Sep 16	Britain's first polaris submarine 'Resolution' is launched
Sep 29	Falkland Islands are raided by Argentina
Sep 30	Bechuanaland gains independence as Botswana
Oct 18	Death of Elizabeth Arden
Oct 21	UK: Inhabitants of Aberfan buried by coal slag heap
Oct 22	Spy George Blake escapes from jail in London
Oct 26	President Johnson visits US troops in Vietnam
Nov 8	Former Hollywood actor, Ronald Wilson Reagan, is elected Governor of California
Nov 9	Italy: Flood ruins many art treasures in Florence
Nov 9	Jack Lynch becomes new Irish PM
Nov 20	Escaped British spy George Blake arrives in Berlin
Nov 26	The World's first major tidal power station opens in Brittany, France
Nov 30	Full independence proclaimed in Barbados
Dec 1	Britain's post office issues first special Christmas stamps
Dec 15	Walt Disney dies
Dec 22	Rhodesia leaves the Commonwealth

The summer of 1966 saw sport dominated by the Soccer World Cup, which was held in England. After a series of exciting matches the final was held at Wembley between West Germany and England in front of a crowd of around 93,000. The English team included many household names such as goalkeeper Gordon Banks, captain Bobby Moore, striker Geoff Hurst as well as the Charlton brothers and Nobby Stiles. Germany scored first, but England rapidly took a 2-1 lead which lasted until the closing seconds when West Germany equalised. In extra time England powered ahead to win 4-2. Leading goal-scorer was Geoff Hurst who became the only man to score a hat-trick in a World Cup final. When the final whistle blew, the fans invaded the pitch. Left: England's captain Bobby Moore holds the coveted World Cup aloft surrounded by his exhausted but exhilarated team.

THE ABERFAN DISASTER

On 21st October a slag heap in the Welsh coal mining village of Aberfa collapsed and slid down hill. Around 2 million tons of mud, rock and eart ploughed into the Pantglas Junior School just as the children were gath ered for morning assembly, burying them beneath 45 feet of debri Townsfolk, firemen and miners from nearby pits rushed to help with mar locals digging with their bare hands before professional help arrived. A fe victims were hauled out alive, but a total of 147 died. The disaster wipe out almost an entire generation of children in the valley and the commu nity grief could almost be touched. Top left: Rescue workers dig throug the rubble of the school in an attempt to find survivors and bodies. Abov Carl Evans, one of the few survivors dug alive from the wrecked schoo carries a floral tribute to the graveside of his classmates. Above left: A fe of the 82 children's coffins buried in Aberfan graveyard on 28th October.

Left: The two astronauts, Armstrong (right) and Scott, of the ill-fated Gemini 8 mis-sion greet their families in Houston, Texas. The pair successfully docked with the Agena craft while in orbit, the first time such a feat had been achieved. The linked space-craft then went out of control and only the skill of the astro-nauts ensured a safe, but nerve-wracking, splash down in the Pacific Ocean. Facing page, bottom left: Indira Gandhi who became the first female Prime Minister of India on 19th January.

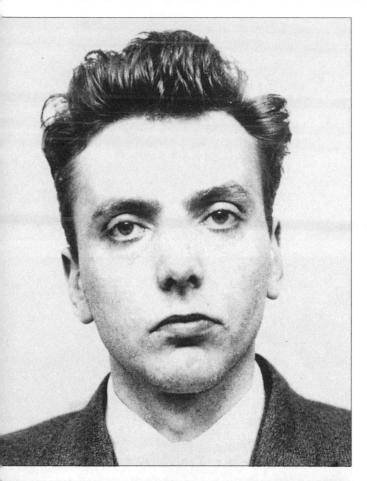

THE MOORS MURDERS

On 6th October police in Manchester received a phone call from a terrified youth named David Smith who blurted out that he had just watched his brother in law, Ian Brady, commit murder. When police burst into Brady's home they found the body of 17 year old Edward Evans, whose head had been smashed by an axe. The horrified police turned up evidence of mass murder carried out by Ian Brady and his lover Myra Hindley. It became clear that the pair had abducted a number of children and tortured them to death before burying their bodies on nearby moorland. Most horrific was the collection of photos and tape recordings which the pair had made of their crimes. When these were replayed in court, the jury wept to hear a young girl plead for her life. The sheer sadism and horror of the crimes shocked the nation, as did the knowledge that there were probably bodies buried on the moors which Brady and Hindley refused to acknowledge and so allow Christian burial. Both killers were sentenced to life imprisonment, the death penalty having been repealed. Above left: Ian Brady. Above right: Myra Hindley.

The Cultural Revolution

In August Mao Tse Tung unleashed the Great Proletarian Cultural Revolution, one of the most damaging mass movements ever inspired by a political leader. The movement was begun by Mao, fearful that he was losing influence within his own government. Calling on the immense reserves of good will he had in the country and on the brutally efficient party organisation, Mao called on all true Chinese to confront "anti-Party, anti-Socialist Rightists" and to fight against foreign influences. Hundreds of thousands of youngsters were recruited in the Red Guards and issued with a Little Red Book of quotations by Mao. The Red Guards marched through all major cities, demanding change. Mao took advantage of the movement to purge his government hierarchy of rivals and disobedient subordinates. The country, meanwhile, suffered a regime of cultural intolerance and political unease unknown since the civil war of the 1930s.

Top left: Mary Quant (right) and Beverly Sasson model some of Quant's ties. Quant epitomised the fashions of the 1960s with a range of cheap but cheerful fashions much in demand by the young of the decade. She was awarded an OBE in 1966 for her contribution to British fashion. Top right: The model Twiggy who snatched world fashion headlines in November by modelling the outrageous new mini skirt. She was in demand for presentations and publicity work as well as for modelling. Above: Buster Keaton, the master comic of the silent movie era who died in 1966. Left: The American pop group The Beach Boys, who invented and popularised a new genre, Surf Music. Epitomising the Californian life style of sun bathing, surfing and hedonistic delight, the Beach Boys' music swept the world.

On 28th May a lone, sea-stained yacht sailed into Plymouth to a stupendous welcome from the watching crowds. The yacht was Gypsy Moth IV, and on board was Francis Chichester. The return to Plymouth marked the end of an epic voyage which had begun the previous August and had taken Chichester around the world on a 28,500 mile voyage. He was the first man to complete such a journey single handed and was knighted by Queen Elizabeth II in recognition of his achievement. Top: The Gypsy Moth IV leaves Sydney Harbour on 29th January. Above: Francis Chichester photographed before his epic voyage.

Jan 3	Death of Jack Ruby, Lee Harvey Oswald's killer
Jan 15	Green Bay Packers win Super Bowl
Jan 16	George Wallace's wife is new Governor of Alabama
Jan 18	Jeremy Thorpe is new Liberal leader
Jan 27	US: 3 astronauts are killed in launch pad rehearsal
Feb 5	Anastasio Somoza is elected President of Nicaragua
Feb 11	Red Army takes over Peking
Feb 14	UK: 100 Labour MPs condemn US bombing of Vietnam
Feb 14	Greece: King Constantine flees country after his attempted coup fails
Feb 18	Death of Robert Oppenheimer, developer of US atomic bomb
Mar 4	UK: First North Sea gas pumped ashore at Easington, County Durham
Mar 6	Death of Hungarian composer Zoltan Kodaly
Mar 9	Svetlana Alliluyeva, daughter of Stalin, defects to the West
Mar 10	US bombs industrial targets in Vietnam
Mar 12	Mrs Gandhi re-elected Prime Minister of India
Mar 18	Oil tanker 'Torrey Canyon' is wrecked off coast of Cornwall
Mar 26	10,000 hippies rally in New York's Central Park
Mar 30	The wrecked oil tanker Torrey Canyon is bombed to destruction
Apr 8	Sandy Shaw wins Eurovision Song Contest for Britain with "Puppet on a String"
Apr 12	The UK pound reaches parity with the US dollar
Apr 15	New York: 100,000 marchers take part in an anti-Vietnam War rally
Apr 24	Soviet Cosmonaut Vladimir Komarov is killed in capsule
Apr 28	Muhammed Ali is stripped of world title for refusing to serve in forces
May 5	Britain launches her first satellite
May 8	US: Muhammed Ali is indicted for draft evasion
May 14	Liverpool's Roman Catholic Cathedral opens
May 25	Celtic becomes first British Club to win the European Cup
May 28	Sir Francis Chichester arrives at Plymouth after sailing round the world
Jun 1	Israel: Moshe Dayan is appointed Defence Minister
Jun 4	Donald Campbell dies on Coniston Water during his attempt to break the world water speed record
Jun 5	Six Day War begins with Israeli air strikes
Jun 7	Death of American writer Dorothy Parker
Jun 17	China explodes her first H-bomb
Jun 29	US actress Jayne Mansfield is killed in car crash
Jul 1	Colour television begins on BBC2
Jul 7	Francis Chichester is knighted with Sir Francis Drake's sword
Jul 8	Death of British actress Vivien Leigh
Aug 15	Bill is passed banning pirate radio stations in Britain
Sep 3	Sweden switches to driving on right hand side of the road
Sep 12	Governor Reagan calls for escalation of Vietnam War
Sep 20	The £26 million liner, the Queen Elizabeth II is launched by her namesake
Sep 30	Radio I begins broadcasting with Tony Blackburn
Oct 8	Death of former British prime minister Clement Atlee
Oct 8	The first breathalyser test takes place in Britain
Oct 9	Death of revolutionary Che Guevara, murdered in Bolivia
Oct 25	Abortion Bill is passed by British Parliament
Nov 27	De Gaulle vetoes Britain's entry to EEC
Dec 3	Christiaan Barnard performs first heart transplant operation
Dec 17	Australian Prime Minister Harold Hold drowns

THE ARAB-ISRAELI WAR

During the summer tension increased between Israel and her Arab neighbours. Egypt, Jordan and Syria formed an alliance which was clearly aimed at Israel, a fact confirmed when Egypt moved troop reinforcements into the Sinai Desert and blocked the Suez to Israeli shipping. Israel gambled by launching a pre-emptive strike before her enemies were ready. On 5th June the Israeli air force, using sophisticated modern weapons and novel tactics, managed to catch the Arab aircraft on the ground and destroy them. The Israeli army then poured into Sinai, smashing through the ill-prepared Egyptian army and driving it back to the Suez Canal. The Jordanian forces were herded back east of the Jordan and the Syrian army thrown off the Golan Heights. The importance of control of the air was reinforced by the startling Israeli successes. On 10th June, Israel called off its offensive actions and settled down to consolidate its hold on the vital strategic prizes of the West Bank, Gaza and the Golan Heights. Facing page, top: An Israeli armoured unit in eastern Jerusalem. Facing page, bottom: Western journalists view the wreckage of a vast Egyptian road convoy destroyed by Israeli forces. Left: Israeli tanks arrive in Bethlehem. Below: Egyptian prisoners captured in Sinai are held at Gaza.

Tragedy In Space Race

The rivalry between the United States and the Soviet Union to win prizes in the space travel industry claimed three victims on 27th January and set back American hopes of putting a human on the Moon. Astronauts Roger Chaffee, Virgil Grissom and Ed White were completing a complex systems check on the Apollo 1 spacecraft on the ground at Cape Kennedy when a tiny spark inside the cramped cabin ignited in the pure oxygen pressurised atmosphere and spread rapidly, killing all three men before the rescue teams could reach them. Officials at the National Aeronautics and Space Administration (NASA) admitted the tragedy would delay the Apollo programme.

The British Protectorate of Aden became increasingly troubled during the mid-1960s as nationalists turned to terrorism to achieve their aims. Britain had gained Aden from the Ottomans in 1839 as a staging post for ships bound for India and it gained some self-government in 1937. The city state became independent in 1967 as Yemen. In 1970 a new constitution imposed a Communist dictatorship, but this was overthrown in May 1990 when Aden joined with the Yemen Arab Republic to form the Republic of Yemen with a liberal constitution. Right: A young British woman, Mrs Ann Frost of Essex, carries a machine gun as she walks her children through Aden.

STALIN'S DAUGHTER DEFECTS

In March Svetlana Alliluyena defected from the Soviet Union to seek asylum in the United States, the event made the headlines as she was the daughter of Soviet dictator Josef Stalin. She walked into the American Embassy in Delhi, India, in April announcing her identity and demanding asylum. The CIA rapidly whisked her to Switzerland where she was kept under surveillance for some time before being allowed into the USA. Her defection came amid talks on arms limitation between the two super powers and was widely judged to be something of an embarrassment to both nations. Right: Svetlana Alliluyena photographed in 1949 when she could enjoy all the privileges her father would bestow.

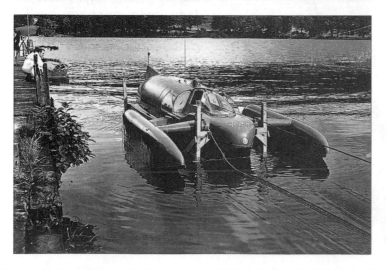

Above left: A BOAC Boeing 707 nose dives into the runway at London's Heathrow Airport after the pilot was forced to land with the nosewheel securely jammed in the fuselage. Pilot Peter Mains-Smith, who had won a DFC and DSO during the war brought the aircraft to a standstill without casualties. Left: The liner **Queen Mary** *arriving in Long Beach California to be moored as a floating hotel after she was scrapped from the Atlantic run. In June Britain was shocked by the violent death of speed enthusiast Donald Campbell, killed on Coniston Water when his power boat crashed at over 300 miles per hour. Below left: Donald Campbell's ill fated* **Bluebird**. *Below: The Bluebird's final moments on Coniston Water.*

Top left: Opera star Maria Callas and Greek shipping magnate Aristotle Onassis who announced their engagement this year. Top right: The British rock group The Rolling Stones enhanced their image as the bad boys of rock by a variety of property breaking stunts. Above centre: The carefree Monkees fostered an image of cheerful youth in their songs and television shows. Left: German statesman Konrad Adenauer who died this year after leading the Christian Democrat Party in West Germany for twenty years. Above: James Callaghan taking up ministerial office, he went on to become Prime Minister.

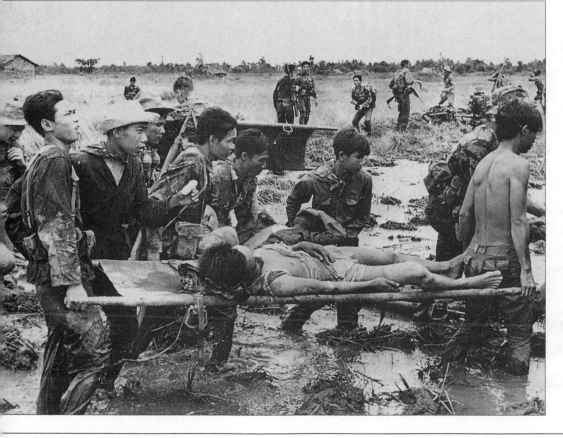

The increasing US involvement in the Vietnam War, and the growing list of US dead caused deep unease in America and elsewhere, particularly when unpleasant facts about the South Vietnamese regime were publicised. *Facing page, top:* On 15th April around 100,000 people marched through New York to Central Park to protest against the war. *Facing page, bottom:* A US F-5 tactical strike aircraft unloads bombs on a Viet Cong camp. *Above left:* A US Paratrooper prepares to dispose of a sign while on an offensive strike near Chu Lai. *Above:* US Marines evacuate the wounded from a battlefield near the Laotian border in May after unexpectedly running up against regular North Vietnamese troops. *Left:* South Vietnamese soldiers regroup and evacuate the wounded after a clash with the Viet Cong in June near Moc Hoc.

1968

Jan 1	Cecil Day Lewis becomes British Poet Laureate		**Aug 21**	Russia invades Czechoslovakia
Jan 31	Mauritius, former British Colony, becomes independent		**Aug 22**	South America gets first ever visit from Pope
Feb 17	Death of British actor Sir Donald Wolfit		**Aug 31**	Gary Sobers became first cricketer to hit 6 sixes off an ove
Feb 20	Death of British film director Anthony Asquith		**Sep 2**	Major earthquake kills 11,000 in Iran
Mar 2	Lockheed wheels out Galaxy, the world's largest aircraft		**Sep 9**	Arthur Ashe becomes first black player to win US Open
Mar 16	UK: Part of the Ronan Point block of flats collapses in the East End of London		**Sep 13**	Press censorship is re-imposed in Czechoslovakia
Mar 16	US: Robert Kennedy says he will run for President		**Oct 2**	Britain's first sextuplets are born
Mar 27	UK: Foreign Secretary says Falklands will stay British		**Oct 3**	UK: A £5,000 'Booker' prize for the best British novel is announced
Mar 27	Russian cosmonaut Yuri Gagarin dies in an air crash		**Oct 12**	19th Olympic Games open in Mexico City
Mar 31	US: President Lyndon Johnson says he will not stand for re-election		**Oct 13**	Death of British publisher Sir Stanley Unwin
Apr 4	Martin Luther King is assassinated		**Oct 14**	Detroit Tigers win World Series
Apr 7	Jim Clark, British motor racing champion, is killed during a race		**Oct 18**	UK: John Lennon and Yoko Ono are arrested on drug charges
Apr 19	A team of Americans reach the North Pole after 42 days, the first to arrive via surface travel		**Oct 20**	Jackie Kennedy weds Aristotle Onassis
Apr 23	5p and 10p coins are issued in UK		**Oct 23**	UK: Rupert Murdoch enters the battle to buy the News of the World
Apr 28	First showing of rock musical 'Hair'		**Nov 5**	US: First black woman is elected to the House of Representatives
May 3	Britain's first heart transplant takes place		**Nov 5**	Republican Richard Nixon is elected as US President
May 8	UK: The Kray twins are arrested		**Nov 10**	Death of novelist John Steinbeck
May 24	France: A policeman is killed during the student unrest		**Nov 15**	The Queen Elizabeth finishes her last voyage
Jun 1	Helen Keller dies		**Nov 28**	Death of British author Enid Blyton
Jun 5	US: Robert Kennedy is fatally shot		**Dec 2**	US: Henry Kissinger is to be the national security adviser
Jun 14	US: Dr Spock is found guilty of draft evasion		**Dec 20**	Spain: Franco banishes Prince Carlos
Jun 24	Death of comedian Anthony Hancock		**Dec 21**	US: Apollo 8 is launched from Cape Kennedy
Aug 1	Nixon says Vietnam War should be scaled down		**Dec 31**	Russia's TU144 becomes first supersonic airliner
Aug 5	Ronald Reagan says he will run for President			

THE PRAGUE SPRING

The early months of 1968 became known as the Prague Spring in Czechoslovakia. The Communist Party leader Alexander Dubcek set out to introduce "Socialism with a human face" by allowing a free press, public debate and other democratic-style reforms. The Czechs welcomed the moves enthusiastically, but neighbouring Communist counties were not so pleased. Dubcek was summoned to talks with the leadership of the Soviet Union who showed their displeasure at his liberalising regime. On 29th April the pressure was stepped up when the Soviets halted food exports to Czechoslovakia. On May 9th the Soviet army staged large scale manoeuvres near the Czech border. On 30th July Dubcek and his ministers met other Eastern bloc leaders in Cierna. A crisis meeting followed with several personal visits by Communist heads of state all of whom pleaded with Dubcek to return to hard-line Communism. Dubcek refused. On 21st August Soviet tanks and hundreds of thousands of men poured into Czechoslovakia. Within just three days the Soviets had overrun all important government buildings and had imprisoned Dubcek and his colleagues. For a few days ordinary citizens rallied around the Czech government in its condemnation of Soviet aggression and demands for continued liberalisation. But on 4th October Dubcek accepted defeat and agreed to reimpose hard line Communist measures. A mass protest on 28th October was held in Prague, but the Soviets had won. It would be two decades before the Prague Spring turned into summer. Facing page: A Czech youth confronts Soviet tanks in Bratislava on 23rd August. Top right: Slogans condemning the invasion being painted on the main road into Prague from Russia on 30th August. Centre right: Soviet trucks set on fire by angry Czechs burn in the streets of Prague on 24th August. Right: A Soviet tank, struck by a petrol bomb, rumbles through Prague.

Below: Senator Robert Kennedy, brother of murdered President John Kennedy, was himself assassinated on 5th June. The murder shocked the nation, and the world coming as it did as a second devastating blow to the political Kennedy clan. Robert Kennedy was running for the Democratic Party's Presidential nomination and had looked set for success. He came to California to campaign in that state's primaries, which he won with ease. On the night of the 5th he was addressing a victory rally at the Ambassador Hotel. It was while he was leaving via the kitchen that Kennedy was shot. The assassin was a young Jordanian named Sirhan Bishara. Sirhan was angered by Democrat backing for Israel. Kennedy was shot twice in the head and died twenty hours later without regaining consciousness.

The United States Presidential elections were sparked in dramatic fashion by President Lyndon B. Johnson (*top*) on 31st March when he declared that he would not be seeking re-election. The announcement was made during a Presidential televised address concerning the war in Vietnam. "I should not permit the Presidency to become involved in the partisan divisions that are developing," declared Johnson. The Democrat candidacy was thus thrown open, though the expected candidate, Robert Kennedy, was murdered during the primary process. The Republicans named Richard Nixon, shown (*above*) with his family, as their candidate with Spiro Agnew as running mate against the Democrats Hubert Humphrey. The election in November ended with a narrow victory for Nixon and Agnew. It was widely regarded as a fine victory for Nixon who had been Vice-President to Eisenhower, but had lost the 1960 Presidential election to John F. Kennedy. One of Johnson's final acts in office was to halt the US bombing in North Vietnam.

Above left: Debris falls from the shattered Ronan Point flats in Plaistow, London. The entire corner of the block collapsed when a gas explosion blew out a section of wall. Three people were killed as the building collapsed. Top right: The wreckage of the BOAC Boeing 707 which crashed on landing at Heathrow Airport on 8th April. Five people were killed but the remaining 121 passengers and crew escaped to safety. Above: The wreckage of the 11,000 ton North Sea oil rig Ocean Prince overturned by high seas in March. The crew of 45 was winched to safety by a helicopter as disaster threatened. Left: An Asian family arriving in Britain from Kenya. The break up of the British Empire left many people in potentially alien lands with few rights of return. The Indians of East Africa constituted the largest such group. Many fled East Africa to find a new home in Britain under the lax immigration rules which then existed. In February new criteria were introduced and there was a rush of Asians seeking to move into Britain before the regulations came into force.

THE PARIS RIOTS

In May France descended into near anarchy and many feared that a revolution was about to take place. Industrial unrest had been simmering for some time when, on 6th May, Parisian students staged a protest at the way the state univèrsities were run. The protest rapidly acquired a political flavour as the more left wing students denounced what they claimed were the evils of the Capitalist System. That night thousands of students rioted and the police moved in with batons and brute force. Some six hundred were injured and police made over four hundred arrests. Four days later fresh battles between police and students took place. Amid this chaos the trades unions called for massive strikes in support of their demands for better pay and job security. President de Gaulle made a dramatic radio and television appeal for calm. By the end of the month thousands of factories were being occupied by workers, the students were barricaded into universities and rioting was commonplace. Only after de Gaulle called on military help was he able to quell the students and persuade the unions to accept a compromise deal. On 30th June the Gaullist party won a massive majority in the elections to the National Assembly and by early July the threat of civil war had receded. Right: Armed police watch as city workmen clear up after the riots of 10th May. Below: Students tear up paving stones and railings to use as weapons during the height of the 6th May riots.

The Biafra Saga

In 1968 a human tragedy of epic scale unfolded in Biafra, a region of Nigeria. In May 1967 the oil-rich region of Biafra, in eastern Nigeria, declared itself independent of Nigeria, itself only newly free of Britain. The Nigerian government retaliated by cutting off economic aid and, in July, war broke out. The war continued into 1968, and it soon became clear that the people of Biafra were starving. Crops were destroyed in the fighting and Nigeria refused to allow food aid to be imported, seeing starvation as a weapon more potent than guns. In August a peace conference was called, but the government demanded little less than total surrender so the war went on. The Biafran leader Odumwega Ojukwu tried desperately to save his people but by the close of the year, tens of thousands were starving to death.

Left: Robert Maxwell arriving at the House of Commons. The Socialist newspaper magnate served as a Labour MP in the 1966-1970 Parliament when Labour were in power. Above: American computer tycoon Ross Perot who was revealed in March to be the fastest money-earning businessman in the world. Starting with just £400 capital, *Perot established a computer data processing service which so matched demand that, backed by Perot's formidable sales skills, it was able to command a market worth of over £70 million just six years later. Unlike Maxwell, Pero expressed no political ambitions i 1968, though that would later change when he ran for Presiden of the United States in 1992.*

Left: American athlete Bob Beamon leaps to victory in the long jump event which he won with a stupendous 8.9 metres, a record which remained unbroken until the 1990's. Below: Bobby Charlton, captain of soccer team Manchester United lifts the UEFA Cup aloft after leading his team to victory at Wembley. Bottom left: Poet C. Day Lewis, who was appointed Poet Laureate in January, with his family. Bottom right: A Chelsea girl sporting a mini skirt, the fashion innovation of the year.

Below: The British pop group the Bee-Gees who swept to fame with a string of chart successes. Right: The comedian Tony Hancock who committed suicide in Australia this year. Hancock was one of the first comedians to become famous through radio work alone with his show **Hancock's Half Hour** which was later adapted to television. A split with his writing team and a succession of failed films and shows preceded his death. Bottom left: Elizabeth Taylor displaying the fabulous diamond ring bought for her by Richard Burton. The ring contained the famous Krupp diamond, one of the largest cut stones in private hands, and cost over £125,000. Bottom right: A winning team for Britain in the Eurovision Song Contest. Singer Cliff Richard (kneeling) was selected to sing the hit **Congratulations**, written by Phil Coulter (left) and Bill Martin (right) on a show hosted by Cilla Black.

MAN ON THE MOON

The great technological achievement of the year was undoubtedly putting a human on the moon. The great event occurred on 20th July and represented the culmination of years of effort. The spacecraft crewed by Neil Armstrong, Michael Collins and Edwin Aldrin took off from Cape Kennedy on 16th July and was the 11th in the Apollo series. The giant Apollo rockets were designed specifically to carry loads heavy enough to equip moon landing missions. Soon after take off, the Apollo craft entered Earth's orbit before swinging out to reach the Moon. After circling the Moon, the spacecraft divided in two, the command module remained in orbit while the lunar module descended to the Moon's surface with Armstrong and Aldrin on board. A soft landing was achieved, despite much worry about the structure of the surface. After some 40 minutes making measurements, Neil Armstrong stepped outside to leave the first human footprints ever on the Moon. He summed up the experience with the famous words "one small step for man, a giant leap for mankind". After 22 hours on the Moon the lunar module blasted off to carry the crew back to the command module and so to return to Earth. The splashdown in the Pacific took place on schedule on 24th July.

Jan 1	Sir Learie Constantine is Britain's first black peer
Jan 4	UK: An airliner crashes into houses near Gatwick airport, killing 50
Jan 20	US: Nixon is sworn in as President
Jan 27	Protestant leader Ian Paisley is jailed in Northern Ireland
Feb 3	Yasser Arafat is new leader of PLO
Feb 3	Death of US actor Boris Karloff
Feb 8	Boeing 747 Jumbo jet makes its first flight
Feb 11	UK: Female Ford workers win equal pay with their male colleagues
Feb 13	A human egg is fertilised in a test tube for the first time
Feb 23	Death of Saudi Arabian King Abd el-Aziz Ibn Saud
Feb 24	US Mariner 6 spacecraft is launched on journey to Mars
Feb 26	Death of Israeli premier Levi Eshkol
Feb 28	US: The request by Sirhan Sirhan, the killer of Bobby Kennedy, to be executed is denied
Mar 2	Concorde makes its maiden flight in France
Mar 4	UK: The Kray twins are found guilty of murder
Mar 10	US: James Earl Ray is jailed for 99 years for the murder of Martin Luther King
Mar 12	Paul McCartney marries Linda Eastman
Mar 17	Israel: Golda Meir becomes Prime Minister
Mar 28	Death of US statesman Dwight D Eisenhower
Apr 1	France formally withdraws from NATO
Apr 9	Britain's Concorde 002 makes her maiden flight
Apr 18	UK: The voting age for women is changed from 21 to 18
Apr 17	Bernadette Devlin becomes youngest woman MP ever at 21 years 359 days
Apr 22	Liner Queen Elizabeth II leaves on maiden voyage
Apr 22	Robert Knox Johnson arrives in Falmouth having completed first non-stop solo circumnavigation of the World
Apr 28	President de Gaulle of France resigns
Apr 29	Ireland: O'Neill resigns as Prime Minister
May 3	Canada: Jimi Hendrix is arrested for possession of heroin
Jun 8	Phased US troop withdrawal from Vietnam is announced
Jun 21	Death of US tennis player Maureen Connolly, 'Little Mo'
Jun 22	Death of Judy Garland, US actress
Jul 1	The Investure of Prince Charles as the Prince of Wales
Jul 16	US: Apollo 11 is launched at Cape Kennedy
Jul 19	John Fairfax arrives in Florida after rowing across Atlantic
Jul 20	Neil Armstrong is first man on moon
Jul 30	US: Edward Kennedy will not run for President
Aug 9	Charles Manson, head of a California commune of hippies, murders the pregnant wife of Roman Polanski
Aug 15	N. Ireland: British troops are deployed on streets of Belfast
Aug 20	US: Bobby Seales, Black Panther leader, is arrested
Aug 31	Rocky Marciano, undefeated boxing champion is killed in an air crash
Sep 1	Colonel Gadafy becomes Head of State of Libya, after leading a military coup
Sep 3	Death of Ho Chi Minh, North Vietnamese leader
Sep 5	ITV makes its first colour transmission in Britain
Sep 12	North Vietnam: Nixon continues B-52 bombing raids
Oct 14	UK: 50p decimal coin is issued
Oct 21	West Germany: Willi Brandt is elected Chancellor
Oct 21	Death of US author and poet Jack Kerouac
Nov 13	UK: Quins born to Irene Hanson of Rayleigh, Essex
Nov 15	US: Huge Vietnam war demonstration in Washington
Nov 19	Pele scores the 1000th goal of his career
Dec 18	UK: The death penalty is officially abolished

GOLDA MEIR TAKES POWER

On 17th March Israeli politician Golda Meir became her nation's fourth premier and first woman leader. Born in the Ukraine in 1898, Meir emigrated to America before moving to Palestine in 1921. There she became involved in politics and gradually assumed leadership of the Zionist Jews as all other prominent politicians were in prison. After independence she served her nation variously as ambassador to the Soviet Union and as foreign secretary. Soon after taking power she authorised preemptive strikes against Egyptian air and military bases. She later took a more conciliatory stance and showed herself willing to discuss even the most intransigent problems with Arab neighbours. The surprise war of 1973 caught Israel almost by surprise and Meir resigned in the following year after criticism of her lack of readiness.

Above: Georges Pompidou who succeeded General de Gaulle as President of France on 20th June. Though a close ally of de Gaulle, Pompidou set out on a new programme by installing the liberal Jacques Chaban-Delmas as Prime Minister. Above right: The Queen presents Charles, Prince of Wales to the Welsh people from the battlements of Caernarvon Castle in July. The ceremonial investment of Charles with the title which belongs by right to the heir to the British throne was a modernised version of mediaeval ritual. Right: Starving children in Biafra where the vicious civil war dragged on throughout the year only to end early in 1970 with the total surrender of the rebel forces.

Above left: Public hangman Harry Allen pours himself a beer in December after his job was ended by Parliament's decision to abolish the death penalty. Left: The three Kray brothers, from left to right Reginald, Charles and Ronald. The twins Reggie and Ronnie for many years ran a violent gang in London's East End which dominated under-world activities and was responsible for numerous crimes. In March the twins were convicted of the murder of underworld rival Jack McVitie and the gang was broken up. Above: Police guard the scene of the horrific murder of film star Sharon Tate and her house guests in August. The murders were carried out by members of a wayward hippy commune led by Charles Manson. Manson set himself up as a semi-divine prophet who foretold a time when his followers would rule the world. Bottom left: The political scandal of the year came when leading American politician Edward Kennedy crashed his car off a bridge at Chappaquiddick in Massachusetts. Also in the car was a pretty young woman named Mary Jo Kopechne and she was drowned as the car sank beneath the waters. Kennedy was severely criticised for leaving the scene of the accident and failing to notify police, although Miss Kopechne was clearly dead.

THE ULSTER TROUBLES

For some time the sectarian rivalry between Catholics an Protestants in northern Ireland had been building up to reach high tension. This tension and bad feeling turned to violence on 12th August as a parade of Protestants celebrating the Siege c Londonderry in 1689, (when the Protestant garrison held out against a Catholic army), passed through the Catholic area of the city. Catholic youths turned out to shout insults and throw stone at the marching Protestants. Clashes developed into fights and b nightfall pitched battles between police and youths were bein fought. As men of the Royal Ulster Constabulary advanced hous by house through the Catholic Bogside region the fragile peace c northern Ireland was vanishing. The riots were the first signs of th Ulster Troubles which were to bring terrorist activity to the regior and to Britain. Top left: Police prepare to advance on stone-throw ing youths in the Bogside area of Londonderry. Above: A membe of the Royal Ulster Constabulary, the RUC, fires a tear gas grenad at rioters in the Bogside region. Left centre: British troops take t the streets of Londonderry in August. Left: A Bogside shop burn unheeded after rioters set it ablaze on 13th August.

Top left: American film star Judy Garland who died this year of a drug overdose in a London hotel room. She was a highly respected musical star with a large following of fans dating from her earliest appearances at the age of just 13. Top right: April Ashley who made history in Britain when her husband sought annulment of the marriage on the grounds that April was a man. She had indeed been a merchant seaman named George Jamieson until a sex-change operation before the marriage. Left: Ann Jones powering her way to victory in the Wimbledon Ladies Singles Final. Above: John Lennon and Yoko Ono in bed at the Hilton Hotel in Amsterdam in March. The highly publicised "bed-ins" were part of the couple's campaign for peace and love in the world.

1970-1979

1970

Jan 1	Princess Anne is made President of Save The Children Fund
Jan 16	Libya: Gaddafi becomes premier
Jan 19	India's first nuclear power stations opens
Jan 22	Boeing 747, world's largest airliner, enters commercial service
Jan 26	Mick Jagger is fined £200 for possession of cannabis
Feb 2	Death of British philosopher Bertrand Russell
Feb 9	PLO leader Yasser Arafat arrives in Moscow for talks
Feb 25	US painter Mark Rothko commits suicide
Mar 2	Rhodesia is declared a republic
Apr 9	The Beatles dissolve their partnership
Apr 9	Champion jockey Lester Piggott rides Nijinsky to victory in the 2,000 Guineas at Newmarket
Apr 21	Bobby Charlton makes 100th appearance for England
Apr 24	China launches her first satellite
Apr 29	US: The judge in the Chappaquiddick case doubts the truth of Senator Kennedy's testimony
May 4	US: 4 students shot dead at Kent State University, Ohio during anti-war demonstrations
Jun 2	Bruce McClaren, New Zealand racing driver, accidentally killed
Jun 7	Death of British author E.M. Forster
Jun 4	Tonga becomes independent of Britain
Jun 17	Decimal postage stamps are issued
Jun 18	Conservatives win election in Britain
Jun 21	Brazil win football's World Cup for the third time
Jul 3	A British Comet airliner crashes in Spain killing 112
Aug 2	British army in Belfast uses rubber bullets for first time
Aug 19	UK: Coronation Street shows its 1,000th episode

Aug 24	UK: Radioactive leak at Windscale power station
Sep 1	King Hussein of Jordan escapes an assassination attempt
Sep 14	Palestinians blow up 3 hijacked jets in Jordan
Sep 18	US rock musician Jimi Hendrix dies of drug overdose
Sep 28	Death of Egyptian statesman Abdel Nasser
Oct 4	Janis Joplin dies of a drug overdose
Oct 5	Anwar Sadat is nominated to succeed Abdel Nasser as President of Egypt
Oct 9	Cambodia is declared a Republic
Oct 10	Fiji becomes independent of Britain
Oct 10	Quebec Minister Pierre Laporte is kidnapped and killed
Oct 10	Death of French statesman Edouard Daladier
Oct 15	Australia: The West Gate Bridge, Melbourne collapses, killing 33
Oct 19	A major oil field is discovered in the North Sea
Nov 1	France: A fire at a dance hall kills 146
Nov 9	Death of French premier Charles de Gaulle
Nov 12	Hurricanes hit Ganges Delta Islands, Bangladesh with 100,000 deaths
Nov 20	Bank of England 10/- note goes out of circulation
Nov 27	Gay Liberation Front marches in London for the first time
Dec 10	Alexander Solzhenitsyn is awarded the Nobel Prize for Literature
Dec 18	Germany: Victims of the drug thalidomide are awarded over £11 million in compensation
Dec 26	British athlete and gold medal winner, Lillian Board dies of cancer at the age of 22

Left: The first of three hijacked airliners is blown up by terrorists in Amman on 14th September. The triple hijacking followed rising tensions in the Middle East. On 28th August the Palestinians rejected a US sponsored peace plan and on 1st September King Hussein of Jordan narrowly escaped an assassination attempt. On the 7th September Arab terrorists captured two American jets bound for New York and two days later hijacked a British jet. In total some 300 passengers and crew were held hostage at Dawson's Field emergency airstrip near Amman. The crisis ended when seven Arabs were released by the West. The terrorists released their prisoners, but destroyed the aircraft. Meanwhile the Palestinians in Jordan turned from guerrilla tactics to outright war in their demands for power. King Hussein unleashed his army and within days Palestinian leader Yasser Arafat had agreed to back down and unite with Hussein against Israel.

Top: The smog which descended on New York City on 27th July. The smog was caused by a quirk of atmospheric conditions which caused the air over the city to remain still and static, stopping the pollution from car exhausts and industry from dispersing as usual. At its peak the sulphur dioxide reached 17 parts per million, nearly double the 10 parts considered to be hazardous to health. Below: West German statesman Willy Brandt who initiated a policy of detente with East Germany and other Communist bloc nations. Brandt was born Herbert Frahm, but adopted his new name when on the run from Nazi persecution in the 1930s. He was elected Mayor of West Berlin in 1957 and became Chancellor of West Germany in 1969.

The British people went to the polling booths on 18th June to elect a government. The Labour Party had been in power for nearly six years and most commentators and opinion polls expected an easy Labour victory. The Conservative Party was led by Edward Heath, a 53 year old bachelor with a passion for sailing and music. His astute use of television broadcasts and media publicity was widely acknowledged. His party targeted women for their message as well as the many thousands of 18-21 year olds who were given the right to vote for the first time in this election. When the Conservatives won with a 31 seat majority in the House of Commons nearly everybody, including many Conservatives, were taken by surprise. Heath at once began implementing his famous "Selsdon Man" proposals of radical economic reform, the breaking of state power and effective anti-union measures. It soon became clear that a trial of strength between the government and vested interests would not be long in coming and the people eagerly awaited the contest. Below: Edward Heath launches the Conservative Party's manifesto entitled *A Better Tomorrow* on 26th May.

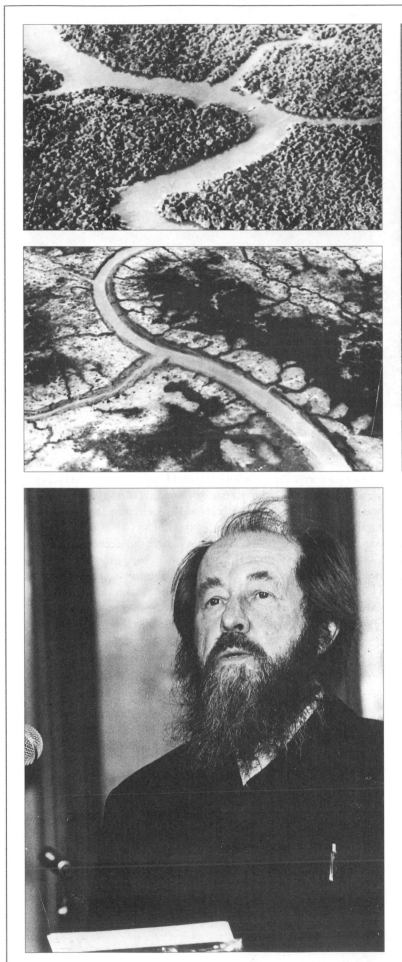

Top left: A stretch of mangrove forest about 60 miles from Saigon in its natural state. Above left: The same stretch of jungle after being sprayed with defoliant. Above: American soldiers of the First Cavalry Division move cautiously through the jungle near the Cambodian border on 5th May. It was on 5th May that President Nixon gave his troops permission to cross the border into Cambodia in *search of Viet Cong insurgents. He promised that the raids would last no more than seven weeks. Left: The Soviet writer Alexander Solzhenitsyn who was awarded the Nobel Prize for Literature this year. He was unable to attend the award ceremony in Sweden due to Soviet disapproval and the risk that, once outside the Soviet Union, he would be refused re-admission and so be separated from his family.*

VIETNAM WAR ESCALATES

The war in Vietnam continued to grow and spread as the struggle between the north and south entered a new phase. Regular United States troops were now deployed in large numbers and were taking part in prolonged jungle fighting. Communist sympathisers in South Vietnam were making great inroads in rural areas, providing secure bases for Viet Cong guerrillas. Communists also established training bases and supply routes through the neighbouring states of Cambodia and Laos. When the US launched air attacks and ground raids into these territories the fighting spread rapidly. In March a terrible incident came to light. It was alleged that a platoon of US troops had massacred an entire village of 567 civilians at Mylai in Vietnam. The trial of the platoon's commanding officer began in March. As the trial continued the conditions of brutality, strain and nervous exhaustion under which US troops operated were revealed as were the haphazard conduct of the war and the lack of discipline among the troops. The long trial served to increase anti-war feeling. Lieutenant Calley was found guilty in March the following year after the enlisted men had been acquitted.

Top left: Tony Jacklin who became the first Briton in fifty years to win the US Open golf tournament in June. Top right: Lillian Board, a British fashion designer, who took the European 800 metres title and died later in the year of cancer. Left: The legendary Pele whose stupendous soccer skills took his native Brazil to victory in the World Cup in a series of matches in which they devastated the opposition. Above: A crushing left punch to the jaw sends Bob Foster crashing to the canvas and a second round knockout defeat. His victor was World Heavyweight Champion Joe Frazier. The fight cleared the way for the much anticipated bout between Joe Frazier and Mohammed Ali, formerly Cassius Clay.

Top left: Louis Armstrong gives an impromptu performance outside his home in Queens, New York. Armstrong was taken seriously ill this year and spent two long periods in hospital. Concerts were held in his honour in both Britain and America as the music world paid tribute to perhaps the greatest jazz trumpeter of the age. Above left: The Who, a British pop group who established themselves as the heroes of the Mods on the streets of Britain. Above: Jimi Hendrix, the legendary rock guitarist who died on 18th September. Hendrix was born in Seattle but first found fame in Britain where his flamboyant style and wild chords ensured success. His return to the USA was accompanied by fantastic innovations in rock guitar work. His early death, aged just 27, from drug abuse was a blow to the music industry. Left: British broadcaster Eamon Andrews with his children after receiving an OBE for services to British television and radio.

Jan 2	Disaster at Ibrox Park football ground, Glasgow when the crowd barriers collapse, 66 are killed
Jan 10	Death of French fashion designer Cooo Chanol
Jan 15	UK: 1/2 p, 1p and 2p coins are issued
Jan 17	Baltimore Colts win Super Bowl
Jan 24	Major-General Idi Amin takes power in Uganda
Jan 31	Apollo 14 is launched
Feb 4	Rolls-Royce are declared bankrupt in the UK
Feb 5	Idi Amin is sworn in as President of Uganda
Feb 5	US spacecraft Apollo 14 lands on moon
Feb 7	Switzerland: Women are given the vote
Feb 9	Ireland: A British soldier is the first to be killed since the arrival of British troops in Ulster
Feb 15	UK: Introduction of decimal currency
Mar 3	Winnie Mandela is jailed for a year in Johannesburg
Mar 6	UK: Over 4000 Women's Lib marchers pass through London
Mar 8	Death of US actor and comedian Harold Lloyd
Mar 16	Death of US politician Thomas Dewey
Mar 23	Ireland: Brian Faulkner becomes new PM of Ulster
Mar 25	Civil War breaks out in Pakistan
Mar 29	US: Murderer Charles Manson is sentenced to death for the murder of Sharon Tate and six others
Mar 31	US: Lt Calley is convicted in My Lai massacre case
Apr 5	Continuing violence in East Pakistan leads to foreigners being airlifted out
Apr 6	Igor Stravinsky, Russian composer, dies
Apr 18	The Federation of Arab Republics is formed by the UAR, Libya and Syria
Apr 19	UK: Unemployment is at 814,819, the highest since 1940
Apr 19	Russia launches the first space station 'Salyut'
Apr 21	Death of Haitian dictator 'Papa Doc' Duvalier
May 12	Mick Jagger marries Bianca Perez Morena de Macias
Jun 10	UK: Joe Gormley is elected President of NUM
Jun 19	UK: Opportunity Knocks is most popular TV programme
Jun 28	US: Muhammed Ali is cleared of draft dodging
Jun 30	Soyuz II crashes on re-entry to atmosphere, killing 3
Jul 3	Jim Morrison dies in a bath in Paris
Jul 6	Death of US singer and trumpeter Louis Armstrong
Jul 25	The first heart and lung transplant takes place
Jul 29	Yugoslavia: Tito is re-elected for another five-year term
Jul 30	Japan: 162 are killed in the world's worst plane crash
Jul 31	Apollo 15 astronauts David Scott and James Irwin ride on moon in specially designed moon buggy
Aug 6	Chay Blyth, the lone yachtsman returns to England after sailing around the world in 293 days
Aug 12	Syria breaks off relations with Jordan
Aug 15	UK: Harvey Smith wins British Showjumping Derby but is disqualified for his use of the two fingered gesture
Sep 3	Ireland: An 18-month-old girl is killed by the bullet of an IRA sniper
Sep 11	Nikita Khrushchev, former Soviet leader, dies
Sep 24	Britain expels 90 Russian diplomats for spying
Oct 1	Disneyworld opens in Florida
Oct 9	Emperor Hirohito arrives in Britain on a state visit
Oct 17	US: Pittsburgh Pirates win World Series
Oct 27	Congo changes its name to Zaire
Nov 5	Princess Anne is named Sportswoman of the Year
Dec 6	India recognises Bangladesh
Nov 10	Ireland: Two Belfast women are tarred and feathered for dating British soldiers
Dec 2	The Queen's salary is doubled to £980,000 per annum
Dec 3	Pakistan and India go to war over Bangladesh
Dec 18	Death of US golfer Bobby Jones
Dec 21	Kurt Waldheim becomes Secretary-General of UN
Dec 25	Worst ever hotel fire, 162 killed in Hotel Daeyungak, Seoul, S. Korea

The Domino Theory

The continuing loss of life and growing suffering in Vietnam went on as the USA persisted in attempts to prop up the South Vietnam regime. As it became increasingly clear that the government of South Vietnam had lost the support of most of its people other considerations came to the fore. Leading these was the so-called Domino Theory which stated that If Vietnam fell to Communism the neighbouring states of Laos, Cambodia and Thailand would similarly collapse. Despite these worries, the US and other nations involved began a gradual withdrawal of troops, By July the Americans could announce that weekly casualties were down to just eleven from a peak of around three hundred. The quarter of a million US troops still in Vietnam were promised that nearly half would be withdrawn by Christmas with more to follow. Australia pledged to pull out completely. It was becoming increasingly clear that South Vietnam was being left to its fate as the cost, in both cash and human terms, of maintaining the state was becoming too much to bear.

Right: Winnie Nomzamo, who married veteran anti-apartheid campaigner Nelson Mandela, was jailed on March 3rd. Winnie Mandela was an active leader of the democracy movement in her own right and would almost eclipse her imprisoned husband in later years before she was disgraced by her connection with a brutal murder in the black townships she dominated.

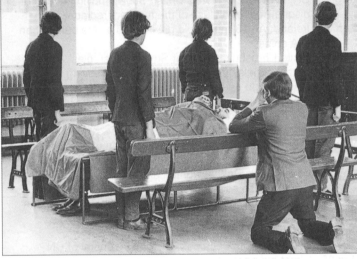

The Ulster Troubles escalated as the IRA resorted to mass terrorism to push their demands for Ulster to be incorporated into the Irish Republic. Earlier civil rights marches turned into brutal confrontations between the Catholic minority and the Protestant majority. Rioting and casual murder reached epidemic proportions and many spoke of civil war. Top left: British soldiers stand guard in the Falls Road district as a factory burns after looting. Above: IRA commander Patrick McAdoxey, aged 25, lies in state in Belfast after being shot dead in an ambush. Above right: A row of terraced houses, inhabited by Protestants, burns after being set alight by IRA terrorists in August. Right: The shattered wreckage of the Post Office Tower in London after an IRA bomb ripped through three stories bringing the Irish troubles to mainland Britain.

THE RISE OF IDI AMIN

The turbulent politics of Black Africa took a surprising turn in January when Uganda acquired a new government by one of the most inept coups ever to succeed. Uganda's President Obote had escaped a murder attempt in December. When he sent for his army chief Idi Amin, the soldier was nowhere to be found and Obote became convinced that Amin had been behind the plot. It actually seems to have been the case that Amin was with a secret lover. On 24th January, Obote was at a conference in Singapore and ordered the arrest of Amin. Amin heard of the impending arrest just minutes before it was due to take place. Dashing to the barracks of a battalion he knew he could rely upon, Amin harangued them about the failures of Obote's rule and led them to the capital Kampala. Finding no organised resistance, Amin seized government offices and declared Obote deposed. East Africa rocked to the news that the relatively unknown soldier ruled Uganda. Above right: General Idi Amin is sworn in as President of Uganda in Kampala on 5th February.

Top left: The Duvalier dynasty which ruled the Caribbean state of Haiti for many years. Papa Doc Duvalier had gained power in 1957 and held it with unremitting ruthlessness until his death on 21st April 1971. The younger Duvalier was just 19 when his father died and he inherited the presidency of Haiti. He abandoned his law studies and took up the reins of power. Above right: Pakistani troops surrender to Indian forces on 18th December. The war was sparked by the decla- *ration of East Pakistan that it was independent as Bangladesh. West Pakistan forces tried to quash the rising, but suffered early reverses. India's clear support for Bangladesh soured relations with Pakistan and led to the short war in December which ended on 17th with the climbdown of the Pakistani government. Right: Austrian diplomat Kurt Waldheim arrives at the United Nations building in New York to take up his post as Secretary General on 22nd December.*

THE APOLLO CLIMAX

This year marked the pinnacle of the American Apollo space programme, and also saw it draw to its end. In February Apollo 14 carried a crew of three to the Moon, two of whom walked on the Moon's surface. The mission followed the abortive Apollo 13 in which mechanical breakdown threatened the lives of the astronauts and disaster was only avoided with care. In July Apollo 15 carried a lunar buggy to the Moon in which astronauts David Scott and James Irwin went on several extensive journeys across the lunar landscape. Two more Apollo flights were to be made in 1972, but already NASA was turning its research towards deep space probes and a reusable space launcher to be dubbed the Space Shuttle. Below: Apollo 14 astronauts sit in a rubber dinghy beside the command module which splashed down in the Pacific on 10th February.

Left: The aftermath of the horrific accident at Ibrox Park in Glasgow when a soccer stand collapsed. The steel and concrete stand crashed to rubble under the weight of the huge crowd watching a needle match between local rivals Celtic and Rangers, leaving sixty six dead and over a hundred injured. On 6th August British sailor Chay Blyth returned to

Britain after completing an arduous single-handed yacht voyage around the World. The ex-Paratrooper made the feat all the more difficult for himself by choosing to sail his yacht British Steel eastwards against prevailing winds and currents. Above: The British Steel sets sail from Southampton. Top right: Chay Blyth before the epic journey.

Left: Coco Chanel, the top Parisienne fashion designer who died on 10th January. Since the flapper era of the 1920s, Coco Chanel had dominated the world of French fashion. She consistently used muted colours and natural fabrics to produce a range of classic but striking clothes. Below: Billionaire J. Paul Getty attends the auctioning of North Sea oil concessions by the British government in August. The North Sea oil fields were to prove a lasting and valuable addition to the British economy. Bottom: The Queen welcomes Emperor Hirohito to Buckingham Palace for a state banquet during the Emperor's extended autumn visit to Europe. Hirohito received a mixed reception as many still recalled the horrors committed in his name during World War II.

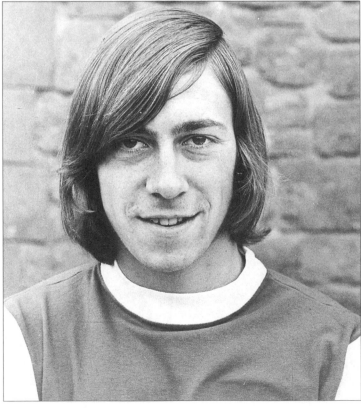

Top left: Princess Anne riding
Purple Star at the Windsor Horse
Trials in April. Her growing skill
in three day eventing was becoming clear for all to see and it was
in this year she won the title of
Sportsman of the Year. Top right:
The pop duo Paul Simon (right)
and Art Garfunkel collecting
Grammy awards at the National
Academy of Recording Arts and
Sciences show in Hollywood on
30th March. Left: Charlie George
the star soccer player who helped
his London team, Arsenal, to win
both the coveted FA Cup and the
League Championship. Above:
The 19 year old Australian tenni
player Evonne Goolagong who
won the Wimbledon Ladies Sing
title with her combination of grac
and power.

Jan 1	Death of French singer and actor Maurice Chevalier
Jan 3	N. Ireland: 50 women and children are injured when the IRA plant a bomb in a department store in Belfast
Jan 9	Liner Queen Elizabeth is destroyed by fire in Hong Kong
Jan 13	UK: A Naval officer is jailed for 21 years for selling secrets to the USSR
Jan 14	Queen Margrethe II accedes to throne of Denmark
Jan 18	First plastic warship HMS Wilton launched at Southampton
Jan 22	Britain, Ireland, Denmark and Norway join the EEC
Jan 30	Bloody Sunday in Northern Ireland
Feb 2	The Winter Olympics begin in Tokyo
Feb 2	The British Embassy in Dublin is destroyed by fire
Feb 15	Death of US writer Edgar Snow
Feb 22	UK: Seven are killed, including a priest, when the IRA bomb the Paratroopers HQ at Aldershot
Feb 23	A Lufthansa jumbo is hijacked by Arab terrorists
Mar 19	Bangladesh signs a Treaty of Friendship with India
Apr 20	Apollo 16 lands on the moon
Apr 22	John Fairfax and Sylvia Cook become the first to row across the Pacific
May 2	US: Death of FBI director J Edgar Hoover
May 15	Governor George Wallace of Alabama, is seriously hurt in assassination attempt
May 21	Rome: Michelangelo's Pieta is damaged by a maniac
May 22	Ceylon becomes Republic of Sri Lanka
May 22	Death of poet Cecil Day Lewis
May 22	Death of British actress Dame Margaret Rutherford
May 20	Death of Duke of Windsor, former British monarch
May 29	President Nixon and Leonid Brezhnev sign the Moscow pact
Jun 8	Rhodesia: An explosion at a pit leaves over 400 miners dead
Jun 18	118 passengers are killed when a BEA Trident crashes minutes after taking off from Heathrow
Jun 11	Colonel Gadaffi says Libya is aiding the IRA
Jun 17	US: Attempted bugging of Democrats' Watergate HQ
Jun 29	Supreme Court abolishes death penalty in US
Jul 6	UK: The Poulson corruption inquiry is set up
Jul 8	Wimbledon: Stan Smith beats Ilie Nastase to win the men's singles title; Billie-Jean King wins the women's singles
Aug 26	Twentieth Olympic Games open in Munich
Aug 26	Death of British yachtsman Sir Francis Chichester
Aug 28	Prince William of Gloucester is killed in an air crash
Sep 5	Arab terrorists kill 11 Israeli athletes at Olympics
Oct 25	Iceland boycotts British goods as part of Cod War
Nov 7	President Nixon is re-elected by a huge majority
Dec 2	Australia: The Labour Party wins the general election
Dec 24	Huge earthquake in Nicaragua, 10,000 are killed
Dec 26	Death of US President Harry S. Truman
Dec 27	Death of Lester Pearson, former PM of Canada
Dec 29	'Life' ends publication after 36 years as the leading pictorial magazine

The Year of The Terrorist

The year 1972 marked, in many ways, the high point for international terrorism. The governments of the world's democracies had not yet organised effective military countermeasures nor were they yet willing to accept civilian casualties to contain the menace. Thus the terrorists had things much their own way throughout 1972. In February a group of Arab terrorists hijacked a German jet liner and successfully negotiated a ransom of $5 million. On 30th May Japanese Communist terrorists stormed Tel Aviv airport with machine guns and hand grenades causing 25 deaths before they shot themselves, one being captured. The following month Palestinian raids on Israel, from bases in southern Lebanon led to Israeli counter raids. September saw the notorious Olympic siege, and also a fire bomb attack on a Montreal nightclub which left 22 dead. October witnessed a second successful Arab hijack of a German airliner with the Olympic terrorists being freed as ransom. In November a letter bomb campaign by Arabs struck several Jewish companies. After the year of violence security measures became increasingly tight. No longer was air travel possible without being searched and armed guards were employed to watch public figures every moment of the day.

On 28th May the Duke of Windsor, once King Edward VIII, died in France. His death marked a brief reconciliation between his widow and the Royal Family. The body of the Duke was flown to an RAF base in Oxfordshire and thence to Windsor Castle where it lay in state for two days. The funeral followed the dying wishes of the former king by being simple and modest in St George's Chapel, Windsor. The Duchess of Windsor, so long ostracised by the Royal Family, attended the funeral on 5th June. The warmth of the greeting (left) between the Duchess and her niece, Queen Elizabeth II, was noted by many. However, following this brief friendly display, the Duchess returned to her home in the Bois de Boulogne where she remained until her death.

Facing page: US President Richard Nixon and USSR President Leonid Brezhnev sign the SALT treaty which aimed to limit nuclear weapons systems on 26th May. The impressive ceremony in the Kremlin's Vladimir Hall was the culmination of a week of talks. The visit was the first to the Soviet Union by a US President and was remarkable for the fact that the two Presidents were content to acknowledge their differences as well as to welcome agreements. Left: President Nixon talking to Chairman Mao Tse-Tung of China in February. The week long visit to China was hailed as a great success with Nixon and his advisor Henry Kissinger establishing new relations with the Chinese regime. During the visit Nixon was honoured at a State banquet in the Great Hall of the People and visited the Great Wall of China. Bottom left: J. Edgar Hoover, first head of the FBI died on 2nd May. He was head of the powerful FBI for nearly 48 years from its inception to his death. It was largely through Hoover's tireless work that the FBI became such a potent force for law and order within the USA. Though some of his actions were criticised after his death the contribution of his organisation to security cannot be doubted.

During 1972 the Vietnamese war entered a new phase. With President Nixon insisting on the gradual disengagement of US ground troops the fighting was left increasingly to South Vietnamese forces, backed by USAAF air strikes. The North Vietnamese were becoming increasingly willing to engage in large scale battles following their acquisition of substantial amounts of Soviet tanks and other modern weapons. In April North Vietnamese forces overran defences around Dong Ha and pushed some thirty miles south to Loc Ninh which was held after weeks of bitter fighting. During the summer the South Vietnamese, aided by accurate US bombing won battles at Binh Din, Kontum and An Loc. In December, after a break, US bombing of North Vietnam resumed at a level unprecedented since the war began. Right: Children flee from a napalm attack at Trang Bang in June.

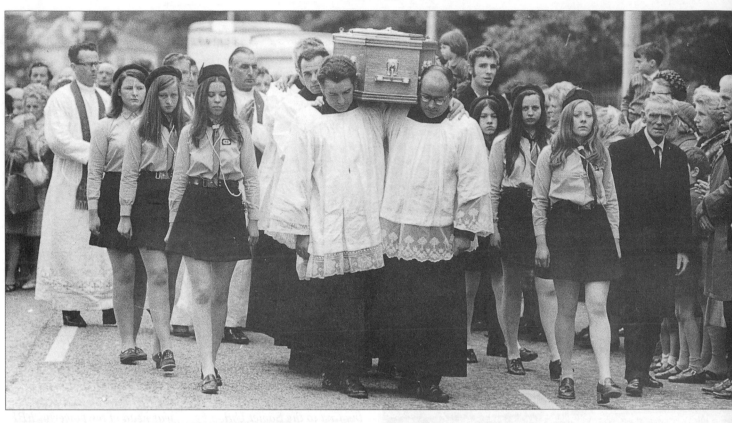

The simmering unrest and sectarian violence of Northern Ireland took a new turn in January with an event which came to be widely known as Bloody Sunday. On Sunday 30th January a march by Republican Catholics in Londonderry took place. Some of the crowd turned on British troops, who were on the streets to preserve order, pelting them with stones. As the crowd became even larger and more hostile, British troops reported seeing armed men at large. Believing these to be IRA snipers, the troops opened fire. In the ensuing confusion and gunfire a total of 13 men were killed. None of the dead could be proved to have been armed and some had been shot in the back. The outcry against the action turned the Ulster Catholics against the army and marked an upsurge in violence. Top: The August funeral of Father Noel Fitzpatrick, cut down in crossfire of a Belfast gun battle. Above: British troops guard a road block during the Londonderry riots of 30th January. Above right: Marchers protest on 2nd February against army tactics on Bloody Sunday. Right: Wounded being carried from a bomb blast in Belfast on 21st March.

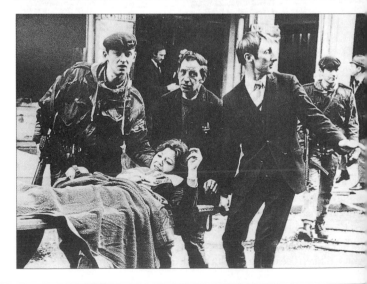

On 22nd January British premier Edward Heath signed the Treaty of Brussels which took Britain into the European Economic Community. The ceremony took place in the Palace d'Egremont in Brussels with Denmark, Ireland and Norway joining Britain in signing the Treaty. The move was hailed as a great step forward for Europe and the cause of European understanding. Under the treaty there were now ten members of the EEC, all pledged to removing trade barriers and co-operating to ensure that international disputes and difficulties would be solved peacefully. Heath viewed the move as one of the most important achievements of his premiership. Though there were some dissenting voices in Britain, the vast majority were enthusiastically in favour of the promised free trade and economic benefits and were unalarmed by talk of a transfer of political power from Britain to Brussels.

The Munich Tragedy
The 1972 Munich Olympics saw a startling terrorist attack which ended in a bloody gunfight. On the 5th September eight Arab terrorists broke into the Israeli athletes apartment, shot 2 dead and captured 9 others. German authorities moved fast to evacuate other athletes and ring the Israeli quarters with troops and armed police. The terrorists demanded the release of 200 fellow Arabs held in Israeli gaols and safe passage out of Germany. Israel refused point blank to release any terrorists. The Germans tried buying the terrorists off with money, but the offer was refused. On 8th September the gunmen agreed to leave on a plane from Munich airport. As the terrorists began crossing the tarmac, German snipers opened fire. The terrorists shot their nine hostages dead while fighting back. When the gunfight had ended 4 Arabs were dead, as was one German. Next day the Israeli air force attacked Palestinian camps in Lebanon which were believed to be strongholds of the Black September group responsible for the attack at Munich. Below: A terrorist on the balcony of the Israeli quarters. Bottom: A member of the International Olympic Committee talks to a masked terrorist on the 5th.

Above: Joe Gormley, President of the National Union of Mineworkers leaves No.10 Downing Street after a marathon fifteen hour session with Edward Heath on 21st February. The talks were called in an effort to find an end to the crippling 6 week strike by coal miners. The strike was damaging British industry due to inter-union co-operation which caused transport workers to refuse to move coal from stockpiles at the collieries to power stations and other customers. The power wielded by the larger industrial trades unions were a direct result of legislation which gave them legal immunities and allowed actions which increased the effectiveness of their actions. There was growing discontent at the power of the unions and many in the Conservative Party began to devise legal restrictions, though they were not put into force by the Heath administration.

The Olympic Games, interrupted by the terrorist attack on Israeli competitors, continued in subdued mood during September. Top left: British athlete Mary Peters taking part in the Women's Pentathlon in which she won the gold medal with a new world record. Top right: David Wilkie competing in the breaststroke event, in which he took the silver medal. Right centre: The Soviet gymnast Olga Korbut who captured the hearts of the audience and a clutch of medals with her dazzling skills. Right: The American swimmer Mark Spitz poses with four of the seven gold medals which he won in the swimming pool. Above: The England soccer player Gordon Banks. His career was tragically cut short by a car crash in 1972 which left him with eye injuries which ruled out professional sport. He had represented his country as goal keeper seventy three times in nine years, including the successful 1966 World Cup.

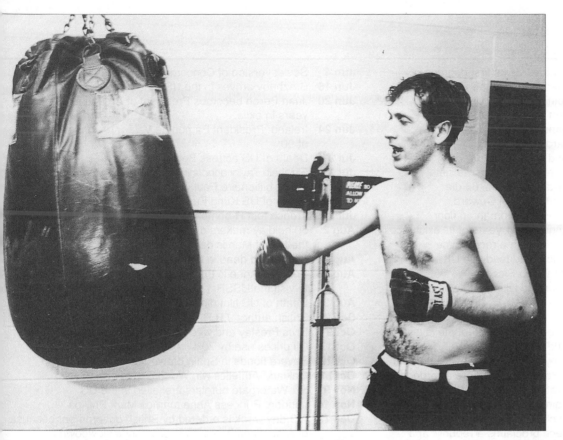

Left: The American chess master Bobby Fischer works on his physical strength in the boxing gym as he limbers up for the intellectual bout with Soviet master Boris Spassky in September. The contest went to Fischer and established him as the world chess champion. Below left: The American singing group, the Osmond Brothers, arriving in London in May for a tour of concerts. The group was massively popular with its perfect harmonies and catchy tunes. Bottom left: Alex Higgins taking a shot in his successful bid for the World Snooker Championship title in November. He won his sobriquet of 'Hurricane Higgins' by his fast and confident play which demolished his opponents. Below: American rock star Chuck Berry arrives in London to take part in a huge concert, which also starred Little Richard, Bill Haley and Jerry Lee Lewis in front of an audience 80,000 strong.

1973

Jan 11	UK: The Open University awards its first degrees
Jan 12	Yasser Arafat is re-elected leader of the PLO
Jan 14	Miami Dolphins win Super Bowl
Jan 22	Death of Ex US President Lyndon B Johnson
Jan 23	5,000 evacuated in Iceland as volcano erupts
Jan 26	Death of US actor Edward G. Robinson
Feb 12	The US dollar is devalued by 10 percent
Feb 22	A Libyan Boeing 727 is shot down by Israeli jets
Mar 5	Two Spanish planes collide in France, 68 die
Mar 26	Death of British playwright Sir Noel Coward
Mar 26	Mrs Susan Shaw becomes first woman on floor of London Stock Exchange in 171 years of its existence
Mar 31	Red Rum wins Grand National in a record time
Apr 1	Value Added Tax (VAT) is introduced into UK
Apr 8	Death of Spanish painter Pablo Picasso
Apr 10	A plane crashes in Switzerland killing 105 women on a shopping trip
Apr 30	Four of President Nixon's aides resign over Watergate
May 4	The Sears Tower in Chicago is completed, the tallest office building in the world
May 5	UK: The FA Cup is won by second division Sunderland
May 7	US: Carl Bernstein and Bob Woodward are awarded the Pulitzer Prize for their Watergate investigation
May 17	US Senate hearings begin on Watergate
May 19	Nine are killed in violent clashes in Northern Ireland
Jun 1	The government in Greece proclaims a republic and abolishes the monarchy
Jun 4	Soviet version of Concorde crashes at Paris air show
Jun 16	Brezhnev arrives in the US for a nine day visit
Jun 20	Juan Peron becomes President of Argentina after 20 years in exile
Jun 24	Ireland: President Eamon de Valera resigns at the age of 90
Jul 2	Death of US actress Betty Grable
Jul 3	Elizabeth Taylor announces her separation from Richard Burton
Jul 15	US oil billionaire Paul Getty's grandson is kidnapped
Jul 19	Death of US Kung Fu film star, Bruce Lee
Jul 21	French test H-bomb in Pacific
Aug 2	50 holdiay makers die when an entertainment complex or the Isle of Man is destroyed by fire
Aug 28	500 feared dead in Mexican earthquake
Aug 28	Princess Anne is the first member of the Royal Family to visit the USSR
Aug 31	Death of US film director John Ford
Sep 2	British author J.R.R. Tolkien dies
Oct 9	Elvis Presley and wife Priscilla get divorced
Oct 17	Oil prices rise by 70%
Oct 19	Severe floods in Spain drown 500
Oct 21	Oakland Athletics win World Series
Nov 9	Six Watergate burglars are jailed in the US
Nov 14	London: Princess Anne marries Mark Phillips
Dec 13	A 3-day week is ordered by British government because of Arab oil embargo and coalminer's slowdown
Dec 17	Arab terrorists hijack US jet, killing 31

On 6th October Egypt and Syria launched a surprise assault on Israeli positions on the Golan Heights and in Sinai. Backed by units from Iraq, Morocco, Saudi Arabia and Jordan, the Arab troops made deep inroads into Israel and Sinai. Soviet missiles caused heavy casualties in the Israeli air force. By the 9th October the situation had stabilised and the Arab advance was halted. By the 16th October Israeli troops had advanced almost to Damascus in the north while in the south a massive tank battle had allowed Israel across the Suez Canal to cut off large numbers of Egyptian troops. When the UN tried to intervene on the 21st the Israelis ignored them, but agreed to a ceasefire on the 25th. By the time peace returned Israel had lost 780 tanks and around 3,000 men compared to combined Arab losses of 1,500 tanks and 19,000 men. Right: Israeli tanks move west in the Sinai, heading for Egyptian troop concentrations.

US PULLS OUT OF VIETNAM

On 27th January treaties were signed in Paris which signalled the end of American involvement in the Vietnam War. President Nixon was convinced that the cost in lives and money of supporting the ailing South Vietnamese regime was too high. A total of 57,000 Americans had been killed and some 300,000 wounded. About $110 billion was estimated to have been spent on the war effort. In addition it was thought that Vietnamese military and civilian casualties had reached 1.2 million. Although the treaties allowed the United States to pull out with some show of success, they in reality represented a strategic withdrawal without victory. The treaties failed to answer the main points at issue between the two Vietnamese regimes and served only to cause a temporary truce in the war. Below: Nixon announces the end of US involvement to the nation. Right: Dr Henry Kissinger, Nixon's foreign affairs advisor in Paris.

*Left: The journalists from the New York Post, Carl Bernstein and Bob Woodward who were largely responsible for bringing the Watergate scandal to light. The scandal begun on 17th June when 5 men were arrested after a break in at the Watergate complex where the Democrat Party were planning their Presidential election campaign. In September the men were brought to court and it was learnt that they had connections with President Nixon or the Republican Party. Two months later Nixon won a landslide election to return to the White House. In February Federal Prosecutor Earl J. Silbert announced that the Watergate investigation would continue after the initial convictions. On 7th May the Pulitzer Prize was awarded to Bernstein and Woodward for their work in uncovering the scandal.
Watergate would eventually bring down the President.*

413

*Below: Princess Anne returning to Buckingham Palace in the glass coach with her new husband Captain Mark Phillips after their wedding at Westminster Abbey. Right: A formal wedding photograph in the Throne Room of Buckingham Palace. Bottom left: Andy Warhol, the epitome of 1960s pop art hit the headlines in January 1973 when a film he had made, claiming it to be highly artistic, was banned from trans-mission on British television on the grounds of bad taste. A film about the Nottingham Craft Centre was shown instead. Bottom right: Sir Noel Coward who died after a lengthy retirement from his mete-oric career as a playwright and musician. His first successful play was **The Vortex**, staged in 1924, but it is his later works such as **Blythe Spirit** (1942) and the movie **Brief Encounter** (1946) which are best remembered.*

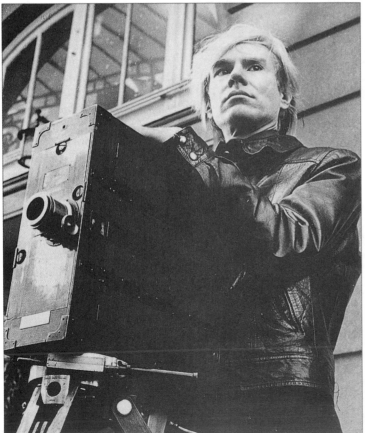

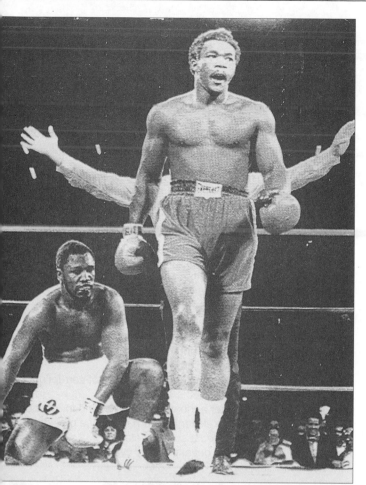

Left: George Foreman walks triumphantly away from Joe Frazier who lost his World Heavyweight Championship to a blow from Foreman's fist in the second round of their fight on 22nd January.
Below: The British rock group Slade who blazed a new trail with their skilful manipulation of the media and extensive use of promotional goods. Despite selling twelve million records in the year, the band members stayed in their Wolverhampton council homes in order to be near their families.
Bottom left: Pablo Picasso being honoured by matadors at a bull fight in 1959. Picasso died on 8th April 1973 after a long lifetime of leading the avant garde in art.
Bottom right: The racehorse Red Rum which won the Grand National, Britain's premier steeplechase event, and went on to become possibly the most successful horse in the history of the sport.

1974

Jan 1	Carlos Navarra is sworn in as prime minister of Spain
Jan 11	First sextuplets to survive born in S. Africa
Jan 31	Death of US film producer Samuel Goldwyn
Feb 4	Following his arrest on Feb 1 the Brazilian government refuses to extradite Ronald Biggs to the UK
Feb 4	US: Patty Hearst is kidnapped
Feb 5	US: Mariner 10 send back pictures of Venus
Feb 7	Grenada becomes independent within the Commonwealth
Feb 10	UK: Coal miners begin a full scale strike
Feb 13	USSR: Author Alexander Solzhenitsyn is deported and stripped of his citizenship
Feb 28	UK: Edward Heath resigns as prime minister
Mar 3	344 are killed in a DC-10 aircrash near Paris, the world's worst air disaster
Mar 6	UK: Harold Wilson is the new prime minister
Mar 10	Harold Wilson ends the state of emergency in the UK and the coal miners return to work
Mar 13	France: Charles de Gaulle Airport is inaugurated
Mar 20	UK: Attempted kidnapping of Princess Anne in the Mall
Mar 24	US: Mariner 10 photographs planet Mercury
Apr 1	Alfonso Michelson is elected president in Colombia's first free presidential election for 16 years
Apr 2	Death of French President Georges Pompidou
Apr 10	Israel: Golda Meir resigns as prime minister
Apr 15	US: Patty Hearst, the kidnapped heiress, is photographed by a hidden camera during a bank raid
Apr 25	Portugal: Dr Caetano is overthrown in a military coup
May 11	Earthquake in Sichuan, China, kills 20,000
May 24	Death of US jazz musician Duke Ellington
May 24	Giscard d'Estaing becomes President of France
Jun 30	US: Mrs Alberta King, the mother of murdered civil rights leader, Martin Luther King, is assassinated in church
Jul 1	Death of Argentinian president Juan Peron
Jul 5	Death of British novelist Georgette Heyer
Aug 8	US: Nixon resigns as President following the Watergate scandal
Aug 9	US: Gerald Ford becomes first unelected President
Sep 4	The US establishes diplomatic relations with East Germany
Sep 8	President Gerald Ford gives Richard Nixon an unconditional pardon
Sep 12	Ethiopia: Emperor Haile Selassie is deposed in military coup
Sep 17	UK: Nurses receive a pay rise of up to 58%
Sep 20	Cyclone Fifi kills 10,000 in Honduras
Oct 5	UK: 5 die when the IRA bomb two Guildford pubs
Oct 11	UK: Labour win second election of the year
Oct 29	Mohammed Ali regains world heavyweight title
Nov 8	UK: Covent Garden moved from central London to Nine Elms
Nov 12	UK: Police seek missing Lord Lucan in connection with the murder of his children's nanny
Nov 26	Japanese PM resigns under suspicion of corruption
Nov 29	IRA is outlawed in UK
Dec 12	US: Jimmy Carter announces he will stand for president
Dec 19	US: Nelson Rockefeller is sworn in as vice president
Dec 20	Ethiopia is declared a socialist state
Dec 25	Darwin, Australia devastated by cyclone 'Tracy'

NIXON AND WATERGATE

On 8th August President Richard Nixon finally accepted the inevitable and resigned from office. The announcement came at the end of the longest running scandal in American political history, the Watergate Affair. The controversy had begun two years earlier when men associated with Nixon and the Republican Party were caught breaking into Democratic Party offices in the Watergate Building. Though in itself the event was embarrassing the real damage was done by the subsequent bungled attempts at a cover up by Nixon and his aides. The story finally centred around the infamous White House tapes, recorded conversations between Nixon and senior party officials which took place in the days after the scandal broke. When these were finally released by Nixon it was clear they had been tampered with in some way. On 5th August Nixon admitted he had withheld information and saw his support suddenly evaporate. Realising he stood in danger of impeachment, Nixon chose to resign rather than have the whole affair dragged out in public even further. The loss of a President in such circumstances was unheard of in US history. The reputation of the Presidency and of the United States reached an all time low.

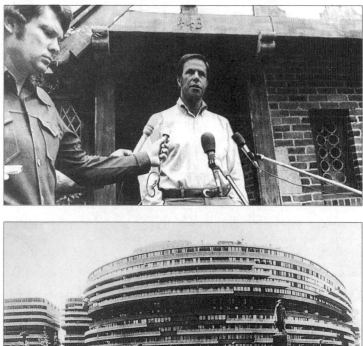

Facing page: Americans on holiday in London eagerly snap up the news. Top left: President Nixon discusses the economic situation with his senior advisers just days before his resignation. Above left: Nixon announces his resignation live on television. Top right: Senior Nixon aide H.R. Haldeman talking to the press outside his home in June denies any secret funds for political purposes. Left: Nixon waves in a gesture more familiar from earlier successful days as he leaves the White House for the last time by helicopter on 9th August. Above: The Watergate Building where the scandal began.

On 4th February Patty Hearst, 19 year old daughter of the newspaper magnate Randolph Hearst, was kidnapped. Two weeks later a demand that $4 million worth of food be given to the poor of America was received from the kidnappers who said they were the Symbionese Liberation Army, a left wing terrorist group. On 15th April Patty Hearst was captured on security cameras helping to rob a bank in San Francisco. It was unclear whether she was acting willingly or under coercion. In May police killed five Symbionese members in a bloody ambush but it was not until September 1975 that Patty Hearst was found and arrested. She was later found guilty of helping the SLA in criminal activities. Right: A photograph issued by the Symbionese Liberation Army in April showing Patty Hearst brandishing a sub-machine gun. Bottom right: John Poulson, the notorious architect, photographed on 18th July after hearing the Home Secretary Reginald Maudling had resigned after allegations of a link between the two.

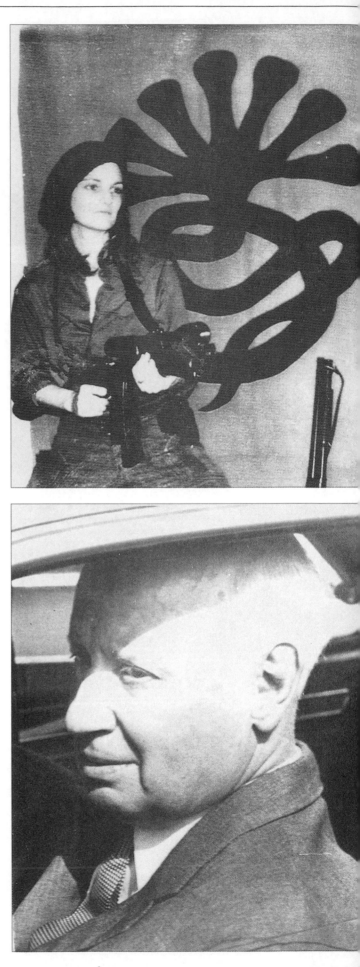

On the evening of 7th November the greatest scandal to rock Britain's nobility in decades began. Lady Lucan, estranged wife of John Bingham, the 7th Earl of Lucan was at home in Belgravia, London, with her children. At about 9 o'clock Lady Lucan went down to the kitchen to find the live in nanny, Sandra Rivett. To her horror she found the kitchen in darkness and Sandra's bleeding body lying on the floor. A large man attacked Lady Lucan, cutting her head and face severely. In terror, Lady Lucan fled upstairs. Moments later her husband appeared and tried to comfort her, but she fled to a nearby pub where drinkers called the police and raced to the Lucan home. Lord Lucan had gone and so had the mysterious killer. A few hours later Lord Lucan arrived at the home of friends and told them that he had been passing his old home when he saw a man break in. Rushing to his wife's aid, he had found the murdered nanny and fled fearing police would suspect him. Lucan was right, the police did suspect him and with some reason. He was known as a great figure in London Society, but was a reckless gambler and heavily in debt. The divorce between the Lucans was going badly for the Earl who faced losing his children and substantial sums of money. By the time police traced Lucan, he had vanished. His car was found abandoned near the south coast. Some thought he had committed suicide rather than face the shame his crime would bring on the Lucan title, others that he had fled abroad to find sanctuary with rich friends. Whatever course the Earl of Lucan chose, he has never been found. Above: Lord and Lady Lucan in happier times.

WAR IN CYPRUS

The island state of Cyprus was plunged into civil war in August after a series of political upheavals. The nation had long been in a state of tension as the Greek and Turkish ethnic groups accused each other of discrimination and violence. When the President, Archbishop Makarios, was overthrown by the military he was replaced by Nicos Sampson, a Greek known for his uncompromisingly anti-Turkish sympathies. The Turks feared for their safety and appealed to Turkey for assistance. On 20th July 30,000 Turkish troops backed by armoured units landed on Cyprus and raced for the capital Nicosia. Within days Sampson had resigned to be replaced by the moderate Glafkos Clerides. The Turks, however, were in no mood to compromise. They conquered the northern third of the island and expelled all Greek residents. The area was proclaimed as the Turkish Republic of Northern Cyprus, though few nations recognised its existence. The island was permanently divided between the Christian-Greek south and the Moslem-Turkish north. Below: Turkish troops drive victoriously through Kyrenia on 22nd July.

Left: Yitzhak Rabin who took over as Prime Minister of Israel on 22nd April. The move followed a devastating split within the ruling Labour Party. Mistakes in military planning were being blamed on Defence Minister Moshe Dayan. Prime Minister Golda Meir stood by Dayan, even to the point of resigning rather than sacking him and so being seen to give way to her party supporters. In Britain industrial unrest led to a change of government. On 5th February the National Union of Miners, led by Joe Gormley, called a strike over wage claims. Prime Minister Edward Heath resisted the calls and the unrest spread. Power cuts became common events and British industry faced being crippled. Heath called a general election for the 28th February in an effort to gain backing from the nation for crushing the strike. In the event the result was so close that Heath could not form a government. Instead Labour, led by Harold Wilson, formed a minority government which relied on the support of smaller parties for power. The coal strike was called off on 10th March and British industry gradually returned to production. Above: Miners at Askern Colliery, Yorkshire, after their first full shift on returning to work.

THE IRA HIT BRITAIN

In 1974 the Irish Republican Army took its campaign of terrorism to the British mainland. On 17th June two bombs struck Westminster Hall and the Tower of London, causing many injuries. On 5th October bombs exploded in two packed pubs in Guildford, Surrey. Four people were killed and many more injured. A month later a pub was bombed in Woolwich, killing two more. Public outrage was intense and the IRA was made a banned organisation in Britain. The days before Christmas saw shoppers in London's West End made the targets for the bombers. Left: Suspects in the Guildford pub bombing case are escorted into court in December. Though found guilty, the suspects were later released after the courts ruled their convictions unsafe. Bottom: Police and firemen outside Harrods store after a bomb tore through the decorating department. Below left: Selfridges after a massive 100lb bomb exploded in Oxford Street on 20th December. Below right: The smashed balcony of the house belonging to Edward Heath, leader of the Conservative Party, struck by a small bomb thrown through the window on 23rd December.

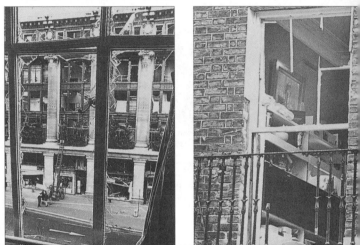

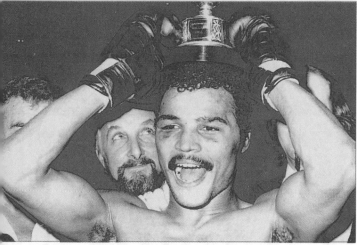

Chaos In Africa

September proved to be a fateful month for several nations in Africa. On 12th a military coup took place in Ethiopia. Formed in 1855 the Empire of Ethiopia was unique in resisting European colonisation under its native rulers. Emperor Haile Selassie had ruled for 58 years when he was driven into exile. He managed to escape the fate of 60 of his government who were executed on the orders of the new Provisional Military Administration. The army invited the Emperor's son, Crown Prince Asfa Wossen, to act as a constitutional monarch while a new democracy was formed. The Crown Prince refused and the new democracy failed to materialise as the military kept a firm grip on affairs. On 30th September President Antonio de Spinola stepped down as President of Portugal. The new government was less keen to retain African colonies. In response, African freedom parties became more active. In Angola bad feeling between the Marxist MPLA and the pro-Western UNITA had tribal origins and rapidly led to civil war. In Mozambique power transferred more peacefully, but was quickly monopolised by the Communist FRELIMO party. The new government was intolerant of opposition and private enterprise in equal degrees leading to much hardship and civil war with the NMR movement. Guinea-Bissau was already in civil war with the rural PAIGC fighting to overthrow the Portuguese-sponsored urban Salazar regime. Changes in Portugal led to rapid peace when Salazar fell.

Top left: The Wimbledon tennis championships saw a double triumph for engaged couple Jimmy Connors and Chris Evert when they took their respective singles titles in thrilling matches. Top right: Miss UK, Helen Morgan, aged 22, who won the title of Miss World in November, but had to retire a few days later after it was revealed that she had had an illegitimate child. Left centre: John Conteh joyfully lifts the World Light Heavyweight trophy which he won by defeating Jorge Ahumba in October. Left: Ronald Biggs, the most notorious of the Great Train Robbers celebrates his release from a Barbados prison where he was held during extradition procedures. The hearings followed a bizarre kidnap plot in which Biggs was snatched from his Brazilian home and put up for auction.

Jan 2	UK: Charlie Chaplin is knighted in the New Years Honours list
Jan 16	Angola wins independence from Portugal
Jan 20	UK: The government abandons plans for a Channel Tunnel
Jan 26	Bangladesh: Prime minister Sheikh Rahman becomes president
Feb 11	UK: Margaret Thatcher is elected leader of the Conservative Party
Feb 14	Death of British scientist Sir Julian Huxley
Feb 14	Death of British-born author P G Wodehouse
Feb 27	UK: PC Stephen Tibble is shot dead by an IRA gunman
Feb 28	UK: Moorgate tube disaster, 35 people are killed
Mar 14	Death of US actress Susan Hayward
Mar 15	Death of Greek shipping magnate Aristotle Onassis
Mar 25	King Faisal of Saudi Arabia is assassinated by his nephew
Apr 5	Death of Chinese statesman Chiang Kai-shek
Apr 11	Death of entertainer Josephine Baker
Apr 13	Fighting erupts between Moslems and Christians in Lebanon
Apr 15	Death of British actor and writer Michael Flanders
Apr 30	South Vietnam surrenders to the North Vietnamese Communists
May 16	Mrs Junko Tobei from Japan becomes the first woman to reach the top of Mount Everest
May 22	Death of British sculptor Dame Barbara Hepworth
Jun 5	The Suez Canal re-opens to international maritime traffic
Jun 5	The people vote to stay in the EEC in the UK's first ever national referendum
Jun 12	India: Prime minister Indira Gandhi is found guilty of corrupt election practices and is told to give up her seat in parliament
Jun 18	The nephew who assassinated King Faisal is publicly beheaded
Jun 19	UK: Lord Lucan is found guilty of the murder of his nanny, but is still missing
Jun 24	US: A plane crashes at Kennedy Airport, killing 109
Jul 5	Arthur Ashe (USA) becomes the first black player to win the men's singles at Wimbledon
Jul 17	The crews of Apollo 18 (USA) and Soyuz 19 (USSR) visit each other's capsules in the first joint space venture between the two countries
Aug 9	Death of Russian composer Dmitri Shostakovich
Aug 10	N. Ireland: A four year old becomes the latest victim of violence in Belfast
Aug 15	UK: The Birmingham Six are sentenced to life imprisonment for planting bombs that killed 21 people in Birmingham
Aug 27	Death of Ethiopian Emperor Haile Selassie
Sep 5	US: An assassination attempt is made on President Gerald Ford
Sep 9	Czech tennis player Martina Navratilova requests political asylum in the USA
Sep 22	US: President Ford escapes a second assassination attempt
Oct 5	Austrian racing driver Niki Lauda becomes world motor racing champion
Nov 11	Australia: Labour Prime Minister, Gough Whitlam, is sacked and a caretaker government is formed
Nov 20	Death of Spanish leader General Francisco Franco

On 11th February Edward Heath, the leader of Britain's Conservative Party, was toppled from power in a leadership bid launched by Margaret Thatcher, the former Education Minister. Known to stand on the right wing of the party, Mrs Thatcher campaigned on a platform based on restricting public spending, curbing the power of the unions and enlarging the private sector in the economy. Though few rated her chances high in the ballot, she swept to victory by defeating first Heath and then that epitome of the Conservative gentleman, Willie Whitelaw. She became the first woman to lead any major British political party and at once made her more vigorous style of Opposition to the Labour government felt in debate. Top: Mrs Thatcher greets the Press as she leaves her Chelsea home for her first day in Parliament as Tory leader, 12th February. Above: Mrs Thatcher and the man she first defeated and then made her deputy, Willie Whitelaw, at a meeting held in March to proclaim her support for Britain's membership of the EEC. Europe was a subject which would haunt her to the end of her political career.

THE BALCOMBE STREET SIEGE

On 6th December four masked IRA gunmen burst into a smart West End restaurant to find the London police ready and waiting, having been tipped off. A desperate chase ended just south of Regent's Park when the gunmen were cornered in Balcombe Street and forced their way into a flat owned by post office worker John Matthews and his wife. Holding the pair hostage, the IRA gunmen demanded safe passage to Eire. The British government refused even to consider the demand. Armed police filled Balcombe Street and cut off the gunmen from contact with the outside world. On 12th December waiting newsmen were pushed right back and the entire area screened off. Word filtered out that the elite army squad, the SAS, were about to be sent into action. The IRA men hastily freed their hostages and then themselves surrendered to waiting police. The tense drama had ended with a major victory for the British government over the IRA. Left: Police train their guns on the flat in Balcombe Street.

Below left: Labour MP John Stonehouse who was arrested in Australia after a catalogue of crime and fraud. Stonehouse vanished when swimming off a Florida beach in 1974 after running up debts, estimated at £800,000. It was thought he had committed suicide to escape disgrace. In fact Stonehouse had fled to Australia with large sums of money using false identity papers and was planning a reunion with his mistress. Australian police were suspicious of the new arrival.

They thought that he was Lord Lucan, the fugitive earl on the run from a murder charge. They arrested the man and only then learnt his true identity. Brought back to Britain in 1975, Stonehouse stood trial for fraud, forgery and theft, found guilty and sentenced to 7 years. Below right: Ambulance men carry the wounded from the Moorgate Underground Station where 29 people were killed when a train ran into a dead-end tunnel at full speed.

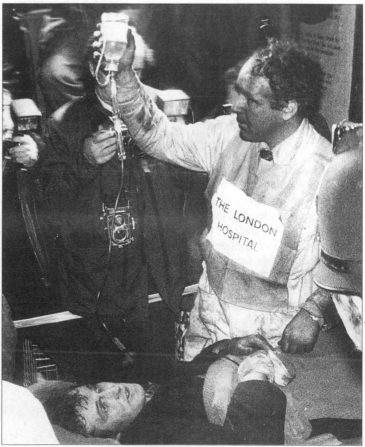

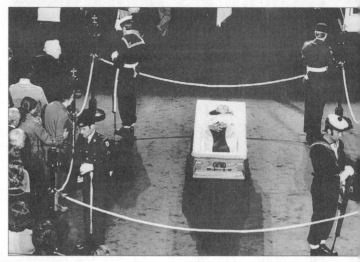

Left: Irish statesman Eamon de Valera who died on 28th August. De Valera was born in New York, but moved to Ireland at an early age and was an active campaigner for Irish independence. He took part in the ill-fated Easter Rising of 1916 and was imprisoned in Britain. While in prison he was elected President of Sinn Fein, the freedom movement. After his release he founded the Fianna Fail party and in 1932 became Prime Minister. He retired from the post in 1959 and was appointed President of his nation, a post he relinquished in 1973. His vision of a united and independent Ireland had been frustrated by the fears of Protestant Ulster about the policies of Catholic Eire and bitter intercommunal violence. His dying words were recorded as "I have done my best for Ireland, and now I am ready to go". Below: de Valera's body lies in state in the Great Hall of Dublin Castle.

Right: Ugandan President Idi Amin meets British Foreign Secretary James Callaghan (left) in July to mark the release of Dennis Hills (right) who had been under sentence of death in Uganda after calling Amin a tyrant. After seizing power in a coup in 1971 Amin had retained a precarious, but firm grip on power. He was a Moslem while over 92% of his peoples were either Christian or pagan. He also came from a minority tribe and so had a weak power base outside the army. He therefore set out to win popularity. He began to slaughter the Acholi and Langi tribes, who had oppressed other tribes in the past. In 1972 he ordered all Asians out of Uganda, forbidding them to take more than they could carry. The Asians were unpopular as their skill in business had allowed them to acquire wealth while native blacks remained poor. The arrest of Mr Hills marked the start of persecution of the British. This new campaign not only gained Amin around $500 million but also gained him immense respect in East Africa as an anti-colonial hard man.

On 20th November, Francisco Franco who had ruled Spain as fascist dictator since winning the Civil War of the 1930s, died. His later years had been largely devoted to finding a successor who could ensure peace and stability in Spain. Franco looked to the Royal Family and chose Prince Don Juan Carlos de Borbon y Borbon. In 1969 Don Juan was sworn in as head of state, though Franco retained real power for himself. The young prince therefore had many years in which to learn the intricacies of Spain's turbulent political make up. Two days after Franco's death Don Juan was enthroned as King Juan Carlos. Equipped with impressive powers of command over the army, control of Parliamentary time and veto over new laws, King Juan Carlos could have seized personal power. He chose instead, to act as a constitutional monarch. Democracy was allowed to flourish and many of the more repressive laws enforced by Franco were repealed. Though he faced many initial difficulties and one attempted coup, the new king proved to be both popular and a force for stability. Below: King Juan Carlos appears before the Cortes with his family to be accepted as the monarch of Spain on 22nd November.

Top left: The Soviet physicist, Andrei Sakharov, who gained fame as a dissident in the Soviet Union won the Nobel Peace Prize in October. Left: King Faisal of Saudi Arabia. The king was murdered on 25th March by his own nephew. The brutal killing occurred in Riyadh at a smart palace reception. The killer, who had been treated for mental illness, suddenly dashed forward and pumped bullets into the 70 year old king. Faisal was a dedicated enemy of Israel, but had always been a moderate voice in Arab meetings. Above: Former Israeli Prime Minister Golda Meir, Foreign Minister Yigel Allon and Prime Minister Yitzhak Rabin vote to approve a peace deal negotiated with Egypt by Rabin in September.

JAN-CARL RASPE

ANDREAS

Above: West German politicians Helmut Schmidt (left) and Willy Brandt celebrate at the annual meeting of the ruling Social Democrat Party. Brandt was confirmed as Chancellor when he took 407 of the 418 votes available for the leadership of the party. Schmidt was confirmed as Deputy Chancellor by a similar margin. Right: The faces of political terrorism in West Germany. The Baader-Meinhof gang, which termed itself the Red Army Faction was a small group of urban guerrillas who were responsible for a series of bomb blasts in West German cities. The gang had been rounded up after a series of bloody gun battles in June 1972, but it was not until 1975 that they were finally brought to trial for their crimes.

The End Of South Vietnam

The gradual withdrawal of foreign armed support for South Vietnam was completed in August 1974 when Congress rejected President Nixon's request for modest resources. In the spring of 1975 newly confident North Vietnamese forces began a massive offensive on all fronts. Towns and cities fell to the Communist troops as they drove south. The final crisis occurred at Xuan Loc in April when a three week battle for the city ended on 26th April with the complete rout of the South Vietnamese. Panic set in and organised resistance ceased to exist. North Vietnamese troops spread out through the central provinces to encircle the capital Saigon. Those who had committed themselves too completely to America or to Thieu to escape punishment were desperate to leave and tragic scenes were enacted throughout South Vietnam, but most especially in Saigon. On 1st May the North Vietnamese army marched into the city and imposed a unification of the two Vietnams on a defeated population. Refugees fled in great numbers over the following years as Communist rule became a reality. Cambodia and Laos were also under Communist rule by the end of the year. The events against which America had fought for so long had come about.

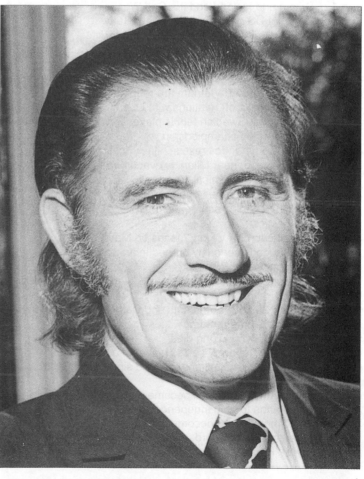

Top left: American tennis star Arthur Ashe grips the Wimbledon Men's Singles trophy which he took by defeating Jimmy Connors in four sets in July. Top right: Billie-Jean King holds aloft the magnificent plate presented to the winner of the Women's Singles title at Wimbledon which she gained by beating Australian Evonne Cawley in straight sets. It was her record sixth triumph at Wimbledon. Right: British motor racing star Graham Hill who was killed in an aircrash this year. Hill had achieved the unique distinction of winning the Formula 1 drivers' championship twice, in 1962 and 1968, as well as the Indianapolis 500 in 1966.

Jan 1	Saudi Arabia: A Lebanese airliner crashes, killing 82
Jan 2	UK: 22 are killed by hurricane force winds
Jan 5	Death of Irish statesman John Costello
Jan 6	Italy: Prime minister Aldo Moro resigns
Jan 8	Death of Chinese statesman Cho En-lai
Jan 12	Death of British novelist Dame Agatha Christie
Jan 15	The Roman Catholic Church condemns sex outside marriage and states that homosexuality can not be condoned
Jan 15	Briton John Curry wins the men's European figure skating championship
Jan 21	The New York Times and The Financial Times go on sale in the USSR
Jan 21	Concorde makes its first commercial flights, simultaneously from London and Paris
Feb 11	John Curry wins a gold medal for figure skating in the Winter Olympic Games
Mar 16	UK: Prime minister Harold Wilson resigns and is succeeded by James Callaghan
Mar 20	US: Patty Hearst is found guilty of assisting her kidnappers, the Symbionese Liberation Army, in an armed bank robbery
Mar 24	President Isabel Peron of Argentina is ousted in a coup by the military leaders
Apr 1	Death of German-born French artist Max Ernst
Apr 5	Death of US tycoon Howard Hughes
Apr 16	India: The minimum marriage ages are raised to 21 for men and 18 for women to curb population growth
Apr 25	Portugal: Socialist Dr Mario Soares is elected premier
Apr 26	Death of South African-born British actor Syd James
Jun 1	Britain and Iceland end the Cod War
Jun 6	Death of US oil tycoon John Paul Getty
Jun 25	Uganda: Idi Amin is made president for life
Jun 25	South Africa: The death toll in the Soweto race riots is 176
Jun 28	The Seychelles gain independence from Britain
Jul 2	North and South Vietnam are reunited
Jul 2	Dusan breaks off relations with Libya
Jul 3	Wimbledon: Swedish tennis player Bjorn Borg wins the men's singles championship
Jul 4	Israeli Commandos rescue hijack hostages at Entebbe
Jul 10	Italy: Seveso, near Milan, is evacuated following an accident at a chemical plant
Jul 17	The Olympic Games opens in Montreal, 14 year old Nadia Comaneci scores the first ever 10 out of 10 for gymnastics
Jul 20	US spaceprobe Viking 1 lands on Mars
Aug 1	Niki Lauda is seriously burned in an accident in the German Grand Prix
Aug 6	UK: John Stonehouse begins a seven year sentence for fraud
Sep 4	Ireland: 25,000 Protestants and Catholics take part in a peace movement march
Sep 18	China: Mao Tse Tung dies
Oct 6	Thailand: The army seizes power in a bloody coup
Oct 10	Cuba: The first elections are held since Fidel Castro came to power
Oct 26	South Africa: Transkei becomes the first of the black homelands to gain independence
Nov 2	US: Jimmy Carter becomes the President of the US, defeating Gerald Ford
Nov 11	Egypt: President Sadat abolishes the single-party system

THE DROUGHT

The summer of 1976 proved to be a remarkable one in Britain, and across much of northern Europe. For some reason the established weather pattern failed to materialise. The rain-bearing depressions which usually swept across the continent from west to east during the summer months passed further north. Britain was instead treated to clear skies and a prolonged dry spell. The dry weather patterns had become clear as early as May, and June was a ferociously hot month in which temperatures soared to record heights for days on end. By July the situation was becoming critical as water supplies dwindled and began to fail. The picture (*above*) shows Water Authority staff inspecting the parched bed of a reservoir normally filled to the brim with water. The British government acted by installing a 'Minister for Drought' and passing emergency measures through Parliament which banned the use of car washes, hosepipes and sprinklers. In the worst affected regions domestic water was rationed and standpipes installed. The drought came at a time when climatologists were predicting an imminent renewal of the ice ages. After the drought they changed their predictions to indicate prolonged global warming.

GOVERNMENT CHANGES

Britain and America saw a changes in supreme political power in 1976. Britain was first when on 16th March Prime Minister Harold Wilson announced that he was stepping down as premier. The news came as a genuine surprise to most of Britain, even to Wilson's cabinet colleagues, but not the Queen. Wilson had confided to her some time previously that he would resign once he had established his Labour Party in power following the 1974 general election victory. The Labour Party at once set in motion the process of electing a successor and chose Foreign Secretary James Callaghan over veteran left-winger Michael Foot. Below: James Callaghan. The accession to power of Jimmy Carter in America was barely less predicted. Gerald Ford, who took over from the disgraced Richard Nixon, had to battle against the slur of Watergate and a reputation for clumsiness. Carter, however, had the traditional handicap of being from the former Confederate states which had not produced a President since their defeat in the Civil War over a century earlier. In the event the result was remarkably close, with Carter edging ahead in crucial industrial states where his Democrat background helped gain the support of workers. Right: Jimmy Carter in November. Below right: President Ford at a state dinner at the White House in July.

Left: Maired Corrigan (left) and Betty Williams (right) who were awarded the Nobel Peace Prize for their campaign for peace in Northern Ireland this year. The campaign was based on an upswell of public opinion against the violence and bloodshed of recent years. Many members of the public found themselves entirely out of sympathy with the actions of terrorists on both sides of the conflict, and with the strict policing of the province. Drawing support from both Protestants and Catholics the peace movement expressed a longing for the return of safer days when it was possible to sit at home or visit a pub without worrying about becoming a victim of a random sectarian killing. The movement attracted much publicity and provided a platform on which the politicians could attempt to build compromise and agreement to placate the majority of the grievances of Ulster's people. However, it failed to affect the terrorists who continued their campaigns unabated.

Above: Mao Tse-Tung who died on 18th September at the age of 82. Since he had led the Communists to victory, Mao had retained personal power based on a combination of hero worship and brute force. His death was long anticipated in government circles and the power struggle to succeed him had apparently already been won in April by Hua Kuo-Feng, though he faced strong opposition from Mao's widow and other radicals in October. Top left: The leader of the Palestine Liberation Organisation Yasser Arafat as he appeared on American television in an NBC interview. The PLO was responsible for numerous terrorist outrages and the interview was not without controversy. Left: The execution of three terrorists who in September attacked the Semiramia Hotel in Damascus. The gunmen left four dead and 34 wounded on their rampage. They were hanged after a peremptory trial at dawn the following day.

THE SEVESO DISASTER

On 10th July the people of Seveso in northern Italy began to suffer from skin rashes and headaches with vomiting and diarrhoea occuring in several of the worst cases. Doctors were inundated as the mystery illness spread through the town. Several pets and wild animals suffered the same symptoms and died. Not until 24th July were the people ordered to leave their homes when it was revealed that there had been an accident in the chemical works in Seveso. A valve had given way under pressure and released some two tons of dioxin, a poisonous chemical, into the atmosphere causing the mystery illness. The Italian people were outraged that nearly two weeks had elapsed before evacuation began and demanded redress. Executives from the company were put on trial, but the courts delayed and prevaricated for so long that the issue lost its importance. Left: About 100 protesters in skull or gasmask headgear marched to the court where the Seveso trial was under way in June 1977. Below: The citizens of Seveso return home in October.

The Mars Landings

The new US programme of unmanned space flights reached Mars in July when *Viking 1* landed on the planet. The landing craft was about six feet tall and was packed with sensitive instruments capable of analysing soil and atmosphere on the red planet. For years man had been fascinated by Mars with its red colouration and distinct seasonal changes. Many had suggested that the planet was so like Earth that it might support life. The Viking probe was designed to test these theories. First indications were disappointing. Photographs revealed a desert landscape of sand scattered with large boulders. Initial soil analyses were more hopeful as they revealed the presence of chemicals essential to life. However, the mission ended with the definitive statement that no organic material had been found. Life on Mars appeared to have been ruled out by the missions.

The world caught its breath at the exploits of Israeli commandos at Entebbe on 4th July. The drama began on 27th June when Palestinian terrorists hijacked an Air France jet and flew it to Entebbe in Uganda. There the terrorists received a favourable welcome from the Moslem President Amin who supplied food and probably weapons as well. The 98 passengers and crew, mainly Jews, were held hostage. The Israeli government made a pretence of negotiating, but in reality were preparing a daring raid. On 4th July 200 commandos flew out of Israel on three darkened aircraft. Landing at Entebbe, the commandos first distracted Ugandan troops with diversionary explosions then stormed the hanger where the terrorists were holding the hostages. All but three hostages were saved and all the terrorists killed in the fighting. Left: A hostage welcomed home by her daughter. Above: One of the commandos, his face blanked for security reasons, is given a hero's welcome on his return to Israel.

Top left: New Zealand runner John Walker wins the 1500 metre Olympic gold medal in a time of 3 minutes 39 seconds. Above right: Britain's John Curry takes the gold medal in the men's figure skating event. The Montreal Olympics were the first in a generation to be affected by politics. The growing unrest in South Africa was condemned by many nations, but the question of sporting links was a matter of controversy. New Zealand sent a rugby team to tour South Africa and in protest many African nations demanded New Zealand's exclusion from the games. When New Zealand participated the black nations pulled out. Above: The badly scarred eyes of Austrian Grand Prix driver Niki Lauda stare out of his helmet as he prepares for the Canadian Grand Prix just weeks after an horrific crash in the German Grand Prix when his car burst into flames. Right: British yachtswoman Clare Francis at the start of the gruelling single-handed race across the Atlantic. She was one of only three women competitors out of over a hundred starters.

Top right: A happy trio celebrating Oscar victories for the movie **One Flew Over the Cuckoo's Nest**. Jack Nicholson (right) won Best Actor and Louise Fletcher (left) took Best Actress in this tale of a mental asylum. Above right: Reality faces art as top Nixon aide John Dean (right) meets Robert Redford and Dustin Hoffman on the set of **All the President's Men**, a movie recreation of the Watergate scandal. Top left: The almost legendary crime writer Agatha Christie whose literary career spanned six decades and established an entire genre of whodunnit mysteries. She died on 12th January as her record-breaking play **The Mousetrap** entered its 24th consecutive year of production. Left: Mick Jagger sings during the Rolling Stones concert in London's Earls Court on 21st May at the start of a tour which cost a reputed £1 million to stage.

1977

Jan 6	UK: EMI sack the Sex Pistols for their outrageous behaviour
Jan 14	Death of British statesman Robert Anthony Eden
Jan 17	US: Convicted murderer Gary Mark Gilmore is executed at his own request by a firing squad
Jan 17	Australia: 80 die in a plane crash in Sydney
Jan 20	US: Jimmy Carter is inaugurated as 39th President
Jan 29	UK: 7 IRA bombs go off in the West End of London
Feb 18	Archbishop of Uganda is murdered by Amin's troops
Feb 19	UK: Antony Crosland, Foreign Secretary, dies
Mar 7	Pakistan: Bhutto wins General Election
Mar 27	Canary Islands: 574 are killed in the world's worst air tragedy when two jumbo jets collide on the runway
Apr 2	UK: Red Rum wins Grand National for record 3rd time
Apr 22	Blow out in N. Sea oil well causes severe pollution
May 9	US: Patty Hearst is freed on five years probation
May 10	Death of US actress Joan Crawford
May 11	The US government says that CFCs will be outlawed as propellants in spray cans in two years time
May 23	105 schoolchildren are held hostage in a hijacked train in the Netherlands by South Moluccan extremists
May 25	China: The ban on Shakespeare is lifted
Jun 1	UK: Lester Piggott wins his eighth Derby
Jun 3	Death of Italian film director Roberto Rossellini
Jun 10	US: James Earl Ray, the killer of Martin Luther King, breaks out of jail
Jun 21	Israel: Menachem Begin takes office as prime minister
Jun 23	Ireland: Premier Cosgrave resigns
Jul 5	Xulfikar Ali Bhutto, the Prime Minister of Pakistan, is ousted
Jul 10	Torrential rain in the South East of France kills 31
Jul 15	US: President Carter approves the admission of 15,000 refugees from Laos, Cambodia and Vietnam
Jul 22	The Gang of Four, Jiang Qing and three fellow radicals are expelled from the Chinese Communist party
Aug 12	US: The space shuttle makes its maiden flight
Aug 16	Death of US singer Elvis Presley, the 'King of Rock and Roll'
Aug 19	Death of US actor and comedian Groucho Marx
Aug 31	Ian Smith's Rhodesian Front wins an overwhelming victor
Sep 12	South Africa: Black leader Steve Biko is found unconsciou in his police cell and later dies from his injuries
Sep 15	South Africa: 1,200 black students are arrested when the gather to mourn the death of Steve Biko
Sep 16	Death of British rock musician Marc Bolan
Sep 17	Death of opera diva Maria Callas
Sep 19	US: Film director Roman Polanski is jailed for three months for having sex with a thirteen year old girl
Sep 26	Freddie Laker's Skytrain takes off from Gatwick
Oct 3	India: Mrs Gandhi is arrested for corruption
Oct 14	Death of US singer Bing Crosby
Oct 18	86 hostages in a hijacked airliner are freed by a German anti-terrorist unit
Oct 19	The body of Hans Martin Schleyer, the kidnapped Germa industrialist, is found in a car boot in Alsace, France
Nov 4	The United Nations bans sales of arms to South Africa
Nov 19	India: A cyclone and tidal wave strike the Southern states killing an estimated 20,000 and leaving 200,000 homeles
Dec 2	South Africa: An inquest rules that no one is to blame for the death of Steve Biko
Dec 4	Malaysia: A hijacked plane crashes, killing 100
Dec 5	Egypt: President Sadat breaks off diplomatic ties with Syria, Iraq, Libya, Algeria and South Yemen
Dec 10	Amnesty International is awarded the Nobel Peace Prize
Dec 25	Charlie Chaplin dies at home in Switzerland

The year 1977 saw the 25th anniversary of the accession of Queen Elizabeth II to the throne of Britain and those Commonwealth nations which acknowledge her as head of state. During February and March the Queen and Prince Philip undertook an extensive tour of the Commonwealth to show their appreciation of the devotion paid to them. Special coins were minted throughout the Commonwealth and stamps were printed to celebrate the Silver Jubilee. Right: The Queen and Prince Philip accepting a miniature of the Bow Bells, mascot of London's Cockneys who traditionally need to be born within sound of the bells of St Mary at Bow. The presentation followed a walkabout of the City of London after a national service of thanksgiving in St Paul's Cathedral.

THE FATE OF RHODESIA

In 1977 Rhodesia became a matter of international concern. In 1965 the country had declared itself independent of Britain in order to prevent handing power over to the Black majority. During the 1970s nationalist groups became increasingly active. ZAPU, based on the Matabele tribe, and ZANU, which drew supporters from the Shona, were banned as political parties and turned to guerrilla warfare to achieve their ends. The Rhodesian government received aid from South Africa and became highly skilled at counter insurgency tactics. However in 1974 both Angola and Mozambique became independent. Their new Black governments gave support to both ZANU and ZAPU. Nkomo, leader of ZAPU and Mugabe, head of ZANU, formed the Patriotic Front to fight against the government led by Ian Smith. By 1977 it was clear that the region was becoming destabilised by the conflict and Britain, America and South Africa began talks to discuss their attitudes towards Rhodesia. The talks would culminate in the Commonwealth Conference of 1979 when a final deal was agreed. Left: British Foreign Secretary David Owen meets US Secretary of State in London in April for talks on the future of Rhodesia.

Above left: British Prime Minister James Callaghan meets with Israeli premier Menachem Begin in December for talks as Egypt and Israel moved towards peace. In June Britain witnessed one of its most bitter industrial disputes at the Grunwick film processing plant in Willesden, north London. A number of workers went on strike when the management refused to allow a closed shop under which all workers would have to join a trade union or lose their jobs. The strikers were sacked and replaced, but they appealed to other unions for help. Large numbers of 'flying pickets' gathered at Grunwick in an attempt to stop workers entering the factory. Police were called in to preserve order. During the height of the dispute 800 police faced 2,000 pickets in the streets and the management went in fear of their lives. Left: Police drag away a demonstrator outside the Grunwick plant. Above: Police help an injured comrade to an ambulance after he was struck by a bottle at Grunwick.

FIRST FLIGHTS

The year 1977 saw two new developments in the world of air travel. The first came in September when the flamboyant entrepreneur Freddie Laker launched his Skytrain service across the Atlantic. The Skytrain was based on the novel premise that passengers would be allowed to buy tickets on the day of departure, rather than being forced to book ahead. More dramatic still was the cost, just £59 one way which considerably undercut the standard air fare. Laker's success seemed assured and his early flights were packed. However, the more established airlines exerted pressure and Laker eventually had to pull out of the service alleging that the market was rigged against small operators. Left: Freddie Laker poses beside his first Skytrain aircraft to enter service. Second to hit the headlines was the first scheduled flight by Concorde across the Atlantic in November. Earlier attempts to start a service were blocked by US authorities. The first flight, on 22nd November, was completed in just under four hours.

The world's worst air crash claimed the lives of five hundred and eighty two people on 27th March when two jumbo jets collided at Tenerife. Both aircraft had been diverted to Los Rodeos Airport due to poor weather. As the Pan Am aircraft manoeuvred across the runway to taxi to a rest a KLM jumbo tore down the runway to take off. At the last moment the KLM pilot saw the danger and tried to lift his aircraft over the other. He failed and the entire crew and passengers were killed as flames engulfed the two jets. Some seventy people scrambled clear of the Pan Am aircraft. It was later found that both aircraft had been using the same radio frequency to receive instructions from the control tower. Confusion was, perhaps, inevitable and in the event was fatal. Left: The wreckage of the KLM Boeing 747.

ZIA TAKES POWER IN PAKISTAN

In March Pakistan went to the polls in a general election for only the second time since the new constitution was adopted following the secession of Bangladesh in 1971. The result was a spectacular victory for Prime Minister Ali Bhutto. Opposition to Bhutto had been so widespread, however, that ballot rigging and fraud were suspected. Riots broke out which took around three hundred lives. Bhutto promptly arrested his political opponents and imposed martial law on the larger cities. Unrest continued and the nation slipped towards anarchy. On 5th July the military Chief of Staff, General Mohammed Zia-ul-Haq, stepped in. He ordered his troops to arrest Bhutto and other ministers. The army had relinquished dictatorship only in 1971 and was now clearly of the opinion that democracy led only to chaos. Zia became President of Pakistan, Bhutto was executed for attempted murder and Islamic law reinforced. New elections were postponed until 1985, by which time Zia felt comfortably in control of the state. Below right: General Zia photographed on his appointment as Chief of Staff in 1976.

The New Napoleon

On 4th December President Bokassa of the Central African Republic crowned himself Emperor Bokassa and renamed his state the Central African Empire. The lavish ceremony cost around $30 million, almost the entire national output for a year and owed much to Bokassa's admiration of the Emperor Napoleon I of France. The throne took the form of a ten foot tall bronze eagle while the crown contained an amazing five thousand diamonds and gems. Bokassa begun his career as an army officer under David Dacko, first President after independence from France in 1960. In 1966 Dacko's rule descended into anarchy and virtual bankruptcy. Bokassa was by then army commander and he staged a coup which drove Dacko into exile. Bokassa at once stifled all political opposition by the simple expedient of having anyone who objected to his rule publicly clubbed to death. However he had an astute economic policy based on the exploitation of his nation's gold and diamond fields and the extensive uranium deposits. The largesse he could distribute from these sources made him popular with the 86% of the population who remained tied to the land in subsistence agriculture. Bokassa's coronation revealed the bizarre side of his character and the French government, which had long supported him, turned against the regime and trouble began which would lead to Bokassa's overthrow in 1979.

Left: The murderer Gary Gilmore who became the first person to be executed in the United States for ten years on 17th January. Gilmore was found guilty in 1976 of killing a hotel clerk, but the death sentence was delayed after action by pressure groups opposed to capital punishment. Gilmore, however, would not accept the delays. He declared himself satisfied with both verdict and sentence. "Let's do it," he said of the execution. On 17th January he was taken out of his Utah state prison cell and shot by firing squad. Below: A protester in Pretoria mourns the death of Steve Biko. Biko, one of the leaders of South Africa's Black Consciousness movement, was arrested under emergency powers passed by government after rioting earlier in the year. His death in police custody occurred in obscure circumstances and many felt that beatings and punishment had contributed to his death. His funeral was attended by 15,000 people in King William's Town.

Facing page, top left: Marc Bolan, British rock star died instantly when the car driven by his girl-friend struck a tree in Barnes, England, on 16th September. Facing page, top right: Bing Crosby photographed while playing golf, his favourite sport. He was on a Spanish course when he collapsed and died on 14th October. Facing page, bottom right: The great Greek opera singer Maria Callas who died in September after a heart attack at the age of 53. Left: The anarchic British pop group The Sex Pistols who enjoyed a brief but dramatic career which included massive record sales, appalling behaviour and drug abuse. Below left: The popular Swedish pop group Abba receive music awards from Prince Rainier and Princess Grace of Monaco. Below: Australian cricket promoter Kerry Packer who revolutionised the sport with evening games, coloured team uniforms and high profile publicity.

On 16th August the greatest star of rock music, Elvis Presley, died at the tragically young age of just 42. Presley leapt to fame in 1953 with his unique renditions of blues and rock and roll music. Hits such as *Jailhouse Rock* and *Heartbreak Hotel* established him as the leading singing star in America. Even more impressive than his singing talents were his stage presence and highly suggestive dancing which amazed his teenage girl fans. His spell in the army did no harm to his career accompanied as it was by a string of highly successful musical movies. From the late 1960s Presley tended to be overweight and dark rumours of drug addiction began to circulate. On 31st December 1976, however, he proved he could still impress an audience with a magnificent show in Michigan. It was the last flash of brilliance. When he was found prostrate on the floor of his mansion, Presley was rushed to hospital but was already dead of heart trouble. Many refused to believe that he had really died and for several years tales of his living in hiding circulated. Facing page, bottom left: Elvis Presley sings in the New Year's Eve concert in Michigan.

Top left: British tennis star Virginia Wade as she realises that her shot has won her the Wimbledon women's singles final against Betty Stove. Wade had been near the top of the tennis profession for years but the Wimbledon title had always eluded her. The win in 1977, Silver Jubilee year, was an emotive triumph. Top right: Tom Watson missing a vital putt during the British Open at Turnberry, a competition he had won two years earlier. Above: British Formula 1 driver and World Champion James Hunt celebrates winning the British Grand Prix at Silverstone on 16th July. Right: John McEnroe, the 18 year old American tennis player who entered Wimbledon as an unseeded player of whom few had heard, but who stormed his way into the semi-finals with some powerful play.

Jan 1	South African Donald Woods, the newspaper editor, arrives in Britain seeking asylum
Jan 1	Bombay: A Boeing 747 explodes in mid-air, killing 213
Jan 3	India: Mrs Gandhi is expelled from the Congress Party
Jan 13	Death of US politician Hubert Humphrey
Feb 13	UK: Anna Ford is ITN's first female newscaster
Feb 17	Belfast: 14 are killed when a bomb explodes in a restaurant
Mar 2	Switzerland: The body of Charlie Chaplin is stolen from a cemetery
Mar 16	The supertanker Amoco Cadiz runs aground off Brittany, spilling 220,000 tonnes of oil
Mar 18	Pakistan: Former prime minister Zulfikar Ali Bhutto is sentenced to death for attempted murder
Mar 19	Former Italian prime minister Aldo Moro is kidnapped by the Red Brigade
Mar 30	UK: The Conservative Party announces that it has hired the advertising agency Saatchi and Saatchi
Apr 7	A copy of the Gutenberg Bible is sold in New York for $2 million
Apr 10	US: Russian UN official Arkady Shevchenko defects to the West
May 9	Italy: Aldo Moro is found dead
May 10	UK: It is announced that Princess Margaret will divorce the Earl of Snowdon
Jun 1	Electronic bugging devices are found in the US embassy in Moscow
Jun 3	UK: Freddie Laker is knighted
Jun 20	UK: Joyce McKinney is sentenced to one year's imprisonment, but she is still missing
Jun 24	Rhodesia: 12 Britons, including a new born baby are massacred at a mission
Jun 25	Argentina win the World Cup
Jul 3	China cuts all aid to Vietnam
Jul 7	EEC members agree to study a propsal linking together EEC currencies
Jul 7	The Solomon Islands gain independence from Britain
Jul 26	UK: Louise Brown, the first 'test tube baby' is born
Jul 27	Portugal: Prime minister Soares is dismissed
Aug 6	Death of Pope Paul VI, who is succeeded by Pope John Paul I
Aug 19	The first balloon crossing of the Atlantic is achieved by three Americans
Aug 22	Nairobi: Jomo Kenyatta, President of Kenya, dies
Aug 25	The Turin Shroud goes on public display
Aug 29	Portugal: Industrialist Alfredo Nobre da Costa becomes prime minister
Sep 15	Bulgarian defector Georgi Markov dies after being stabbed in the leg by a poison umbrella
Sep 20	South Africa: Prime Minister Vorster resigns
Sep 21	Nigeria lifts a 12 year state of emergency
Sep 28	South Africa: Botha is new prime minister
Sep 28	Newly elected Pope John Paul I dies suddenly
Oct 5	Swedish prime minister Falldin resigns and is replaced by Ola Ullsten
Oct 25	Portugal: Carlos Alberto da Mota Pinto is new PM
Nov 3	The US and Vietnam sign a 25-year treaty of friendship and co-operation in economic, scientific and technical endeavors
Nov 3	Dominica gains its independence within the Commonwealth
Nov 15	Death of US anthropologist Margaret Mead
Nov 19	Guyana: 909 members of the American religious cult, the People's Temple are found dead from suicide by cyanide
Dec 8	Death of Israeli prime minister Golda Meir

Left: Israeli Prime Minister Menachem Begin and Egyptian President Anwar Sadat shake hands at Camp David in September where they met with US President Jimmy Carter to discuss the Middle East. The talks were the culmination of months of careful diplomacy. During the talks Carter achieved much with his unique brand of diplomacy and cajolery. By the conference end on the 18th two documents had been signed by Israel and Egypt. The first promised that Israel would recognise the rights of the Palestinians living in occupied lands and would withdraw troops. The second allowed for diplomatic relations between the two states and a formal peace to be declared in return for Israeli withdrawal from the Sinai. Both leaders paid tribute to Carter.

THE DEATH OF ALDO MORO

Political terrorism grabbed the headlines in Italy when guerrillas kidnapped former premier Aldo Moro on 19th March. The Red Brigade was a well known Communist group which had already carried out several assassinations of government officials. The captors demanded the immediate release of several fellow Communists imprisoned on criminal charges. The Italian government refused, and the Red Brigade reacted by murdering a leading prison official. On 5th May the kidnappers announced they would kill Moro if their demands were not met at once. On the 9th Moro's bullet-riddled body was found in the boot of a car near Rome's Communist Party headquarters. Pope Paul VI celebrated a requiem mass for Moro, the first time that a pope had celebrated such a service for anyone other than a high church official. Left: Aldo Moro pictured in 1966 as he accepts appointment as Prime Minister. Below: The body of Aldo Moro as it was found in a Renault car in Rome in May.

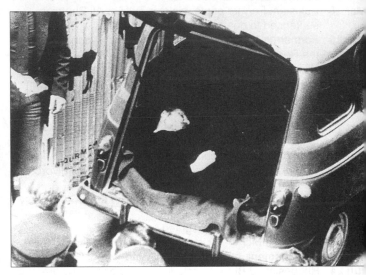

Right: South African politician Pieter Botha took over as Prime Minister of his nation on 28th September. The move came after unrest at home and turbulent foreign relations had shaken the confidence of the ruling Nationalist Party. The previous premier Johannes Vorster had been in power for a total of 12 years before his resignation. During the previous year intercommunal violence had increased markedly in South Africa. The Johannesburg township of Soweto exploded in riots after police broke up a demonstration of schoolchildren demanding to be taught in English and fighting spread rapidly to other towns. The United Nations passed a resolution condemning apartheid. Vorster was a strong supporter of apartheid but in the face of unrest met with black leaders. The views of Botha were little known and the policies he would pursue were awaited with both eagerness and caution.

Britain was amazed by the case of a missing Mormon missionary in the autumn. The details of the case as they slowly unfolded almost defied belief. The missionary, Kirk Anderson, had been snatched from a Surrey street by his blonde ex-girlfriend, Joyce McKinney who still harboured a passion for the man. After Anderson's release he told a bizarre tale of how he had been held against his will, manacled to a bed and forced to have sex with the voluptuous McKinney. The accused girl responded that Anderson had been a willing partner and that the handcuffs were simply part of a 'game' he liked to play. The preliminary hearings were inconclusive and McKinney jumped bail before the trial proper could open. Perhaps the most famous incident came when McKinney declared that her love for Anderson was so great that "I loved him so much I would have skied down Mount Everest in the nude with a carnation up my nose". The tabloid newspapers loved the entire scandal and were rather disappointed to be robbed of the trial. Left: The tearful Joyce McKinney arrives at court in Epsom to be charged with kidnapping. Below left: A mass demonstration in Teheran by supporters of Ayatollah Khomeini protest at the westernising reforms of the Shah.

MASS RELIGIOUS SUICIDE

During the 1960s and 1970s several religious movements had sprung up in California. Most were harmless, but a few were evil. In 1969 Charles Manson had led his hippy followers on a trail of murder. In 1978 the People's Temple movement of James Jones outdid even Manson in gruesome horror. The cult centred around Jones, known as Reverend Jim, and his messianic pronouncements. Having recruited over a thousand followers, Rev. Jim purchased an estate, renamed Jonestown, in the rainforests of Guyana and transplanted most of his followers, leaving only a small People's Temple outpost in California. Soon ominous rumours were leaking out of Guyana. On 17th November Congressman Leo Ryan set out to Guyana to investigate claims that Jones was brainwashing his followers, stripping them of their wealth and forcing them to indulge in perverted sexual acts. On his way to Jonestown Ryan and his party were ambushed and murdered. NBC newsman Robert Brown kept his camera going until he was killed, collecting enough evidence to identify Jones's followers as the killers. Two days later Guyanan officials following up Ryan's murder arrived at Jonestown. They found the bodies of 909 members of the People's Temple. They had apparently committed suicide by drinking a cyanide-laced fruit drink. Jones had shot himself through the head. The few survivors told how Jones had ordered the mass suicide after he realised the Ryan killings would be discovered. He had told his followers that they would be together in a glorious afterlife if they obeyed his instructions. Most willingly did so, even killing their children, and only a handful fled to the jungle. Right: The scene at Jonestown on the 20th November.

Top left: American golfer Jack Nicklaus hugs the British Open Trophy after winning the silver prize at St Andrew's, Scotland, on 15th July. Top right: John Travolta and Olivia Newton-John at the gala premiere of the movie **Grease**. The film was the box-office smash of the year. Based on a successful Broadway show, the film launched both lead players into star status, though it proved to be shortlived for both as Travolta reverted to stage work and Newton-John to her singing career. Above: Mick Mills, captain of Ipswich Football Club kisses the FA Cup after receiving it from Princess Alexandra following his team's sensational 1-0 victory over Arsenal. Right: Martina Navratilova reaches for a powerful forehand during her 6-2 6-3 victory over Tracey Austin for the women's singles title at Wimbledon.

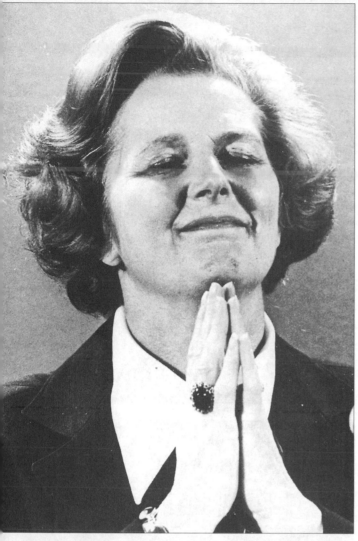

THE THATCHER TRIUMPH

On 3rd May Britain voted at a General Election which was to prove to be one of the most decisive in recent years. The Labour government of James Callaghan had held on for almost its full term before going to the country. The winter just finished had been widely dubbed the Winter of Discontent due to the massive industrial unrest and hardship. The government had been further humiliated by the need to go to the International Monetary Fund for financial help and the general collapse of the economy. The Conservative Party offered a radically different agenda. The Tory leader, Margaret Thatcher, declared her open hostility to the power of the trades unions and her belief that the government should retrench, leaving more decisions to individuals and so cut expenditure and taxes. Three million more Britons voted Conservative than in 1979, sweeping the Tories to power with a majority of 43 in the House of Commons. The government at once set out on the programme of union reform, monetarist theory economics and privatisation of state monopolies which was to become known as Thatcherism. Above: Margaret Thatcher joins the Conservative Party in prayer at the start of the Party Conference in October.

Jan 1	Diplomatic relations are formally established between China and the US
Jan 1	The European Monetary System(EMS) is introduced
Jan 8	Cambodia falls to the Vietnamese
Jan 16	Iran: Shah Muhammad Reza Pahlavi is forced to leave after months of riots
Jan 26	Death of US Republican politician Nelson Rockefeller
Feb 1	Iran: Religious leader Ayatollah Khomeini returns after a fifteen year exile
Feb 2	Ex-Sex Pistols member Sid Vicious dies of a heroin overdose
Feb 9	Trevor Francis becomes football's first £1 million player
Feb 13	Death of French film director Jean Renoir
Feb 14	Afghanistan: US ambassador is abducted and killed
Feb 17	China invades Vietnam
Feb 22	St Lucia gains independence within the Commonwealth
Mar 26	President Sadat of Egypt and Prime Minister Begin of Israel sign a peace treaty ending over 30 years of war
Mar 28	US: An accident at the Three Mile Island nuclear power station caused the greatest nuclear crisis to date
Mar 28	UK: The Labour government collapses over home rule vote - parliament is dissolved
Mar 30	UK: Airey Neave, MP and opposition spokesman on Northern Ireland is killed by an IRA car bomb
Apr 4	Pakistan: Former president Bhutto is executed
Apr 11	Idi Amin is deposed by a Ugandan exile force
Apr 17	Rhodesia: The first one-man one-vote elections take place
May 3	UK: Conservative party leader Mrs Margaret Thatcher becomes the first female PM in Europe
May 22	Canada: Joseph Clark, leader of the Progressive Conservative Party becomes youngest ever PM
May 29	Death of Canadian-born US actress Mary Pickford
Jun 2	Poland: John Paul II is first Pope to visit an eastern bloc country since the end of World War II
Jun 11	Death of US actor John Wayne
Jun 22	UK: Jeremy Thorpe is found not guilty of plotting murder
Jul 19	Maria Pintassilgo becomes Portugal's first woman PM
Jul 22	Indonesia: A tidal wave hits the island of Lomblen, killing over 700
Aug 11	Nigeria returns to civilian rule after 13 years of military leadership
Aug 14	UK: Eighteen yachtsmen are killed in storms during the Fastnet International Sailing Race
Aug 15	UK: Sebastian Coe becomes the first athlete to hold the 800m, 1500m and mile world records simultaneously
Aug 15	USSR: Two Aeroflot airliners collide over the Ukraine
Aug 23	Russian ballet dancer Alexander Godunov defects to the USA during a Bolshoi ballet tour
Aug 27	UK: Earl Mountbatten of Burma, the last British viceroy of India is killed by an IRA bomb on his boat
Oct 1	Panama takes control of the American Canal Zone
Oct 26	President Park Chung Hee of South Korea is assassinated by his head of intelligence
Oct 27	St Kitts and the Grenadines achieve independence
Nov 4	Iranian militants storm the US embassy in Tehran
Nov 21	UK: Antony Blunt is named as 4th man in spy scandal
Dec 2	Iran: Ayatollah Khomeini is made absolute leader for life
Dec 23	Czechoslovakia: Playwright Vaclav Haval is convicted of subversion
Dec 25	The USSR begins an invasion of Afghanistan

THE FIGHT AGAINST TERRORISM

The international nature of terrorism came increasingly to light in 1979, as did the scope of the struggle to contain the threat. Increasing numbers of groups with a grievance were turning to terrorism as a means of achieving their ends, or at least gaining publicity for their cause. However the established proponents of terrorism continued to be the most active. In the Middle East the PLO was continuing its struggle for an independent Palestine with attacks on Israeli targets. These increasingly took on the form of a guerrilla war and led to reprisals from the regular Israeli army in form of raids on PLO bases. The IRA, in contrast, remained a terrorist group with a small number of activists. It was nonetheless effective and evidence was growing of contact and co-operation between the IRA and other groups, such as the PLO and Mafia. The IRA murdered both the Earl Mountbatten and leading politician Airey Neave this year. In response the British government introduced more sophisticated security and anti-terrorist measures aimed at containing the freedom of action enjoyed by the IRA killers.

Top left: Irish premier Charles Haughey. Top right: British politician Airey Neave who was killed by an IRA car bomb as he left the Palace of Westminster in the heart of London on 30th March. Neave had been the Conservative Party spokesman on Northern Ireland and a robust opponent of the IRA. His murder sparked a major review of security in Britain and led to increased protection for pub-

lic figures. Right: The funeral of Earl Mountbatten on 5th September in London. The Earl, cousin to the Queen, was murdered by the IRA who planted a bomb on his small fishing boat. Mountbatten was spending the summer as usual at his Irish home at Mullaghmore. The assassination of the former Viceroy of India and war hero caused a wave of revulsion in Britain and Ireland.

The situation in Rhodesia reached crisis point in 1979 with the long running guerrilla campaign on the edge of precipitating anarchy. At Lusaka in August it was agreed to hold a Constitutional Conference in London in September to sort out the situation. Other African leaders would pressurise the guerrilla leaders Joshua Nkomo and Robert Mugabe into compromise while the British government would work on Bishop Muzorewa and Ian Smith. In London a deal was finally hammered out which guaranteed the Whites some say in government, but otherwise introduced democracy. In the following elections Robert Mugabe's ZANU party gained a majority of seats in the Parliament. Right: The scene at the final signing of the Lancaster House Agreement on 21st December. From left to right are: Bishop Abel Muzorewa, Dr S. Mundawarara, Robert Mugabe and Joshua Nkomo.

The SALT II arms treaty was signed between the two super powers in the splendid setting of Vienna's Hofburg Palace on June 18. The agreement placed restrictions on the numbers of strategic nuclear missiles but did not go as far as limiting the number of warheads. Mr Brezhnev said "We are helping to defend the most sacred right of every man, the right to live." Although NATO reaction was favourable many European countries were uneasy over the fact that the agreement left them vulnerable to the Soviets massive build up of the medium range SS-20 missiles. Jimmy Carter also faced strong opposition from Congress who did not feel it actually restrained Russian arms build up. In the event the US Senate failed to ratify the treaty. Below: President Carter gets to his feet while Soviet leader Leonid Brezhnev talks to Austrian President Rudolph Kirchschlaeger during the SALT II negotiations. Left: The executions of eleven Kurdish rebels and supporters of the Shah after summary trials found them guilty of crimes against the new Islamic state of Iran.

Three Mile Island

The potential dangers of nuclear power stations was revealed starkly on 28th March at Three Mile Island in Pennsylvania. A fault in the water cooling system caused a section of the uranium core to melt, fusing with fuel rods. Safety measures at once cut in to shut down the power station, but not before some radioactivity had leaked into the atmosphere. State Governor Dick Thornburgh ordered pregnant women and children to be evacuated from the immediate area, but no general evacuation took place. For a while there was genuine worry that an explosion caused by hydrogen gas pockets would rip the core open, spraying the surrounding land which highly radioactive particles or that core meltdown might occur. Both eventualities were avoided and the plant brought back under control within days. Both sides in the nuclear debate used the incident to their advantage. The anti-nuclear protesters pointed to Three Mile Island as a warning of disaster, those in favour of nuclear power declared that safety procedures had been shown to be effective and that there was no need for concern.

CIVIL WAR IN NICARAGUA

A civil war which had lasted, off and on, for 17 years ended when the Somoza family relinquished control of Nicaragua to a coalition of opposing forces. Though the Somozas had managed to resist all pressure for a total of 47 years, largely through judicious use of US backing, the end came swiftly. The guerrilla campaign waged by the Sandinista Front had broken out of its rural base to reach the capital Managua. Up to 20% of the population was homeless because of the fighting. The US, which had earlier given up an option on the naval base in the Bay of Fonseca, refused to see a close neighbour torn apart in such a way. President Jimmy Carter sent in negotiators to fix a settlement. On 25th July President Anastasio Somoza resigned, turning over power to the Sandinistas. Guerrillas ran amok destroying every monument to the Somoza regime in Managua. The new government began by restoring human rights and abolishing summary execution. However, the uneasy alliance of the groups which made up the Sandinistas could not long survive. The Communists rapidly staged a takeover, nationalising major companies and stifling private enterprise as they enforced a regime as harsh in its way as that of Somoza. Left: Troops loyal to Somoza prepare to attack Sandinista positions in a suburb of Managua. Below left: Citizens protest at a Somoza decree forcing them to hand in all high denomination notes to the banks in order to starve the Sandinistas of cash. Below: A refugee from the country arrives in Managua.

Right: A crowd of Pakistan People's Party members gather in Rawalpindi to offer funeral prayers for their leader Ali Bhutto who was executed early on the morning of 4th April after being found guilty of the attempted murder of a political enemy. During his time as Prime Minister Bhutto had made great strides in economic growth and had established parliamentary democracy in Pakistan. Much of this good work was undone when Bhutto resorted to repressive measures in order to silence the opposition. He won a handsome victory in the elections of 1977 but the opposition were unhappy. General Zia took over and imposed martial law. Zia was determined to establish the military as the ultimate authority and ruthlessly removed any opposition to his plans. The execution of the former Prime Minister Bhutto bought widespread condemnation of Zia and his military government.

THE AYATOLLAH RETURNS

The unrest which had become widespread in Iran reached breaking point in January. Shah Mohammed Reza Pahlavi had attempted to modernise his nation by introducing western-style reforms and economics. His people, however, were more traditionally minded and resented the rejection of Islamic teaching and the repression with which the Shah enforced his will. Mass demonstrations occurred and the government machinery began to show signs of break down. On 16th January the Shah bade farewell to his Imperial Guard and boarded an aircraft for Egypt. He said he was taking a vacation to recuperate and give his nation time to settle down. Few thought he would ever return. On 1st February the great religious leader Ayatollah Ruhollah Khomeini arrived in Iran after fifteen years exile in Paris. He at once proclaimed a provisional government as rival to the Shah's ministers led by Dr Bakhtiar. Three million people turned out on to the streets of Teheran to back the Ayatollah. Dr Bakhtiar accepted defeat and left while Khomeini declared "A great Satan has fled". Within weeks the government of the Ayatollah had overthrown the hated reforms of the Shah and erected a revolutionary Islamic state in their place. Religious fervour came to take the place of political debate. Top left: The Shah on 6th January just days before his fall from power. Top right: The Ayatollah speaks to the world's press as he takes the reins of power. Left: Ayatollah Khomeini descends from an Air France jet to arrive in Iran for the first time in fifteen years. Above: Troops loyal to Khomeini execute rebels against Islamic law in August.

THE THORPE SCANDAL

The British political system was rocked by a bizarre scandal in 1979. The extraordinary case first came to light when a former male model, Norman Scott, charged with a minor crime, grumbled that the authorities were persecuting him because he was Jeremy Thorpe's homosexual lover. Jeremy Thorpe MP was the widely regarded leader of the Liberal Party, the third largest in the House of Commons. The case took a turn from sexual scandal to criminal trial when it was alleged that Thorpe had hired a hitman to murder Scott when the ex-lover began to be an embarrassment. Thorpe wisely resigned his party's leadership before he was formally charged with conspiracy to murder. The fact that the alleged hitman had apparently muffed the job and shot Scott's dog in mistake added to the glee of the press and provided a subject for numerous cartoons and jokes. On 22nd June Thorpe and the three men accused with him were acquitted of attempted murder. Thorpe's political career was, however, at an end. Below: Jeremy Thorpe and his wife face the press after he was cleared of conspiracy to murder.

Top right: Sir Anthony Blunt who was revealed to have been a Soviet spy in 1979. Son of a vicar Blunt was recruited to Soviet intelligence by Guy Burgess when both were studying at Cambridge. Blunt then took an academic life in the Arts, eventually rising to become Surveyor of the Queen's Pictures, but continued to work as a Soviet spy. In 1940 Blunt joined MI5. Throughout the war he worked tirelessly for the KGB, handing over every secret to which he had access. He regularly betrayed pro-Western agents in eastern Europe and many were killed by the Russians. Blunt's treachery came to light in 1964 when an American confessed to the FBI that he had been a Communist in his youth and had been approached by the KGB. He named Blunt as the Soviet agent in question and the FBI told MI5. Blunt was questioned and confessed much in return for immunity from prosecution. From then until his unmasking in 1979 Blunt continued to live his privileged life as a member of the Art Establishment. When Press speculation and pressure from backbench MPs forced his naming by Mrs Thatcher, Blunt lost everything and plunged into disgrace. Left: Mother Teresa of Calcutta who was awarded the Nobel Peace Prize in 1979 for her work among the poor of India. Above: The toddler Louise Brown, the world's first test tube baby, appeared with her parents on American television in September.

Top left: British punk rock star Sid Vicious with his girlfriend Nancy Spungen. It was while awaiting trial for her murder in New York that Vicious died of a heroin overdose on 2nd February. Top right: British soccer star Trevor Francis who became the first million pound player this year. Left: Severiano Ballesteros of Spain holds aloft the British Open Golf Championship Trophy which he won in August. Above: British pop star Elton John before his historic concert in Moscow in May. Many hoped that the granting of permission for a Western rock star to perform in the Soviet Union heralded a softening of Communist attitudes to the West, but such hopes proved ill-founded.

1980-1989

Jan 3	Death of Austrian-born naturalist Joy Adamson
Jan 6	India: Indira Gandhi is re-elected as prime minister
Jan 22	Dissident physicist Andrei Sakharov is exiled from Moscow
Feb 3	US: Rioting at the New Mexico state penitentiary leaves 50 prisoners dead
Feb 4	Teheran: Bani Sadr becomes Iran's first president
Feb 12	The Winter Olympics open at Lake Placid, NY State
Feb 18	Canada: Pierre Trudeau is returned to power in the general election
Feb 18	Death of British photographer and designer Sir Cecil Beaton
Feb 27	Colombia: Left-wing terrorists storm the Dominican Embassy and take 80 hostages
Mar 4	Robert Mugabe is elected premier of Zimbabwe
Mar 23	Sweden: National referendum approves use of nuclear power
Mar 28	The Alexander Kielland oil platform in the North Sea collapses,
Mar 31	Death of US athlete Jesse Owens
Apr 15	Death of French writer and philosopher Jean-Paul Sartre
Apr 25	Iran: US commando mission to rescue hostages is abandoned when a helicopter hits a transport plane, killing 8
Apr 29	Death of British film director Sir Alfred Hitchcock
Apr 30	UK: Armed gunmen seize the Iranian embassy in London, demanding the relese of political prisoners in Iran
Apr 30	Princess Beatrix becomes Queen of the Netherlands on the abdication of her mother, Queen Juliana
May 4	Death of Joseph Tito, ruler of Yugoslavia

May 5	UK: SAS troops storm the Iranian embassy, rescuing 19 hostages and killing 5 terrorists
May 19	US: The long-dormant volcano, Mount St. Helens, erupts
Jun 12	Death of Japanese prime minister Masayoshi Ohira
Jun 23	The son of Indira Gandhi, Sanjay, is killed in a plane crash
Jun 30	US: The Sioux Indian nation wins $122.5 million in compensation and interest for the federal government's illegal seizure of their land in 1877
Jul 5	Bjorn Borg of Sweden becomes the first player to win five successive men's singles titles at Wimbledon
Jul 17	US: Ronald Reagan is chosen as the presidential candidate for the Republican party
Jul 19	The Olympic Games open in Moscow
Jul 23	Death of film actor Peter Sellers
Aug 2	Italy: 84 die and 200 are injured by a terrorist bomb in Bologna station
Aug 30	Poland: Lech Walesa, strike leader, wins the right for independent trades unions
Sep 15	War breaks out in the Persian Gulf as Iraq invades Iran
Oct 3	A bomb explodes outside a synagogue in Paris, killing 4
Oct 14	British biochemist Dr Frederick Sanger wins his second Nobel Prize
Nov 7	Death of US actor Steve McQueen
Nov 21	The episode of 'Dallas' in which it is revealed who shot JR breaks viewing records
Dec 8	John Lennon is shot dead in New York by a deranged fan

On 19th May the volcanic Mount St Helens ripped itself apart in the most powerful explosion seen on Earth for decades. The titanic eruption followed months of increasing volcanic activity around the mountain. Geologists noticed an ominous bulge building on the north slope of the mountain and issued warnings. Most residents of the surrounding area of Washington State were evacuated. A handful of news photographers moved to the area in the hope of achieving a scoop photograph. The force of the explosion was reckoned to be equivalent to about 1000 atomic bombs of the type dropped on Hiroshima. Some 5,000 feet of the mountain were torn away and blasted in to the air in the form of rock and dust. The landslide set up released millions of tons of rock, mud and water which cascaded down the Toutle River Valley, destroying everything in its path. A total of 24 people are known to have been killed, but some 40 others were missing. Left The yawning chasm left by the explosion as seen on the 30th May

THE GANG OF FOUR

In November the trial opened of China's 'Gang of Four' who had launched a bid for supreme power after the death of Chairman Mao, but had lost. Led by Mao's widow, Jiang Qing, were the Communist Party Vice Chairman Wang Hung-Wen, Vice Premier Chang Chu-Chiao and ideologist and leading government strategist Yao Wen-Yuan, all of whom were stripped of office by the government before their trial began. The vicious nature of the factional in-fighting which followed Mao's death found expression in the rhetoric which it produced. The winner of power, Hua Kuo-Feng described the Gang of Four as "bourgeois revisionists and fascists". As far as outsiders could judge, the disgraced four had been in favour of putting the Communist government on a more radical course which would have led to increased regimentation of the populace and culture, while their opponents looked more favourably on dispersing authority and allowing some extension of freedoms. Far left: Wang Hung-Wen. Left: Chang Chu-Chiao. Below left: Yao Wen-Yuan. Below: Jian Qing in the dock during her trial. Bottom right: Caricatured effigies of the Gang of Four are paraded through the streets of Canton by Communist Party loyalists.

The Boycott Olympics

The Olympic Games of 1980 were held in Moscow, which led to an unfortunate display of international indignation. At the start of the year everything had seemed set for the most successful Games ever with the Soviet Union supplying magnificent stadia and facilities and an unprecedented number of athletes scheduled to take part. But in January it became clear that Soviet troops in Afghanistan were not there at the invitation of the legitimate government of Hafizullah Amin which was struggling with rebellious tribes, but was an invasion force intent on putting its own puppet ruler Babrak Karmal in power. The religious leaders of Islam proclaimed a *Jihad*, or holy war, against the Soviet invaders. The western governments recognised the invasion as a culmination of policy begun under the Tsars to push Soviet influence south to the Indian Ocean. Pakistan and India naturally were alarmed and gave help to the rebels who termed themselves the *mujahedin*. America ordered a boycott of the Moscow Olympics in protest at Soviet aggression. West Germany and Japan followed suit, but the response of other western nations was not so clear. Several refused to attend under their own national banners and instead sent athletes as individuals. The political controversy threatened to overwhelm the Olympic Ideal of friendly competition without rancour. The siting of the 1984 Games in America promised more trouble in store if the Soviets chose to retaliate.

THE IRAN-IRAQ WAR

The imposition of Islamic law and rule by clerics in Iran after the fall of the Shah grated on the people of Khuzistan. The province was in a volatile position being not only rich in oil but on the border with Iraq, which had an historic claim to the region. When the local populace rioted against Iranian rule Iraq's President Saddam Hussein sent his troops to the border. Ostensibly in support of the rioters, Hussein invaded Iran across the strategic Shatt-al-Arab waterway on 15th September. His troops quickly seized the vital port of Khorramshahr and swept on to encircle Abadan. This oil centre held out against heavy attacks and by the close of the year was under a siege which would last for nearly two years. Heavy air attacks by both sides led to massive destruction of oil wells, refineries and dock facilities. By the end of December both nations looked set for a long war. Left: Iraqi troops advance through the village of Khomaisse. Below: A pro-Iraqi civilian poses with an Iraqi tank at Shalmaja, some ten miles inside Iran, on 27th September.

The Iran hostage crisis reached new heights of tension in April. The previous November 53 US Embassy staff had been seized by fanatical Iranian students in protest at America's medical treatment of the ailing Shah. The Iranian government made no attempts to free the hostages. Carter froze all Iranian assets in the US and began a determined diplomatic campaign. By April 1980 it was clear that Khomeini had no intention of releasing the hostages so President Carter agreed to a desperate plan. Eight helicopters packed with marine commandos flew into Iran to launch a rescue mission. Three helicopters had to turn back because of breakdown while a fourth collided with its supply plane and crashed into the desert killing eight of those on board. The mission was aborted. The Iranians moved the hostages from Teheran and became more intransigent than ever. Above: The burned bodies of American marines scattered around the wreckage of their helicopters. Right: US hostage Richard Queen, released in July, warned journalists that his Iranian captors were quite prepared to hold the remaining hostages for a long time before release.

On 4th November the Republican candidate for President of the US, Ronald Reagan, stormed home with a massive majority. Reagan secured 489 votes in the electoral college, leaving just 49 to his rival President Jimmy Carter. The massive majority was a reflection of disillusionment with Carter as much as of enthusiasm for Reagan. The Carter administration, elected in response to the Watergate scandal, had scored some successes, but was widely regarded as ineffectual. In foreign policy many felt their nation had been pushed around by smaller states, the Iran hostage fiasco adding to that impression. The economy was also in decline. Reagan offered to solve both problems with a combination of forthright patriotism and free market economics which had wide appeal. Reagan's approach to control of the economy largely amounted to allowing the markets a free hand within government guidelines was dubbed Reaganomics, a rare example of a President's name entering the language. Below: Ronald Reagan (left) and George Bush at their first press conference after the election result was announced.

On 30th April six Arab gunmen burst into the Iranian Embassy in London and took the staff and visitors prisoner. The terrorists were members of the Sunni sect of Islam, persecuted by the Iranian Shiite regime. They demanded the release of 91 prisoners held in Iran. The British police surrounded the Embassy and began negotiations. On 5th May the talks showed signs of breaking down. The terrorists shot two hostages dead. Just hours later the crack Special Air Services unit was sent in to free the remaining hostages. Using grenades to cover their advance, the SAS stormed the building, shot dead five of the gunmen and released all hostages unharmed. Above: An SAS man clambers on to the Embassy balcony before bursting in to attack the terrorists. Top right: Firemen tackle the flames in the Iranian Embassy started by SAS grenades, but without success. The building was gutted.

In 1980 Poland, always a troublesome Soviet satellite state, erupted into political disorder. The unrest had long been simmering, but was sparked by a rise in official meat prices. The move led to demands for increased wages which produced a rash of strikes across the nation. Among the best organised was that in the massive Lenin Shipyards in Gdansk where the strikers were organised by Lech Walesa. On 31st August the government agreed to the Gdansk Agreement which for the first time in a Communist state allowed the formation of an independent trade union. Within weeks dozens of unions had sprung up in various industries and on 17th September they joined together in a national organisation dubbed Solidarity. Walesa became leader of Solidarity and it soon became clear that the workers were intent on using the union for political purposes. As the Polish government found itself increasingly under pressure to introduce reforms, the Soviet Union massed its armies on the Polish borders. With memories of Hungary in 1956 and Czechoslovakia in 1968 being stirred up, President Reagan of the USA called a meeting of NATO members and issued a blunt warning to the Soviet Union to leave Poland alone. Right: Lech Walesa is carried through the Lenin Shipyard in Gdansk by fellow workers after he concluded the Gdansk Agreement.

Left: President Joseph Tito of Yugoslavia. The death of this idiosyncratic Communist ruler threatened to destabilise the Balkans. Since 1948 Tito had enforced a repressive Communist regime on his federation of diverse nationalities while preserving a strict independence from Soviet authority. His regime had even gone so far as to embrace trade with the West and to welcome tourists. Many feared that with the death of the strong man, the Soviets would find the temptation to intervene overwhelming. In the event the Soviets restrained themselves. The new nation of Zimbabwe entered a troubled phase in 1980. President Robert Mugabe moved against his colleague in government and former ally in the civil war, Joshua Nkomo by arresting five prominent Nkomo supporters and severely restraining Nkomo's influence in government. The distrust between the two was of tribal origins, Nkomo championing the numerically inferior Matabele against Mugabe's Shona, though there were ideological differences between the two. Below: Robert Mugabe (left) and Joshua Nkomo when they worked together before Mugabe's bid for sole power in 1980.

The Pink Panther Passes On

On 23rd July Peter Sellers, one of the great comics of the British screen, died tragically aged of 54. Born in Hampshire in 1925, Sellers followed his parents on to the stage and scored early success with ENSA during the war. His ability to produce silly voices and to mimic the voices of public figures earned him regular spots on radio. It was his superb portrayal of a bungling crook in the movie *The Ladykillers* in 1955 which brought him real stardom. He appeared in British comedies for several years, starring in classics such as *I'm All Right Jack* and *The Wrong Arm of the Law*, but it was *The Pink Panther* in 1963 which shot him to international fame. Sellers always turned in magnificent performances, being nominated twice for an Oscar, but had a reputation for being moody on set and demanding from others the same perfectionism he displayed himself. His sudden death from a heart attack came as a blow to his many friends and marked a loss to the world of movies.

In 1980 the Soviets began their invasion of Afghanistan, though at first it was unclear to the outside world exactly what was happening. In April 1978 a palace coup overthrew President Mohammed Daoud and replaced his regime with one led by Hafizullah Amin, which professed friendship to Moscow. A Treaty of Friendship was duly signed. In December 1979 Soviet troops were flown to Kabul, apparently acting under the terms of the treaty, to help Amin reimpose order in his nation. Instead the Soviets overthrew Amin and installed Babrak Karmal in power. It rapidly became clear that Karmal was a Soviet puppet ruler and that Afghanistan was due to become a part of the Soviet Empire. Left: Soviet troops repair a vehicle while on patrol in a suburb of Kabul in December. The streets of the capital were relatively safe at this period, most unrest being confined to the hill country.

POLITICAL UNREST IN ITALY

The Italian political system is one of great complexity which allows for rapid changes of government without any great change in the make-up of the political classes. As a result government edicts are widely ignored though some are frustrated by the lack of accountability of state institutions. These feelings have led more than one political terrorist group to spring up in anger at the system and embark on criminal terrorist activities. The infamous Red Brigade was a Communist-inspired group which wreaked havoc while the ominously named Ordine Nero, the Black Order, based its message on that of Fascist dictator Benito Mussolini. It has been suggested, though without much evidence, that these groups are backed by the Mafia or by Freemasonic orders. Left: Mario Tuti, believed to be the leader of the Ordine Nero, gives the Fascist salute as he is led handcuffed to his trial in Bologna in June. Above: Marco Affatigato is led to a waiting police van at Bologna Airport after extradition from France on charges of planting bombs for a right-wing group.

Mass Beheadings In Saudi Arabia

On 9th January a total of 63 prisoners were led out into a public square in Saudi Arabia and ceremonially beheaded by the state executioner. This, the largest mass execution seen for many years, followed dramatic events the previous November which managed to combine politics, religion and violence in a dangerous combination. On 20th November 1979 a force of about 700 men stormed the holy mosque at Mecca, shooting their way past the Saudi guards. For four days the insurgents held out until the Saudi Army retook the building. It was revealed that the assault had been led by a self-proclaimed *Mahdi*, or prophet, called Juseiman bin Seif who had led his followers out of the Saudi desert to storm the religious capital of Islam. It was at first thought that the raid was backed by Iran's Shiite government to embarrass the Saudi royal family who adhere to the Sunni sect, but this suggestion was later dropped. It appeared that Seif had been motivated by genuine religious fervour blended with a desire to purify the mosque of what he saw as secular control by the Saudis. The rebels not executed were subjected to 'religious education' while serving their prison sentences.

THE KILLING OF JOHN LENNON

On 8th December the former Beatle John Lennon was shot dead outside his New York apartment. Lennon was returning to his home in the Dakota Building at 10.45 pm after a recording session. As he walked across the sidewalk to the front door a man pushed forward as if about to ask for an autograph. Instead he drew a pistol and pumped two bullets into Lennon. As Lennon's dying body fell into the arms of his wife, Yoko Ono, the killer calmly sat down and began to read from a book he had brought with him. The murderer was later named as Mark Chapman from Hawaii. Chapman was found to have had an obsessive interest in Lennon, going so far as to use Lennon's name on occasion. It was found Chapman had been mentally incompetent at the time of the killing. The death shocked many for Lennon had epitomised much of the peace movement of the late 1960s and early 1970s. His music spoke for a large section of the decade's youth while his lifestyle was admired by many. Facing page, top left: Part of the 50,000 strong crowd which gathered outside Lennon's flat for a silent vigil for their hero on 14th December.

On 28th March a floating rig in the North Sea capsized, killing 123 of those on board. The rig had been fitted out as a hotel and recreation centre for the many men employed on the various oil drilling rigs in the surrounding Edda Field, and this accounted for the tragically high number of deaths. The disaster happened when one of the five supporting legs suddenly gave way. Below: Survivors from the stricken oil rig who were rescued from the icy waters of the North Sea are comforted at Stavanger Airport, Norway, where they were waiting for hospital treatment. Far left: A distraught man stands on the wreckage of his home in Lioni, one of several Italian mountain villages devastated by the earthquake of 26th November. It was estimated that some 3,000 people were killed by collapsing buildings, and the landslides and flash floods which accompanied the earthquake. Above right: The space shuttle Columbia, the first of several to be built, is bathed in powerful searchlights as it arrives on the launchpad at the Kennedy Space Center after a tantalisingly slow seven hour journey from the Vehicle Assembly Building a short distance away.

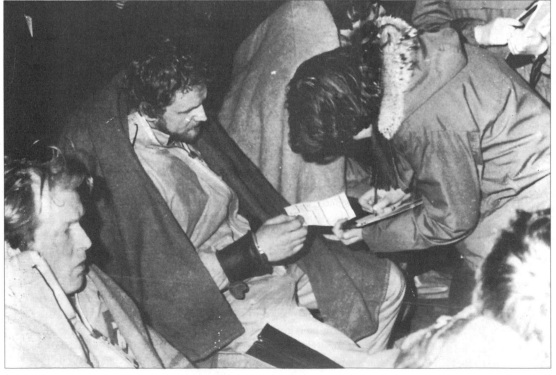

Above left: The movie star Steve McQueen who died on 7th November at the age of just 50. McQueen was born in Indiana in 1930 and turned to acting after serving in the Marines. After some small parts in the 1950s, McQueen starred in the classic western **The Magnificent Seven** *which won him both popularity and a string of parts as a tough man with a cool exterior. Above: The author Joy Adamson who won fame as the author of the book* **Born Free***, the story of Elsa the lioness, died this year. Left: The master of film suspense, Sir Alfred Hitchcock, who died on 29th April aged 80. He first entered movies in 1919, directing his first film in 1926. He went on to direct a total of 53. His movies include such classics as* **Psycho** *in 1960, and* **The Birds** *in 1963, but his only Oscar came for* **Rebecca** *in 1940. Some considered that he deserved more recognition from the industry he served so well for over fifty years.*

Top left: Britain's Robin Cousins (centre) celebrates his gold medal in the men's figure skating championships together with silver medallist Jan Hoffmann of East Germany and bronze medallist Charlie Tickner from the USA. Top right: The British boxer Alan Minter is carried shoulder high by his team after taking the Middleweight World Championship from Vito Antuofermo in Las Vegas on 16th March. Above: The agony and exhilaration of victory in the Olympics is clearly shown on the face of British runner Sebastian Coe as he breasts the tape to take the gold medal in the 1,500 metre race. Right: Steve Ovett acknowledges the cheers of the crowd after taking the gold medal in the Olympic 800 metre race.

Jan 1	Greece becomes the 10th member of the EEC
Jan 5	UK: 'The Yorkshire Ripper', Peter Sutcliffe, is charged
Jan 20	Iran releases all 52 US Embassy hostages
Jan 20	Ronald Reagan is inaugurated as US president
Jan 29	Adolfo Suarez resigns as PM of Spain
Feb 9	Poland: PM is forced to resign after 5 months of unrest
Feb 0	Death of US rock singer Bill Haley
Mar 2	A Pakistani plane with 148 on board is hijacked
Mar 26	UK: The Gang of Four launch the Social Democratic Party
Mar 29	UK: 6,700 runners compete in the first London marathon
Mar 30	US: President Reagan and three aides are shot in an assassination attempt in Washington
Apr 4	UK: Oxford wins Boat Race with first ever lady cox
Apr 11	UK: Over 300 people are injured in violent rioting in Brixton
Apr 12	US: The launch of the first reusable manned space vehicle, the space shuttle Columbia
Apr 12	Death of US boxer Joe Louis
May 5	Robert Sands is the first IRA hunger striker to die in the Hillsborough prison
May 6	The USA expels all Libyan diplomats
May 10	France: Francois Mitterand is elected the first Socialist President of France since the foundation of the Fifth Republic
May 11	Death of Jamaican musician and black rights activist Bob Marley

May 13	Pope John-Paul II is seriously wounded by a gunman
May 26	Italy: Arnaldo Frolani's government resigns after revelations of links between top officials and an illegal secret Masonic lodge
May 30	Bangladesh: President Ziaur Rahman is shot dead in an attempted military coup
Jun 8	Israeli planes bomb a nuclear power plant being built near Baghdad
Jul 17	UK: Opening of the Humber Bridge, the longest single span bridge in the world
Jul 24	Israel and the PLO endorse ceasefire agreements
Jul 29	A worldwide TV audience of over 700 million watches the wedding of the Prince of Wales to Lady Diana Spencer
Jul 30	Ireland: Dr Garret Fitzgerald becomes prime minister
Aug 7	Poland: 1 million Solidarity members go on strike
Aug 19	US fighter aircraft shoot down two Libyan jets
Aug 30	Iran: A terrorist bomb kills 15, including Prime Minister Bahomar and President Rajaj
Oct 6	President Anwar Sadat of Egypt is assassinated by extremist Moslem soldiers
Oct 18	The first socialist government in Greece is elected under Andreas Papandreou
Nov 29	Death of US actress Natalie Wood
Dec 31	Doctors warn of new disease that destroys the immune system and appears to be common in homosexuals

Solidarity In Poland

In a year which saw terrorism, assassination and the imposition of totalitarian governments in many parts of the world, Poland provided a bright ray of hope for those who believed in democracy. Even here the year was to end in tragedy. In 1979 workers had won the right to organise free trades unions, which came together under the Solidarity organisation headed by Lech Walesa. On 24th January Solidarity called a strike to back demands for a five day working week, winning their claim on the 31st. On 9th February the Communist Party ousted premier Pinkowski and installed General Wojciech Jaruzelski in his place On 8th June events became ominous when Soviet leaders issued a statement urging Jaruzelski to crackdown on "counter-revolutionaries" in a clear reference to Solidarity. In August protests about poor food supplies led to government repression and a strike threat from Solidarity. Soviet leader Brezhnev visited Poland to put backbone into the Polish government in its struggle with Solidarity, which was rapidly acquiring a political facet. Two weeks later a Soviet army 100,000 strong was sent to the Polish border on 'manoeuvres'. Jaruzelski sent for Walesa and warned him that the actions of Solidarity were risking a Soviet invasion along the lines of Hungary and Czechoslovakia. The two leaders tried to reach a compromise on many issues, but the talks eventually broke down. Solidarity asked for a referendum on the future of the government in December. Fearing Soviet invasion, Jaruzelski imposed martial law and sent the Polish army on to the streets to impose order. Walesa and other leaders were arrested, Solidarity appeared crushed.

Left: A startlingly clear photograph of Saturn obtained in September by the Voyager 2 space probe which was launched by NASA. The probe took the picture when it was some 13 million miles distant from Saturn. As it drew closer to the planet and its satellite moons, Voyager 2 transmitted images back to Earth which provided much information and data previously unknown to scientists.

In the spring of 1981 several British cities saw districts descend into riot and civil disorder. First to erupt was Brixton, a region of south London with a particularly high concentration of Black immigrants. A police operation designed to catch criminals was construed by local youths as harassment. On the evening of 11th April the ill feeling boiled over into direct confrontation. This rapidly escalated into a major riot. A total of 97 police were injured in the fighting and 70 arrests were made in a night which saw 780 crimes, mostly shop looting, committed. The rioting continued for several nights before peace returned. Similar riots later broke out in the Toxteth area of Liverpool and West London, though the causes were substantially different. Below: The wreckage in Mayall Road, Brixton, on 12th April as firemen damp down remaining smouldering fires. Right: Firemen stand on the pile of rubble which marks the site of The George, a pub in Brixton which was destroyed by a petrol bomb attack on the night of 11th April.

Left: Newspapers announce the arrest of Peter Sutcliffe, later convicted of the Yorkshire Ripper murders. Sutcliffe killed for the first time on 30th October 1975. The murder of Wilma McCann, a Leeds prostitute, was brutal with the skull being crushed and the body stabbed repeatedly. Three months later a second prostitute was killed in the same way, and police knew a serial killer was at large. The press dubbed him the Yorkshire Ripper, as the injuries he inflicted reminded some of Jack the Ripper in the 1880s. In all Sutcliffe murdered twelve women and made seven abortive attacks before his arrest. He was finally caught by local police who arrested a man picking up a prostitute in a car with false number plates. In the car were weapons identified with the injurie inflicted by the Yorkshire Ripper. Sutcliffe was found guilty of the ser al killings in May 1981. Above: The bus attacked by an IRA bomb as it carried an army band back t Chelsea Barracks after a concert on 10th October. The bomb injured eight bandsmen and killed one woman passerby.

The Hostage Crisis Ends

The year long Iran-US hostage crisis came to an end in January amid confusion and recrimination typical of the whole affair. The deal between the USA and Iran over the release of US Embassy staff held hostage in Teheran by revolutionary students backing the Khomeini regime was complex and controversial. The US agreed to unfreeze Iranian government funds, impounded when the Shah was overthrown by revolution. America also agreed to freeze the substantial personal fortune of the ex-Shah until it could be decided if these were indeed personal assets or national wealth. Trade sanctions were also to be ended. Some accused President Carter of effectively giving in to terrorism and paying ransom for the release of the 52 hostages after 444 days. The release was scheduled for Carter's last full day in the White House, but Iran delayed until Reagan had been sworn in. Some saw this as a final snub to Carter. Reagan allowed Carter to fly to Germany to greet the hostages formally, thus neatly ending a crisis which had been Carter's throughout.

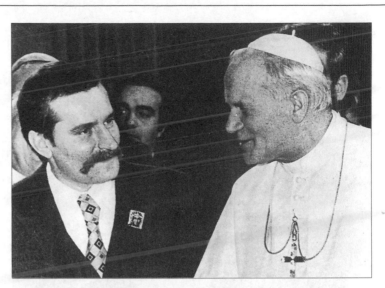

THE YEAR OF ASSASSINATION

The year 1981 was marked by dramatic attempts to murder political leaders. First to take the assassin's bullet was US President Ronald Reagan. On 30th March the President was shot in the chest as he left a meeting at the Washington Hilton Hotel. Also shot were two security men and Reagan's press secretary James Brady. Police pounced on the gunman, later identified as John Hinckley of Colorado who was found not guilty due to insanity at his trial in June 1982. Reagan left hospital after 12 days. Bottom left: Secret service agents grab Hinckley (*right*) while others watch the crowd for further trouble or tend the wounded. Second to be shot was Pope John Paul II, gunned down in St Peter's Square in front of ten thousand worshippers. The gunman was a 23 year old Turk named Mehmet Agca who was a neo-Nazi on the run from a murder charge in Turkey. The Pope underwent an emergency five hour operation, but survived. Top right: The Pope welcomes Lech Walesa to the Vatican on 15th January. Above left: Turk Mehmet Agca being led to prison by police. More dramatic still was the murder of Egypt's President Sadat on 6th October. During a military parade, five soldiers wheeled out of line and dashed to the Presidential stand which they attacked with grenades and machine guns. Security guards cut down the assassins, killing three, but not before Sadat and ten close officials had been killed. Vice-President Hosni Mubarak took over power, blaming Moslem fundamentalists angered over the peace treaty with Israel for the brutal attack. Above: President Sadat's coffin is carried to a Cairo mosque for a funeral service.

Above: Ken Livingstone, the charismatic left wing politician who rose to be leader of the Labour controlled Greater London Council. Livingstone's unique brand of populism and far left policies made him a dynamic figure in local politics who became well known far beyond London. He later entered Parliament as the Labour MP for Brent East. Top right: Shirley Williams arrives at Westminster to take her seat as Social Democratic Party MP for Crosby after a bye-election in November. Williams was a former Labour Cabinet Minister and was once tipped as a candidate to be Britain's first woman Prime Minister. It was largely the conflict between moderate Socialists, such as Williams, and more idealistic thinkers in the Livingstone mould, which led to the split in the Labour Party which led to the formation of the SDP. The decision by Labour MPs to leave Labour to join the newly formed Social Democrats at first promised great things, but ultimately led to a decline in their careers. Right centre: Shirley Williams and William Rogers applaud a speech by Dr David Owen, another former Labour minister who in 1981 joined the SDP. Right: Mrs Thatcher welcomes President Mitterand of France to London in October for bilateral talks on the direction of the EEC.

The most important wedding of the year was that of Charles, Prince of Wales, to Lady Diana Spencer on 29 July. The engagement was announced on 24th February, and Diana had been subjected to intense press attention throughout the spring and summer. The wedding was a magnificent event, with all the ceremonial of royal events and graced by the presence of numerous state figures. Charles was dressed in naval uniform, but it was Lady Diana's sumptuous ivory silk wedding dress that captured the headlines. Below: Prince Charles and Lady Diana Spencer taking part in a television interview a few days before the wedding. Left: The royal couple returning to Buckingham Palace after the service in St Paul's Cathedral. Bottom left: The joint winners of London's first public marathon, run on 29th March. Norwegian Inge Simosen (right) and American Dick Beardsley crossed the line in a time of 2 hours 11 minutes and 48 seconds.

Rebellion In Spain

King Juan Carlos faced severe tests in 1981 as first terrorism then an attempted coup threatened to rock his kingdom. The terrorist threat came from the Basque separatists of northeastern Spain whose unique cultural and linguistic heritage was distinct from that of the rest of Spain. Known as ETA, the movement had both a political and terrorist wing. The terrorists specialised in kidnapping or murdering state officials and police officers. On 23rd February a squad of Civil Guard troops led by Colonel Antonio Tejero Molino stormed the Cortes Building and held the Parliament at gunpoint. The chamber was the scene of gunfire and threats as the colonel attempted to bully the deputies and senators into following his orders. Military leaders, however, remained loyal and a million people flooded into the streets to protest loyalty to the king. King Juan Carlos was able to restore order rapidly, gaining increased public respect for his firm handling of the crisis.

Right: British explorer Sir Ranulf Fiennes sells equipment left over from his intrepid Transglobe Expedition which circled the planet via the poles, rather than the more usual east-west route. Sir Ranulf acquired an impressive reputation for daring journeys, usually for the benefit of charity fundraising. Below: The Jamaican reggae singer Bob Marley. The international star died in Miami on 11th May after a long fight against cancer. Although his music and Rastafarian religion were deeply rooted in Jamaica, Marley abandoned the island after gunmen tried to kill him at his home in 1976. Below right: Harrison Ford who starred in the massive box-office hit movie **Raiders of the Lost Ark** *in this year. The success followed up his roles in* **Star Wars** *and* **The Empire Strikes Back** *to establish him as a major star.*

In 1981 the world motor industry was dazzled by a startlingly modern sports car built with the exclusive luxury market firmly in mind. The De Lorean two seater became an accepted standard of excellence and featured in movies and advertising, as an unequalled status symbol. The vehicle was the result of collaboration between US automobile industry executive John De Lorean and the British Government. Faced by rising levels of both unemployment and terrorism in Northern Ireland in the late 1970s, the Government agreed to put large sums of capital at the disposal of De Lorean for the founding of his company and the tooling up required by any new vehicle manufacturer. In the event the enterprise was to fail dismally as the luxury car market shrank alarmingly. De Lorean was later convicted of drugs dealing in America after he fell into a trap laid by drugs enforcement officers. Left: De Lorean sits in one of his futuristic sports cars at the Earl's Court Motor Fair in October.

Above: The wedding of ex-Beatle Ringo Starr to film actress Barbara Bach drew crowds to an otherwise obscure London Register Office on 27th April. Above right: The British actor Sir Alec Guinness who was awarded an honorary Oscar in 1981 for his contributions to the movie industry. Sir Alec Guinness's career had begun on stage in the 1930s but after serving in the Royal Navy during World War II, he turned to the movies with the Dicken's classic **Oliver Twist**. His fame was assured in the comedy **Kind Hearts and Coronets** in 1949 after which he appeared in a large number of films and television dramas in both Britain and America. Right: The British rock star Rod Stewart who stunned American critics with his flamboyant show in New York's Madison Square Garden on 27th November when he appeared in fake leopard skin trousers.

Jan 12 Mark Thatcher, son of Margaret, goes missing in the Sahara while taking part in a rally

Jan 13 US: 78 people are killed when a jet crashes on take-off into the frozen Potomac River

Feb 4 The cut-rate transatlantic passenger service, Laker Airways collapses with debts of £276 million

Feb 19 Belfast: John De Lorean's luxury motor car company is put into receivership

Mar 9 Dublin: Charles Haughey is sworn in as prime minister

Mar 19 UK: 15 cricketers who made an unofficial tour to South Africa are banned from international cricket for three years

Mar 26 UK: The first test-tube twins are born

Apr 2 Argentinian forces invade the Falkland Islands and overthrow the British administration

Apr 3 The UN Security Council votes in favour of a resolution demanding that Argentina withdraw from the Falklands

Apr 4 The first ships of a Royal Navy task force leave Britain for the Falklands

Apr 15 Cairo: Five men found guilty of killing Sadat are executed

May 2 The Argentinian cruiser General Belgrano is sunk by a British submarine, killing 368

May 4 Falklands: HMS Sheffield is sunk by an Exocet

May 19 Sophia Loren begins a month long sentence for tax evasion

Jun 13 Death of King Khaled of Saudi Arabia

Jun 14 British forces take command of the Falkland Islands

Jun 19 UK: Italian banker, Roberto Calvi, is found hanging from a London bridge

Jun 21 The Princess of Wales gives birth to a son, William

Jul 7 UK: An intruder at Buckingham Palace, Michael Fagan, gets into the Queen's bedroom

Jul 11 Italy wins the World Cup with a 3-1 victory against West Germany in Madrid

Jul 13 Iran invades Iraq

Jul 20 IRA bombs explode in London's Regent's Park and Hyde Park, killing 11 soldiers

Aug 12 Death of US actor Henry Fonda

Aug 29 65-year old Ashby Harper becomes the oldest person to swim the English Channel

Aug 30 Death of Swedish actress Ingrid Bergman

Sep 1 Mexico: Inflation is at 70 percent and around eight million are out of work

Sep 5 Death of British airman Sir Douglas Bader

Sep 10 Poul Schluter becomes prime minister of Denmark

Sep 14 Princess Grace of Monaco dies after a car crash

Sep 14 President-elect of Lebanon, Bashir Gemayel, is killed in a bomb explosion in Beirut

Oct 11 Henry VIII's flagship, The Mary Rose, is raised 400 years after she sank

Oct 13 Australia: Lindy and Michael Chamberlain go on trial for murder after claiming a dingo killed their baby

Oct 15 Halley's Comet is sighted for the first time since 1911

Nov 10 Soviet president Leonid Brezhnev dies of a heart attack

Nov 12 Poland: Lech Walesa is freed after one years detention

Nov 14 UK: Over 20,000 women surround the Greenham Common airbase in a peaceful protest against the installation of US cruise missiles

Dec 2 Felipe Gonzalez is worn in as the first Socialist prime minister of Spain

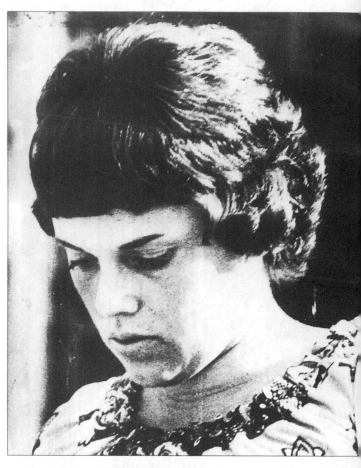

THE DINGO BABY CASE

In October 1982 one of Australia's most baffling murder trials seized the headlines, not only in the Northern Territory where it was held but around the world. On trial was a 30 year old mother accused of murdering her baby. The case had begun on 17th August 1980 when Lindy Chamberlain, her husband, Michael, and three children camped at Ayers Rock in the Outback. As the Chamberlains joined other families in a barbecue, Lindy went to check on 9 week old Azaria. She returned screaming that a dingo had taken the baby. Witnesses stated that the tent was indeed empty of the baby, but there was no sign of a dingo. A week later the baby's bloodstained clothes were found a short distance away. Dingoes were not known for attacks on humans and intense local gossip had it that the baby girl had been murdered. In February 1981 the coroner gave his verdict that he thought a dingo was responsible. But the case did not rest for police had found new forensic evidence. Traces of blood were found around the front seat of the Chamberlains car and the baby's clothes showed signs of being cut with a knife rather than torn by dog's teeth. The pattern of blood was said to be indicative of a cleanly cut throat, rather than the more uneven marks of bite wounds. In defence, Lindy Chamberlain stuck to her dingo story and explained the blood in the car as being the result of giving a lift to an injured man some time earlier, and the man testified the truth of this. Nevertheless, the jury convicted Lindy Chamberlain of murder and in 1983 the Court of Appeal backed the decision. In 1986, however, more of Azaria's clothing was found and new forensic evidence was produced, leading to the release of Lindy Chamberlain. Above: Lindy Chamberlain photographed as she left the court in Darwin on 18th October.

The announcement that Britain was to be host to US cruise missiles was greeted with indignation by the British anti-nuclear movement. The intermediate range missiles were equipped with nuclear warheads and were capable of delivering the weapon to targets thousands of miles away with great precision and reliability. The development of such weapons was a sophisticated response to new Soviet missiles and a calculated hard bargaining counter in US-Soviet arms talks. The protesters viewed the missiles as an escalation of the danger of nuclear war and objected to Britain playing host to a US weapons system. When President Reagan announced the 'Star Wars' initiative aimed at making intercontinental ballistic missiles effectively useless, the protesters redoubled their efforts. Large scale demonstrations took place outside the Greenham Common base in Berkshire where cruise missiles were to be based and a permanent camp of women protesters was established near the gates of the airfield. Right: The debris left behind by the protest at the Greenham Common base against the installation of cruise missiles on 14th November, the day the first missiles arrived.

The Mary Rose

Maritime history was made on 11th October when a flagship of the Royal Navy was raised from the seabed 437 years after she sank. The *Mary Rose*, pride of King Henry VIII's fleet, sank in the Solent as she set sail to engage a French invasion fleet on 19th July. The ship appears to have sunk when a sudden gust of wind allowed the sea in through open gunports. The wreck, much of it preserved in soft mud, was discovered in 1968. By 1982 enough money and expertise to raise the wooden hull had been gathered. First all the movable artifacts, such as guns and carriages, were removed. A large metal cage was built around the hull and, on 11th October, the lifting began. As the timbers broke the surface, part of the cage gave way threatening to plunge the ship back to its grave, but the main struts held secure. The ship was moved slowly to dry dock where she is now on view to the public. The finding of a ship virtually intact was a major discovery which allowed historians to reconstruct for the first time life at sea in the 1540s and to gain an idea of battle tactics. The ship was armed with heavy guns and light weapons capable of crippling but not sinking an enemy. Large numbers of troops equipped with bows, swords and daggers were also carried, presumably to board and capture a ship after it was disabled by gunfire.

Above left: A detachment of the Household Cavalry ride through Hyde Park, passing the spot where four of their comrades were killed and many civilians injured by an IRA bomb on 20th July. The bomb was packed with nails to inflict horrific injuries. A second bomb at an army band concert killed seven more troops. On 13th January an Air Florida jet crashed into the Potomac River while lifting off from Washington Airport. Five passengers were killed, as were six people on the ground. The debris scattered across the 14th Street Bridge caused a massive traffic jam which hampered rescue teams trying to reach the scene of the disaster. The crash occurred after a heavy snowstorm and icing problems were suspected to be a contributory factor. Left: The tail-section of the Air Florida jet is hoisted from the Potomac five days after the crash.

471

Below: Nurses belonging to the COHSE union demonstrate outside the Palace of Westminster in support of their demand for a 12% pay rise. The government resisted the call as part of its attempts to restrict public spending and so help to control inflation. Right: Empty rail tracks at Waterloo Station in London as a national rail strike began in July. Right centre: Passengers queue for coaches at Victoria coach station on 15th July as the rail strike made long distance rail travel virtually impossible. British Rail was threatening to sack any staff who did not return to work within

days. Bottom right: Yasser Arafat, leader of the PLO, defiantly waves a gun as he tours positions held by his Palestinian gunmen in southern Lebanon on 15th June. The Israeli invasion of Lebanon launched on 6th June was designed to destroy the bases from which PLO fighters had been raiding northern Israel. Fighting ended with a ceasefire on 25th June after which Israel occupied a thirty mile wide strip of southern Lebanon and the PLO were forced to leave Lebanon. Facing page, bottom: A PLO sentry stares out across Beirut during an Israeli air strike on the Lebanese capital.

A NEW SOVIET LEADER

Facing page, top: The body of Soviet leader Leonid Brezhnev lies in state in Moscow. His death followed a long heart and lung illness. Soviet leaders moved swiftly to appoint a successor, the KGB chief Yuri Andropov being created General Secretary of the Communist Party just two days later. Brezhnev had ruled the Soviet Union with a tough record of repression for eighteen years. Born in 1906 in the Ukraine he trained as an engineer before joining the Party. His rise under Stalin and Khrushchev was rapid, joining the Politburo when only 51. He was instrumental in plotting the overthrow of Khrushchev in a cunning ploy which fully exploited the officially democratic nature of the Communist Party. His rule was early characterised by the Brezhnev Doctrine which stated the Soviet Union would interfere if any Communist regime appeared in danger of collapse. In 1968 he put the doctrine into brutal force with the invasion of Czechoslovakia and at the time of his death was threatening to repeat the move in Poland. Detente with the Western powers was combined with ruthless determination to extend Soviet influence in Africa and the Third World. His successor, Andropov, promised to be equally ruthless but to scorn the softening influences of detente. His first speech glorified the 'invincible might of the Soviet armed forces'.

THE FALKLANDS WAR

The long standing dispute between Britain and Argentina over ownership of the Falkland Islands erupted into warfare in April. The Argentinian government believed from diplomatic contact that Britain was not prepared to fight to retain the islands if force were used. Just before dawn on 2nd April Argentinians stormed Port Stanley, the islands' capital, with overwhelming forces of troops, light armour and naval guns and the 61 British marines surrendered. Remote South Georgia was taken the next day. At once the British Prime Minister, Mrs Thatcher dispatched a task force to retake the islands. As the ships sailed south and the forces were gathered for the coming struggle, diplomats tried to negotiate a peace. The US Secretary of State flew repeatedly between the two nations in an attempt to find common ground, but without success. On 2nd May a British submarine torpedoed and sank the battleship General Belgrano causing some 350 deaths. Two days later HMS Sheffield was sunk by Argentinian air attack. The war was on in earnest. On 21st May British troops landed in the relatively undefended San Carlos harbour and losses mounted rapidly. Within days two British frigates had been sunk and 14 Argentinian aircraft shot down. On 29th May the strategic Goose Green fell to the British after stiff fighting and two days later Mount Kent was taken. By the 14th June Port Stanley was surrounded and British forces prepared for the final assault, but the Argentinian commander, General Menendez surrendered his troops. In all some 256 British and 750 Argentinians were killed in the fighting which restored the islands to Britain and emphasised that Western powers were still capable of impressive military operations when circumstances demanded.

Right: Mrs Thatcher welcomes US Secretary of State Alexander Haig to No.10 Downing Street on 8th April during his shuttle diplomacy. Top right: Men of M Company 42 Commando pose on South Georgia after recapturing the island on 25th April. It was M Company, known to comrades as the Mighty Munch, which retook South Georgia with help from the SAS, after the island had been occupied for just over three weeks. Centre right: Deck crew on HMS Hermes, protected by anti-flash masks, await the return of aircraft on anti-submarine patrol on 19th April. The threat posed by the Argentine submarines was a worry throughout the campaign. Above: A survivor from HMS Sheffield is helped by medical orderlies to the sick bay on HMS Hermes on 26th May.

Top: The frantic scene aboard HMS Hermes as Sea King helicopters and Sea Harrier jets are prepared for combat as the ship sails south from Ascension Island. Above left: British Royal Engineers probe the marshy ground for mines before an area around Port Stanley is cleared for civilian use after the fighting. Above: An Argentinian captured on 17th June near Port Howard is searched by a 40 Commando Marine. Left: Small craft decked with flags turn out to welcome SS Canberra and her complement of troops to Southampton on 11th July.

Above: Henry Fonda who died on 12th August aged 77. He began his career at college, reaching Broadway in 1934 before moving to films in 1939 when he played the title role of **The Young Mr Lincoln.** *Fonda usually played the hero, a man of honesty and integrity often faced by corrupt or uncaring authority. His last film* **On Golden Pond** *was highly acclaimed and won him an Oscar. Above left: Princess Grace of Monaco, formerly the film star Grace Kelly, was killed at the age of just 52 when she was involved in a road crash. Her car plunged over a mountain slope in southern France on 10th September. Her daughter, Princess Stephanie was injured in the crash. Left: Douglas Bader, the British pilot who won great fame during the Battle of Britain, died in 1982. Bader was an exceptionally gifted pilot who led his squadron with daring during the heaviest fighting, managing all this after losing both legs during an air crash before the war.*

The Atlanta Strangler

On 27th February a US jury found Wayne Williams guilty of a series of murders which had brought fear to the streets of Atlanta, Georgia. The murders by the killer dubbed the Atlanta Strangler had mounted alarmingly over previous months and showed a brutal pattern. The victims were almost without exception young black children, mostly boys, who were strangled by being caught in a powerful arm lock from behind. Police were puzzled not only by the lack of clues but also by the lack of motive for none of the children were sexually assaulted or robbed. By the winter of 1980 killings were taking place with terrifying regularity. In the poor black neighbourhoods vigilante groups roamed the streets and parents kept a close eye on children. Yet still the murders continued. Dark rumours of a racial motive circulated and police began to fear for public order. In May 1981 when 26 deaths had occurred, police saw a large object dumped into a river from a bridge. Drivers on the bridge were stopped and questioned while divers searched the river and found the body of a black youth. Among those on the bridge was Wayne Williams, a quiet 23 year old Black who lived with his parents. Police noted the fact that he was known to listen to police radio and race to the sites of crimes, but they had no evidence. Then Williams began to behave oddly. On 3rd June he held a press conference to proclaim his innocence of the murders. He declared himself a genius and raved about police intimidation. But the police gathered evidence and found that fibres in Williams's car matched those of victims clothing. When the trial opened evidence was thin, relying on forensics of an inconclusive nature and identifications which were not the strongest on record. More telling for the jury was the fact that the regular monthly killings had stopped since Williams was arrested. He was found guilty and sentenced to life.

Top left: The sultry Italian movie star Sophia Loren who was imprisoned for a month after conviction for tax evasion in this year. She emerged full of thanks to the authorities and looking healthier than when she had entered. Above: Princess Diana emerges from St Mary's Hospital in London on 22nd June with her first son, born the previous day. He was later christened William, continuing a distinguished royal name which had already belonged to four kings of England. Left: Burt Reynolds and Dolly Parton who starred in the movie **The Best Little Whorehouse in Texas** *this year.*

Top left: Austrian Grand Prix dri-ver Niki Lauda acknowledges the crowd after winning the British Grand Prix at Brands Hatch on 18th July. Top right: The crowds shelter beneath umbrellas as tor-rential rain stops play at Wimbledon three times in a single day on 18th June. The two week tennis competition proved to be one of the wettest on record. Right centre: The victorious Italian soc-cer team parades around Santiago Stadium in Spain with the coveted World Cup which they won on 11th July. Above: Golfer Tom Watson celebrating his win of the British Open on 18th July. Right: Briton Daley Thompson wraps himself in the Union Jack after taking the decathlon gold medal at the European Championships and setting a new world record in the process.

Jan 5	UK: Two policewomen and a policeman die trying to save a man who was trying to rescue his drowning dog
Jan 14	UK: Police opened fire on Stephen Waldorf, mistaking him for an escaped prisoner
Jan 17	Breakfast television begins in the UK for the first time
Feb 9	Ireland: The winner of the 1981 Derby, Shergar, is kidnapped and a £2 million ransom is demanded
Feb 10	The remains of 17 people are found at a house in London, a civil servant is later accused of the murders
Feb 13	Italy: 63 die in a fire in a theatre in Turin
Feb 15	The Lebanese army takes complete control of Beirut
Feb 16	Australia: 68 die in bush fires
Feb 25	Death of US playwright Tennessee Williams
Mar 5	Australia: The Labour party wins the election under Hawke
Mar 8	The Australian $ is devalued by 10 percent
Mar 23	US: President Reagan announces the beginning of the 'Star Wars' programme
Apr 4	UK: £7 million is stolen in cash from a Security Express van
Apr 18	The US Embassy in Beirut is bombed, killing over 30
Apr 19	UK: Anna Ford and Angela Rippon are sacked from breakfast television
May 25	Egypt: 500 die when a Nile steamer sinks in crocodile-infested waters
Jun 9	UK: Conservative party under Mrs Thatcher is reelected
Jun 13	US: Pioneer 10 becomes the first spacecraft to travel beyond the known planets

Jun 18	Sally Ride becomes the first US woman in space
Jun 24	Syria expels PLO leader Yasser Arafat
Jul 11	An airliner flies into a mountain in Ecuador, killing 119
Jul 25	Sri Lanka: Racial violence leads to the death of over 100
Jul 29	Death of British actor David Niven
Aug 6	A Spanish supertanker splits in two, resulting in a 20 mile oil slick off the Cape coast of South Africa
Sep 1	A South Korean passenger plane is shot down by a Soviet war plane, all 269 on board are killed
Sep 15	Israeli Prime Minister Menachem Begin resigns
Sep 25	Northern Ireland: 134 members of the IRA eacape from the Maze prison in a mass breakout
Sep 26	Australia II becomes the first boat to take the Americas Cup from the New York Yacht Club
Oct 2	UK: Neil Kinnock becomes new leader of the Labour Party
Oct 4	UK: Richard Noble takes the world land-speed record, reaching 633.6 mph in Nevada, USA
Oct 14	UK: Cecil Parkinson resigns from the cabinet in disgrace
Oct 23	Suicide terrorists set off explosives at US and French barracks in Beirut killing over 300 members of the peace keeping force
Oct 24	US Marines go ashore in Grenada
Nov 25	Thieves steal £26 million worth of gold bullion and diamonds from a warehouse near Heathrow Airport
Dec 17	A car bomb planted by the IRA explodes outside Harrods in London, killing 6 and wounding 90

In April the German magazine Stern made a startling announcement. They said that reporter Gert Heidemann had located diaries written by Adolf Hitler between 1932 and 1945. Stern announced its intention of publishing extracts from the diaries and began negotiating with foreign newspapers and book publishers. It was said that the diaries had been lost when an aircraft carrying secret documents from Berlin in 1945 was shot down. Heidemann claimed to have located a man in East Germany who stole various artifacts, including the diaries, from the wreck. Handwriting experts and top historians were called in to inspect the documents. At first the diaries appeared genuine. However forensic tests revealed anomalies and Heidemann's supplier admitted forgery before fleeing abroad. Left: Gert Heidemann with one of the alleged Hitler diaries at a press conference in April. He is accompanied by (left) Stern's Editor in Chief Peter Koch and (centre) Editor Dr Thomas Walde.

THE INVASION OF GRENADA

In October the internal turmoil of a small Caribbean state led to a full scale US invasion which sparked international tension. The crisis began on 19th October when Maurice Bishop, Prime Minister of Grenada, led a march of his supporters to a military base where General Hudson Austin, the Marxist army chief, had several politicians under arrest. Austin ordered his men to intern Bishop, which they did after savagely dispersing the march. Deputy Prime Minister Bernard Coard headed for the base and forged an alliance with Austin. Bishop and other ministers were executed as Coard and Austin set about establishing a new regime. US President Reagan was alarmed for both Board and Austin were Marxists with strong Soviet links. When martial law was enforced and construction of a new airstrip suitable for Cuban jets was begun, neighbouring islands states appealed to Reagan for help. Reagan decided to use force to unseat the new regime, citing danger to the 1,000 US citizens in Grenada as reason to act. On 24th October a force of nearly 2,000 US Marines stormed ashore, backed by sophisticated naval and aerial forces. For five days fighting raged across the island, but by the 29th all resistance had ceased. A state of emergency was imposed for two weeks, during which time new elections were organised and a provisional government set up under a Bishop loyalist, Nicholas Braithwaite. The invasion was a clear signal from the US to both Cuba and the Soviet Union that no Marxist regime would be tolerated in the Americas. Many in the international community, however, condemned the invasion as flagrant aggression. Britain's Queen Elizabeth, also head of state of Grenada, was reportedly angry at the lack of consultation before the attack and relations with the White House cooled noticeably. Facing page, top: US paratroops lead a blindfolded suspect to a detention centre on 13th November. Left: US Marines on patrol in St George's on 30th October.

The NASA space programme entered a new phase of public relations in June. The prototype Space Shuttle **Enterprise** *was sent on a global good will tour. When it reached Stanstead Airport in Britain a crowd of around 175,000 turned out to watch. Over the following three weeks the prototype, used for high-altitude flight tests, was on show and tens of thousands more visited Stanstead to view the historic aircraft. The Enterprise later visited Canada and Iceland as part of its tour. Facing page, bottom: The Enterprise arrives at Stanstead riding piggy-back on the specially modified Boeing 747 transport. Right: US President Ronald Reagan laughs at a joke made by Queen Elizabeth during a formal dinner at the de Young Museum in San Francisco. The Queen was paying a state visit to the United States with no hint of the difficulties which would erupt between the White House and Buckingham Palace in the autumn following the Grenada Crisis.*

THE KILLING OF A RIVAL

On 21st August a major political assassination was caught live on television when Philippino politics took a bloody turn. Benigno Aquino, leader of the opposition to the autocratic rule of President Marcos, was shot dead in Manila by an unknown man, but many blamed Marcos for the death. Aquino had spent the previous three years in the USA in protest at the rule of Ferdinand Marcos. His return on 21st August had been widely publicised and tens of thousands of his supporters turned out to cheer him on arrival at Manila Airport. Television cameras trained on the aircraft steps clearly showed a man step past the military guard, push a revolver into the back of Aquino's head and fire. As Aquino tumbled forwards, blood pouring from his head, the guards shot the killer dead. It was widely rumoured that Marcos had been behind the killing, intending to silence for ever his most vociferous critic, but the charges were never proved. Left: President Marcos at a press conference on 22nd August denies any part in the murder. Below: Benigno Aquino's blood-spattered corpse lies in state at his home on the same day as Marcos's press conference.

Korean Jumbo Shot Down

On 1st September a Korean civil Boeing 747 with 269 passengers and crew was shot down by Soviet fighters, killing everyone on board. The first the outside world knew of the disaster was when air traffic controllers reported losing contact with the jet off Sakhalin. For a week the Soviets remained silent before admitting that they had shot down what they claimed was a spy aircraft over Soviet territory. The Soviet air force claimed that they had picked up the jet on radar flying over strategic bases on Sakhalin. The aircraft had refused to answer radio calls, so a fighter was sent to investigate. The pilot reported a large aircraft, without lights apparently dodging into bad weather to escape detection. With still no radio reply received, the Soviets ordered their pilot to "stop the intruder", which he did by blasting it with a missile. On 15th September the US Senate passed a unanimous motion condemning the Soviet action, and President Reagan described the shooting as barbarous and brutal. It remains most likely, however, that the tragedy was a result of a terrible mistake. It was thought that the Korean aircraft may have been on automatic pilot, which may have caused it drift off course in the heavy winds. Why the pilot failed to answer the radio messages sent by the Soviets remains a mystery.

In October a political sex scandal rocked the Conservative Party just weeks after the Tories had secured a massive majority in a general election. Conservative Party Chairman, Cecil Parkinson, had been instrumental in the tactics which led to electoral success. After the victory celebrations died down, Prime Minister Margaret Thatcher made Parkinson a member of the Cabinet as Trade and Industry Secretary. Popular and widely tipped as a future Prime Minister himself, Parkinson had a secret. It was revealed in October when his former secretary, Sara Keays, claimed she had been his mistress and was pregnant with his child. Parkinson, who had earlier confessed to Mrs Thatcher, admitted the truth of the allegations. On 13th October he addressed the Conservative Party Conference in Blackpool. His speech was sound, and the thousands of party workers present rose to give him a standing ovation, but his fellow ministers remained firmly seated. Realising he had lost the confidence of his colleagues, Parkinson resigned. He later returned to government as Transport Secretary and in 1992 was ennobled and elevated to the House of Lords. Right: Cecil Parkinson at the Conservative Party Conference on 13th October.

The Nilsen Murders

In February the owner of No.23 Cranley Gardens, Muswell Hill, London sent for the plumbers. His tenants had complained about smelly drains. Michael Cottran, the plumber, realised the main drain was blocked and set about clearing the obstruction. Instead of the expected leaves or kitchen waste, Cottran found part of a human hand. He called the police, who wasted little time in questioning the only tenant who had not complained about the drains, Dennis Nilsen. In his top floor flat Nilsen showed no surprise when the police told him about the human remains. "Where is the rest of the body?" asked the police, and Nilsen revealed two plastic bags filled with disjointed flesh hidden in a cupboard. Worried about the amount of flesh, the police asked if they were dealing with one murder or two. Nilsen quite calmly announced it was fifteen, or possibly sixteen, he wasn't certain. It turned out that the quiet civil servant was the worst mass murderer in England. His killings had begun in a drunken stupor in December 1978 when he murdered an unknown Irishman he had met in a pub and invited back to his flat. A year later he murdered a Canadian tourist in similar circumstances. After that the murders came more regularly. Police were baffled as to the motive, and Nilsen did little to dispel the mystery. No sexual motive was evident, nor was robbery a factor. The only clue was the bizarre fact that Nilsen carefully scrubbed clean each corpse after the murder, before dismembering it for disposal. In November Nilsen was found guilty of murder and imprisoned for life.

Above left: The new leader of the Labour Party, Neil Kinnock (left) leads his party in singing Auld Lang Syne at the Party Conference in Brighton on 7th October. He is accompanied by Michael Foot (right) and Eric Heffer. Left: Irish nationalist politician Gerry Adams after being released by Special Branch police in London. Adams, leader of Sinn Fein, the political wing of the terrorist IRA, was visiting Britain to participate in an Oxford Union debate on political violence. Above: Flamboyant leader of the Greater London Council, Ken Livingstone (left) hands in a payment demand to the Prime Minister with his deputy leader Iltydd Harrington on 18th April. It was publicity stunts such as this which earnt Ken Livingston his fame. Top right: Women peace protesters clamber over the boundary fence of Greenham Common air base, where US cruise missiles were based, to demonstrate against nuclear weapons. Several of the women were dressed as the wild animals they claimed were under threat from the weapons.

BLOODSHED IN BEIRUT

Beirut, capital of Lebanon, was a city of anarchy ruled by rival warlords each backed by a formidable militia drawn from the many factions within the nation. The international peacekeeping force, in place since August 1982, came under consistent and vicious attack from all sides as their presence was widely resented. On 18th April a van was driven at high speed directly into the US Embassy. The explosives packed within it were detonated by the suicide driver, bringing down much of the building and killing 60 of the staff within. Over the following months the violence continued to escalate with the warlords setting up fortified enclaves in the city and surrounding countryside. The peacekeepers were increasingly finding themselves under siege. On 23rd October two more suicide attacks on western troops were made. In one a lorry containing some 5,000 pounds of high explosive was rammed through the security fencing around the US Marine HQ. The resulting blast killed 260 men, injuring many more. Simultaneously a second bomb killed around 50 French troops. The western world was stunned by the scale of the killings, and gradually came to the conclusion that the price of holding a precarious peace in Lebanon was too high. Left: US Marines guard the wrecked US Embassy on 18th April. Below: Singer Gloria Gaynor signs photographs for servicemen during an entertainment trip to Beirut. Bottom left: Naval and Marine personnel search through the wreckage of the US Marine HQ just hours after the blast on 23rd October. Bottom right: A Marine reads a newspaper carrying initial reports of the October bombings.

In 1983 the coveted America's Cup, premier trophy in the yachting world, was being competed for yet again. The rules of the competition favoured the holder and, indeed, the Americans had not lost the competition for over a century. That was changed by Australian tycoon Alan Bond who financed the construction of a revolutionary new yacht with a radical split keel design. It swept aside all other challengers and then took on the Americans to win a spectacular final race. Top left: The Australian 12-metre yacht **Australia II** during its qualifying race against the Italian vessel **Azzurra** on 2nd August. Centre: Stars of British television gather to toast Britain's first independent breakfast TV show, launched on 17th January. The presenters are, from left to right: Robert Kee, Angela Rippon, David Frost, Anna Ford and Michael Parkinson. Bottom: Richard Attenborough (left) and Ben Kingsley hold aloft the Oscars which they won for Best Director, Best Picture and Best Actor at the 1983 Oscar Ceremony for their movie **Gandhi**. Top right: The heavily sponsored speed car of Briton Richard Noble thunders across the Black Rock Desert in Nevada to establish a new world land speed record of 633 miles per hour on 4th October.

Jan 1	Brunei achieves independence from Britain
Jan 20	Death of US actor and athlete Johnny Weissmuller
Feb 2	US: The first successful embryo transplant is performed
Feb 7	US astronaut Bruce McCandless becomes the first man to fly in space without a safety line
Feb 9	Death of Soviet premier Yuri Andropov
Feb 14	British skaters Jayne Torvill and Christopher Dean win the Olympic gold medal with their Ravel's Bolero routine
Feb 29	Pierre Trudeau, Prime Minister of Canada, resigns
Mar 14	Northern Ireland: Sinn Fein leader Gerry Adams is shot and seriously wounded by Loyalist gunmen
Mar 24	Italy: Red Brigade terrorists rob a Rome security company of $21.8 million
Mar 24	UK: Civil servant Sarah Tisdall is jailed for six months for passing on classified information to a daily newspaper
Apr 1	Death of US singer Marvin Gaye, shot dead in a violent argument with his father
Apr 5	Death of British Commander Marshal of the RAF, 'Bomber' Harris
Apr 17	UK: Policewoman Yvonne Fletcher is killed when a gunman fires from the Libyan embassy on demonstrators in London
Apr 23	US: The discovery of the AIDS virus is announced
May 4	Death of British actress Diana Dors
May 19	Death of British Poet Laureate Sir John Betjeman
May 29	Steven Spielberg's film, 'Indiana Jones and the Temple of Doom' has grossed a record $45.7 million in its first week
May 29	Death of British comedian Eric Morecambe
Jun 22	The first Virgin Atlantic flight leaves Gatwick for New York, a single fare costs £99
Jul 7	Czech-born tennis star Martina Navratilova, now a US citizen wins the women's singles title at Wimbledon for the 5th time
Jul 18	US: 21 die when a gunman opens fire at a MacDonalds hamburger restaurant near San Diego
Jul 27	Death of British actor James Mason
Aug 1	Ireland: Peatcutter Andy Mould discovers the body of 'Lindow Man', preserved in a peat bog for over 2,000 years
Aug 5	Death of Welsh-born actor Richard Burton
Aug 13	British, US and French warships go to the Suez Canal to clear mines laid by unknown terrorists
Aug 25	A French freighter carrying radioactive cargo collides with a ferry and sinks in the North Sea
Sep 3	South Africa: 14 are killed in rioting in Sharpeville and other black townships
Sep 20	Lebanon: A bomb explosion at the US embassy in Beirut kills 20
Oct 12	UK: 5 die when a bomb explodes at the Grand Hotel in Brighton during the Conservative party annual conference
Oct 24	The Ethiopian government appeals for help from the West to save an estimated 6.4 million facing starvation
Oct 30	Poland: Father Jerzy Popieluszko is found murdered after being kidnapped by the police
Oct 31	Indian prime minister Indira Gandhi is assassinated
Nov 6	US: Ronald Reagan is re-elected in a landslide victory
Nov 20	UK: British Telecom shares go on sale, the largest share issue in the world
Dec 19	India: Rajiv Gandhi wins the general election by a huge majority

THE BRIGHTON BOMB BLAST

In October the IRA came close to pulling off a major terrorist outrage when they attempted to murder British Prime Minister Margaret Thatcher and her cabinet in a single bomb blast, and only failed due to a simple misunderstanding. The terrorists chose the Conservative Party Conference for their attack, knowing that most senior ministers would be gathered together for the event. The terrorists hired a prestige room in the Grand Hotel some weeks before the Conference and planted a massive bomb in the wall of the room. They reasoned that the more important ministers would stay in the main rooms and timed the bomb to explode in the early hours of the morning, hoping to catch the government in bed. The bomb exploded as planned and though five people were killed, none were senior ministers. The bombers had not realised that many meetings and bar gossipings go on late into the night at such a Conference and that the vast majority of ministers were still wide awake and far from their rooms when the bomb went off. Only Norman Tebbit was caught by the blast, and he escaped with relatively light injuries though his wife was seriously crippled. Police evacuated the area and began a belated search for other bombs. It was reported that some conference-goers were happily continuing with their meeting having ignored the explosion, when police arrived to evacuate the building. The Conference continued as planned with the PM appearing on the platform next day as scheduled. Above: The scarred face of the Grand Hotel in Brighton on the morning after the blast.

THE MINERS STRIKE

In 1984 the simmering conflict between the government and the trades unions which had been growing for over a decade erupted into open dispute. The former Conservative Prime Minister, Edward Heath, had attempted to reform the unions in 1972, but had been brought down by a prolonged strike. His successor, Mrs Thatcher, was determined to succeed where he had failed. After the Conservative victory in the General Election of 1983 it was clear a major conflict was coming. The government was pushing through new laws to restrict union power. The major clash came with the miners, traditionally the most militant and determined of workers, led by Arthur Scargill. The government prepared carefully for the strike, building up vast stocks of coal and preparing power stations to use oil and gas. In March Scargill called the Yorkshire miners out on strike, others rapidly followed although the Nottinghamshire miners continued to work. Massive pickets and demonstrations were organised by Scargill. Confrontations between police and pickets became commonplace and, at times, degenerated into pitched battles. Many felt that the strike was a test of will between the union movement as a whole and a government determined to reform industry. Public sympathy was clearly not with the strikers, preferring to back the elected government. After many months of often bitter dispute, the miners were forced to concede defeat and call off the strike. Below: Miners from Yorkshire with buckets to collect contributions from the public take part in a mass TUC march in London on 29th March. Centre right: Arthur Scargill, leader of the striking miners. Bottom right: Police arrest a Yorkshire miner picketing outside a Nottinghamshire colliery in an attempt to persuade the workers there to join the strike.

Right: The Australian premier Bob Hawke breaks down and weeps at a news conference called on 20th September after allegations about his private life were made in Parliament by the Leader of the Opposition. Hawke quickly regained his composure and continued with the conference, but his apparent vulnerability had a large impact on the public who saw it. Below: Soviet politburo member Mikhail Gorbachev is welcomed to the British House of Commons on 19th December by Neil Kinnock, leader of the socialist Labour Party and his senior colleague Dennis Healey. Gorbachev also met Prime Minister Thatcher.

Religious disputes in India turned to violence and claimed the life of Prime Minister Indira Gandhi this year. The Sikhs made increasingly vociferous demands for increased autonomy for their proposed religious state based on the Punjab. Indira Gandhi refused. When Sikh nationalists turned to terrorism, she acted swiftly. The Golden Temple in Amritsar, holiest shrine of the Sikhs, was stormed by Indian troops intent on removing the large stocks of guns and explosives said to be stored there. The Sikhs fought back with courage and several hundred people were killed before the temple was captured. The Sikhs threatened revenge. On 31st October two members of Prime Minister Gandhi's personal bodyguard, both Sikhs, turned on her and shot her dead. The mantle of power passed to Indira's son Rajiv, though some doubted if he had the strength to hold the country together. Above: Rajiv Gandhi and his wife Sonia watch the blazing funeral pyre of Indira Gandhi on the banks of the Yamuna River. Right: Rajiv Gandhi is welcomed to London by Prime Minister Thatcher on 14th October.

MEDICAL EQUIPMENT
HAWA MAHAL ROAD
PEER GATE BHOPAL

THE BHOPAL DISASTER

In the early hours of 13th December a gas valve fractured at a chemical plant in Bhopal, India. Within a few hours some 2000 people had died and many more were seriously injured. The valve had released around three tons of the deadly methyl isocyanate gas, used in the manufacture of insecticides. Nearly 250,000 people were treated in hospital for breathing difficulties and blindness as the gas cloud spread out over 40 square kilometres around the plant. The owners of the chemical works, Union Carbide, were blamed for slack working practices. The five top officials were arrested on charges of criminal negligence and a $15 billion law suit begun against the company. The Indian Prime Minister, Rajiv Gandhi demanded compensation and tough new safety measures. When it was announced that the plant would reopen nearly a quarter of a million people fled Bhopal. Left: A woman who lost 13 members of her family, leaving just one young daughter, in the disaster. Below: Firemen spray canvas screens around the Bhopal plant with water in an attempt to minimise gas seepage on 16th December.

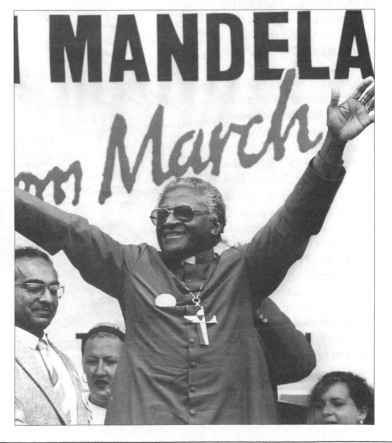

Above: Some of the fifty bodies found by the Peruvian police in shallow mass graves in a rural area near Huanta. The victims had been tied, gagged and beaten before being shot dead. The police had been tipped off by local peasants and the rebellious forces of drug barons and Communist guerrillas were widely blamed for the massacre. Right: Archbishop Desmond Tutu, this year's winner of the Nobel Peace Prize, addresses a rally in London. The meeting, attended by thousands of people in Hyde Park, called for the release of Nelson Mandela, the Black South African activist imprisoned by the South African government for political offences.

In the early 1980s drought affected a wide area of northern Africa. The sahel regions of dry grassland bordering the Sahara saw the rains fail for several seasons. Millions of people saw their crops and livestock destroyed by the relentless heat and drought as 1984 progressed. About six hundred thousand are thought to have died. The famine was worst in Ethiopia where civil war and an insensitive regime exacerbated the problems. Massive relief operations were begun by the western world, but ran into immense problems of distribution over appalling roads and obstruction from government officials. It was widely thought that the policies of the hardline Communist Ethiopian government had devastated the local economy and contributed to the collapse of agriculture. Top left: Village chiefs oversee the distribution of food relief in Upper Volta. Right: Part of a massive refugee camp at Alamata in Ethiopia where food was doled out by the World Vision charity. Top right: A mother and child at the Ebanat refugee camp near Gondar where thousands of herdsmen and their families gathered after the drought killed their cattle. Above: A child at the Bochum camp in Lebowa, South Africa, where drought was also causing problems.

Left: American astronaut Bruce McCandless makes space history on 7th February. Using the revolutionary Manned Manoeuvring Unit (MMU), McCandless roamed freely through space reaching a distance of 309 feet from the spacecraft. Bottom right: The official portrait of the Prince and Princess of Wales taken to celebrate the birth of their second son, Prince Henry, born on 15th September. Bottom left: British entrepreneur Richard Branson, aged just 33, launched his bold bid for a place in the risky air traffic business at a London press conference on 29th February. Below: American evangelist Billy Graham and the Archbishop of Canterbury Dr Robert Runcie. The pair met at Lambeth Palace on 16 January to discuss plans for Graham's planned visit to Britain during which he hoped to convert many citizens to Christianity.

The Murder Of A Polish Preist

Since 1981 when the Polish government banned the free trade union Solidarity, Poland had appeared to be slipping back into Communist totalitarianism. The government felt confident enough to lift martial law and release Solidarity leader, Lech Walesa, in 1983. Beneath the surface, however, unrest continued to seethe. The discontent with Communist rule found a fresh focus when a parish priest was found tortured and murdered in October. Jerzy Popieluszko had come out strongly in favour of Solidarity in 1980 and had continued to call for more freedoms in his sermons. His masses became enormously popular and sometimes as many as 10,000 would attend his church in Warsaw. On 19th October Popieluszko vanished. Neighbours claimed he had been visited by members of the state security police. Eleven days later his body was found dumped in a reservoir. A massive crowd of 200,000 attended his funeral on 3rd November and suddenly the Solidarity issue was back in the spotlight. Within weeks four secret policemen were arrested and convicted for the murder. Popular unrest, however, could not be contained and soon reforms were again on the political agenda in Poland, much to the fury of the Soviet Union.

*Below: The comedian magician, Tommy Cooper, who collapsed and died this year. Cooper was widely regarded as one of the most original and inventive comics of his generation. His bungled stage magic and comic stories combined with a manic appearance to devastating effect. Right: Marvin Gaye, top American rhythm and blues singer who was shot dead by his father during a domestic argument on 1st April. Bottom left: American pop star Michael Jackson emerged from his role as youngest of the Motown Jackson Brothers group to become a superstar in his own right. He established a reputation for inventive dancing and catchy tunes which took the pop industry by storm. Right centre: British composer Andrew Lloyd Webber celebrates the continuing success of his London stage musicals **Cats** and **Starlight Express**. Bottom right: British pop star Boy George who shot to stardom with a string of catchy hits and his deliberately androgynous look.*

THE HOLLYWOOD OLYMPICS

The Los Angeles Olympics were marked by a showbiz-style presentation worthy of Hollywood and by political troubles. The opening ceremony was a magnificent display of colour, music and drama watched by millions worldwide. Unfortunately the games were marred by the absence of the Soviet Union and its satellite Communist states in retaliation for the US boycott of the 1980 Moscow Olympics. Top left: British skaters Jayne Torvill and Christopher Dean on their way to a gold medal in the ice dance competition which they won with the highest marks ever awarded in the event. Top right: American hero Carl Lewis waves his national flag after taking the gold medal in the 100 metres , one of three gold medals he collected. Left: Zola Budd, the South African athlete who competed under her adopted British nationality. Her race against American Mary Decker in the 3000 metres was eagerly anticipated, but ended in dispute when the two runners collided, leaving Decker sprawled on the ground (*above*).

1985

Jan 13	Africa: 390 are killed when a train falls into a ravine
Jan 16	UK: The Dorchester Hotel is bought by the Sultan of Brunei
Jan 20	US: President Reagan is sworn in for a second term of office
Feb 5	Gibraltar: The frontier with Spain is reopened after 16 years
Feb 5	Libya releases four detained UK nationals after negotiations by Terry Waite
Feb 11	West Germany: 19 are killed, including 17 RAF bandsmen when a bus collides with a petrol tanker
Feb 11	UK: The pound falls below $1.10
Feb 26	UK: The rapist known as The Fox is given 6 life sentences
Feb 28	Northern Ireland: Eight police and a civilian die in an IRA bomb attack in Co. Down
Mar 10	Death of Soviet premier Konstantin Chernenko
Mar 11	USSR: Mikhail Gorbachev is new General Secretary of the Communist party
Mar 21	South Africa: 19 die when police fire on a crowd of blacks on the 25th anniversary of the Sharpeville Massacre
Apr 9	Japan: The prime minister urges his fellow countrymen to buy foreign goods
Apr 15	South Africa: The ban on mixed marriages ends
Apr 22	Brazil: Jose Sarney becomes first civilian president for 21 years
May 11	UK: 40 soccer fans are killed when fire sweeps through Bradford City football ground
May 29	Belgium: 41 die at Heysel Stadium as a result of British soccer hooliganism against Italian and Belgian fans
Jun 2	The UEFA bans UK soccer clubs from Europe indefinitely
Jun 3	Italy: Compulsory Roman Catholic instruction in schools ends and Roman Catholicism is no longer the state religion
Jun 23	An Air India plane explodes in mid-air killing 325
Jul 4	UK: 13 year old maths genius, Ruth Lawrence, wins a first-class degree at Oxford
Jul 7	West German Boris Becker becomes the youngest winner of the men's singles title at Wimbledon at age 17
Jul 10	Greenpeace ship, 'The Rainbow Warrior' is destroyed by explosions in Auckland Harbour, NZ.
Jul 13	Singer Bob Geldof brings together international stars in 2 simultaneous Live Aid concerts in London and Philadelphia
Jul 27	Ugandan president Milton Obote is ousted in bloodless coup
Sep 17	Death of fashion designer Laura Ashley
Sep 19	Mexico: 20,000 die in a massive earthquake in Mexico City
Oct 2	Death of film actor Rock Hudson after a long struggle against AIDS
Oct 7	UK: Riots erupt in Tottenham after a black woman, Cherry Groce, is shot during a police raid
Oct 10	Death of US film director Orson Welles
Oct 10	Death of US actor Yul Brynner
Nov 14	Colombia: 25,000 die when Nevado del Ruiz volcano erupts, swamping the town of Armero
Nov 19	President Reagan and Mikhail Gorbachev meet in Geneva and issue a joint statement that nuclear war could not be won and must never be fought
Dec 19	US: Edward Kennedy says he will not run for President

The Geneva Summit

For two days in November the Presidents of the USA and USSR met in Geneva in a series of meetings which were immediately recognised as being strikingly different from previous summits. The new tone was set on the first day when a meeting between Presidents Reagan and Gorbachev lasted a full hour instead of the scheduled fifteen minutes. A second similar meeting lasted two hours, and became known as 'the fireside chat', by diplomats. The wives of the two leaders appeared to get on very well indeed and attended many joint functions in a startling break with tradition. The formal talks, however, were not as productive as many had wished ending with a rather bland commitment to peace. There was, however, a noticeable warmth in the relationship of the two men and a commitment was made to meet again the following year.

On 10th March the Soviet leader Konstantin Chernenko died, the third leader to die in as many years. Chernenko had been ill ever since taking over the top position in Soviet politics, so his death was not unexpected. Into his shoes stepped his number two, Mikhail Gorbachev. Aged just 54, Gorbachev was the youngest man to rule the Soviet Union since Stalin, and the first to have been born after the Revolution which installed the Communists in power. It had already been realised that he was a quite different character to the more usual Soviet leaders. During a trip to western Europe the previous autumn, Gorbachev had impressed Mrs Thatcher as "a man we can do business with", while his wife went shopping in Paris. US Vice-President George Bush met Gorbachev at the funeral of Chernenko and came away convinced of a real possibility for making progress in East-West understanding. Right: Mikhail Gorbachev photographed just a few weeks before his elevation to the top position in the the Soviet Union.

Left: Police, armed with crowd control gas pistols, await the call to join the struggle against rioters in Tottenham, north London on 7th October. The nights of rioting and street fighting followed a police operation to crack down on drugs dealing which was interpreted by many in the local Black community as harassment and an assault on their cultural identity. At one point the police feared that they would be unable to contain the situation, but determined action and skilled use of anti-riot weapons restored order. Below: The Rev Ian Paisley (left) and James Molyneaux, both leaders of the Protestant community in Northern Ireland, leaving No.10 Downing Street after long talks with Mrs Thatcher in advance of the Anglo-Irish Agreement which agreed new and revolutionary methods for controlling terrorism and administering government in Ulster.*

THE PONTING AFFAIR

In January the trial opened of British civil servant Clive Ponting who was charged under the Official Secrets Act of improperly disclosing information gained through his position as a servant of the state. Ponting had been the senior Defence Ministry official who prepared a brief for Defence Secretary Michael Heseltine so that he could answer questions relating to the sinking of the Argentinian battleship *General Belgrano* during the Falklands War. Ponting was angered when Heseltine actually gave an answer not in line with the brief but, in Ponting's opinion, misleading. Ponting believed that his loyalty as a civil servant was to Parliament rather than to the Government. He therefore sent documents to Labour MP Tam Dalyell which were used to embarrass the government. When the leaked documents were traced back to Ponting, he confessed and offered to resign. Instead he was prosecuted. The government wanted to establish the principle that ministers took the decision on which documents to make public and that a civil servant owed loyalty to the Government. In his defence Ponting maintained his loyalty lay to Parliament and that a civil servant was acting correctly if he gave information to Parliament which his minister would prefer kept secret. After the long hearing, the judge summed up by instructing the jury to address only the letter of the law, not to rely on sympathy for Ponting as a person. Despite this clear summing up for the prosecution, the jury found Ponting not guilty. The Official Secrets Act was discredited, and calls for it to be reformed were made. *Left: Clive Ponting arrives at the Old Bailey to face charges on 7th February.*

MIDDLE EAST HIJACKINGS

The year was marked by two dramatic hijackings. The first was that of the TWA flight 847 which was captured by Palestinian terrorists of the Hezbollah faction minutes after take off from Athens. After a lengthy flight the aircraft landed at Beirut. The pilot, Captain John Testrak (*above*), gained fame and praise for his calm handling of the situation, even after the terrorists murdered passenger Robert Stetham on discovering he served in the US Navy. On the second day of the drama the non-American passengers were released. These included the singer Demis Roussos (*centre left*) and his secretary. The remaining 39 on board, all Americans, were kept hostage for a further 15 days. Top left: The hijackers wave to photographers during the long siege which followed. The hijackers demanded that US President Reagan pressure Israel into releasing 700 Moslem prisoners, but Reagan flatly refused. Instead he began to threaten a commando raid on Beirut in retaliation and sent a naval task force to cruise off the coast. Syrian officials then stepped in and persuaded the hijackers that Reagan would not give in to their demands. Eventually the hijackers released their prisoners before melting away into the streets of Beirut where they were assured of a warm welcome. The second major hijack was that of the Italian cruise liner *Achille Lauro* on 7th October. The PLO gunmen shot dead an elderly American Jew before accepting an Egyptian offer of a free aircraft journey to safety. The aircraft was dramatically forced down by US jets on Sicily and the hijackers arrested. The leader Abu Abbas (*left*) was later released by the Italian courts. Centre right: A Moslem militiaman fires on Christian positions in Beirut as the fighting which formed the backdrop to the hijackings continued unabated.

NATURAL DISASTERS

On 19th September a massive earthquake, measuring 7.8 on the Richter Scale, struck Mexico, tumbling Mexico City into ruin. Many of the most modern buildings in the city collapsed in seconds, killing everyone inside. It was thought that as many as 10,000 may have been killed in the city alone. An aftershock, nearly as powerful as the main earthquake struck the following day, bringing already damaged buildings down on top of rescue workers digging in the rubble for survivors. Left: Rescue workers stand atop the wreckage of the National College of Professional Education which collapsed like a pack of cards. Two months later, on 14th November, a volcanic eruption in Colombia caused nearly 20,000 casualties. The heat of the eruption melted snow on the volcano's summit causing a massive mudslide which engulfed parts of the towns of Armero and Chinchina. Below: Rescue workers help a mud-covered woman from the marsh where the flash flood had left her.

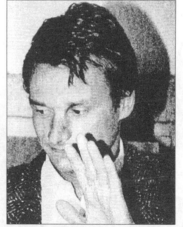

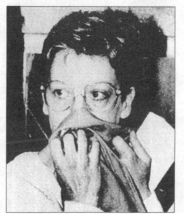

On 10th July the Greenpeace ship Rainbow Warrior was sunk in Auckland Harbour and a member of the crew killed. The ship had been about to set sail to protest against French nuclear tests in the South Pacific. A few days later a couple carrying Swiss passports were arrested and on 23rd appeared in court. It was revealed that they were a French couple named Alain and Sophie Turenge (small pictures). Rumours that the French government had ordered the sinking began to circulate, but were not confirmed until 26th September when the French Defence Minister resigned after admitting that his secret services had inspired the action. On 3rd November the Turenges pleaded guilty to the sinking. Centre left: The Rainbow Warrior in 1978 on an anti-whaling mission in the North Atlantic. Bottom left: The ship resting on the bottom of Auckland Harbour the day after the sinking.

On 23rd June an Air India Boeing 747 vanished from air traffic controllers' radar screens when about 150 miles west of Shannon in Ireland. All the 329 passengers and crew on board were killed. No distress message was received, leading to suspicions of foul play. The suspicions were confirmed when a Sikh terrorist group claimed responsibility. Top left: A body is carried from an RAF helicopter at Cork Airport. Top right: The blazing stand at Bradford soccer stadium which erupted into flames during a match on 11th May killing 56 spectators. The disaster was blamed on rubbish under the stand and on the fact that at least one safety door was locked. Centre right: The wreckage of the British Airways Boeing 737 which crashed on 22nd August during take off from Manchester Airport. Nearly 60 of the 131 on board were killed. Left: The wreckage spread across a mountainside on Mount Osutaka near Tokyo after a Japan Air Lines Boeing 747 plunged into the hillside.

Bloodshed In South Africa

The long running conflicts between whites and the various black tribal groupings in South Africa erupted into bloodshed once again this year. The first sign of impending trouble came in mid-February. Cape Town authorities ordered that thousands of squatters be moved from their illegal shanty town to a new site. The blacks, largely families of migrant workers, refused. Police were called in to enforce the eviction and the situation deteriorated into street fighting. A few weeks later the conflict reopened and 17 were killed by police gunfire. The USA responded by voting for limited economic sanctions in June and international condemnation was widespread. Preoccupied with maintaining law and order, however, the South African government imposed emergency powers in July, leading the French to withdraw their ambassador. In August more died in battles between police and squatters. Anti-Apartheid campaigner Archbishop Tutu blocked talks with the government and resorted to colourful condemnations of the regime. The stock exchanges were frozen and in September foreign debt payments were halted and economic sanctions became widespread as eleven major nations followed America's lead. The year ended in high tension with the African National Conference openly refusing a peaceful settlement as more street fighting erupted.

On 29th May the European Cup Final turned to tragedy when 41 people were killed at the Heysel Stadium in Belgium. As the crowd waited impatiently for the match to begin, fighting erupted between fans of the British club Liverpool and Italy's Juventus. The Liverpudlians attacked vigorously, forcing the Italians to surge back against a solid wall. When the wall collapsed in a tangle of bricks and metal, the Italian fans were hurled over a sheer drop to be crushed by rubble and others following them. The incident led to British teams being banned from european competition. Left: Police carry the body of a victim away from the fatal wall. Above: The moment of tragedy as the wall collapses and fans struggle to escape the crush. Below: A British Airways Concorde touches down at Sydney, Australia, on 14th February after establishing a new record of 17 hours 3 minutes for the journey from London.

The desperate plight of the starving millions in Africa touched ma[ny] hearts, but none more productively than that of Irish rock star Bob Geld[of]. Determined to raise money for the relief needed, Geldof set about persua[d]ing fellow stars to participate in firstly a record "Do they know [it's] Christmas?" which was followed by plans for a concert. The result was L[ive] Aid, the greatest rock concert ever. Held on 13th July simultaneously [in] stadia in Philadelphia and London, the concert was broadcast to 152 cou[n]tries in the largest satellite broadcast ever. The mammoth show produce[d a] surplus of some $70 million to be spent on helping victims of the Afric[an] famine and served as a model for later charity events staged by show b[usi]ness. Top left: Prince Charles meets Bob Geldof after the show. Cen[tre] left: Princess Diana with Elton John after his stage appearance in the co[n]cert. Top right: David Bowie on stage. Left: Sting (right) and Phil Coll[ins] acknowledge the cheers of the crowd after their set. Above: Bob Gel[dof] collects a cheque for the Japanese contribution to his charity fund.

Left: The British rock duo Wham, George Michael and Andrew Ridgeley, in Peking's Forbidden City before a concert held on 7th April. Bottom right: A poster for the smash movie **Rambo** which confirmed actor Sylvester Stallone as a star of action movies and spawned a number of imitations. Below left: British broadcaster Roy Plomley who died this year. Plomley's most enduring contribution to radio was his **Desert Island Discs** programme in which celebrities chose the music they could not do without if stranded on a desert island. First broadcast in the 1940s, the show ran without interruption to his death and is still a regular feature on the BBC. Below right: Film star Rock Hudson who died on 2nd October. Throughout his career Hudson had played tough romantic leads, opposite some of the greatest female stars Hollywood could produce. It came as a shock to his fans, and the public at large, when he announced that he was not only homosexual but dying from the disease AIDS which was ravaging the West Coast gay community. He had guarded his secret jealously for years in order to safeguard his career, and only those closest to Hudson knew his reputation as a female heart-throb was a fraud. Bottom left: A scene form the film **Out of Africa**, starring Meryl Streep and Robert Redford, which picked up a record 11 Oscar nominations.

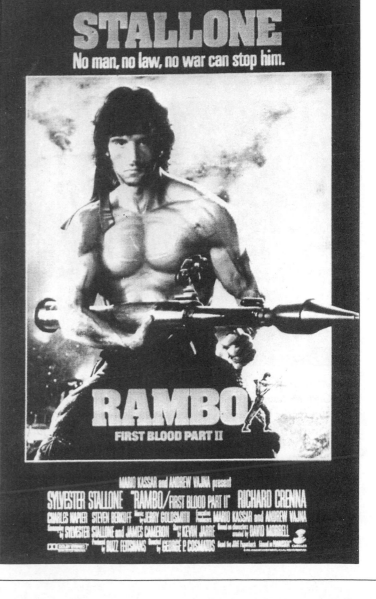

STALLONE
No man, no law, no war can stop him.

RAMBO
FIRST BLOOD PART II

MARIO KASSAR and ANDREW VAJNA present
SYLVESTER STALLONE "RAMBO/FIRST BLOOD PART II" RICHARD CRENNA
CHARLES NAPIER, STEVEN BERKOFF Music by JERRY GOLDSMITH Produced by MARIO KASSAR and ANDREW VAJNA
Screenplay by SYLVESTER STALLONE and JAMES CAMERON Story by KEVIN JARRE Based on characters created by DAVID MORRELL
Executive Producer BUZZ FEITSHANS Directed by GEORGE P. COSMATOS

Top left: The popular 17 year old West German tennis ace Boris Becker kisses the Wimbledon Men's Singles trophy after beating Kevin Curren in a gruelling four set final on 7th July. Top right: Britain's top boxers, the heavyweight Frank Bruno and featherweight Barry McGuigan pose together to publicise the boxing tournament of 26th March in which both fought. Above: The historic moment as US Ryder Cup team captain Lee Trevino hands the coveted cup to European captain Tony Jacklin after the American team lost for the first time in 28 years. The climactic match took place at The Belfry golf course, Sutton Coldfield, on 15th September. Right: Sam Torrance playing to victory for the European team in the Ryder Cup competition.

Jan 1	Spain and Portugal become the 11th and 12th members of the EEC	**Apr 26**	Chernobyl nuclear reactor no. 4 explodes leading to a huge release of radioactivity
Jan 8	US: President Reagan freezes all Libyan government assets in the USA	**Jun 27**	The International Court of Justice at The Hague rule that US aid to Contra rebels in Nicaragua is illegal
Jan 20	US: The Martin Luther King holiday celebrated for first time	**Jul 7**	Malaysia: Two Australians become the first foreigners to be hanged for drug trafficking
Jan 28	US: Space shuttle Challenger explodes shortly after take-off, killing its seven astronauts including schoolteacher Christa McAuliffe	**Jul 23**	UK: Prince Andrew marries Sarah Ferguson

Jan 1 — Spain and Portugal become the 11th and 12th members of the EEC

Jan 8 — US: President Reagan freezes all Libyan government assets in the USA

Jan 20 — US: The Martin Luther King holiday celebrated for first time

Jan 28 — US: Space shuttle Challenger explodes shortly after take-off, killing its seven astronauts including schoolteacher Christa McAuliffe

Feb 7 — Haiti: Baby Doc Duvalier, President for Life, flees to France after widespread demonstrations against his regime

Feb 7 — Philippines: President Marcos is declared winner of the presidential election despite widespread allegations of ballot-rigging

Feb 12 — Channel Tunnel Treaty between Britain and France is signed

Feb 16 — Portugal: Dr Mario Soares becomes president

Feb 27 — Philippines: President Marcos flees abroad with US assistance

Feb 28 — Swedish PM Olaf Palme is assassinated in Stockholm

Mar 2 — The Australia Bill formally severs Australia's constitutional ties with the UK

Mar 30 — Death of US actor James Cagney

Apr 14 — Death of French author, philosopher and feminist Simone de Beauvoir

Apr 15 — US bombers cary out air raids on targets around Tripoli in an attempt to wipe out terrorist bases

Apr 23 — Death of English cricketer Jim Laker

Apr 24 — Death of US born Duchess of Windsor

Apr 26 — Chernobyl nuclear reactor no. 4 explodes leading to a huge release of radioactivity

Jun 27 — The International Court of Justice at The Hague rule that US aid to Contra rebels in Nicaragua is illegal

Jul 7 — Malaysia: Two Australians become the first foreigners to be hanged for drug trafficking

Jul 23 — UK: Prince Andrew marries Sarah Ferguson

Jul 29 — UK: Pop singer Boy George is convicted of possessing heroin

Jul 30 — UK: Estate agent Suzy Lamplugh is reported missing

Aug 21 — At least 1,700 die in Cameroon after toxic gases erupt from volcanic Lake Nyos

Aug 31 — Death of British sculptor Henry Moore

Sep 17 — A terrorist bomb kills 4 in a Paris department store

Sep 21 — UK: Prince Charles states on TV that he talks to his plants

Nov 2 — US hostage David Jacobsen is freed after 18 months in Beirut

Nov 13 — US: In a televised speech, Reagan admits secret arms deals with Iran

Nov 22 — Mike Tyson becomes the youngest holder of the WBC world heavyweight title

Nov 25 — US Vice-Admiral Poindexter and Lt Col Oliver North are dismissed from the National Security Council after it is revealed that money from arms sales to Iran has been channelled to Nicaraguan Contra rebels

Nov 29 — Death of British-born US actor Cary Grant

Dec 19 — Dissident scientist Andrei Sakharov is permitted to return to Moscow after seven years' internal exile

Left: The **Virgin Atlantic II** *speeds through London's Tower Bridge as fire barges spray water in the traditional Docklands welcome for a famous ship. The massive power boat gained fame from its epic voyage across the Atlantic Ocean, piloted by its millionaire entrepreneur owner Richard Branson. The high speed crossing was an attempt to snatch the coveted Blue Riband, the prize for the fastest sea crossing of the Ocean. The record was held by the liner* **United States**, *which completed the crossing in just three days and ten hours in July 1952. Branson's first attempt to break the record failed when his craft sank, but in the Virgin Atlantic II, he powered to victory by an easy margin. Unfortunately the American holders of the Blue Riband refused to accept Branson's victory. They maintained that the trophy was exclusively for passenger liners, not specially constructed speed boats and so kept hold of their title.*

NEW REGIME IN THE PHILIPPINES

The twenty year long rule of President Ferdinand Marcos ended in the Philippines amid bloodshed and confusion. The countdown to disaster for Marcos began when opposition leader Mrs Cory Aquino announced she would stand in the Presidential elections of February 1986. During the run-up to the ballot, allegations of intimidation were made against both candidates. On 7th February the official results were announced, giving Marcos a large majority. However, suspicions of ballot-rigging were so widespread that Aquino refused to accept the result. When Marcos was sworn in for a new term as President, Aquino had herself sworn in as Provisional President, pending the overthrow of Marcos. On 11th February the Aquino campaign manager was shot dead and three days later ten prominent Aquino supporters were found beheaded in Quirino. A few days later, with popular unrest rising, a group of army officers defected to the Aquino camp. Other generals refused to mobilise their troops to back Marcos and his regime appeared in deadly trouble. However, the final collapse came when US President Reagan announced that Marcos should accept the inevitable and resign. Marcos, a life-long supporter of the USA, was devastated by the announcement which he regarded as a betrayal of trust. On 27th February Marcos fled the Philippines with American help and moved to Hawaii where he hoped to find sanctuary. In the Philippines, Mrs Aquino *(top right)* set about establishing an administration which, she hoped, would prove both popular and enduring.

In February the Duvalier family lost its grip on power in Haiti. The regime had begun in 1957 when Francois Duvalier was elected President. Duvalier tightened his grip on power until he was a virtual dictator. On his death in 1971 his son, Jean-Claude, took over the reins of power. He took the autocratic tendencies of his father to new extremes with the backing of the secret police, the Tonton Macoutes. Unrest and discontent spread through all layers of society during the early 1980s and by the start of 1986 had reached the highest political levels. On 7th February, Duvalier fled to France taking with him a sizeable private fortune. In Haiti power fell to General Henry Namphy who set up a Council of Government who pledged a return to democracy. Right: Haitians dance in the streets of St Marc on 9th February to celebrate the end of the Duvalier dynasty. Above right: A Swedish taxi driver describes how he saw Prime Minister Olaf Palme shot dead in Stockholm on 28th February. It was at first thought a lunatic was responsible, but later links to a political movement working for the independence of Croatia were found. Above left: John Demjanjuk arrives at Israel's Ben Gurion Airport to face war crimes charges. After a controversial trial Demjanjuk was convicted of being a brutal concentration commander nicknamed Ivan the Terrible by his victims.

THE WESTLAND AFFAIR

In January 1986 the British Government plunged into crisis as open warfare broke out between Prime Minister Margaret Thatcher and Defence Secretary Michael Heseltine in what became known as the Westland Crisis. The trouble began when British helicopter manufacturers Westland found themselves in financial difficulties. The management recommended a takeover by American rival Sikorsky as the way out. Defence Secretary Heseltine preferred to see a European buy-out and set about supporting one. Mrs Thatcher and her Trade Secretary, Leon Brittan, preferred the government to stay out of commercial decisions. The dispute was heightened by the long running clash between Thatcher and Heseltine. On 3rd January Heseltine wrote a public letter to the European consortium. The letter contained an error and the Prime Minister asked Brittan to instruct the Solicitor-General to write a private but formal letter pointing out the "material inaccuracies". The letter was written on 6th January and within four hours it was in the hands of the Press. Exactly how it was leaked has never been made clear, but Heseltine blamed Thatcher. At the next cabinet meeting, on the 9th, Heseltine stormed out, ministers thought to calm his nerves, but in fact Heseltine resigned from the government. In the row which followed Thatcher was accused of deliberately leaking the letter to discredit her own minister, though no charges could be made to stick. Brittan was forced to resign when it became clear that his office had leaked the letter, though whether on his instructions remained obscure. At one point it seemed as if Mrs Thatcher might have to resign, but the Tory party rallied round her and by the end of February her position was once again secure. Centre right: Michael Heseltine before his resignation. Far right: Leon Brittan photographed in the weeks leading up to his resignation .

Right: Religious unrest continued in India as Sikh extremists stormed the holy Golden Temple in Amritsar. Urged on by the widow of a Sikh killed after assassinating Prime Minister Indira Gandhi in 1985, a large crowd of Sikhs hacked down the official guards of the Temple, one of who is seen in this picture being mobbed by demonstrators. The militants occupied the Golden Temple, reiterating the long standing demands for political autonomy from the Hindu majority in India. Above: Pro-Government militia in Afghanistan. The fighting in the hill country was carried out largely between such auxiliary forces, armed with a variety of weapons some dating back to the First World War. Behind the facade of pro-Soviet government and anti-Communist Islamic forces was often hidden a reality of old tribal feuds and past scores. Top right: Neil Kinnock, leader of the Labour Party, meets Soviet Foreign Minister Eduard Schevardnadze at the Commons during a visit by the Soviet minister to Britain in July.

SPACE SHUTTLE TRAGEDY

The NASA space programme received a devastating setback when the space shuttle *Challenger* exploded during launch on 28th January, killing the entire crew of seven astronauts. Media attention had focussed on the mission because a civilian, teacher Christa McAuliffe, was to be included on a mission for the first time. After a delay caused by bad weather, the launch took place at 11.38 am. At first everything went well. The booster rockets fired on time and the massive craft soared skywards. After seventy four seconds the craft was engulfed in an orange fireball. The two thrusters span wildly out of the huge ball while debris and wreckage flew in all directions. The vast crowd which had gathered was stunned into silence. After diligent investigation of the wreckage and film of the launch the cause was traced to one of the twin booster rockets. Suspicion that the accident could have been avoided by better management procedures within NASA led to a number of resignations. Right: The blast which tore the shuttle apart, spraying debris across a wide area. Centre left: Christa McAuliffe's family watches the tragedy in horrified disbelief. Centre right: The crew of *Challenger* walk towards the shuttle on the morning of the launch.

Terry Waite In Action

The Archbishop of Canterbury appointed a special envoy whose task it was to visit trouble spots in an attempt to relieve suffering and to investigate allegations. The man chosen was Terry Waite, a large and imposing man with a genuine concern for his fellow humans. In June Terry Waite visited South Africa to investigate the troubles there and to confer with leaders of the Anglican community. The South African government pointedly refused him a visa which would cover 12th June, the date of expected demonstrations to mark the 10th anniversary of the Soweto riot. More famous were Waite's visits to the Middle East. In Lebanon Waite met and talked to the various factions fighting for control of the country torn apart by civil war. In particular he met with the Islamic factions which were holding Westerners hostage. Waite was instrumental in securing the release of several hostages and appeared to be on relatively good terms with the Islamic guerrillas. His bearded face became one of the most familiar on news reports from the region. Left: Terry Waite at a news conference on 13th June.

On the night of 15th April a force of American aircraft bombed targets in Libya. The air strikes came after US President Reagan had been presented with what he described as "direct evidence of Libyan involvement" in a number of recent terrorist attacks on Americans. Targets singled out for attack were the airport and docks of Tripoli, air bases near Benghazi and Gaddafi's personal headquarters. The A6 aircraft from American carriers in the Mediterranean and F-111s from bases in Britain struck without warning and although some bombs hit residential areas, the main targets were hit. The raid caused enormous controversy in the free world as many felt Reagan had gone too far in bombing a country at which his nation was not at war. Others backed his strong stand against terrorism and saw the raid as a warning to other regimes involved with backing international terrorist groups. Below: General Moammar Gaddafi, head of the Revolutionary Council which rules Libya. Bottom: The shattered remains of the French Embassy in Tripoli, one of several non-target buildings damaged in the raid.

THE CHERNOBYL DISASTER

On 26th April scientists in Denmark and Sweden noticed their radioactivity meters jumping wildly. Indications pointed to a major rise in background radiation, but it was not until it was realised that the radiation was moving northwest with the wind that an explanation was suspected. There had clearly been a major radiation leak to the southeast, somewhere in the Communist bloc. The Soviet authorities admitted that there had been a leak at Chernobyl, but it was not until the 30th that they announced the full scale of the disaster. An entire reactor was burning out of control, spewing highly radioactive particles into the atmosphere and threatening meltdown. Experts from the West raced to help their Soviet counterparts in getting the situation under control, but this was not achieved before two men had been killed and dozens of others subjected to dangerous levels of radiation. The radioactive dust continued to spread across western Europe, depositing its fatal load across the countryside. In several areas, mostly high rainfall upland regions, livestock was slaughtered and pasture remained unusable for years. Above: Soviet police check vehicles entering the restricted zone around Chernobyl on 13th June. Top left: West German border guards spray vehicles entering from the East which show signs of radioactive contamination.

Left: The Duke and Duchess of York emerge from Westminster Abbey after their marriage on 23rd July. Prince Andrew was the Queen's second son and had served as a Royal Navy helicopter pilot during the Falklands War. He chose to marry in his naval uniform with the medals he had earned. Miss Sarah Ferguson was a lively young woman who showed every promise of being a major character within the Royal Family. Her ivory silk gown was

in an Edwardian style and was liberally decorated with naval symbols. Bottom right: Clint Eastwood, the Hollywood tough man, who achieved fame when he was elected to be Mayor of his native city, Carmel-by-Sea in California. Eastwood won an overwhelming majority in the voting and set out to try to unite the various factions in local politics. His one-liners from the Mayoral Chair became legendary. Bottom left: Australian comic actor Paul Hogan who this year progressed from national television shows to international movie fame. His movie **Crocodile Dundee** *told the tale of a tough, resilient Outback man deposited in New York City and was wildly popular, leading to a sequel soon after. Left: The novelist Kingsley Amis celebrates winning the Booker Prize, Britain's premier literary award, with his book* **The Old Devils**. *Amis had been short-listed twice before, but this was his first win.*

Top right: Irish snooker player Dennis Taylor who shot to fame in 1986 by winning snooker's World Championship in the final frame of his match with Steve Davies. His specially constructed spectacles which gave him uninterrupted view along the cue became his hall-mark. Top left: The Argentinian football star Maradona whose skills earnt him fame during the World Cup tournament in June. His undoubted skills were somewhat marred by a clear determination which, during a match against England, led him to handle the ball. Above: American boxer Mike Tyson weighs in for his World Heavyweight challenge against champion Trevor Berbick in November, a fight Tyson won with convincing ease. Right: British runner Steve Cram powering his way to a gold medal in the 1500 metres event of the Commonwealth Games in August.

1987

Jan 1	Beijing: Thousands of students march on Tiananmen Square	**May 15**	Death of US actress Rita Hayworth
Jan 2	The traditional black golliwogs in Enid Blyton's Noddy books are to be replaced with neutral gnomes in an attempt to remove any taint of racism	**May 17**	Iraqi Exocet missiles hit USS Stark in the gulf, killing 37
Jan 9	UK: Ernest Saunders resigns as Guinness chief executive over the DTI probe into the Distillers' takeover	**May 28**	19 year old West German pilot Mathias Rust lands his plane in Moscow's Red Square
Jan 20	Ireland: Dr Fitzgerald's coalition collapses	**Jun 11**	UK: Margaret Thatcher becomes the first British prime minister for 160 years to be re-elected for a third term
Jan 20	The Archbishop of Canterbury's envoy Terry Waite disappears in Beirut while seeking to negotiate the release of Western hostages	**Jun 19**	Spain: 17 die in a Basque separatist car bomb attack
Jan 25	US: A hotel in Puerto Rico collapses killing 96	**Jun 22**	Death of US dancer and actor Fred Astaire
Feb 2	Philippines: Referendum approves new US style constitution	**Jul 4**	Nazi Klaus Barbie, known as 'The Butcher of Lyon' is jailed for life for war crimes
Feb 4	Death of US pianist Liberace, unofficially he dies of AIDS	**Jul 22**	US navy warships begin escorting Kuwaiti tankers in the Persian Gulf after Iranian threats against shipping
Feb 22	Death of US artist Andy Warhol	**Aug 17**	Ex-Nazi leader Rudolf Hess commits suicide in Spandau prison, Berlin, after spending 40 years locked up
Mar 3	Death of US actor and comedian Danny Kaye	**Aug 19**	In the UK's worst ever mass shooting, 14 die when Michael Ryan kills his neighbours in Hungerford, Berkshire and then shoots himself
Mar 6	UK: The ferry Herald of Free Enterprise capsizes off Zeebrugge, Belgium, killing at least 188		
Mar 10	Ireland: Haughey takes over as PM for the third time	**Sep 10**	Ethiopia is declared a republic
Mar 10	Roman Catholic church bans conception by artificial methods	**Oct 16**	UK: In the worst storm for 300 years, 17 people are killed and 15 million trees are felled by winds of 149 kph
Mar 30	Christie's in London sell Van Gogh's 'Sunflowers' for £24.75 million ($39.9 million)	**Nov 9**	11 die when an IRA bomb explodes at a Remembrance Day service in Co. Fermanagh
Apr 2	At a sale in Geneva, jewelry owned by the late Duchess of Windsor sells for £31 million	**Nov 18**	UK: 31 die in a fire at Kings Cross underground station
May 8	US: Gary Hart withdraws from the presidential campaign after press exposure of his relationship with Donna Rice	**Dec 16**	Italy: 338 people are convicted in biggest Mafia trial ever
May 11	Philippines: First democratic elections are held for 16 years	**Dec 21**	Nearly 3,000 die when a ferry collides with an oil tanker in the Philippines

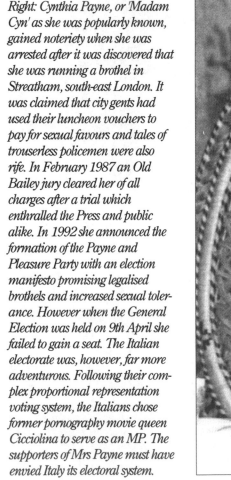

Right: Cynthia Payne, or 'Madam Cyn' as she was popularly known, gained noteriety when she was arrested after it was discovered that she was running a brothel in Streatham, south-east London. It was claimed that city gents had used their luncheon vouchers to pay for sexual favours and tales of trouserless policemen were also rife. In February 1987 an Old Bailey jury cleared her of all charges after a trial which enthralled the Press and public alike. In 1992 she announced the formation of the Payne and Pleasure Party with an election manifesto promising legalised brothels and increased sexual tolerance. However when the General Election was held on 9th April she failed to gain a seat. The Italian electorate was, however, far more adventurous. Following their complex proportional representation voting system, the Italians chose former pornography movie queen Cicciolina to serve as an MP. The supporters of Mrs Payne must have envied Italy its electoral system.

The Great Gale

As midnight drew near on 15th October a depression moved eastwards into the English Channel. The weather forecasters predicted strongish winds and much rain. When a woman telephoned to ask if a hurricane was on the way, the forecasters were not impressed. In a television broadcast which became legendary the BBC weatherman repeated the woman's anxieties before assuring his audience that no hurricane was coming. Two hours later the hurricane struck. Winds well over 100 mph lashed across southern England. As the depression moved inland it became deeper and more powerful. By 2 o'clock London was being battered by winds not witnessed since the historic Great Storm of 1703. By 6 o'clock the winds had reached East Anglia. Many people cowered in cellars as the forces of nature demonstrated their power in terrifying manner. By the time the hurricane had abated, the sheer scale of the damage was revealed. Nineteen people had been killed by falling trees and masonry, a total mercifully small as most people were at home in bed when the winds struck. A total of fifteen million trees, some four hundred years old, had been destroyed, their roots torn out of the rain-sodden ground to lie prostrate. Buildings were shattered leaving hundreds homeless and the damage bill ran into millions of pounds. Below: A local Council worker uses a chainsaw to slice up a fallen tree in London. Right: Trees block a residential street in Orpington, Kent. It took several days to clear all the roads.

Two sensational court cases were heard in London this year. First was the libel action brought by novelist and Conservative activist Jeffrey Archer against a newspaper article which accused him of having sex with a prostitute. The case acquired great notoriety for its rather convoluted chain of events. The newspaper alleged that Mr Archer had paid £2,000 to the prostitute to keep her quiet after she threatened to tell her story publicly. Archer admitted paying money, but refuted the allegations. His wife Mary was a prominent witness and stood by her husband, confirming his version of events. After a lengthy trial, which was enlivened by numerous ribald remarks, the jury found for Jeffrey Archer. Left: Jeffrey Archer and his wife. The second, and far more serious, case was the major City scandal over the acquisition of the Irish brewers Guinness by Distillers, a Scottish whisky company. The trial followed the high profile takeover battle between the two companies which had led to much ill feeling and disquiet in the City. Allegations that shares had been traded improperly and without due regard to the laws of the City of London formed the foundation for the charges, which were proved only after an extremely long and complex trial. Above: Ernest Saunders, former Chairman of Guinness, leaves Bow Street Court on 13th October after an initial hearing.

On 9th November the people of Enniskillen in Ulster gathered around their war memorial to pay tribute to the war dead. The town was home to the Royal Inniskilling Fusiliers and the 6th Dragoons, both premier regiments in the British army, raised primarily from Ulster Protestants. They were thus considered a legitimate target by the IRA. As the crowds gathered for the Remembrance Day service a massive bomb exploded just behind the war memorial. Eleven people were killed and more than sixty were injured. The fact that the IRA had attacked a religious service attended largely by civilians brought severe condemnation. Right: Police forensic experts prepare to start sifting through the wreckage in their search for evidence.

Two major transport disasters struck Britain in 1987. On 6th March the cross-channel ferry *Herald of Free Enterprise* steamed out of Zeebrugge with over 500 people on board. A few minutes later the ship lurched to port and rolled on to her side. Only the shallowness of the sea near the harbour entrance saved the ship from sinking within minutes. A total of 184 passengers and crew were killed. The subsequent inquiry discovered that the bow doors, by which vehicles entered the ship, were left open as the ship got underway. As the waves broke over the bow, they poured sea water across the single deck which ran the entire length and width of the ship. The inrush of water destabilised the ship causing the rapid capsize. Left: The *Herald of Free Enterprise* lies on her side after the disaster. The second disaster occurred when fire broke out on the London Underground railway at King's Cross station. A small fire turned into a giant fireball in the main ticket hall when flammable materials were ignited and toxic gasses filled the network of tunnels which make up the station. Firemen found the fire difficult to control and the station virtually impenetrable. One firemen lost his life in the blaze joining the 31 passengers and staff who died as the fireball swept though the station. Above: A fire inspector moves through the scene of the fire in a search for clues as to its cause.

The City of London's financial markets were stunned by the collapse of share prices on what became known as Black Monday. On Friday 16th October share prices in New York had fallen dramatically, about twice as far as the Wall Street Crash of 1929. When London markets opened on Monday 19th the prices went into free fall. More money was wiped off the value of shares in a single day than ever before. A market which had seen gradually rising prices for a decade was stunned by the sudden collapse which followed a loss of confidence in industry. Black Monday caused not only hardship for those with money invested in stocks and shares, but also for pension holders. In the UK the government's privatisation issue of BP shares was threatened. It also caused many governments to fear a collapse in the economy on a scale similar to that of 1929 which precipitated world wide slump. They therefore took action to help the economy, though events proved such moves were not needed, and the effect was to boost inflation and cause economic problems for future years. Below: A young future's dealer catches up with the bad news at the end of the week.

On 19th August the worst mass killing in British history began in the quiet market town of Hungerford. Early in the evening of the fatal day a young man named Michael Ryan shot his mother in the house they shared on the outskirts of the town. Leaving her body lying sprawled on the floor, he set fire to the house and set out with his gun. Marching into town, Ryan blasted everyone he met. Witnesses who survived reported him as walking in a trance. Some escaped by playing dead, others by diving into cover. Within a few minutes, Ryan had shot dead 14 people. After this rampage, Ryan shot himself through the head. Bewildered police and survivors could only guess at his motives. Top: A policeman stands guard outside the gutted home of Michael Ryan. Above: Viscount Rothermere, Rupert Murdoch and Robert Maxwell. The newspapers these three men controlled together accounted for the bulk of the popular circulation of daily and weekly papers in the British Isles.

On 28th May a tourist in Red Square, Moscow, was surprised to hear an aircraft engine. Swinging his camera away from the minarets of St Basil's Cathedral, the tourist captured an historic event. Dodging low over the massive bastions of the Kremlin came a small, single-engined aircraft. Dropping lightly to the ground, the aircraft ran to a halt and a young man clambered from the cockpit. Soviet police hastily arrested the intruder who was dragged off for questioning. It emerged that the man was Mathias Rust, a 19 year old West German, who had an amateur pilot's licence. Mathias revealed that he had flown alone from Helsinki without filing details of his flight plan. Somehow evading the most sophisticated Soviet air defences, Mathias had reached Moscow undetected and touched down observed only by the tourist and police. Given a sentence by a tough Soviet court for his daring exploit, Rust was release a few months later to return to his home.

THE TANKER WAR

The war between Iran and Iraq had begun in 1980. Within months the ma[in] front had bogged down in virtual stalemate. A ceasefire in 1984 broke dow[n] within six months and the Battle of Marshes in 1985 failed to produce a de[ci]sive result. In early 1987 the war took a fresh turn when the Battle of t[he] Tankers began. The object of both sides was to cripple the economic might [of] the other. Iran began with an advantage as almost all Iraq's oil was forced [to] leave by tanker through the Straits of Hormuz, passing within a few miles [of] Iranian soil. Iran, by contrast, could export via pipelines. The attacks [on] tankers serving Iraqi oil supplies began with harassment and intimidation, b[ut] before long Iranian naval forces were interfering with tankers. More unpr[e]dictable were the Revolutionary Guard gunboats which were both fast a[nd] liable to launch sudden attacks without warning. American and British nav[al] forces were dispatched to the Persian Gulf to act as escorts to national tank[ers] making the hazardous journey to the Iraqi oil ports. Insurers slapped war zo[ne] premiums on any vessels making the voyage. Attacks on neutral shippi[ng] appeared to pose the threat of escalation of the war, but Iran stopped short [of] the final confrontation. Top left: A US Navy helicopter rescues the crew [of] the Cypriot tanker *Pivot*, sinking after an attack by an Iranian frigate, on 12[th] December. Below: Saddam Hussein, the leader of Iraq, at a pan-Arab confe[r]ence called in November in a futile attempt to end the war.

Centre left: A photograph of Robert Polhill issued by his captors on 29th January. Polhill was held hostage in the Lebanon by a militant Islamic organisation which owed allegiance to Iran. The group threatened to shoot Polhill and other Western hostages if the United States were to interfere in the tortuous internal rivalries of that country. Left: In Bangladesh

relief workers distribute sterilised water to survivors of the floods in September which covered thousands of square miles of the Gang[es] Delta. Millions of people saw the[ir] homes inundated and crops ruin[ed] by the floods. About 200,000 wer[e] thought to have contracted illnes[s] through drinking polluted water, making the distribution of clean water a high priority.

Top left: Peter Wright, the former British secret service agent whose memoirs, **Spycatcher**, caused a massive row in 1987. The British government maintained that the information in the book had been obtained by Wright only by virtue of the post he held in the secret service and that such information was therefore classified and could not be published. Wright was living in Australia at the time, so the injunction demanding that his book was not sold was heard in an Australian court. On 13th March the court found against the British government and permitted publication. The book proved to contain little not already known by the public, though its allegations of Soviet penetration of the British security forces were embarrassing confirmation of what until then had been merely rumour. Scandal engulfed the US services when the Irangate affair became public. It emerged that the administration had been selling arms to Iran, officially a banned practice, and using the profits to finance the Contra guerrilla movement in Nicaragua after Congress had expressly forbidden monies to be used for this purpose. Star of the hearings was Colonel Oliver North (above) who had handled the complex deals. North's testimony revealed him to be an uncompromising patriot who believed his actions to be consistent with his duty to America. His attractive secretary, Fawn Hall (left), loyally backed up all his evidence. Political opponents of President Reagan hoped that the affair might turn into another Watergate, but North and others firmly testified that they had acted on their own initiative and without orders from the White House. Reagan thus earned his reputation as the Teflon President, to whom no scandal could stick.

In June 1987 Britain went to the polls in a general election, the result of which was in little doubt. Labour, wracked by internal disputes about philosophy and what message it should be presenting to the electorate, opted for glossy packaging and suave presentation. The Conservative government, under Mrs Thatcher, chose to emphasise the economic success achieved by eight years of determined monetarist policies and a passionate commitment to individual liberty and retrenchment of the state. In the weeks running up to the vote, opinion polls put the Tories well ahead of Labour, although the Liberal-Democrats patchy popularity made the final results difficult to calculate with any accuracy. When the votes were counted in the early hours of 12th June it was found that the Conservatives had achieved a tremendous victory taking 375 seats in Parliament to Labour's 229. Top left: Neil Kinnock and his wife Glenys. Top right: Mrs Thatcher waves to supporters after hearing confirmation of her victory in the early hours of the morning. Above: Mrs Thatcher meets Soviet leader Mikhail Gorbachev in Moscow on 30th March. The two leaders met for a series of talks aimed at increased understanding between the two regimes and significant progress towards mutual disarmament. Right: Disarmament of a different kind was proposed by the CND marchers who gathered in their thousands on London's Victoria Embankment on 25th April to demand a nuclear-free Britain.

Left: English cricketer Ian Botham returns to the pavilion after his innings against the Pakistan test team on 10th August. Botham was, for many, the finest cricketer to play for England. His debut in 1977 against the Australians was marked by a bowling spell which took five wickets for just 21 runs. During the 1981 Ashes series Botham dominated the series with astonishing displays of batsmanship and bowling, including a string of centuries and five wickets for one run. By 1987 Botham's youthful brilliance was less predictable but he remained no less a superb player. Bottom left: American yachtsman Denis Conner skippers the yacht **Stars and Stripes** to victory in the America's Cup on 31st January off Fremantle, Australia, regaining the prestigious trophy for his nation. Below: David Kirk, captain of the All Blacks, lifts the Ellis Trophy, the Rugby Union World Cup, after leading his team to victory in June in front of a passionate home crowd at Auckland, New Zealand. Bottom centre: Nick Faldo, leading British golf player, kisses the British Open Golf Trophy after taking the title on 19th July at Muirfield in Scotland.

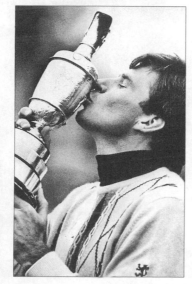

Top left: The Irish rock group U2. Formed by Dublin teenagers looking for a creative career, U2 scored a string of hits this year, establishing themselves as the leading Irish pop music group. Above: Genesis, the British rock group, long famous for their succession of high quality and popular albums were basking in the limelight of high profile celebrity status. Above right: Paul McCartney lifts a large slice of birthday cake at a party held on 1st June. Celebrating its 20th birthday was the Beatle album Sergeant Pepper's Lonely Hearts Club Band, released in 1967. The party was held at the Abbey Road Studios, where the album was recorded. Right: American pianist Liberace who died this year. Liberace established himself as an enormously popular entertainer in the early 1950s with his flamboyant stage persona and addiction to bright costumes and ostentatious luxury. His sheer skill as a pianist complemented the image and ensured that he was taken seriously as a musician.

Jan 17 Lebanon: Lt-Col. Higgins, chief of the UN Truce Supervising Organisation is kidnapped by Moslem extremists

Feb 5 USSR: Mikhail Gorbachev rehabilitates 21 people that had been erased from history by Stalin

Feb 8 USSR: Mikhail Gorbachev announces that Soviet troops will withdraw from Afghanistan

Feb 18 USSR: Mikhail Gorbachev sacks Boris Yeltsin

Feb 21 US: Leading evangelist, Jimmy Swaggart, confesses that he consorted with a prostitute

Feb 26 Panama: President Delvalle is forced to resign after attempting to dismiss General Manuel Noriega

Feb 29 South Africa: Archbishop Desmond Tutu is arrested

Mar 6 Gibraltar: Three suspected IRA terrorists are shot dead by British SAS forces

Mar 8 Five hijackers are killed when USSR security forces storm the plane at Leningrad

Mar 10 An avalanche sweeps one member of the royal ski party to his death, the Prince of Wales narrowly escapes

Mar 16 Panama: A US-backed coup to oust Noriega fails

Mar 16 A Loyalist gunman kills three mourners at a funeral in Belfast

Apr 3 Ethiopia and Somalia conclude a peace agreement ending 11 years of border conflict

Apr 5 Shia Moslem extremists hijack a Kuwaiti Airways jumbo jet and two passengers are shot dead

Apr 18 US planes and warships destroy two Iranian oil platforms, cripple two frigates and sink a patrol boat in the Persian Gulf

May 8 France: Francois Mitterand is reelected as president

Jun 8 Death of British writer and broadcaster Russell Harty

Jul 3 US warship Vincennes shoots down an Iranian civilian airliner in the Gulf with the loss of 290 lives

Jul 6 166 people are killed by a gas explosion on the British oil rig Piper Alpha in the North Sea

Jul 18 A concert is held to campaign for the release of Nelson Mandela

Jul 28 UK: Paddy Ashdown is elected leader of the Social and Liberal Democrats

Aug 17 Pakistani premier General Zia, the US ambassador and 33 others are killed when their plane explodes in mid-air

Aug 28 West Germany: 33 die when Italian air force jets collide at an airshow

Aug 31 Bangladesh: Widespread flooding leaves 25 million homeless

Sep 30 Ben Johnson is stripped of his gold medal for drug use

Nov 8 US: In the presidential elections Vice-President George Bush defeats Michael Dukakis

Nov 22 US: Stealth bomber, invisible to radar and heat-seaking missiles, makes its first public appearance

Dec 7 Armenia: 50,000 are killed and 500,000 are made homeless by a massive earthquake

Dec 12 UK: 36 people are killed in the Clapham Junction rail disaster

Dec 22 UK: A Pan Am Boeing 747 crashes at Lockerbie, Scotland killing 259 aboard and 11 on the ground, a terrorist bomb is responsible

The 1988 Winter Olympics opened with everyone determined that these games would be different. The summer games at Los Angeles in 1984 and Moscow in 1980 had been marred by boycotts and everyone was hoping that the Winter Olympics and the summer games in Seoul later in the year would prove to be an opportunity to re-establish the Olympic Ideal of friendly competition between the nations. One man did more to promote the feeling of levity, Edward Edwards of Cheltenham in England. Edwards entered himself for the 90 metre ski jump event, despite never having ski jumped in his life and having skied only on his local dry slope. Quickly dubbed "Eddie the Eagle" by the Press, the athlete missed his practice jump when his equipment was damaged. The avid Press demanded a conference, which was duly organised, though Eddie the Eagle had trouble getting in as the security guard did not recognise him. With huge support among the crowd, Edwards competed in the great event. He came a spectacular last, surprising many commentators by staying upright. So proud was Cheltenham of their son that they organised a civic reception complete with a tour around the town in an open-top bus. Other competitors in the Olympics were reported to be upset that all the publicity had been grabbed by a man with no skiing skills at all.

The scandal of the Seoul Olympics burst while the Games were still in progress. The Canadian athlete Ben Johnson had a formidable reputation as one of the fastest men in the world. His track record was unassailable and few doubted that he would return home loaded with medals. In the 100 metre final Johnson stormed to victory smashing both the Olympic and World Records. His glory did not last long. Traces of banned drugs were found in his blood samples during a routine test. Johnson was stripped of his gold medal and records and he was sent home to Canada in disgrace. Left: Ben Johnson attempting to avoid press photographers at Seoul's Kimpo Airport as he waits the flight home on 27th September.

THE LOCKERBIE BOMB

The Lockerbie Bomb was one of the most bloody and effective acts of international terrorism in the history of the 20th Century. At 7.19 pm on 22nd December the citizens of Lockerbie, a small town in western Scotland, were horrified to see a massive ball of flame plunging from the sky towards their town. The blazing mass plunged into a suburban street, erupting into an explosion which sent flames 300 feet high before bouncing on into open countryside. As the horrified emergency services raced to the scene it was confirmed the object had been a jetliner. The crash had destroyed 40 houses and gouged a crater 150 feet long and 50 deep. There were no survivors either from the aircraft or the houses. A total of 270 people had died. The aircraft was found to be Pan Am flight 103 bound from Frankfurt to New York, carrying Americans home for Christmas. The bomb was blamed on Islamic terror groups who were protesting against American involvement in the Middle East. After the blast the number of passengers crossing the Atlantic fell dramatically, leading to economic crisis for the airlines. Below: The nose section of the aircraft. Right: British Prime Minister Margaret Thatcher visits the wreckage on 23rd December.

Left: A policeman inspects the smoking wreckage of the Airbus A-320 which crashed at the Habsheim Air Show in France on 26th June. The Airbus, a brand new model of the successful jetliner, was on a demonstration flight with 129 dignitaries and potential buyers on board. As the aircraft flew low over the airfield, it seemed to clip the tops of trees at the end of the runway. With apparent slowness, the aircraft settled into the forest, tearing a path through the trees. It was the pilot skill which restricted casualities a mere four deaths. More catastrophic was the accident at the Ramstein Air Show on 29th August. During a formation flyi display, three Italian military jet collided just feet above the groun One aircraft burst into flames a ploughed into crowd, killing sixty six of the audience in addition to the crew. Above: The injured receive medical attention at Ramstein from USAF volunteer

In the early hours of 6th July a small explosion took place on the oil rig Piper Alpha, 120 miles off the Scottish coast. The flames spread rapidly to cause a second and much larger explosion which virtually destroyed the rig. Flames shot over 400 feet into the air as the oil rig was enveloped in flames. One hundred and sixty six workers were killed in those first seconds. Only sixty two managed to leap into the sea to escape the searing heat and await rescue ships. As the ships pulled the survivors from the sea, the heat from the platform was unbearable, and could be clearly felt up to a mile distant. After that night of horror the rig continued to burn for several days until Texan oil fire expert Red Adair was called in with his expert team who managed to cap the burning wells. Left: The smoking wreckage of Piper Alpha on 8th July. Below left: Red Adair views the burning oil platform from the support vessel Tharos on 9th July as he attempts to formulate plans for dousing the flames.

Trouble In Armenia

The Soviet republic of Armenia was a troublespot in 1988, but it was a natural disaster which overwhelmed the area after months of human-induced disaster. Trouble first flared in February when riots broke out in Nagorno Karabakh. This region was densely populated by Armenians, but for administrative reasons lay in the republic of Azarbaijan. The Armenians had been agitating for the region to be transferred to their home republic, but all such demands were resisted. The riots of February were put down, but civil unrest continued to disrupt life as ethnic ill feeling spread to other regions in the area. During the autumn massive demonstrations led to street fighting and around thirty deaths. In October Soviet tanks and troops took to the streets in an attempt to quell the unrest. It was amid this turmoil that a series of massive earthquakes struck on 9th and 10th of December. The major cities of Leninakan and Spitak were flattened and many villages destroyed. About one hundred thousand were killed immediately and millions more threatened by disease and exposure to the winter weather. Survivors of the earthquake scrabbled through the wreckage of their homes in a desperate attempt to find relatives and friends. The local authorities were clearly unable to cope with a major disaster on top of their disorder. Soviet President Mikhail Gorbachev travelled to the area and took personal control of the relief effort. At once conditions improved and the threatened mass deaths failed to materialise. The ethnic violence abated as the community tried to recover, but regained strength as the earthquake damage was repaired.

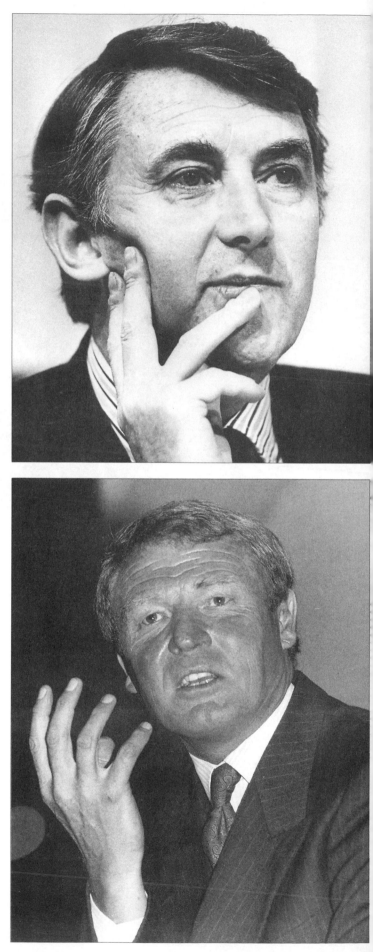

The failure of the Liberal-Social Democrat Alliance to boost the number of Members of Parliament in the 1987 General Election called into question the leadership of both parties. Much soul searching in the months after the election led to a realignment. Many Social Democrats joined the Liberals to form a new party dubbed the Social Liberal Democrats, though many saw this as simply an extension of the Liberal Party. Other Social Democrats reverted their allegiance to Labour, now more moderate than when they had left. A few retained their independence as Social Democrats and were led by the redoubtable David Owen. Top right: David Steel at a press conference before his resignation as leader of the Liberal Party. Right: The new Social Liberal Democrat leader Paddy Ashdown MP makes a point with a typically strong gesture. Above: Irish premier Charles Haughey addresses the United Nations on 2nd June in a year when British and Irish authorities were cooperating more closely than ever before to quell the terrorist menace in Ulster. Top left: British MP Edwina Currie who blazed a high publicity career through British politics with a series of controversial and dramatic statements. She eventually had to resign her post as a junior health minister after she made unscripted comments about salmonella infection in the British poultry industry.

Right: Peter Clowes arrives in the City of London for questioning on 15th June. Clowes had a reputation and track record which many city financiers must have envied. His Barlow-Clowes Fund Management Group consistently out performed others and seemed secure. But his arrest in June marked the start of complex fraud investigations which were to delve deeply into Chinese Walls and other City structures. Clowes maintained he was a victim of collusion among more established city figures. After a lengthy investigation and trial, the jury disagreed with Clowes and found him guilty of fraud.

ULSTER TROUBLES

The struggle against terrorism in Ulster continued unabated in 1988. The new atmosphere of co-operation between the authorities of Britain and Eire bore fruit in the form of better intelligence gathering on the activities and plans of the terrorists. On 7th March IRA activists Sean Savage, Danny McCann and Mairead Farrell travelled to Gibraltar to plant a bomb at a military parade. They were trailed by the SAS and shot dead soon after crossing the border from Spain. Though the circumstances of the shooting later led to some disquiet, the SAS had successfully foiled an IRA bomb plot. Below: A British soldier inspects the wreckage of a coach in which eight of his comrades were killed by an IRA bomb at Ballygawley on 21st August. Right centre: Masked IRA gunmen fire a symbolic salute to their colleague Kevin McCracken on the day of his funeral in march. McCracken, a trained IRA sniper was shot dead in a skirmish with British soldiers on 14th March. Bottom right: Mourners dive for cover as grenades explode and shots are fired at the funeral of the IRA activists shot on Gibraltar. A gunman was seen hiding behind tombstones of Miltown Cemetery in West Belfast and lobbing grenades at the Republican crowd. After the attack he fled, but was caught and named as Loyalist terrorist Michael Stone.

THE CLAPHAM RAIL CRASH

During the morning rush hour of December 12 a London-bound commuter train stopped just outside Clapham Junction in response to a signal. Moments later a packed express train bound for Waterloo Station slammed into the back of the stationary train at high speed. Carriages were torn apart and flung across the lines by the impact of the collision. Seconds later a third train collided with the wreckage and a fourth only escaped because of the swift action of a guard in applying the brakes. Emergency services arrived at scene of the accident with great speed and skillfully dragged survivors clear of the tangled trains. A total of thirty six were killed in the accident and over a hundred needed hospital treatment. Left: Firemen, ambulancemen, police and British Rail staff desperately search the wreckage for survivors. Above: As hope of finding survivors fade, work concentrates more on sifting wreckage for evidence as to the cause of the crash and on clearing the tracks for other trains.

The complex politics of the Middle East continued to plague international relations. On 15th January riots in Jerusalem marked the start of an uprising of Palestinians living in Israeli occupied lands in support of a free Palestinian state. On 16th April Abu Jihad, the deputy leader of the PLO, was shot dead by unknown gunmen in Tunisia. Meanwhile a Kuwaiti airliner (right) was hijacked and its passengers and crew held hostage in Algiers for 16 days before release came on 20th April. Violence continued in the occupied lands and in September the Islamic forces in Lebanon released the picture (facing page, bottom left). The photo shows the hostages Allan Steen, Mithileshwar Singh, Robert Polhill and Jesse Turner holding a banner asking their governments to back the Palestinians in return for their own release.

Left: Pakistani politician Benazir Bhutto who became Prime Minister of a minority administration after elections. A decisive shift in power in Pakistan followed the death of General Zia on 15th August. Zia had been President and autocratic ruler of the nation since his accession to power in 1978. Miss Bhutto had been gathering popular opposition to Zia's rule, who responded with repressive measures. When Zia's aircraft exploded in mid-air shortly after take off it was suspected that he had been murdered by political enemies, though no saboteur was convicted. Benazir Bhutto's Pakistan People Party won more seats in the November elections than any other party and formed a new administration. As autumn closed in on Alaska and the seas froze newsmen came across a story which would capture the attention of the world. Three Californian grey whales had failed to swim through the Bering Straits to warmer seas before the ice formed. The small hole through which they could surface to breathe was rapidly closing. Wildlife officials worked ceaselessly to batter at the ice and keep the hole open. In an attempt to save the whales a series of holes was opened leading towards open sea, but the ice formed too quickly for this to save the whales and one died. Eventually Soviet ice-breakers, who were in the area, battered a path through the ice to the whales, which were then freed to begin the long swim south. Below: The two grey whales surface through one of the artificial holes cut in the ice for their benefit on 27th October while awaiting the arrival of the ice breakers.

NAVAL WAR IN THE GULF

The Gulf War between Iran and Iraq continued to take a heavy toll on both combatants and civilians. The fact that both sides frequently attacked neutral shipping in an attempt to disrupt the other's trade and economic ability to continue the war necessitated the presence of naval units to protect shipping. The bulk of the force was provided by the US and the Royal Navy, though other nations were involved. Despite the presence of modern warships, the attacks on merchant craft, particularly tankers, continued. Right: The US Navy missile destroyer *Vincennes* in the straits of Hormuz on 2nd July. While on a regular patrol in the Persian Gulf on 3rd July the *Vincennes*'s radar picked up what appeared to be a rapidly approaching jet. Fearing a repeat of earlier air attacks, Captain Rogers took evasive action before launching a missile at the unidentified intruder. Only after the aircraft was destroyed was it realised that it was an Iranian civil jet with nearly three hundred on board, all of whom were killed.

Right: British comedian Kenneth Williams who died this year. Williams starred in a string of highly successful British comedy films in the post war era. Perhaps the best known were the Carry On movies in which Williams played characters as diverse as a British Secret Service man, an Indian prince and a conscripted British soldier. Williams's ability to produce a range of voices and his impressive facial mobility enabled him to take on a wide range of character parts, with comedy as his chosen vehicle. Below centre: The Prince and Princess of Wales return to

Britain from Austria on 11th March after the tragic Alpine skiing holiday during which their close friend Major Hugh Lindsay was killed in an avalanche from which the Prince himself only narrowly escaped. Below: American rock singer Roy Orbison who died on 6th December. His death did nothing to lessen his popularity and his songs continued to score top ten hit status for some years. Below right: Christina Onassis, heiress to the Onassis shipping empire died on 19th November at the age of just 37. Her fortune passed to her four year old daughter Athina.

The Greatest Birthday Party

On 26th January 1788 a fleet of ships sailed into Australian waters to found the colony of New South Wales. The voyage followed the path blazed by Captain James Cook, the British naval explorer who mapped the eastern coast of Australia in 1770. Cook's reports of a fertile land with good natural harbours so enthralled the British government that they decided to colonise the new land. As a first settlement the authorities chose a penal colony with strong military presence. Only later were civilians tempted to travel in large numbers to populate the strange new continent. The settlement founded by the First Fleet flourished and grew into Sydney. Two centuries later the Australian government decided the celebrate the founding of their nation. A replica of that First Fleet was constructed and sailed from Britain to Sydney Harbour. For weeks beforehand the celebrations had been gaining in strength. Across the nation from the big cities to the tiny Outback settlements the people were getting ready for a monster celebration. The Prince and Princess of Wales travelled to Australia to take part in the festivities which culminated with a magnificent firework display over Sydney Harbour and massive civic celebrations. Later that year the Queen and Prince Philip also visited the country. The celebrations were not shared by representatives of the Aboriginals who viewed the arrival of the First Fleet more as an invasion than the arrival of founding fathers and some protests were made.

Top left: US rock superstar Bruce Springsteen performing at the Human Rights Concert organised by Amnesty International to raise money for the cause of political prisoners across the globe. The concert was held on 2nd September at Wembley Stadium in London. Top right: British television personality Russell Harty who died in this year. Left: The happy smiles of Cher and Michael Douglas with the Oscars they won for Best Actress and Best Actor. Above: Singer Simon Le Bon leads pop group Duran Duran in their concert at Wembley which was held on 23rd December. Duran Duran were at the height of their success this year, with a string of hits.

1989

Jan 1	Namibia is granted independence from South Africa
Jan 7	Death of Hirohito, emperor of Japan since 1926
Jan 9	UK: 42 people die when a Boeing 737 aircraft crashes on to the M1 motorway
Jan 20	George Bush in inaugurated as 41st president of the US
Jan 23	Death of Spanish surrealist painter Salvador Dali
Feb 14	Iran: Ayatollah Khomeini issues a death sentence against British author Salman Rushdie
Feb 15	The last Soviet troops leave Afghanistan
Mar 7	Iran severs relations with the UK
Mar 7	The Chinese government imposes martial law on Tibet
Mar 26	USSR: The first democratic elections take place
May 13	China: 3,000 students begin a hunger strike in Tiananmen Square
Mar 25	US: The Exxon Valdez ruptures on reefs in Alaska, spilling an estimated 10 million gallons of oil
Apr 15	UK: 95 Liverpool football fans are crushed to death at Hillsborough Stadium in Sheffield
Apr 25	Prime minister Takeshita of Japan resigns amidst a corruption scandal
May 14	Peronist Carlos Saul Menem is elected president in the first free elections in Argentina
Jun 3	Death of Ayatollah Khomeini
Jun 4	A gas explosion on the trans-Siberian railway kills over 460
Jun 21	China: The first public executions of demonstrators at Tiananmen Square take place
Jul 11	Death of British actor Sir Laurence Olivier
Aug 14	South Africa: P W Botha resigns as president, F W de Klerk becomes acting president
Aug 20	UK: 51 people die when a pleasure cruiser collides with a dredger on the River Thames

Aug 24	Poland: Tadeusz Mazowiecki is the first democratically elected prime minister
Sep 10	The Hungarian government opens its border with Austria and permits thousands of East Germans to seek a new life elsewhere
Sep 19	UK: 10 soldiers are killed when an IRA bomb explodes at the Royal Marines' School of Music
Sep 27	UK: The government announces its plans to give an unspecified number of Hong Kong citizens the right to immigrate into the UK after Hong Kong reverts to China
Sep 28	Death of Ex-president Marcos of Philippines
Oct 18	East Germany: Head of State Erich Honecker is ousted
Oct 18	An earthquake devastates the Bay area of San Francisco
Oct 19	Hungary: 40 years of one-party Communist rule ends
Oct 19	UK: An appeal court finds the 'Guildford Four' innocent
Oct 23	A new Hungarian Republic is declared
Oct 29	The US authorities seize 20 tonnes of cocaine in California, the largest drugs seizure worldwide to date
Nov 9	The Berlin Wall is opened after nearly 30 years
Nov 10	The President of Bulgaria and leader of the Communist Party resigns
Nov 24	Czechoslovak leaders resign, after a week of demonstrations demanding democracy
Dec 14	Death of Soviet physicist and dissident Andrei Sakharov
Dec 21	Panama: Manuel Noriega is ousted from power following the invasion by American troops
Dec 25	Rumania: Ex President Ceausescu and his wife Elena are executed
Dec 26	Death of Irish playwright Samuel Beckett
Dec 29	Vaclav Havel, writer, philospher and anti-government protestor becomes president of Czechoslovakia

Left: The inauguration of George Bush as President on 20th January as his wife, Barbara, looks on. Bush owed his electoral victory largely to his solid performance as Vice-President to Ronald Reagan and his achievements in that role. Coming from a family which could trace its American roots back to 1755 he had a conventionally firm New England ancestry, though he moved to Texas early in his career as an oil man. From being a member of the House of Representatives for Houston in 1966 Bush progressed through various diplomatic and party political offices until his installation as Vice President in 1980. During his Presidency, Bush was to concentrate on foreign affairs where he scored many successes, though his success with his domestic policies was far less impressive.

CRISIS IN ISLAM
In February the Moslem world was plunged into conflict over a book written by top Islamic author, Salman Rushdie. The book, The Satanic Verses, dealt, in part, with the private life of the Prophet Mohammed alleging, in fictional form, various behaviour of which Moslems would not approve. Rushdie maintained he had written his book to encourage contemplation of the faith, but its effect was to produce an angry reaction of massive proportions. Widely seen as being blasphemous, the book was banned in many Islamic countries and the Ayatollah Khomeini issued a death sentence on Rushdie. The author went into hiding to protect himself from the assassins he felt certain Khomeini would unleash. Above: Moslem demonstrators on the streets of Sheffield protest against the publication of The Satanic Verses and demand its banning on grounds of religious offence. On 4th June it was announced that the Ayatollah had died. His funeral on 6th June turned into an hysterical scene as mourners whipped themselves and drew blood to display their emotion. Left: Part of the emotional crowd at the funeral in Teheran. Above left: PLO leader Yasser Arafat meets with British Foreign Minister Waldegrave in a secret rendezvous in Tunis on 13th January as fruitless talks to find a solution to the Palestinian situation continued.

TIANANMEN SQUARE

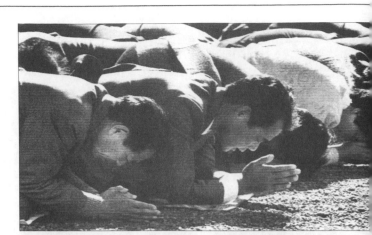

The Chinese Communist system showed its repressive nature in June when hundreds of protesters were massacred in Peking's Tiananmen Square. In April Hu Yaobang, the leading Communist figure most friendly to calls for democracy and freedom of the press, died. Some of his supporters massed in Tiananmen Square, the largest open space in Peking which is often used for parades and rallies. The Yaobang faction was joined after a few days by students who also favoured reform of the repressive government machine which suppressed any non-Communist ideas at universities. In May Soviet leader Mikhail Gorbachev visited Peking, but his official schedule was disrupted by the protesters. By now there were many thousands of students and workers gathered in the Square. They erected a statue dubbed the goddess of liberty and began to make calls for more specific action to topple the leadership. The Communist leaders decided that the protest would have to end. They calculated, correctly, that the protests were supported by only a small number of urban workers and that the vast mass of peasants had no sympathy for reform. After some harassment and threats, which caused most of the demonstrators to abandon the protest, the army was sent in. On 4th June tanks and massed infantry formations stormed into the Square. Hundreds were killed by the withering fire of the army, perhaps as many as two thousand died. Within hours the demonstration had been smashed. Tiananmen Square reverted to its official use for pro-Communist rallies. International condemnation was widespread, but the Communists remained in firm control of China. Below: A lone protester blocks the advancing tanks on 4th June.

Top: Part of the large crowd which gathered outside the Imperial Palace in Tokyo to pray for the health of Emperor Hirohito after it was learnt that the 87 year old monarch was seriously ill. Above left: Hirohito, the Emperor of Japan who died on 7th January. His reign began in 1926 and though he had little direct power, he encouraged the westernisation of his nation. He ruled over his nation's empire building in the 1930s and attack on America in 1941. Allowed to remain Emperor, but as merely a figurehead, after the defeat of Japan in 1945, Hirohito continued to guide his people. His death was widely mourned in Japan where, when Hirohito was born, Emperors were regarded as living gods. Above right: Afghan Communist general Abdul Had Ullumi announces crushing losses in a battle around Jallalabad on 11th March. Most felt that the regime would not survive for long.

A major environmental disaster struck Alaska on 25th March when the tanker **Exxon Valdez** ran aground while carrying a full load of Alaskan oil out of Prince William Sound. A massive hole was ripped in the side of the tanker and ten million gallons of crude oil gushed out. The oil spread rapidly to engulf a hundred miles of coastline and thousands of square miles of ocean. Thousands of birds, seals and sea otters were killed by the slick and marine flora was severely disrupted throughout the area. Top left: A volunteer worker carries an oil-soaked bird near Valdez on 3rd April. Top right: The wrecked jetliner, US Air flight 5050, which skidded off the runway of New York's La Guardia Airport and plunged into the East River on 20th September. The vast majority of those on board escaped with few injuries. Above: The collapsed flyover of Interstate Highway 880 in Oakland California. The area was hit by an earthquake on 18th October which claimed around 200 lives but fell far short of the long predicted earthquake expected to devastate San Francisco at some time in the future. Left: General Noriega, dictator of Panama. After a coup failed in October 1989, Noriega blamed the USA for the attempt and declared war on 15th December. Five days later US Marines invaded Panama. Troops loyal to Noriega fought back and the invasion went slowly. Noriega managed to elude the snatch squads sent to capture him. He eventually sought sanctuary in the Vatican Embassy. There he was surrounded by US forces who played loud rock music at him until he surrendered. He was taken to America to stand trial on charges of drug trafficking.

On 15th April a soccer match turned to tragedy. Thousands of Liverpool fans travelled to Hillsborough Stadium in Sheffield to watch their team in an FA Cup match. As the kick off approached, many fans had not found their places. Police opened a new, larger gate which precipitated a rush into the stadium. Fans already inside found themselves crushed against security fencing by the sudden influx of people. Unable to escape the incredible pressure, 95 fans were suffocated or crushed to death. Above: Floral tributes laid by families of the dead at Hillsborough Stadium. Top right: Royal Marine bandsmen march through Deal on 29th September. The parade followed an IRA bomb at the Marine's School of Music just seven days earlier which killed ten bandsmen. The places of the dead were left poignantly empty in the parade. On the night of 20th August the Thames pleasure boat **Marchioness**, packed with party goers, was rammed by the dredger **Bow Bell**. The party boat capsized and sank within seconds, trapping many inside. A total of fifty one died in the tragedy which led to a full scale investigation of river safety. Right centre: Relatives and friends of the dead pay their own tribute on the Thames on 21st August. Right: The wreckage of the British Midland Boeing 737 which struck an embankment beside the M1 near Birmingham. The pilot was attempting to make an emergency landing at the East Midlands Airport on the night of 9th January after reporting that both engines had failed. Forty four people were killed, but over eighty scrambled free of the aircraft.

In the early winter months of 1989 an intrepid team of explorers manhandled sleds loaded with supplies as they walked to the North Pole. It was the first time that the Pole had been reached by manhauling, an exploration technique largely abandoned since motorised snow sleds were invented. Below: British Prime Minister Margaret Thatcher welcomes the international Icewalk Team to No.10 Downing Street for an official reception on 19th May. Bottom left: Prince Charles meets the opera singer Placido Domingo backstage at the Royal Opera House, Covent Garden, after a gala performance of Verdi's **Il Trovatore** on 7th June. Right: A grim-faced Jimmy Swaggart faces reporters on 30th January. The press conference in Baton Rouge followed allegations from model Catherine Kampen that she had had an affair with the television gospel evangelist.

KYLIE SHOOTS TO FAME

One of this year's sensations of the pop world was Kylie Minogue. She first found international fame as lead teenage heartthrob of the Australian soap *Neighbours*. Her screen marriage to next door neighbour Scott Robinson, played by Jason Donovan, hit all time highs for audience figures wherever the series was shown. Already established as a singer in Australia, Kylie capitalised on her new fame to launch her singing career overseas. Teaming up with record producers Stock, Aitken Waterman of London, Kylie launched a series of mammoth hits, including *I Should be so Lucky*, *Got to be Certain* and *Love at First Sight*. In 1989 the image of a chirpy neighbour was replaced by that of a more sophisticated international girl, though Kylie lost a court case in November to suppress earlier videos which might have undermined the new image. Right: A 1989 publicity shot of Kylie Minogue released to help enhance her new image.

END OF A COUNTRY
BIRTH OF A NATION

The Communist regime in East Germany approached collapse, bringing nearer the time when Germany could reunite. For months mass demonstrations in the cities of East Germany had articulated popular discontent with the Communist regime. The clear signal from Mikhail Gorbachev that Soviet military might would not be used to prop up Communist regimes gave the opposition hope of the success which had been crushed in Hungary in 1956 and Czechoslovakia in 1968. The first tangible sign of change came in Hungary when the borders to the West were opened in September. Tens of thousands of East Germans flooded through Hungary to Austria and thence to West Germany. Top left: A woman cries with relief on hearing that she was being allowed across the border in September. East German leader Erich Honecker (*bottom left*) tried to stop the flow of refugees by bolstering the Communist system, but on 18th October he was forced to resign. His place was taken by Egon Krenz who at once eased border controls. On 9th November Krenz dramatically removed all restrictions on travel between East and West. The Berlin Wall, long the symbol of a divided nation was thrown open. Millions round the world watched live on television as bulldozers flattened entire sections to allow for ease of movement. The citizens of Berlin turned out in their millions to join in impromptu parties. Below: An East German youth hammers away at the Wall an action for which, just days earlier, he would have been shot. Centre left: Berliners dance on the Wall in front of the Brandenburg Gate, historic symbol of Berlin.

As reform and revolution swept across Communist Eastern Europe, one regime remained stubbornly repressive. President Nicolae Ceausescu of Rumania had ruled his nation with increasingly autocratic measures since 1965. At the Communist Conference in November 1989 he told his obediently cheering audience that Rumania would have nothing to do with the Imperialist reforms of Poland, Hungary and Czechoslovakia. News agencies clamped down on news from other nations as Ceausescu sought to retain power. But rumours of what was happening elsewhere started up and the Rumanians began agitating for reform. On 15th December secret police tried to arrest Protestant preacher Laszlo Tokes in his home city of Timisoara. The scuffle with parish-
ioners escalated into a major antigovernment demonstration. This spread rapidly to other cities. On 21st the unrest reached the capital Bucharest and a state of emergency was declared. The military was ordered to open fire on the demonstrators, but after a few skirmishes, the troops changed sides. Ceausescu fled with his wife but was captured and, after a summary trial on 25th December, he was shot. Fighting continued for two more days and it is thought around 8,000 were killed during the revolution. Left: President Ceausescu speaks to the party faithful on 24th November when he believed himself to be in full and permanent control of his nation. Below: A young boy swings from the barrel of tank gun on 26th December after the execution of Ceausescu had been announced.

The Velvet Revolution

When the overthrow of Czechoslovak Communism came it was with remarkable ease and lack of violence. The Communist regime had taken power as a minority government in a democratically elected Parliament in 1946. The subsequent grip on power was buttressed by Soviet might. The reform movement of 1968, the so-called Prague Spring led by Alexander Dubcek, was crushed by Soviet armies. Opposition had never been entirely destroyed and centred around the dissident Charter 77 movement. In late 1989, encouraged by reforms in other Communist European states, those opposed to Communist rule formed the Civic Forum and in November organised the first of many mass demonstrations. On 17th November one of these was brutally broken up by the authorities. After this incident President Milos Jakes and the entire Politburo was forced to resign and two weeks later the Communist Party's constitutional right to govern was abolished by Communist deputies in the Federal Assembly. On 3rd December the government fell and on the 10th a new administration including many Civic Forum leaders was established. The liberal playwright Vaclav Havel, who had been a major force in the opposition became President and Dubcek was brought out of retirement to be chairman of the parliament. Left: Vaclav Havel listens to a nun during one of the demonstrations.

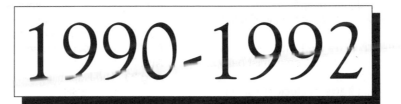

1990

Jan 4	At least 225 are killed in a train crash in south Pakistan
Jan 19	US: Marion Barry, the black mayor of Washington, is secretly filmed smoking 'crack' and faces a possible prison sentence
Jan 22	Yugoslavia: A landslide vote at the congress of the Communist party to abandon the one-party system
Jan 28	Around 150 are feared dead when a river ferry collides with another vessel in Bangladesh
Feb 1	Communist leaders in Bulgaria resign
Feb 1	Yugoslavia: Troops and tanks are sent in to Kosovo to quell ethinic violence
Feb 2	South Africa: President F W de Klerk lifts the 30-year ban on the ANC and the South African Communist party
Feb 11	Nelson Mandela is released from jail in South Africa
Feb 14	The Perrier company withdraws its stock of 160 million bottles of mineral water after traces of benzine are found
Feb 24	USSR: The first genuine multiparty elections since 1917 are held for the new Lithuanian parliament
Feb 26	President Daniel Ortega of Nicaragua is defeated
Feb 26	President Valcav Havel announcees that all Soviet troops will be withdrawn from Czechoslovakia by July 1991
Mar 6	The USSR parliament passes a law sanctioning the ownership of private property
Mar 10	The military leader of Haiti, Prosper Avril, is ousted
Mar 11	Lithuania declares independence with Vytautas Landsbergis as leader
Mar 18	East Germany holds its first genuinely democratic election
Apr 1	UK: A riot erupts in Strangeways prison, with prisoners taking control of the buildings
Apr 25	The Strangeways prison siege ends

May 4	The Latvian parliament votes for independence from the Soviet Union
May 30	France joins the USSR, Austria and Germany in banning imports of British beef and cattle due to fears of the cattle disease BSE
Jun 22	An earthquake in northwest Iran kills 40,000
Jul 7	Martina Navratilova of the USA wins a record 9th singles title at Wimbledon
Jul 7	Kenya: Rioting breaks out in Nairobi after a rally to demand multiparty democracy
Aug 2	Iran invades Kuwait
Aug 7	US troops are sent to the Gulf
Aug 7	Pakistan: Prime minister Benazir Bhutto is sacked
Aug 23	The Republic of Armenia declares its independence from the USSR
Oct 2	German Reunification Day
Oct 8	Israeli border police shoot dead 21 Arabs during rioting in Jerusalem
Oct 8	UK formally joins the Exchange Rate Mechanism
Oct 19	USSR: The Supreme Soviet endorses the introduction of the market economy
Nov 22	UK: Margaret Thatcher announces that she will not fight on for the Tory party leadership
Nov 27	UK: John Major defeats Michael Heseltine and Douglas Hurd to become Tory Party leader and prime minister
Dec 1	French and British workers shake hands, having dug through to each other in the Channel Tunnel
Dec 4	Germany: Helmut Kohl's Christian Democrats win the first nationwide elections since 1933
Dec 9	Poland: Lech Walesa wins a landslide victory

*Left: The spectacular night blast off of the Space Shuttle **Atlantis** on 28th February. The launch of **Atlantis** marked the definitive recovery of the Space Shuttle programme after the destruction of the Challenger which exploded, killing its entire crew. The Shuttle programme was begun in 1972 when NASA was becoming increasingly disenchanted with the disposable rocket launchers in use at that time and sought a reusable launcher for future missions. Each Shuttle consists of a delta-winged orbiter about 110 feet long and having a 79 foot wingspan. The craft is sent into orbit by three powerful booster rockets, a central liquid hydrogen fuelled booster and two solid fuel side boosters. It was a fault in one of the solid-fuel rockets which caused the Challenger disaster. On its successful launch the Atlantis carried a top secret military payload.*

Bottom left: British ships, HMS York and HMS Jupiter on patrol in the Persian Gulf on 14th August with orders to seize any ship carrying goods to Iraq. Left: Saddam Hussein, President of Iraq, who ordered the invasion of Kuwait. Far left: US soldiers manning a battery of Patriot missiles, capable of intercepting and knocking out the SCUD missiles which gave Iraq the power to attack Allied bases. Below: King Fahd of Saudi Arabia at the emergency Arab Summit called on 10th August in Cairo to discuss the Iraqi invasion of Kuwait.

THE GATHERING STORM

Throughout the autumn of 1990 the world waited as the storm of war gathered over the Persian Gulf. On 2nd August vastly superior Iraqi forces invaded Kuwait, sweeping aside the small forces of the tiny Emirate. Amir Jabir Al-Sabah escaped to Saudi Arabia, but his brother Sheik Fahd Al-Sabah was killed in the fighting. Iraq had a long standing claim to Kuwait which had precipitated a crisis in 1962 which led to a British garrison being established in Kuwait, though this had been withdrawn within a few years. The claim had its origins in the complex web of inter-Arab agreements and rivalries which began during the collapse of the Ottoman Empire in the 19th century. Amir Jabir set up a government in exile at Taif in Saudi Arabia and appealed to the United Nations for help. The United Nations responded by passing a resolution condemning the unprovoked aggression of President Saddam Hussein of Iraq and demanding the withdrawal of all Iraqi forces by 15th January 1991. Throughout August and the following months a massive military build up took place. Having first obtained an alliance with Saudi Arabia and other Arab states, the United Nations consented to vast numbers of American and British forces on both land and sea, together with smaller forces from Italy, France and other nations, being sent to the region. By Christmas it was clear the Iraqis would not pull out voluntarily and the world waited to see if the Americans and British would actually go to war for the sake of Kuwait.

THE END OF AN ERA

At the end of November Britain's Prime Minister of thirteen years, Mrs Margaret Thatcher, was ousted from office by her own party. The extraordinary events which caused the upheaval at the highest levels of British politics split the Conservative Party and baffled many. By the autumn it was clear that Mrs Thatcher was losing the confidence of many Tory MPs. Those with marginal seats feared that aggressive and unpopular policies, such as the Community Charge, would cost them their seats at an election, due within two years. Mrs Thatcher had also managed to offend several elder statesmen within the party over the years. These distrustful elements gathered around Michael Heseltine, the former Defence Secretary, who had left government over the Westland Affair in 1986. Heseltine assiduously courted backbenchers and lost few opportunities to put forward his alternative list of policies for the government. At the Conservative Party Conference in October party activists picked up this unease and put on an impressive demonstration of their support for Mrs Thatcher. The MPs were in no mood to listen. Just weeks later Sir Geoffrey Howe, Deputy Prime Minister, resigned. In his resignation speech in the House of Commons, Howe launched a highly personal attack on Mrs Thatcher and urged others to join him. Heseltine rose to the challenge by standing against Mrs Thatcher for the leadership of the Parliamentary Party. Mrs Thatcher won the first ballot of Tory MPs, but not by a large enough margin to win outright. There followed days of intense scheming and backroom manoeuvring, the truth of which has not yet emerged. Mrs Thatcher announced that she would not stand in the second ballot but instead allowed two cabinet ministers, Douglas Hurd and John Major, to stand against Heseltine. The winner of the second ballot was John Major who thus became Prime Minister. At the following year's Tory Conference the party activists, who angrily felt that they had been betrayed by their Parliamentary Party, rose to give Mrs Thatcher a noisy and enthusiastic standing ovation the moment she appeared. The feeling of betrayal continued to fester. Facing page: John Major, MP for Huntingdon, whose MP three centuries earlier had been Oliver Cromwell who rose to be Lord Protector of England and virtual dictator. Top left: Mrs Thatcher leaving No. 10 Downing Street on her way to Buckingham Palace to tender her formal resignation to the Queen. Top centre: Michael Heseltine whose bid for power brought down Mrs Thatcher. Below: Workmen remove Mrs Thatcher's personal belongings from Downing Street on 25th November. Left: A demonstration against the Poll Tax in March, one of the issues worrying Conservative MPs at the time of the leadership challenge.

Choosing A Prime Minister

The methods by which Britain gains its Prime Minister are complex. Constitutionally the Prime Minister is appointed by the monarch, who can choose whoever she wishes. In practice, however, the Prime Minister needs the support of the House of Commons. This means that the leader of the majority party in the House is invited by the monarch to become premier. The Labour Party has long had a definite method for choosing their Parliamentary leader, though the system has varied over the years. Similarly the Liberals have enjoyed a set procedure for producing a leader. Until recently, however, the Tories had no such system. A leader would 'emerge', meaning that one MP would be selected by party grandees, the infamous Men in Grey Suits, to be recommended to the monarch. These Men in Grey Suits made their choice by chatting to other MPs and discussing the problem with Tory peers. Clearly it was not a system which was suitable to a parliamentary democracy and was abolished. Instead the Parliamentary Party adopted a highly complex electoral system which produced the peculiar situation in 1990 that Mrs Thatcher lost although she gained a majority of the votes while Mr Major won although he gained a minority of votes. After the ousting of Mrs Thatcher angry demands were made by party activists that the system be changed, but the Parliamentary Party took no action and the system remains in force. It is widely recognised that the Men in Grey Suits continue to wield significant power.

Germany was dismembered into the Communist German Democratic Republic and the capitalist German Federal Republic after the wartime Allies failed to reach agreement on the future of the nation. Following the collapse of the hardline Communist regime in the East in November 1989 Chancellor Kohl of the Federal Republic published a proposal for reunification. This led to talks in May 1990 between the two Germanies and representatives of the four wartime Allies, France, Britain, America and the Soviet Union, which became known as the 2+4 Talks. On 18th May the Germanies agreed that the currency, monetary and social legislation of the West should be adopted in the East. On 23rd August the East German parliament voted to cease to exist in favour of a new united German parliament based on that of West Germany. The treaty setting out how this would be achieved was signed on 12th September and came into force on 2nd October. On the day of reunification huge celebrations, both official and private, took place throughout the new nation, the Federal Republic of Germany. Left: German youths wave the flag of Federal Republic and Democratic Republic, with the Communist symbol crossed out, at the Brandenburg Gate on 2nd October.

Above right: President Mikhail Gorbachev in Vilnius during his three day visit to Lithuania in January. Lithuania had been overrun by the Soviet Union during World War II and forcibly incorporated into the USSR as a constituent Republic. Opposition to Soviet rule was widespread and during the autumn of 1989 led to demonstrations and open calls for independence as East European nations threw off the shackles of Communism. Gorbachev's visit was, in part, an attempt to quieten such agitation. His efforts failed and in March the Lithuanian Soviet voted unanimously for total independence from the Soviet

Union. The USSR refused to accept the move and confrontation between the two authorities continued through the summer. Above: Brian Keenan, the Irishman held hostage in Lebanon by Islamic terrorists hugs his sisters after his release on 25th August. Right: The South African political leader Nelson Mandela salutes well-wishers as he grips his wife's hand on leaving prison where he had been held by the government for 28 years. Mandela backed the ANC, a political organisation which was largely based on Xhosa tribe support and had strong links with Communist organisations and policies.

DEMOCRACY IN POLAND

In May democracy achieved its final victory in Poland when the first free local elections were held following the fall of Communism at a national level the previous autumn. Left: Solidarity leader Lech Walesa casts his vote for a new City Council in Gdansk, where he first founded the trades union movement Solidarity. Poland was one of the first European nations to experiment with democracy, having a form of elective monarchy during the Renaissance. The system gave too much power to the nobles who contentedly saw Poland absorbed by neighbours in return for privileges. In 1918 Poland again became independent and introduced a democratic constitution which was too easily dominated by military strongmen. The imposition of Communism in 1947 stifled democratic urges until the summer of 1989. In June of that year a general election created a Sejm, or Parliament, which had a strong Solidarity presence. The Communist leader Czeslaw Kiszczak had a stormy few weeks in office before he resigned on 14th August in the face of determined Solidarity opposition. On 24th August the Sejm elected Tadeusz Mazowiecki, a Solidarity nominee, to be Prime Minister. Poland's 38 million people seemed assured of a democratic future and the local elections of May 1990 completed the process.

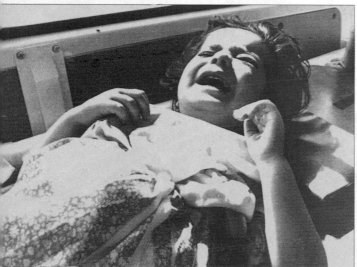

bove: A three year old victim of
e earthquake which struck
orthern Iran on 22nd June. The
ung girl was pulled from the
ibble of her home in Manjil, a
wn which lost thousands of peo-
le in the quake. Top right: A
nall boat packed with fifty four
ietnamese refugees which sailed
to Hong Kong Harbour on 26th
pril. Harbour Police impounded
e craft and escorted the refugees
a detention centre where they

joined thousands of their compa-
triots. The Vietnamese were flee-
ing the Communist regime but
had nowhere to go and Hong
Kong was becoming increasingly
restive at playing host to the horde
of Boat People. Right: An omi-
nously masked gunman in
Managua, capital of Nicaragua
prepares to defend the pro-govern-
ment radio station Radio Catolica
against a march of strikers intent
on stopping broadcasts.

The Channel Tunnel

Plans to dig a tunnel beneath the English Channel date back many centuries. Emperor Napoleon I considered constructing a tunnel to supply his army of invasion in 1805, but abandoned the scheme after Admiral Nelson destroyed the French and Spanish fleets at the Battle of Trafalgar. Joint plans between the French and British governments were discussed several times in the 20th century and in the 1970s tunnelling work began, only to be abandoned after technical problems caused a rise in costs. The final, successful attempt came into being after British PM Mrs Thatcher refused government money and insisted that private enterprise play the lead. The company Trans Manche Link was formed and raised tens of millions of pounds on the money market. The first breakthrough was made in December, after which work continued on completing the rail tunnels which would carry trains at high speed from England to France. Right: The moment of breakthrough. British tunnel worker Graham Fagg greets Frenchman Philippe Cozette beneath the English Channel on 1st December.

The training of military pilots over heavily populated areas of Italy came under scrutiny after an accident on the 6th December. A jet on a training flight crashed into the village school at Casalecchio di Reno, near Bologna. The flaming wreckage caused a dozen deaths and many injuries. Above: Injured school children lie on the grass of their playground as they receive first aid from local volunteers at Casalecchio di Reno. Right: Rioting prisoners hurl slates from the roof of Strangeways Prison in Manchester. The riot at Strangeways was the longest and most serious outbreak of violence at a British prison. The riot started in the chapel during Sunday service on 1st April. Initial reports suggested that up to twenty inmates had been killed as the prisoners paid off scores and settled feuds, but these proved to be unfounded rumours when the authorities restored order.

Below: Actress Jessica Tandy celebrates winning the Oscar as Best Actress for her role in **Driving Miss Daisy**. Before this triumph, Tandy was best known to film audiences as the disturbed Tippi Hedren in Hitchcock's classic **The Birds** in 1963. Most of her career was devoted to the stage, often partnered by husband Hume Cronyn. Right: American pop star Madonna in her flamboyant Jean Paul Gaultier stage costume at the Flaminio Stadium in Rome on 10th July. Her seemingly endless desire to startle and amaze drove her career from strength to strength. Bottom left: Washington Mayor Marion Barry and his wife Effi leave court on 17th September. Barry was found guilty of possessing cocaine, but had a dozen other charges of drug and perjury offences dropped after the most sensational trial in years. Bottom right: Asil Nadir, the dashing entrepreneur who built up the massive Polly Peck industrial conglomerate, leaves court with his lawyer on 22nd October after posting a £3.5 million bail. He was charged with more than sixty individual charges of theft relating to financial irregularities within the Polly Peck companies.

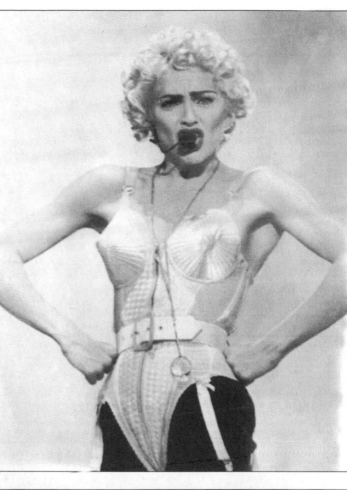

Left: Geordie soccer star Paul Gascoigne kisses his team jersey after playing a spectacular game for England in the World Cup semi-final. England lost the match 4-3 to West Germany after a series of penalty kicks settled a 1-1 draw. Gascoigne's superb soccer skills and larger than life personality earned him a massive following in England. Below: Mechanics and fans crowd around the Jaguar XJR12 which won the Le Mans 24 Hour Race on 17th June, re-establishing the dominance of Jaguar which had been at its height in the 1950s before the company pulled out of the event for a number of years. Bottom left: US tennis star Martina Navratilova holds aloft the Wimbledon Women's Singles Trophy which she won for a record-breaking ninth time on 7th July, beating the previous record set by Billie Jean King. Bottom right: World Middleweight Boxing Champion Nigel Benn (left) prepares a right hook which floored challenger Iran Barkley in the first round of the title fight on 18th August in Las Vegas.

Jan 15	UN deadline for Iraqi withdrawal from Kuwait passes		Apr 9	Georgia proclaims formal independence from Moscow
Jan 16	War breaks out in the Gulf when US-led allied forces launch an air strike on Baghdad		May 18	Britain's first astronaut, Helen Sharman, goes into space
Jan 17	Death of King Olav of Norway		May 21	India: Rajiv Gandhi, former prime minister, is killed in a bomb attack
Jan 18	Iraq fires Scud missiles at Israeli cities			
Jan 20	Iraq shows captured Allied airmen on TV		Jun 12	Philippines: Mount Pinatubo erupts threatening to obliterate the US 13th Air Force at Clark Air Base
Jan 24	The Allies liberate the first piece of Kuwait, the island of Qaruh		Jun 20	The German parliament votes to move the country's seat of government from Bonn to Berlin
Feb 1	South Africa: President FW de Klerk promises end of all apartheid legislation		Jul 17	The G7 Summit takes place in London
Feb 1	An earthquake in Pakistan kills 1,500		Aug 9	John McCarthy, UK hostage in Beirut is released after 1,943 days
Feb 3	The Italian Communist party disbands itself and is renamed the Democratic Party of the Left		Aug 19	President Gorbachev is imprisoned at his holiday villa by hardline Communist conspirators carrying out a coup
Feb 7	UK: The IRA attack Downing Street with mortars			
Feb 13	Civilians are killed during an Allied bombing of an Iraqi bunker		Aug 22	The attempted coup in the USSR crumbles and Gorbachev is restored as president
Feb 21	Death of ballerina Margot Fonteyn		Aug 25	Gorbachev resigns as leader of the Communist party and the party prepares to dissolve, ending 70 years of Communist supremacy
Feb 23	The Government of Thailand is toppled by a military coup			
Feb 24	The Allied land offensive begins in the Gulf			
Feb 28	US president George Bush announces that the war to liberate Kuwait has been won		Nov 5	Publishing tycoon Robert Maxwell dies after falling over board from his yacht while in the Canary Islands
Mar 14	UK: The 'Birmingham Six' are released after serving 16 years for a crime they did not commit		Nov 19	UK: Envoy to the Archbishop of Canterbury, Terry Waite, returns to England after being held hostage in Beirut
Mar 21	UK: The government announces abolishment of poll tax		Nov 21	Death of British rock musician Freddy Mercury, lead singer of 'Queen'
Mar 27	The IOC readmits South Africa to the Olympics after a 30 year absence			
Apr 3	Death of British writer Graham Greene		Dec 5	American hostage Terry Anderson is released from Beirut and sees his 6 year old daughter for first time

The year 1991 saw tumultuous events throughout the world. There was talk of a New World Order and a Peace Dividend to be gained from it. The collapse of the Communist grip in Eastern Europe had been accompanied by the sudden cessation of Soviet support and aid to Marxist regimes throughout the world. In Africa totalitarian regimes eagerly began the process of reform in an attempt to gain Western favour and support. Eastern Europe was occupied with establishing democratic constitutions which would provide stable but changeable governments. Many nations began the process of disarmament, believing the threat of global war to be over. Money previously earmarked for defence was distributed elsewhere. But 1991 clearly showed that the New World Order would not be the simple peaceful process which had been portrayed. In the Persian Gulf the Western nations went to war against Iraq to preserve Kuwaiti sovereignty and oil supplies. Yugoslavia degenerated into civil war as the new freedoms gave vent to years of suppressed ethnic anger and feuds. Most dangerous of all, however, was the coup in the Soviet Union launched by hard line Communists in an attempt to reimpose their regime in place of the reformist Mikhail Gorbachev. The results of the coup were to prove long lasting and unpredictable.

Growing awareness of environmental issues dominated much of the world in 1991. The discovery of a hole in the planet's ozone layer above Antarctica was widely blamed on the use of CFC gasses in aerosol cans and cooling plants. Antarctica itself became the focus of international attention in October when the Madrid Treaty was signed by nations with an interest in and claim on territory in Antarctica. Military activity had long been banned on the continent, but the Madrid Treaty also forbade oil and mineral exploration and established procedures for measuring the impact of humanity on the landmass.

Right: A photograph of the refuse tip near the US base at McMurdo Sound highlights the environmental impact of humans on the frozen continent.

THE HOSTAGES COME HOME

The long saga of the hostages in Lebanon ended in 1991. The taking of hostages has a long history in Middle East politics, but is alien to Western culture. When the Islamic guerrillas of the Lebanon began taking Western hostages to hold as bargaining counters with the Western powers the resulting deadlock reflected a clash of cultures as much as one of wills. Some nations gave in to demands made by the captors, though not always directly, but the majority held firm. By 1991 signs were emerging that the guerrillas were realising that they were gaining little but condemnation by holding on to the hostages. On 9th August John McCarthy, a British journalist held for five years, was released bearing a message from the hostage takers to the United Nations. Over the following few weeks, through Syrian intermediaries, all the remaining hostages, including Terry Waite, were released. Left: US hostage Terry Anderson hugs his 6 year old daughter Sulome as he meets his family at Wiesbaden US Air Force Hospital for the first time since his release on 5th December. Below: John McCarthy (*left*) hands over the note from his captors to UN Secretary General Perez de Cuellar at RAF Lyneham on 11th August.

In 1974 the IRA had carried its campaign of terror and murder to mainland Britain for the first time in many years, and with startling results. Bombs were planted in pubs in Guildford, Woolwich and Birmingham. The two blasts in Birmingham were most horrific claiming 21 lives and injuring nearly 200. Neither the pubs nor the victims had army connections. Shortly after the police arrested their suspects. Eventually six men were convicted of the Birmingham bombings at a trial in 1975. Both the convicted men and the IRA denied that they had planted the bombs, and other doubts about their convictions surfaced. After much lobbying the Home Secretary agreed to reopen the case in 1991 and a court hearing in London ruled that the convictions had been unsafe. Right: The Birmingham Six after their release following a court hearing on 14th March.

July was notable for the meeting of the G7 leaders which this year included a number of guests. The G7 Summits were originally an informal gathering of the leaders of the seven leading industrialised nations called at intervals to discuss world economic problems and difficulties. By 1991 the meetings had become far more formalised and the leaders were attended by large entourages of civil servants and diplomats who had been excluded from earlier meetings. The 1991 meeting was also attended by the Dutch Prime Minister and by Jacques Delors, President of the European Economic Community's Commission. More important was the presence of Soviet leader Mikhail Gorbachev, the first time a Soviet President had been present at a G7 Summit. Gorbachev asked for export credits and help in revitalising the industry and economy of the Soviet Union. The G7 leaders offered advice and some help, but not on a grandiose scale. Top: The leaders of the G7 meet at Lancaster House in London on 17th July. Front row, from left: President George Bush, President Mikhail Gorbachev, Prime Minister John Major, President Francois Mitterand, Chancellor Kohl. Rear row left to right: Jacques Delors, Italian premier Giulio Andreotti, Canada's leader Brian Mulroney, Japan's Prime Minister Toshiki Kaifu and Dutch premier Ruud Lubbers. Left: The new gates installed at the entrance to Downing Street. An IRA mortar attack on the street took place on 7th February. Although the Prime Minister and senior government officials were present at No. 10 they all escaped injury.

THE SOVIET COUP

On 19th August the world held its breath. Soviet radio announced that President Mikhail Gorbachev was ill and that a Committee of top Communists had taken over the Soviet Union. It was clear that a hard line Communist coup was under way. Gorbachev was under heavy guard at his Black Sea holiday home and nobody knew of his fate. In Moscow and other major cities the tanks took to the streets as the new regime enforced its rule. The conspirators had reckoned without the maverick Boris Yeltsin and his massive popular support. Head of the Russian Soviet, Yeltsin was committed to reforms and to dismantling the monolithic Communist regime. Using his sophisticated communications network, Yeltsin called on the Russian people to defy the coup. Barricading himself in the Russian Parliament Building, Yeltsin declared the coup leaders had no authority in Russia. When the tanks arrived, Yeltsin climbed on top of one to appeal directly to the troops. After two days the coup leaders acted. They sent the army into Moscow to take the Russian Parliament. After fighting and demonstrations in which two civilians died, the army withdrew. One crack division marched to the Russian Parliament to declare support for Yeltsin. The coup had failed and on 22nd Gorbachev was released and flew back to Moscow. He found a totally changed situation. His power and influence were gone. Yeltsin was the hero of the hour and set in motion reforms more radical and wide ranging than Gorbachev had dreamed possible, including banning the Communist Party. Top right: Tanks guard Red Square and the Spassky Gate entrance to the Kremlin on 19th August. Below: Gorbachev arriving at Moscow Airport on 22nd August to be met by Russian Prime Minister Ivan Silayev. Right: The dramatic scene as Boris Yeltsin forces his views on Gorbachev in front of the Russian Parliament on 17th December, signalling the transfer of power.

Right: South Africa's President Frederik de Klerk addresses MPs at the Opening of Parliament on 1st February. It was during this session of Parliament that he announced the final dismantling of Apartheid, the state institutionalising of racial discrimination. No longer would the Whites and various Black tribes be encouraged to seek the separate development of Apartheid. Instead the tribes and races would be allowed to mix free of legal impediment. Residential areas would no longer be reserved for particular groups, nor would Blacks be obliged to register themselves. The abolition of this legislation was widely viewed as the final acceptance by South Africa of a new multi-racial future for the state. Exactly what that future would be was the subject of heated debate.

Yugoslavia plunged into civil war as long hidden ethnic rivalries surfaced. Under the autocratic rule of Communist General Tito Yugoslavia had been kept repressed, but peaceful, as the secret police brutally crushed any opposition. After Tito's death, however, the various nationalistic pressures began to re-emerge. As the largest republic Serbia naturally had a leading role in Yugoslav affairs, but this was resented by smaller republics, especially Croatia and Slovenia. So bitter had this dispute become that at the end of 1990 both Croatia and Slovenia declared independence. The Federal Yugoslav authorities refused to accept the break up of their multi-national state and sent the army against the secessionist states. Warfare flared in Croatia as the local Croat and Slovene militias took on the heavily equipped army. Soon the situation became more confused. Serbia imposed customs dues on its borders within the Federal state, an action ruled illegal by the Constitutional Court. Militias rose in numbers and fighting broke out as the Serb minorities in the secessionist states demanded that they be allowed to separate from the new states and join with Serbia. The ethnic and cultural melting pot of Yugoslavia appeared set to boil over. Right: A Serb militiaman in Croatia gives a victory salute in the shattered town of Vukovar, recently captured from the Croats, on 22nd November.

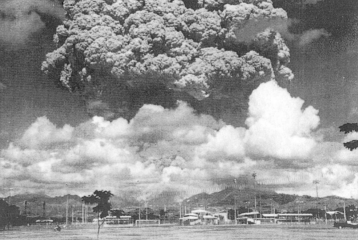

Top left: Polish President Lech Walesa acknowledges a standing ovation as he addresses the US Chamber of Commerce. The former trades union leader realised that the future of his nation hinged on economic prosperity. During his trip to Washington he called for investment in Poland to help the burgeoning market economy. Left: Imelda Marcos, widow of the former Philippino dictator Ferdinand Marcos, prepares to return to her home country after years in exile. She announced that she wanted to bury her husband at home, but some suspected a political motive. Above: The massive 20 kilometre tall cloud of smoke and ash which spewed from Mount Pinatubo when that volcano erupted on 12th June. Vast areas of the Philippines were plunged into darkness and covered with ash as the eruption brought life to a halt.

The year opened with war almost inevitable in the Arabian desert. The United Nations had set the date of 15th January as the deadline for Iraqi withdrawal from Kuwait. Far from showing signs of retreating, Iraqi forces were digging in and preparing their defences. Just hours after the deadline passed US and British aircraft attacked Iraq. A Western television crew still in Baghdad sent live pictures of the air strikes on the city. For days the air assaults continued. Military bases, arms dumps and communications were targeted. Factories, state buildings and nearly every major bridge in Iraq were destroyed by Allied aircraft in a determined attempt to disrupt the capacity of Iraq to wage war. Cruise missiles and smart bombs were used to achieve pinpoint accuracy, though civilian casualties were inflicted. Naval manoeuvres off the coast suggested an armed landing in Kuwait and Iraqi forces were diverted from the land border to guard against this move. On 24th February the long awaited ground assault began. Allied troops smashed through the bomb-dazed Iraq front line. While American troops pushed into Kuwait and Anglo-American forces raced northwards through Iraq west of Kuwait to swing round and reach the coast, thus cutting off the Iraqi occupation army from its home bases. The war, planned methodically and with great eye for detail by US General Norman Schwartzkopf, went almost exactly to the Allied plans. Vast numbers of Iraqi soldiers were killed or captured by the technologically superior Western forces. Within just four days Kuwait had been cleared of Iraqis and the front line had moved deep into Iraq itself. US President Bush called a halt to the fighting when it became clear that the battle had become a rout. Kuwait had been freed, but the after effects of the war were more persistent. Before retreating the Iraqis had set ablaze the oil wells of Kuwait. The smoke blotted out the mid day sun while crude oil poured into the sea to pollute the Persian Gulf.

Top right: A reconnaissance squadron of the 1st Queen's Dragoon Guards takes a rest in Kuwait on 10th March. Centre right: A heavily armed soldier of the 1st Battalion, The King's Own Scottish Borderers, adopts local headgear as relief against the sun on 6th February, the day the battalion left its camp to take up positions in the desert. Left: An Iraqi and his child wait for food distribution from American servicemen in the refugee camp of Safwan in southern Iraq on 3rd April. Many of those dis- *placed by the fighting found their way here. Above: Sheik Jabir al-Sabah congratulates the oil well fire fighters on 6th November as the last of the burning wells was brought under control. Facing page, top: US General Norman Schwartzkopf, universally known as "Stormin' Norman", inspects a guard of honour of the Coldstream Guards during a visit to London on 25th July. Facing page, bottom: A scene of devastation left by the Iraqis. Oil well fires are reflected in a lake of crude oil swamping the desert.*

Far right: Professor Anita Hill arriving at Oklahoma University School of Law on 15th October as the row concerning her and Judge Clarence Thomas rumbled on in Washington. Judge Thomas was President Bush's nominee for a place on the Supreme Court, but his alleged sexual harassment of Professor Hill some years earlier was seized upon by those who opposed his appointment as a means of showing he was unfit to hold office. After lengthy Congressional hearings and questioning of witnesses and colleagues of Thomas and Hill, the Congress voted to accept Judge Thomas on the Supreme Court. Right: Burmese opposition leader Aung San Suu Kyi addressing a large crowd in Rangoon in 1989, one of her last public appearances before being confined by the military government. In 1991 her persistent work for human rights and opposition to General

Saw Maung won her the Nobel Peace Prize. Top: The Right Reverend George Carey with his grandchildren at a press conference called to announce that he had been chosen to replace Robert Runcie as Archbishop of Canterbury and primate of the Anglican Church. Carey had a well-known stance within the Church and his primacy promised to be one of major changes.

BRITAIN'S FIRST ASTRONAUT

Britain's first astronaut entered space orbit in May when Helen Sharman blasted off with a Soviet crew on a routine mission to undertake various experiments and researches in the zero gravity of orbit. Sharman was selected from several hopefuls before travelling to the Soviet Union for intensive training in the skills demanded of a cosmonaut. Only when the Soviets were fully satisfied as to her abilities was she allowed to participate in the mission which began on 18th May with lift off from the Baikonur Space Complex. Below: Helen Sharman with (left) flight commander Anatoly Artsebarsky and (centre) flight engineer Sergei Krikalev.

Top right: The youthful American tennis star Jennifer Capriati powering a backhand during her climb to dominance in the US Open in August. Left: The Austrian motor racing ace Niki Lauda at a press conference at Vienna Airport on 29th May. Having abandoned motor racing, Lauda founded his own airline, Lauda Air. The Conference was called to make a statement about the crash of a Lauda Air Boeing 767-300 in Thailand. Above: British runner Liz McColgan with the gold medal she won in the 10,000 metre run at the World Athletics Championships in Tokyo on 30th August.

Left: The Hollywood actress Julia Roberts who took the Oscar for Best Actress for her role in the movie **Pretty Woman**. Roberts played a prostitute finding true love in a modern reworking of the Cinderella theme. Below: Kevin Costner holds aloft the golden globe awards for Best Director and Best Motion Picture for his movie **Dances With Wolves** which concentrated on the relationship between a US Army officer and a tribe of Indians. The film went on to break box office records and to win a clutch of Oscars. Bottom left: The Prince and Princess of Wales, both drenched by heavy rain, meet Italian opera singer Luciano Pavarotti after the open air concert in Hyde Park which attracted over 100,000 spectators despite the appalling weather. Bottom right: Hollywood heartthrob Warren Beatty and his girlfriend Annette Bening. In July it was announced that the couple were expecting a baby, though marriage was still not mentioned.

Global Warming

Gaining ground in environmental circles and becoming a matter of public concern was the phenomenon of Global Warming. The theories behind the concept began circulating in the early 1980s, as meteorological scientists abandoned the idea of an imminent Ice Age. The new theory held that increasing levels of carbon dioxide in the atmosphere, due to the burning of fossil fuels and general human activity, was causing a greenhouse effect and forcing up global air temperatures. This, in turn, would lead to the melting of the polar ice caps, massive flooding of low lying areas and general disasters and mayhem for mankind. Some Pacific island nations, it was confidently predicted, would cease to exist. Impressive data was collected to back up the Global Warming predictions including a general rise in climatic temperatures over the past century and the rising levels of carbon dioxide. However, other scientists pointed out the lack of correlation between amounts of fossil fuels burnt and carbon dioxide in the atmosphere and the fact that satellites had failed to reveal a rise in global air temperatures over the 1970s and 1980s. Those who doubted the existence of Global Warming had as much scientific evidence on their side, but were generally ignored by their more cataclysmic minded colleagues.

Jan 1	Russia: Panic buying sets in ahead of Yeltsin's price increases
Jan 7	Yugoslavia: 5 EC peace monitors are killed in their helicopter by Federal forces
Jan 13	UK: The Maxwell brothers refuse to answer MP's questions about the pension funds
Jan 15	The EEC recognise Croatia and Slovenia as independent states
Jan 22	Ireland: Haughey denies Involvement in phone tapping scandal
Mar 19	UK: Announcement is made that the Duke and Duchess of York are to separate
Mar 23	A plane crashes at La Guardia airport, NY, killing 26
Mar 26	US: Mike Tyson is sentenced to 6 years in jail for rape
Apr 2	US: Gotti is found guilty of murder and racketeering
Apr 8	A plane carrying PLO leader Yasser Arafat crashes in the desert, three crew members are killed but Arafat survives
Apr 9	US: General Manuel Noriega is convicted of drug and racketeering charges
Apr 9	UK: John Major's Conservatives win the general election
Apr 10	UK: IRA bomb explodes in the City of London, killing 3 people
Apr 13	UK: Neil Kinnock resigns as leader of the Labour party
Apr 19	Death of British comedian Frankie Howerd
Apr 23	US: NASA makes a breakthrough in the discovery of the origins of the universe
Apr 30	US: Rioting begins in Los Angeles following the acquittal of 4 policemen who assaulted a black driver
May 6	Death of Marlene Dietrich
Jul 18	UK: John Smith and Margaret Beckett are elected leader and deputy leader of the Labour Party
Jul 25	The Olympic Games open in Barcelona
Aug 16	UK: Nigel Mansell is the new motor racing world champion
Aug 20	UK: Daily Mirror publishes topless pictures of Duchess of York
Aug 23	US: 1 million people are evacuated from Florida as Hurricane Andrew heads for the coast
Aug 24	Florida is declared a disaster area in wake of Hurricane Andrew
Sep 24	UK: David Mellor resigns as Heritage Secretary following a series of scandals
Oct 4	Amsterdam: An Israeli cargo plane crashes into a block of flats with the loss of at least 75 lives
Oct 13	UK: British Coal announces 31 pit closures and the loss of 30,000 jobs
Oct 13	Egypt: An earthquake devastates Cairo, over 400 are feared dead
Nov 3	Bill Clinton is the elected the new President of the USA
Nov 5	Elton John signs the biggest record deal in music history, worth £26 million

The Gatt Talks

Arguably the most important international negotiations of the year were the GATT Talks. The General Agreement on Tariffs and Trade was being renegotiated in a series of long and complex discussions. First made in 1947 the General Agreement was signed by 23 leading economic countries as a preliminary to establishing a Trade Organisation under the auspices of the United Nations. The Organisation was never formed, but GATT remained a major treaty allowing free trade and regulating government involvement in commerce. There have been nine 'Rounds' of negotiation, each aimed at widening GATT to cover more nations and increasing freedom of trade. In 1986 the Uruguay Round was begun. The immensely difficult and technical agreements and details of disputes progressed steadily until December 1990 when a major obstacle emerged in the form of the European Economic Community's Common Agricultural Policy which other members of GATT considered to be an unfair subsidy of farm products. The EEC made changes to CAP, but not enough to satisfy the USA which, in October 1992, threatened to introduce import tariffs on EEC farm produce to compensate for the subsidies. The threat to destroy GATT and spark a major trade war with results highly destructive to world trade seemed very real. Ray McSharry, the EEC negotiator, resigned complaining that EEC Commission President Jacques Delors had been interfering improperly on the side of French farmers who wanted to keep their subsidies. In November as the deadline for agreement was only days away, a final agreement was reached.

Left: Andrei Tchikatilo, the Soviet mass murderer, at his trial in Rostov on 21st April. The horrific crimes of Tchikatilo were previously unheard of in the Soviet Union, where such depraved and criminal excesses were generally suppressed. At his trial, Tchikatilo was accused of 55 murders, though the police believed he was responsible for many more, committed between 1978 and 1990. The victims were mostly young men and women who Tchikatilo lured into woods or remote country areas where they were brutally killed, their bodies hacked to pieces and parts eaten by Tchikatilo. Despite this, the 'Cannibal Killer', as the Russian press labelled him, was a devoted father and grandfather. During the police investigation it was realised that another man had been convicted of a Tchikatilo killing and subsequently executed. Tchikatilo was convicted and sentenced to death.

The US Presidential Election of 1992 was a dramatic and exciting race for office with three candidates involved. The incumbent President George Bush was highly respected for his foreign affairs successes, such as the defeat of Saddam Hussein in the Gulf War of 1991, the release of US hostages in Lebanon and the ending of the Cold War with the Soviet Union. However, his domestic policies were less successful with the US economy in deep recession and trouble between the various ethnic groups rising. The Democrat candidate was Governor Bill Clinton of Arkansas. Successfully exploiting the discontent with the economic turndown under Bush, Clinton pointed to the success enjoyed by Arkansas under his governorship and promised a radical new agenda for government which would pay particular attention to health care and similar domestic issues. The wild card of independent candidate Ross Perot, a Texan multi-millionaire, was difficult to assess. With little in the way of an orthodox political platform, Perot drew a large following with a blend of down-home wisdom and charismatic leadership. His support faded in the last days of the campaign. When the votes were counted, Clinton cruised to victory with a large majority in the electoral college. Facing page: Bill Clinton makes a point at the first televised debate of candidates on 11th October. Below: Bill Clinton and Al Gore salute the crowd which gathered at the Old State House in Little Rock to celebrate their victory on the night of 3rd November. Right: President George Bush during the televised debate between the candidates on 11th October at Washington University in St Louis.

Los Angeles erupted into violent rioting and civil violence in May after a controversial court case whipped up ethnic and community emotions to fever pitch. Four white policemen were charged with assaulting black motorist Rodney King after stopping him for a traffic offence. A passerby caught the incident on a home video camera and the tape was broadcast widely on television news programmes. The defence maintained, however, that before the video had been shot King had been resisting arrest and assaulting the policemen. A jury found the four policemen not guilty on 30th April. Sensing a collusion between Whites to secure a discharge, the Blacks of impoverished areas in the city mounted protests and demonstrations which degenerated into riots and looting. Nine people were killed and over one hundred injured before order was restored. Left: A protester tears the American flag in half while colleagues block traffic outside the Los Angeles courthouse after the jury delivered a not guilty verdict in the Rodney King case on 30th April. Above: A National Guard trooper stands guard over looters, penned in a makeshift cell, in reality a ransacked toy store in Los Angeles.

The civil war in Yugoslavia between those states wishing to secede from the federal structure and the federal government became more hardened and bitter as the year progressed. Slovenia and Croatia secured international recognition of their independence on 15th January, largely on German insistence, and fought the Serb dominated federal army to stalemate. Bosnia-Herzegovina was torn apart as the Serb minority sought to join their regions to Serbia as Bosnia sought independence. The diverse Moslem and Christian Bosnians found themselves attacked by both Bosnian-Serb irregulars and the Serb army. Fighting grew intense as the Serbs punched a Serb Corridor to link their population centres in eastern and northern Bosnia. The bloodshed was particularly intense around the capital Sarajevo which was virtually under siege. The United Nations Peacekeeping Force came under attack from the warring factions and sustained casualities and on 7 January five EC peace monitors were killed when their helicopter was shot down. Various politicians including Paddy Ashdown, leader of the Liberal Democrats, visited the area and the summer saw a concerted attempt by David Owen and Cyrus Vance to find common ground on which to secure an end to the fighting. Above: Canadian armoured vehicles, acting under UN orders, patrol near Daruvar in Croatia. Top right: A Bosnian soldier takes a break in Sarajevo. Centre right: Belgian UN supply convoy near the Slovenian town of Sombor. Right: Dutch UN women soldiers in Zagreb, Croatia.

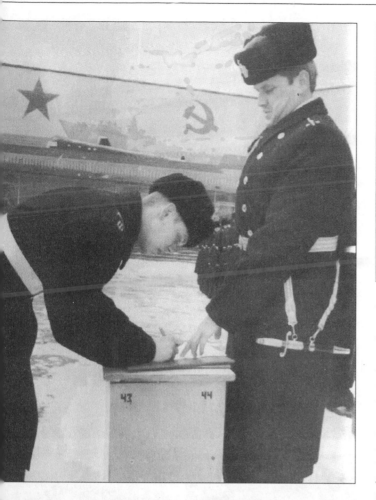

The Soviet Union Ends

Following the dramatic events of the failed Communist Coup of 1991 the Soviet Union collapsed. First to break away from central control were the three Baltic States of Latvia, Lithuania and Estonia which had been forcibly added to the Union in 1940 and had craved independence ever since. Boris Yeltsin threw off central control of the Russian Republic, of which he was President, and gathered powers under his own control. Other republics followed suit, with the Ukraine, Moldavia and Kazakhstan leading the way. Republic leaders suggested forming a Confederation of Independent States to replace the USSR with far more powers held by the republics and the central power being reduced to little more than a coordinating body. Disputes between the republics over ownership of resources and trade arrangements led to bitter disputes about the exact form which the CIS authority should take. By the close of 1992 it was still unclear to outside observers how the various republics would eventually emerge from the political disputes and economic meltdown which was enveloping the former USSR.

Left: A sailor of the former Soviet Black Sea Fleet pledges his allegiance to the Ukraine. The division of the powerful Black Sea Fleet had been a major point of disagreement between Russia and the Ukraine with the personnel being drawn from throughout the Soviet Union. An agreement was finally reached which shared ships and shore installations between the two republics. Below left: New York hotel magnate Leona Helmsley who acquired a notorious reputation for her tough business deals and difficult personal relationships, enters the Federal Courthouse in Manhattan on 18th March to be sentenced to four years in prison for tax evasion. Below: Alessandra Mussolini, granddaughter of the dictator Benito Mussolini, arriving at the Italian Parliament to take her seat after being elected in the elections of 23rd April. Miss Mussolini stood for the Italian Social Movement Party which had many policy similarities with her grandfather's regime.

The British Government followed a roller coaster ride as bad fortune succeeded good. During the spring the Conservative Government was consistently outpaced in the opinion polls by the Labour opposition. Nevertheless Prime Minister John Major decided to hold the general election on 9th April. Throughout the robust campaign Labour remained ahead in the polls, but when the actual votes were counted the Conservatives held on to power, though the majority in the House of Commons was cut from 102 to 23. The good fortune did not last long for European and economic policies coincided disastrously. Membership of the ERM system meant British interest rates had to remain high to match those in Germany, although British industry demanded low rates. In September, on a day to be known as Black Wednesday, the Chancellor of the Exchequer, Norman Lamont, pulled the pound out of the ERM as the level against the deutschmark could not be defended. Next to come under attack was the Maastricht Treaty on European Union which John Major had negotiated with other EEC leaders. At the Conservative Party Conference in October the issue dominated all and led to John Major being hissed by his own supporters, an event never before seen. At a vital vote in the House of Commons in November, Major only won when he made dramatic concessions to those Tory MPs opposed to the Treaty. Meanwhile plans to cut the coal industry led to a huge public outcry and a quick rethink on how the closures were to be handled. In November a major scandal involving sales of arms making equipment to Iraq threatened to engulf leading ministers including Michael Heseltine, Kenneth Clark and Tristan Garel-Jones. Top right: Prime Minister John Major at the Conservative Party Conference. Below: French schoolchildren read campaign posters urging the French electorate to vote No to Maastricht. In the event the French voted in favour of the Maastricht Treaty. Such a referendum was not considered for Britain. Centre: Chancellor of the Exchequer Norman Lamont. Far right: President of the Board of Trade Michael Heseltine. Bottom right: The new leader of the Labour Party, John Smith who took over on 18th July. The former leader Neil Kinnock had resigned on 13th April following his failure to lead his party to victory in the General Election.

Top right: The jagged gash torn in an apartment block in Amsterdam when an El Al cargo jet crashed soon after takeoff on the 4th October. The apartments were home to many immigrants, some of them illegal, and the authorities were unable to determine how many had been in the building when disaster struck. Initial estimates of 12 dead and 30 injured rose alarmingly as the true scale of the tragedy emerged. Centre: Relatives of the dead grieve at the commemoration service held on 11th October by which time the known death toll had risen to 75. The crash was at first blamed on a terrorist attack, but structural weakness was later considered more likely. Right: The hole torn in the ground by the IRA bomb planted in the City of London on 10th April. Three people were killed and many others injured by the blast which rocked the Baltic Exchange causing millions of pounds worth of damage and lost business. Top left: Two hundred people were killed on 22nd April as Mexico City fell victim to a bizarre disaster. Gasses built up in the city sewers to such an extent that the mixture became highly inflammable. An accidental spark ignited the mixture which exploded with terrific force, ripping away the foundations of several buildings which collapsed on those within.

Right: British athlete Linford Christie celebrates winning the Olympic Gold Medal for the 100 metres sprint on 1st August. Below: Doctor Jose Gonzales, one of the Olympic doctors who tested samples from athletes for banned drugs. The stringent tests resulted in several athletes being sent home from the Barcelona Olympics in disgrace. Bottom right: British rowers Jonathan and Greg Searle with cox Garry Herbert listen to the British national anthem after winning the Olympic gold medal in the coxed pair event. Below centre: British Formula 1 racing driver Nigel Mansell awaits the start of the Brazilian Grand Prix on 5th April. The race was to end in victory for Mansell, his third win in a season which would see him win the World Championship. Below right: Andre Agassis, the flamboyant tennis star, who captured the support of the crowd at Wimbledon in his successful bid to take the men's singles championship. Bottom left: Paul Gascoigne, transferred to the Italian club Lazio for the 1993 season, watches his team draw 1-1 with Parma in the first match of the new season on September 1st.

*Top left: Freddie Mercury, lead singer of the British rock group Queen, who died of AIDS in 1991. Mercury was a highly talented performer whose powerful voice was a vital ingredient in many Queen hits such as **Bohemian Rhapsody** and **We are the Champions** . His death was marked by much mourning in the pop world and led the other members of Queen to organise a huge charity concert in support of AIDS research in the summer of 1992. Top right: Another victim of AIDS was the British actor Denholm Elliott, famed for his superb playing of character parts in a long succession of movies and plays, who died in October. Left: Diana, Princess of Wales. A biography of her by Andrew Morton contained allegations of marital unhappiness and personal tragedy which made headlines around the world but were denied by Buckingham Palace. However in December the Prince and Princess of Wales announced their separation, ending 11 years of marriage. Above: The Duchess of York who separated from Prince Andrew earlier in the year.*

1993

Jan 5	The oil tanker Braer runs aground in the Shetland Islands
Jan 6	Death of Russian ballet dancer Rudolf Nureyev
Jan 17	UK: The Sunday Mirror & The People publish transcript of the 'Camillagate Tape', an alleged telephone conversation between Prince Charles & Camilla Parker-Bowles
Jan 20	Bill Clinton is inaugurated as 42nd President of the US
Feb 2	US tennis player Arthur Ashe dies of AIDS
Feb 11	UK: Buckingham Palace announce the Queen's intention to start paying income tax in April
Feb 24	Former England soccer captain Bobby Moore dies of cancer
Feb 28	US: A siege begins at HQ of a religious cult in Waco, Texas
Mar 1	UK: Funeral of 2 year old James Bulger who was murdered
Mar 20	UK: IRA bomb in Warrington town centre kills a child
Mar 28	Dublin: Peace rally following the IRA bomb in Warrington is attended by thousands
Apr 10	SA: Communist Party leader Chris Hani is assassinated
Apr 19	US: 86 people die as the 51 day siege at Waco, Texas ends
May 13	France: A siege begins in a Paris nursery school when a gunman takes a class of children and their teacher hostage
May 15	The Paris nursery siege ends when the gunman is shot dead
May 17	Briton Rebecca Stephens reaches summit of Everest
May 18	The Danes vote 'yes' to the Maastricht Treaty
May 27	UK: Norman Lamont resigns as Chancellor of the Exchequer.
May 29	Germany: 5 Turks die in a neo-Nazi arson attack
Jun 3	9 people die when BP owned oil tanker British Trent collides with a cargo ship off the coast of Belgium
Jun 10	British comedian Les Dawson dies
Jun 15	Former Formula One world champion James Hunt dies
Jun 17	UK: A 5th gay man is murdered in London. Police believe they are dealing with a serial killer
Jul 16	The city of St. Louis floods as the Mississippi breaks its banks
Jul 19	Ian Botham retires from first class cricket
Jul 20	Thailand: Britons Patricia Cahill & Karyn Smith are given a royal pardon and released from prison in Bangkok after serving 3 years for drug smuggling offences
Jul 21	Colin Ireland is charged with the murder of Andrew Collier, one of the 5 gays murdered in London
Jul 25	Israeli forces attack guerilla positions in southern Lebanon
Jul 29	Israel: John Demjanjuk is acquitted of war crime atrocities and released from prison
Jul 30	UK: Derek Bentley is pardoned 40 years after he was executed
Aug 13	500 are feared missing when a hotel collapses in Thailand
Aug 15	Linford Christie wins the 100 metres at World Championships
Aug 15	'Operation Irma' airlifts 21 sick & injured people from Sarajevo
Sep 8	SA: 19 die when gunmen open fire on a bus queue
Sep 13	Israeli PM Yitzhak Rabin and PLO leader Yasser Arafat sign a peace treaty in Washington DC
Sep 21	Boris Yeltsin dissolves the Russian parliament
Sep 22	Alabama: At least 44 die when a train crashes into swamp
Sep 30	India: A massive earthquake hits the state of Maharashta at least 20,000 die
Oct 4	Boris Yeltsin wins street battle for control of Russian parliament building
Oct 23	N. Ireland: IRA bomb in shop kills 10 in the Shankhill Road
Oct 30	N. Ireland: 7 people are massacred by Loyalist terrorists
Nov 11	Laura Davies dies after 2 multiple transplant operations
Nov 17	UK: 10 children and a teacher die in a minibus crash on M40
Nov 24	Two 11 year old boys are found guilty of the murder of James Bulger, aged 2
Dec 3	Princess of Wales announces her retirement from public life
Dec 10	Iraq: Paul Ride and 2 other Britons are released from prison
Dec 20	Colin Ireland, the 'gay slayer', is given 5 life sentences

On the 5th January the tanker Braer, heavily laden with 85 tons of light crude oil, ran into trouble in heavy seas and storm force winds off the coast of the Shetland Islands. The coastguards managed to rescue the crew but despite repeated attempts to salvage the ship and her cargo, the extreme weather conditions forced her onto the rocks at Garths Ness on the 12th January and she broke into three pieces. Thousands of tons of oil spewed into the sea as the tanker broke up. Many feared an ecological disaster. However, damage to wildlife was not as great as at first feared due to the violent seas quickly breaking up the oil slick. Left: Masked against the fumes of the oil spilling from the tanker, members of the media view the stricken Braer

PRESIDENT CLINTON

The 42nd President of the United States of America was sworn in on 20th January in Washington DC. Brought to power by a landslide electoral victory over the incumbent President George Bush, Bill Clinton, the 46 year old former govenor of Arkansas, promised the end of an "era of deadlock and drift" and declared the start of a season of renewal. However within 13 days of taking office Clinton had made several mistakes and, according to opinion polls, a third of Americans were disappointed with his performance. The Democratic Party were also unhappy. Clinton had fought his campaign efficiently and put himself forward as an honest middle-of-the-road American. This seemed at odds with the man who, upon taking office, tried to appoint corporate lawyer Zoe Baird as Attorney-General despite the fact she was known to have broken the law; championed the cause of homosexuals in the armed forces and floated an energy tax which hit middle-class, working Americans the hardest. Government spending targets seemed to promise more large tax increases while the much-vaunted health care reforms quickly proved to be an impractical commitment. The role of Hillary Clinton in the administration remained ambivalent and open to criticism. The early promise seemed to have vanished remarkably quickly.

p left: Bill and Hillary *linton wave to the crowds* *ter Bill Clinton was sworn* *as the 42nd President of* *e USA on 20th January in* *ashington DC. Above* *ght: The Presidential* *earing-in was preceded by* *ur days of parties and* *lebrations. On 17th* *nuary President Clinton* *d his daughter Chelsea* *ined Michael Jackson and* *iana Ross to sing "We are* *e World" at the Lincoln*

Memorial. Above: Paul Ride, *the British citizen who* *strayed over the border from* *Kuwait into Iraq and was* *arrested by Iraqi officials. He* *received a sentence of 7* *years imprisonment for his* *crime, leading to a wave of* *international condemnation* *of Iraq. Paul Ride joined* *another Briton who had also* *been imprisoned by the* *Iraqis. Michael Wainwright* *was serving a sentence for a* *similar crime.*

Stalemate in Iraq

Following the Gulf War, fought to free Kuwait from Iraq, the UN imposed tough sanctions and measures against Saddam Hussein and his nation. One of the sanctions was a ban on Iraqi ownership of long range missiles and chemical or biological warheads. Such resolutions were carried with little opposition, even from Arab states, at the UN, but enforcing them proved to be far more difficult. In January the US, Britain and France were involved in air and missile attacks on Iraqi military targets in an attempt to get Saddam to toe the line. A dispute between Iraq and the UN then arose over a building which the Iraqis claimed was the Agriculture Ministry, but which UN investigators believed to hold vital information on missile testing. For days the UN staff waited outside the building while the Iraqis refused them entrance on various pretexts. Eventually the UN gained access, to find that any incriminating evidence which had existed had been spirited away. For months the cat and mouse game continued until in June President Clinton again sanctioned the use of force. Cruise missiles were fired from US warships in the Persian Gulf and struck selected targets within Iraq. Clinton's unexpected toughness indicated that in foreign policy at least he was prepared to be every bit as determined as had his predecessor, George Bush. Soon after the missile strike the Iraqis and the UN investigators announced that the stalemate was over and that investigations were going smoothly. Several wondered how long Hussein would remain co-operative.

THE WACO SIEGE

Waco, Texas, was the setting for a dramatic siege and shoot out between US Federal agents and members of the Branch Davidian religious sect. The trouble began on 28th February when federal Alcohol, Tobacco and Firearms agents arrived at the headquarters of the sect to arrest the leader David Koresh for suspected firearms offences. The Sect members opened fire killing four federal agents and injuring more than a dozen in the following gun battle. Government troops in armoured vehicles surrounded the ranch. The stalemate continued for 51 days. The apocalyptic end to the siege came on the 19th April amid allegations of an FBI fiasco. The wooden compound was set alight by cult members several hours after agents had surrounded the compound with tanks and fired tear gas into the buildings. The heavily armed compound was reduced to ashes in less than an hour. Eighty six people including the cult's leader and 17 children, died in the inferno.

THE HANDSHAKE OF PEACE

On the 13th September on the lawns of the White House, Shimon Peres, the Israeli foreign minister and Mahmoud Abbas, the PLO deputy chief, signed an agreement promising Palestinian self rule. The agreement followed months of secret negotiations led by a team of Norwegians. Moments after the signing, the real drama of the occasion happened when the PLO leader, Yassir Arafat, held out his hand to the Israeli Prime Minister, Yitzhak Rabin. After a slight hesitation and a nudge from President Clinton, Mr Rabin shook hands with Arafat (*below*) and hopefully years of bitterness and bloodshed were over. It was a difficult occasion for both men who have spent most of their adult lives bent on each others destruction. In his address Mr Rabin (*left*) spoke about the bloodshed and his sorrow for all the victims of war. In a direct message to the Palestinian people he said "We say to you today, in a loud and clear voice: 'Enough of blood and tears. Enough'." Yassir Arafat, dressed in service uniform instead of his customary battle fatigues and gun, said "Today marks the beginning of the end of a chapter of pain and suffering which has lasted throughout this century," but he warned "The battle for peace is the most difficult of our lives." The agreement signals the beginning of a new era in the Middle East. In the days following the White House ceremony the peace process gathered momentum with Mr Rabin flying to Morocco to establish diplomatic ties and the Jordanians initialling an accord with the Israelis which laid the foundation for a peace treaty between the two nations.

Right: The Queen Mother leaving the Aberdeen Royal Infirmary on 23rd May after a three day stay. She had undergone an operation to remove a piece of fish lodged in her throat. Below: Camilla Parker-Bowles. Her friendship with the Prince of Wales hit the headlines in January with the publication of the transcript of an alleged intimate phone call between the two of them. Below right: The Princess of Wales took her sons on holiday to the West Indies in January. Diana continued with her royal duties despite her separation from Prince Charles and in the first half of 1993 undertook two overseas tours. Bottom right: Princess Anne with her second husband Commander Timothy Laurence at a rugby international between Scotland and France. They married in a quiet private ceremony in January.

CRIMES IN ENGLAND

Two major crimes dominated the headlines in England. In London a serial killer preying on homosexuals stalked the streets. Andrew Collier (*right*), Peter Walker (*far right*) and Emanuel Spiteri (*below*) were three of the five victims. The killer made phone calls to the police after each murder giving details of his crimes which convinced the police that the calls were genuine. The man wanted in connection with the murders was caught on a security camera at Charing Cross station accompanying the fifth victim, Emanuel Spiteri, on the evening of his death. The picture was widely circulated and on July 21 Colin Ireland, an unemployed man, surrendered to the police and was charged with the murder of Andrew Collier. The trial of the kidnapper of Stephanie Slater (*below right*) took place in June. Quickly convicted of her kidnapping and unlawful imprisonment, Michael Sams was also tried for the kidnapping and murder of Julie Dart, which had taken place six months earlier than the Slater kidnapping. In his summing up the judge described Sams as a cold blooded killer who showed no remorse. He was given 4 life sentences. Sams was caught after an appeal was broadcast on BBC's Crimewatch UK. Sams first wife Susan Oakes saw the programme and was convinced the description of the suspect - a man obsessed with railways and with an artificial leg - was her ex-husband. She telephoned the police and Sams was arrested and almost immediately confessed to the Slater offences. He denied murdering Julie Dart, blaming it on a friend. However forensic evidence linked the rope and sheet on Dart's body with Sams cottage. After his conviction Sams confessed to the murder.

Left: Woody Allen and Mia Farrow photographed during the early days of their romance which ended with acrimony in the New York Courts in 1993. The previous year it had been revealed that Allen was having an affair with Farrow's 21 year old adopted daughter Soon-Yi Previn while ostensibly continuing his relationship with Farrow herself. Though they had never married and lived in separate homes, the Allen-Farrow relationship was felt by friends to be permanent. Further allegations by Mia Farrow against Woody Allen included sexual abuse of the couple's other children. New York Society pored over the salacious gossip which emerged during the court case, the details of which baffled most independent observers.*

Left: Firemen gaze at the burnt out shell of the Saint-Francois psychiatric clinic in Rennes, France, where 17 people died and many more were injured during a night time blaze on 25th June. Below: Fire tugs spray water onto the smoking hulk of the BP owned oil tanker British Trent. The tanker, ladened with 24,000 tons of unleaded petrol, caught fire on 3rd June after it was involved in a collision with the Panamanian registered cargo ship Western Winner in thick fog 15 miles from Oostende Harbour. The ship were traversing a sharp angle in a narrow navigation channel at the time of the collision which left 10 people dead and 27 injured. Many of the survivors had to swim through a sea of burning fuel to safety. Below: South African Communist Party leader Chris Hani, who was assassinated outside his home in Johannesburg on April 10.

POLITICAL VIOLENCE IN SOUTH AFRICA

Continuing political unrest in South Africa claimed a victim of international renown on 10th April. Chris Hani, leader of the South African Communist Party and a prominent figure in the ANC, was shot outside his home in Johannesburg. Witnesses to the assassination said the killer, believed to be a member of a right wing terrorist group, fired from close range, hitting Hani repeatedly in the head. A 40 year old South African of Polish descent was arrested and charged with the crime, but the assassination was merely the most notable of hundreds of political murders taking place in the country. Attempts by the White government to come to terms with the ANC alienated the Inkhata Movement and served to increase the smouldering feud between the ANC and Inkhata which had already claimed thousands of lives. Over the following months murders and violence spread with right wing whites holding armed parades and breaking into multiparty talks. On 25th July at least 10 people were killed and 53 injured when hooded gunmen burst into a church in Cape Town during Evensong and opened fire with automatic weapons. The attack was blamed on the Azanian People's Liberation Army (APLA), the armed wing of the Pan African Congress. The outrage occured on the eve of the publication of a new interim constitution for South Africa which was expected to go a long way to solving the differences between the political parties, both black and white.

On 30th May neo-Nazi demonstrators launched a murderous fire-bomb attack on a hostel for Turkish migrant workers in the steel town of Solingen in Germany. Five people died in the blaze including two children. Witnesses said they had seen four skinheads leaving the scene as the fire took hold. A teenager, with links to neo-Nazi groups, was arrested and the government offered a reward of DM100,000 (£38,000) for evidence leading to more arrests. This was the worst of several attacks targeted at Turks in Germany. The government responded by a tight clamp down on neo-Nazi organisations and with the promise of tighter immigration controls. Left: The body of a victim is carried from the burned out hostel in Solingen. Right: Mourners at the funeral of a Solingen victim.

Maastricht

Through 1993 the name of the small Dutch town of Maastricht became synonymous with a crisis within the European Economic Community and complex legal and judicial wrangling in several nations. The Treaty signed in Maastricht was designed to create a new Union among the European states but it ran into bitter opposition in many quarters. The Danes voted against the Treaty in June 1992, but for it in a repeat referendum in May 1993. In Germany the Treaty received a relatively easy ride until challenges were lodged at the Supreme Court alleging that it contravened the basic German constitution. The hearing lasted months, long into the autumn. In Britain, the passage of the Treaty through Parliament was marked by heated debate, knife-edge votes and accusations of outright bullying by the Government. In July Britain, too, saw a legal challenge to the Treaty and a fresh round of mayhem ensued. What had begun in such hope was foundering in ill will.

ove right: Distraught hotel ner Barry Turner, facing mera, inspects the ruins of Holbeck Hall Hotel with uctural engineers as the tel continues to collapse to the sea in the South Cliff ea of Scarborough in June. ght: Equally upset were the ce-goers at Aintree on 3rd ril who saw the famous and National declared void *after two false starts and a bungled recall, which led to many horses pulling up and others completing the course. Sir Michael Connell, a High Court judge and member of the Jockey Club, was appointed to head an inquiry into the fiasco. The inquiry was highly critical of the flagman at the starting line for failing to raise his flag.*

IRA BOMBING CAMPAIGN

The IRA campaign of violence struck the UK mainland again in th[e] year. On saturday 20th March two explosions rocked Warrington [in] Merseyside. The blasts tore through the town centre crowded wi[th] children shopping for Mother's day presents and killed several victim[s] including 3 year old Johnathon Ball. A second child, 12 year o[ld] Timothy Parry, died of his injuries later in the week. A coded warni[ng] had been given to the Samaritans at midday about a bomb outsi[de] Boots The Chemist in Liverpool. Fourteen minutes later the bom[b] exploded in Warrington, some 16 miles away. Although police [in] Warrington had been warned, they had no time to evacuate the are[a.] Left: A policewoman weeps during the funeral of bomb victi[m] Timothy Parry. A later blast destroyed properties in the City [of] London, causing millions of pounds worth of damage. The blast led [to] new security gates around the financial district. Police were success[ful] in arresting IRA sympathisers, but the campaign of terror went o[n] leading to tougher security arrangements throughout Britain.

Yugoslavia in Turmoil

The bitter fighting in the former Yugoslavia continued to gather pace, with little sign of peace in sight. The situation was made all the more difficult for those attempting to broker peace by the fact that every faction believed passionately in the moral right of its cause and had plenty of past grievances to use as justification for its actions. Fighting in Bosnia took a fresh turn when the Croats, formerly allies of the Moslems against the Serbs, turned on the Moslems in search of new territory to conquer. Feeling betrayed by the Western Powers who had failed to supply help on the ground to back up their rhetoric of support, the Moslems launched determined counter-attacks on their new enemies which resulted in much bloodshed. Ethnic cleansing, the removal of families from their homes for ethnic reasons, produced some memorable horrors. Despite attempts at peace, the war continued.

Right: British Colonel Bob Stewart of the Cheshire Regiment speaks to UN Security Council Deputy President Diego Arria during a UN fact-finding mission in Bosnia-Hercegovina. Lieutenant-Colonel Stewart took the UN team to the village of Ahmici where war crimes had been committed, allegedly by Croat troops persecuting Moslem civilians. On 16th March he met the Prince of Wales who had flown to the war-stricken region to meet some of the 2,500 British troops who formed part of the UN peace-keeping force. Lieutenant-Colonel Stewart's readiness to talk to the press and his commanding presence made him a well-known figure in the tortuous and bloody conflict which was Bosnia.

OPERATION RESTORE HOPE

The escalating violence in Somalia prompted the US to send troops to the country at the end of 1992. The aim was to halt the factional clan feuding which was destroying the country and disrupting trade and agriculture to such an extent that many thousands of people were in danger of starving to death. Other countries followed the US initiative and on 1 May 1993 all foreign troops were placed under UN command. After many initial successes, the UN forces found themselves being increasingly dragged into local rivalries and feuds. The formidable General Aidid became a target for UN hostility, although he protested his innocence of alleged crimes. Casualties mounted and by the late summer the role for the UN in Somalia was being seriously questioned. Its original aims had not been achieved and its troops seemed to some to be fighting a neo-colonial war of pacification and subjugation. Top left: A US Marine preparing for his departure to Somalia in December. About 16,000 US Marines from Camp Pendleton took part in Operation Restore Hope. Top right: A Somali family walk past a UN armoured vehicle manned by Nigerian soldiers. Above: Pakistani UN troops who played a leading role in the growing conflict. Left: A Belgian UN soldier stands guard at a ceremony for the opening of a bridge built by the US army to allow relief supplies to reach the famine stricken areas in southern Somalia.

On May 13 a hooded gunman walked into a nursery school in Neuilly-sur-Seine, a wealthy Paris suburb, and held 21 children and their teacher hostage, demanding a ransom of 100 million francs. During the first 24 hours the gunman, Eric Schmitt, released 15 children. He allowed food to be brought in for the remaining hostages and the police seized the opportunity to smuggle in a video camera to monitor events. Early on the morning of 15 May the gunman was dozing and armed police crept into the classroom. As Schmitt woke he was shot by marksmen using silencers on their guns in order not to frighten the children. *Right:* A child, released early in the siege, is hugged by his mother. *Below:* Laurence Dreyfus, the school teacher caught up in the hostage drama. *Below right:* The children being carried out of the school by police after the death of the gunman. *Bottom right:* A hostage being reunited with his parents.

Left: No. 1 men's seed Pete Sampras kisses the Wimbledon Challenge Cup after taking the singles title for the first time by beating fellow American Jim Courier. Below: The World's No.1 Ladies player Monica Seles after winning the Australian Open in January. On April 30 she was playing in the Hamburg Open tournament when a man appeared from the crowd and stabbed her in the back. She was taken to hospital and treated for a 2cm wound. Bottom left: Arsenal player Ian Wright clowns with the FA Cup after his goal assured his club of victory in a 2-1 final replay against Sheffield Wednesday. The unfortunate Sheffield Wednesday had also lost the League Cup to Arsenal in April. Bottom right: The Cambridge University crew celebrate a sweet victory over Oxford in the University boat race after 6 successive defeats.

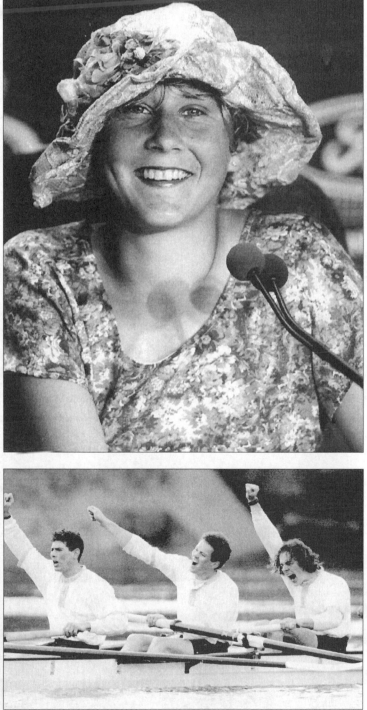

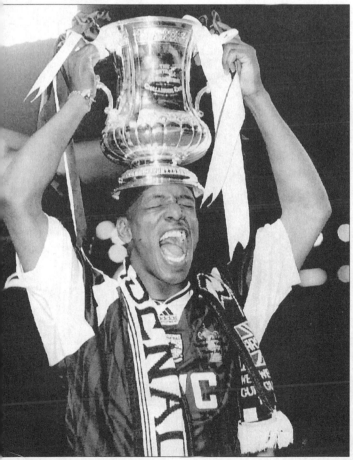

577

The Greatest Living Explorer

England's eccentric traveller Sir Ranulf Fiennes (facing page) has been called the greatest living explorer in honour of his extraordinary journeys. In February 1993 he completed a project which he had attempted, unsuccessfully, in 1989. Sir Ranulf and Dr. Michael Stroud completed a walk across the Antarctic continent unsupported by external supply squads or rescue teams. The two men dragged everything they needed for the journey on sleds which had to carry not only tents and food but also navigation equipment, spare tools and scientific instruments. During the weeks they were on the march, the explorers were beset by blizzards, freezing rain and unimaginable cold. Fiennes and Stroud completed their arduous walk, the first men ever to do so, with severe frostbite and other injuries. On his return to London Sir Ranulf described his feat as the 'nastiest' 4 months of his life. Like his previous exploits, this trek was designed to raise money for charity and Sir Ranulf was able to donate large sums to charities helping those with disabling diseases.

Top left: Briton James Hunt, the former Formula 1 world champion, who died of a heart attack in his sleep in June. Top centre: Arthur Ashe, former Wimbledon champion, who died of AIDS which he had contracted through infected blood given to him during an operation. Left: The great British comedian Les Dawson who died suddenly in July. Top right: Dizzy Gillespie the legendary jazz trumpeter who died this year. Above: Russian ballet dancer Rudolf Nureyev. He died in Paris on January 6 at the age of 54 of what his doctor described as "cardiac complications following a cruel illness". Nuryev was arguably the greatest ballet dancer the world has ever seen. Born in 1938, he became the leading dancer with the famous Kirov Ballet. In June 1961 he caused a sensation when he defected to the West. He returned to dance with the Kirov in 1989 towards the end of his career.

Jan 5	UK: Tim Yeo resigns from government following newspaper revelations about an illegitimate child
Jan 9	UK: Lord Caithness resigns from government after his wife commits suicide
Jan 17	US: Los Angeles is hit by an earthquake measuring 6.6 on the Richter Scale
Jan 20	Sir Matt Busby, former Manchester United manager, dies
Jan 25	Michael Jackson pays an undisclosed sum to the boy in the sex allegation scandal
Jan 26	Sydney: A student fires 2 blank shots at Prince Charles
Jan 26	France: 3 die and 94 are injured when the roof of a supermarket falls on shoppers in Nice
Jan 27	Terry Venables is appointed England football manager
Jan 28	British aid worker Paul Goodall is murdered in Bosnia
Jan 29	Five British doctors die in an avalanche while skiing in the French Alps

The beginning of 1994 brought torrential rain to the UK, with the south being very badly hit. Above: Children from Chichester use their initiative to travel through the flood waters after the River Lavant burst its banks and flooded the city for the second time in a week. The army was called in to help with the emergency after many main roads on the south coast became impassable. Below: The Environment

Minister Tim Yeo was forced resign from the government o January 5 following newspape revelations that he had had a extra marital affair resulting in an illegitimate daughter. A second minister, Lord Caithness, resigned on Janua 9 after his wife commited suicide. The government, who "back to basics" policy placed emphasis on the moral welfar of society, faced the new year behind in all the opinion polls

The legendary manager of Manchester United, Sir Matt Busby (*above*), died on January 20 aged 84. During his 24 years at the club, he transformed United from a struggling side to one of the greatest clubs in the history of football. Matt Busby began his career at Manchester United in 1945 when the club was in debt and struggling for form. By 1952 the team had won the FA Cup and become League Champions. During the 1950s Busby built the first team around his youth players which earnt them the nickname 'Busby Babes'. In 1958 United was devastated by the Munich air disaster which claimed, among others, 8 members of the team. Despite suffering near fatal injuries and losing many great players, Busby fought his way back to create another great team in the 1960s which won 2 League Championships and the FA Cup. The climax to his career came in May 1968 when United beat Benfica 4-1 to win the European Cup.

At the end of the previous year Michael Jackson (*below*) cancelled his world tour and was admitted to hospital for the treatment of drug addiction. At the same time he was the centre of a scandal concerning child sex abuse. Fourteen year old Jordan Chandler had brought civil proceedings against Jackson, claiming that the star had molested him on numerous occasions. On January 25th lawyers announced that Jackson was to pay an undisclosed sum, thought to be between 5 and 50 million dollars, in return for the dropping of all charges against him.

the early hours of January 7th Los Angeles was hit by a owerful earthquake which used enormous damage to e city and its surrounds. At st 28 people died and the mage is estimated at $7 lion. Above: A resident arches for her belongings in e wreck of her apartment ck. Above right: A mother d daughter eat their breakfast er camping the night in a LA rk. Thousands slept outside e to the fear of powerful ershocks. Right: Rescue rkers continue their search of e Northridge Meadows artments where 16 people d when the building llapsed during the earthquake.

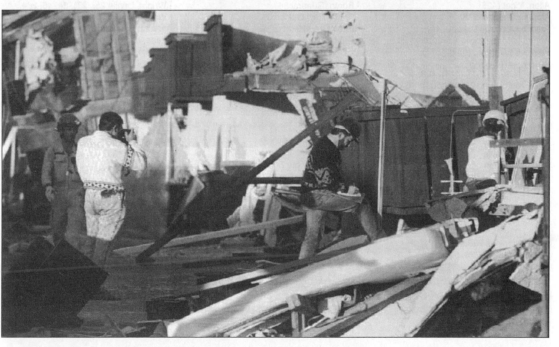

INDEX

Page numbers in brackets indicate text and illustration references. Page numbers without brackets refer to text and chronology entries.